The British Empire and its Italian Prisoners of War, 1940–1947

Bob Moore
and
Kent Fedorowich

D1457711

palgrave

First published 2002 by
PALGRAVE
Houndmills, Basingstoke, Hampshire RG21 6XS and
175 Fifth Avenue, New York, N.Y. 10010
Companies and representatives throughout the world

PALGRAVE is the new global academic imprint of
St. Martin's Press LLC Scholarly and Reference Division and
Palgrave Publishers Ltd (formerly Macmillan Press Ltd).

ISBN 0–333–73892–6

This book is printed on paper suitable for recycling and made from fully managed and sustained forest sources.

A catalogue record for this book is available from the British Library.

Library of Congress Cataloging-in-Publication Data
Moore, Bob, 1954-
    The British Empire and its Italian Prisoners of war,
    1940–1947 / Bob Moore and Kent Fedorowich.
        p. cm. – (Studies in military and strategic history)
    Includes bibliographical references and index.
    ISBN 0–333–73892–6 (cloth)
        1. World War, 1939–1945 – Prisoners and prisons, British.
    2. Prisoners of war – Italy – History – 20th century. 3. Prisoners
    of war – Commonwealth countries – History – 20th century.
    4. Repatriation – Italy – History – 20th century. I. Fedorowich,
    Kent, 1959-II. Title. III. Studies in military and strategic history
    (Palgrave (Firm))
    D805.G7M66 2002
    940.54'7241 – dc21   2001054581

10   9   8   7   6   5   4   3   2   1
11   10   09   08   07   06   05   04   03   02

Printed and bound in Great Britain by
Antony Rowe Ltd, Chippenham, Wiltshire

Contents

List of Tables and Maps

Table

Map

Preface

The origins of this book go back to the late 1980s when the authors were both employed at the former Bristol Polytechnic and had adjacent rooms in the (now condemned) attic of 'The Conifers', the School of History's former office building. This prompted extensive general discussions on the military history of the Second World War, but the catalyst for further investigation into prisoners-of-war came with the supervision of an undergraduate dissertation based on materials in the Public Record Office written by Heather Parkin on the Italians in British hands. This helped to demonstrate how little was known about the history of prisoners-of-war in this, or in any other modern conflict, and led to an ongoing collaboration which has so far seen the publication of an edited collection, *Prisoners of War and their Captors in World War II* (Oxford, 1996), and a series of journal articles, written jointly or individually. In this context, we would like to express our thanks to the editors of the *International History Review* and *Intelligence and National Security* for permission to publish reworked material which first appeared in their journals in 1996 and 1999 respectively.

No book of this nature could be attempted without extensive primary research and we are delighted to acknowledge the financial assistance provided by the British Academy, Scouloudi Foundation, Australian War Memorial, Australian Army, UWE (University of the West of England) Bristol, Faculty of Humanities Research Committee, and the History Department, Manchester Metropolitan University. Collectively, they facilitated visits to libraries and archives in Australia, South Africa, New Zealand, Canada, and the United Kingdom. Bob Moore would also like to thank the Department of War Studies, King's College London, whose award of a non-stipendiary fellowship in 1999 greatly assisted in the completion of several chapters in this book.

The co-operation we have received from archivists and librarians across the world has been exemplary, and we would like to record our gratitude to the directors, staffs and librarians of the Australian Archives (Canberra, Melbourne and Sydney); Australian War Memorial; National Archives of Canada; National Archives of New Zealand; South African National Archives, Pretoria and Cape Town; South African Department of Defence Archives (Ms A. van der Westhuizen and Mr Steve de Agrela); Zonderwater Prison (Ernest Collins); Killie Campbell Africana Library,

University of Natal, Durban; India Office Records and Library, British Museum, London; Mass Observation Archive, Sussex (Dorothy Sheridan); British Library of Political and Economic Science, London; National Archives of Scotland, Edinburgh; Churchill College Archive Centre, Cambridge; Imperial War Museum; Liddell Hart Centre for Military Archives, King's College London; Rhodes House Library, Oxford; the John Rylands University Library, Manchester; the Public Record Office of Northern Ireland, Belfast; and the Public Record Office, Kew, London.

On a more personal note, the authors owe debts of gratitude to many friends and fellow scholars who work in this field of study. Firstly we would like to record our thanks to Professor Michael Dockrill (London) in whose series this book appears. His support and continuing interest have been invaluable. We would also like to thank a number of other historians whose work has informed our own, namely Gerry Douds and David Rolf (Worcester), Martin Thomas (UWE, Bristol), Keith Jeffrey (Jordanstown), Martin Alexander (Aberystwyth), Carl Bridge (London), David Killingray (School of Oriental and African Studies), Andrew Porter (King's College, London), Anthony Hellen (Newcastle), Graham Thompson (Edinburgh) and Barbara Hately-Broad (Sheffield) in the United Kingdom; Günther Bischof (New Orleans) and Paul MacKenzie (South Carolina) in the United States; Joan Beaumont (Deakin) in Australia; Rüdiger Overmans (Freiburg) in Germany and Barbara Stelzl-Marx (Graz) in Austria. Equally important has been the linguistic and bibliographical help given to us by Rob Mallett (Birmingham), Dick van Galen Last (Amsterdam) and Nicola Iannelli (Rome), all of whom gave freely of their time and expertise to help us. And finally to Chris Hearmon (UWE, Bristol) for his technical wizardry with the maps.

In a different way, but no less valuable, are the friends who looked after us so very well on our travels over the last six years: Jeff and Gina Grey (Canberra), Adrian and Linda Fitz-Alan (Sydney), Bruce Faraday (Canberra), Nic Thomas (Melbourne), Gareth Hughes (Bangkok), Jane and Hugh Patrickson (Pretoria), Peter Dennis and family (Canberra), Rex and Simonè Tomlinson (Johannesburg), Daryl and Sandra François (Durban), Ian and Nöelle van der Waag (Saldhana Bay) and 'Bwana' Bob Keffen and 'friends' in the Pilansberg National Park, near Sun City. There have also been a number of bars and restaurants which have played an important role in the gestation and completion of this project, notably the Blaythwayt Arms (Bath), Doyles Restaurant (Watsons Bay, Sydney), the Taras Bulba Steakhouse (Pretoria), the Butcher Boys (Durban) and the Konaki Greek Restaurant (Bloomsbury, London). Last but certainly not least, we both owe an enormous debt of gratitude to our respective wives and families who, in spite of extended absences on research trips overseas and houses littered with books, papers and the detritus of this project over many years, have supported us with love and understanding.

BOB MOORE
KENT FEDOROWICH

List of Abbreviations

AA	Australian Archives
AG	Adjutant-General
AIF	Australian Imperial Force
AMF	Australian Military Force
AWM	Australian War Memorial
CCC	Churchill College Archive Centre
CGS	Chief of the General Staff
CIB	Commonwealth Investigation Branch
CID	Committee of Imperial Defence
C-in-C	Commander-in-Chief
COS	British Chiefs of Staff
CSDIC	Combined Services Detailed Interrogation Centre
DDMI	Deputy Director of Military Intelligence
DMI	Director of Military Intelligence
DPW	Directorate of Prisoners of War
DPW&I	Directorate of Prisoners of War and Internees
GHQ	General Headquarters
GOC	General Officer Commanding
GPO	General Post Office
HD(S)E	Home Defence (Security) Executive
HMT	His Majesty's Transport
ICRC	International Committee of the Red Cross
IPOWC	Imperial Prisoners of War Committee
IWM	Imperial War Museum
JIC	Joint Intelligence Committee
LHCMA	Liddell Hart Centre for Military Archives
MIR	Military Intelligence Research
NAC	National Archive of Canada
NANZ	National Archive of New Zealand
NCO	Non-Commissioned Officer
NFU	National Farmers Union
NRB	National Roads Board (South Africa)
NSO	National Service Officer
PID	Political Intelligence Department
POW	Prisoner of War
POWs	Prisoners of War

PRO	Public Record Office
PRONI	Public Record Office of Northern Ireland
PWD	Prisoners of War Department
PWE	Political Warfare Executive
PWIS	Prisoner of War Interrogation Service
QMG	Quartermaster-General
RHL	Rhodes House Library
SADDA	South African Department of Defence Archive
SANA	South African National Archive
SOE	Special Operations Executive
SAR&H	South African Railways and Harbours
UDF	Union Defence Force

Introduction

On 10 June 1940, and against the advice of his Foreign Minister, Count Ciano, and his military leaders, Benito Mussolini took Italy into the war against a beleaguered Anglo-French alliance. Ultimately, it would lead to the defeat of his armed forces and the collapse of the Fascist regime he had created, but in the summer of 1940, with German arms apparently victorious on all fronts, *Il Duce* failed to see or at least acknowledge the dangers that might lie ahead. In entering the war, he undoubtedly hoped to obtain some cheap military successes at the expense of the French, but was primarily concerned with aligning Italy belatedly with her German partner, whom he had so signally failed to support in September 1939, and to obtain a seat at the peace conference which would follow the imminent Axis victory.[1] While Mussolini's intervention contributed little or nothing to the German victories in Western Europe, his involvement against Britain and her Empire served to extend the war into another continent and opened a series of new military fronts in North and East Africa where British and Italian imperial territories shared common borders.

With hindsight, it is surprising how little consideration Mussolini and his government had given to war with the British Empire. The Italian military leadership had asserted that they could only mount a defensive campaign in Africa, and it rapidly became clear that Mussolini's immediate territorial ambitions lay not in Africa, but in extending Italian control from a recently conquered Albania outwards into the Balkans. A planned Italian invasion of Yugoslavia was vetoed by Hitler in August 1940, but undeterred by this setback, Mussolini began a series of provocations which culminated in a declaration of war against Greece on 28 October 1940. Ignoring the British threat to the African empire may have seemed foolhardy, but it was based on the twin premises that

Britain was still licking her wounds after the retreat from Dunkirk, and that in any case either the Germans would succeed in an invasion or the Churchill cabinet would accept a negotiated peace.

Towards the end of 1940, it became increasingly clear that Mussolini's gamble had not paid off. The expected German victory over Britain had not materialised and Churchill was proving impervious to any suggestions of negotiations. At the same time, Italian troops had failed to make headway against the Greeks and had suffered the embarrassment of being driven back onto Albanian soil. In Africa, however, the full impact of Mussolini's miscalculations took time to emerge. Although intending to mount defensive campaigns, the Italian commanders in East Africa and Libya initially achieved some modest successes against the British. From Abyssinia, the Duke D'Aosta was able to mount raids into Kenya and the Sudan with a force of 91,000 Italian and 182,000 colonial troops, and also successfully captured British Somaliland.[2] From Libya, Marshal Graziani's Tenth Army managed to advance more than 100 kilometres into Egypt before his forces under the command of General Mario Berti were repulsed at Sidi Barrani on 9–11 September 1940. Three months later, Operation 'Compass', which started as a raid to assess Italian strength, turned into a full-scale victory and provided the first mass of Axis troops to fall into British hands,[3] prompting the famous despatch from the Coldstream Guards that they had had no time to count their prisoners yet, but held 'about five acres of officers and two hundred acres of other ranks'.[4] In three days a total of 38,300 Italian regular army and colonial soldiers including four generals were captured for the loss of 624 Allied servicemen.

Less than a month later, on 4 January 1941, the 6th Australian Division overran the fortified town of Bardia, capturing 40,000 men. Indeed, according to one intelligence summary, the advance of the 16th Australian Brigade had been 'so sudden and unexpected' that the Italian garrison gave in with 'scarcely a struggle'. Late that evening the brigade commander, General A. S. 'Tubby' Allen, received an envoy from the Italian divisional commander in the northern sector saying that he and 7,000 men were prepared to surrender. 'Embarrassed already with thousands more prisoners than he could handle', Allen allegedly replied, 'that it would be more convenient if they left it till the morning!'. The suggestion was accepted.[5] Finally in February, after heavy fighting at Beda Fomm, the 13th British Corps encircled the retreating Tenth Army, taking a further 25,000 prisoners, thus removing the immediate Italian threat to Egypt. This prompted the British Foreign Secretary, Anthony Eden, to gibe, never had 'so much been surrendered by so many to so few'.[6]

By the beginning of January 1941, this somewhat unexpected series of victories allowed General Sir Archibald Wavell, Commander-in-Chief Middle East, to report the capture of around 73,000 prisoners-of-war (POWs).[7] In the subsequent months, the victory at Beda Fomm and the campaign in Abyssinia added yet more captured or surrendered Italian personnel so that by August of 1941 the total had reached almost 200,000.[8] Already representing a huge logistical problem for their hard-pressed captors, these men were later joined by many thousands of others, taken prisoner as the pendulum in the North African campaign ultimately swung in the Allies' favour, not least after the Eighth Army breakthrough at El Alamein in October 1942. As the British, now in concert with the Americans, rolled up Axis resistance in Tunisia in May 1943, and then mounted the invasion of Sicily and southern Italy in the summer, further captures followed. Thus by 8 September, when the Italian government now under Marshal Badoglio surrendered to the Western Allies, more than half a million Italian servicemen had been taken prisoner by British forces, and a further 130,000 by their American allies.[9]

These are the raw statistics which chart, more clearly than any map, the gradual failure and ultimate military collapse of the Italian war effort. Yet the military history on its own can only tell part of the story. In dealing with numbers on this scale and the collective experience they represent, it is important not to lose sight of the fact that they are also the summation of hundreds of thousands of individual stories – of military service, combat, surrender, captivity, eventual release, and for the vast majority, repatriation to a postwar Italy trying to forget its Fascist past. While some experiences were common to large numbers of men, such as those involved in the mass surrenders in East and later North Africa, it remains impossible to suggest that there was a single, easily identifiable prisoner-of-war story. While large numbers of prisoners were taken on the battlefield, many others were surrounded and/or surrendered by their officers without firing a shot in anger. The men's initial feelings beyond capture will doubtless have been of fear of what the enemy might do to them. However, once over this initial phase and reassured by the behaviour of their captors, the individual's reaction to being a prisoner was conditioned by a myriad of factors; for example the conditions experienced during their military service, the nature and competence of their leaders, their commitment to the Fascist imperial cause, or the strength of their desire to be out of the war. Some will have seen their capture as a frustration, a disappointment or as a personal humiliation, others as a blessed release from the dangers of warfare and fighting for a cause in which they did not believe.[10]

British security and political imperatives dictated that huge numbers of these Italian prisoners had to be evacuated from the theatres in which they had been captured, and while the 1929 Geneva Convention placed some general restrictions on where they could be taken, the fact that the British Empire was considered as a single entity meant that there was enormous scope for captives to be taken to all parts of the globe. As this book will make clear, the dispersal of prisoners to specific destinations was governed by a range of factors which, inevitably, changed over time. Officers were almost invariably segregated from other ranks, and many thousands of them were shipped to camps in India to see out the war. Yet even ordinary soldiers from the same unit captured at the same time often had widely divergent experiences of captivity. Some were sent to East or South Africa, others to Australia, India and the United Kingdom. Further groups found themselves handed over to other detaining powers such as the United States, or more controversially, the Free French. During the latter stages of the war some were transported to West Africa and suggestions were even made to employ Italian POWs in the Persian Gulf.[11] As far as the British were concerned, the dispersal of Italian prisoners was conditioned largely by their usefulness as a labour supply. Apart from officers being segregated from other ranks, committed Fascists were likewise removed to separate camps. From amongst the remainder, trained craftsmen and those with particular skills were sent where they could be best used. Most of the remainder were employed in unskilled work; road building in East Africa, forestry in Wales and agriculture almost everywhere else. Later, after Italy had become a co-belligerent of the Allies, the types of work involved increased exponentially and incentives such as better pay and conditions were offered for prisoners to engage in all manner of tasks directly connected with the British and imperial war effort.

The placement of prisoners, and therefore their experiences, were also dictated to some extent by other factors. Captives were seen as a source of battlefield intelligence in the first hours and days after their capture. Later, those perceived as having specialist knowledge of the Italian war effort and Mussolini's regime in general were also screened for information. In parallel with this, there were limited British attempts made by the Political Warfare Executive (PWE) to foster an anti-Fascist resistance among Italian captives. This war for the hearts and minds not only of the prisoners but of the Italian population as a whole, took on a greater importance when London was given the responsibility for the administration and reconstruction of a surrendered Italy. Thus after September 1943 there was a more concerted attempt to win over prisoners to a western view (i.e. anti-Fascist and anti-Communist) of a reconstructed Italy. These included a series of attempts to win over those prisoners with little or no commitment to Fascism and to inculcate in them western ideas on capitalism and democracy to form the basis for a future Italian state. Thus, prisoners were screened and labelled according to their supposed political proclivities. Ultimately, the extent of these political education campaigns remained limited, but those willing to be involved were again provided with certain incentives in the form of better treatment. The success of these programmes was also limited; undermined by the crudity of the propaganda, the lack of coherence and funding, but ultimately by the alienation felt by many prisoners about their treatment and prolonged incarceration after the collapse of Fascism and the Italian surrender.

Adjustment to a new and alien environment would inevitably take time. One wonders how the soldier used to the heat of his native homeland and the parched conditions of the Libyan desert adjusted to the cold and damp of England or the severe winters of Scotland. With the benefit of hindsight, it is clear that in comparison with their counterparts who fell into Russian or German hands, the Italians were not badly treated by their British captors. Indeed, throughout the war, London adhered carefully and more-or-less completely to the stipulations of the Geneva Convention, giving relatively little scope for real complaints to be raised by their captives or the Italian government. Nevertheless, confronted with an apparently open-ended period of captivity and unlimited time to contemplate their situation, prisoners tended to see the smallest injustices in their treatment as major issues. To all intents and purposes, the camp became their entire world. While the slow provision of Red Cross parcels or erratic delivery of mail from home may have seemed a minor inconvenience to the military and civilian authorities, they were the very centre of life for the prisoners dealing with the tedium of captivity in a foreign land and in alien conditions. The lack of news from home was a major issue for many prisoners and all manner of conspiracy theories were created to explain why the British were apparently withholding mail. However elaborate the theories, the reality was usually far more mundane – Italian government inefficiency, transport problems, the sinking of boats carrying mail or censoring problems associated with the bulk rather than the content of the mails. The sense of frustration was undoubtedly aggravated by news of the armistice and Italian surrender in September 1943. Worries about family became paramount as the Allied troops moved into southern Italy and the Germans poured in from the north. This was exacerbated as news reached the prisoners about the conditions at home – either under Allied or German control. Stories of destruction and deprivation at home all contributed to a feeling of complete powerlessness. If capture had been interpreted by prisoners as a humiliation and a slur on their masculinity, then the reports from home merely served to heighten such feelings of inadequacy and impotence. Incarcerated in foreign lands miles from home with no immediate prospect of repatriation, they were unable to fulfil traditional patriarchal functions as breadwinner, protector of the family or role model for children. While worries about family were common to most prisoners (and these could be fuelled both by news or by lack of news), it is nevertheless important not to stereotype reactions. Inevitably, some prisoners adjusted better to long-term captivity than others and the most adaptable made the best of their situation – wherever they were sent.

Frustrations also increased when it became apparent that the armistice represented a false dawn for those in captivity. The end of the Mussolini regime and Marshal Badoglio's negotiated surrender did not precipitate a wholesale repatriation of Italian prisoners, even for those who came from territory liberated by the Allies. The designation of Italy as a co-belligerent rather than as an allied power undoubtedly owed something to the importance of the Italian prisoners. While the outcome of the war against Germany and Japan was still in doubt, the POWs were seen as an invaluable asset for the British as a docile labour force, and London made every effort to keep them in captivity for as long as possible. Only when they could be replaced by large numbers of captured Germans – effectively after the end of the war in Europe – was some consideration given to allowing the Italians to go home. Yet even then, there were apparently innumerable obstacles, with the fate of men from a defeated former enemy low on the list of Allied priorities. Thus only in 1946 was shipping made available to repatriate the mass of Italians still held in various corners of the Empire, and the last prisoners were not released from captivity until October 1947.

The sources for this study come primarily from an extensive range of official documents from across the former British Empire, other archives, and published accounts of prisoners' lives in captivity. This latter category includes the contemporary records and memoirs of captors, civilian bystanders and, of course, the prisoners themselves. While no attempt has been made to make a comprehensive survey of prisoner autobiographies and memoirs, a few have been used to provide an appropriate counterweight to the 'official' British view of their Italian captives.[12] Research in British and overseas archives has uncovered a wealth of relevant material spread over a wide range of government and military departments, in Whitehall, the former dominions and colonies. In addition to the Foreign Office and War Office departments concerned specifically with prisoners-of-war, references to the Italians appear throughout the public records, from Churchill's prime ministerial files at the top, to the deepest recesses of the Ministry of Labour and its dealings with County War Agricultural Committees.[13] Missing, however, are most of the records relating to individual camps, their organisation, administration and history. With only a few files being retained as examples, much has been destroyed or lost with the result that information about particular camps is scarce and usually has to be derived from non-official sources. Beyond the national records, local histories and archives also shed important light on the subject. One remarkable facet of this was that in the course of research for this book, mention of the Italian soldiers in Britain invariably elicited recollections from those old enough to remember – or their offspring – of stories about the prisoners in their particular neighbourhood.

English-language historiography on the Second World War generally has tended to marginalise the role of Italy as an enemy in favour of a concentration on Nazi Germany and Imperial Japan as the principal belligerents. This has meant that the Italian military experience in North and East Africa is not particularly prominent in the major histories of the various campaigns involved. Moreover, there is some evidence to suggest that wartime assumptions and propaganda have influenced postwar judgements to a disportionate extent with Italian military leadership usually being dismissed as inept and the contribution of their soldiers as unimportant to the outcome of the conflict in North Africa.[14] The stories and jokes about the Italian Armed Forces, which gained such general currency towards the end of the war, have provided an enduring and detrimental image which has only been offset by publications in Italian. While these also have many faults, it is worth bearing in mind the judgements, both by British military authorities at the time, and by historians subsequently, that the Italian soldier was no better or worse than his British counterpart, but suffered from obsolescent equipment, poor training, poor victualling and clothing, but above all, from poor leadership.[15]

If the participation of Italian servicemen in the Second World War has been subjected to a denigrating bias, their subsequent history as captives has been all but ignored, by both English and Italian authors. Published works on prisoners-of-war in general during the Second World War are scarce. Although the taking of prisoners has some marginal importance for military historians in terms of measuring the scale of victory or defeat, the subsequent treatment of captives beyond actual military campaigns seems to have held no interest for them whatsoever. Similarly, their incarceration by the various belligerent powers has provided no more than footnotes for the social histories of the countries concerned. Most English writers have inevitably tended to concentrate on the British and Commonwealth experiences of captivity, and primarily on those in German and Japanese hands, with only a passing mention of the many thousands held by the Italians. There are, of course, exceptions – most notably *Behind Barbed Wire*, by A. J. Barker, which provides a thematic analysis of war prisoners' experiences throughout the twentieth century.[16] More recently Gerald Davis and, especially, Paul MacKenzie have looked at questions about the general treatment of prisoners in the First World War and the Second World War.[17] Nevertheless, even these articles give little attention to the Italian experiences, and detailed study of the Italians in British imperial hands has remained limited to a small number of book chapters, journal articles and local studies.[18] These have provided a basic outline of the development of British policy towards Italian prisoners and some understanding of the captives' reaction to their treatment, but nothing approaching an overall synthesis of the issues involved. Of some comparative relevance to this study are two major works that deal wholly or partially with the United States' treatment of their Italian prisoners. A general work by George C. Lewis and John Mewha gives a wide perspective on the way policy had been developed over the previous two centuries, but the most comprehensive volume on the subject is that of Louis E. Keefer, *Italian Prisoners of War in America 1942–1946: Captives or Allies?*, which deals with all aspects of American policy towards the Italians. In addition, there have also been studies of particular localities or camps where prisoners were held which use oral history and other archival sources to portray the relationships between the inmates and the communities with which they came into contact.[19]

Until the 1980s, the Italian-language historiography on Italian prisoners-of-war had been confined to two distinct experiences: firstly the harsh treatment meted out to Italian soldiers by their erstwhile Axis partners the Germans after the Italian surrender in 1943 when some 650,000 were interned and shipped northwards to act as a supplementary labour supply for the Nazi war effort;[20] secondly, there was the fate of the 84,830 soldiers unaccounted for on the Eastern front. At the end of the war, the Soviet Union admitted to having around 20,000 men who had been taken prisoner by the Red Army, but only approximately

12,000 survived long enough to return home.[21] While it is undoubtedly true that the victims of these two captivities suffered far more severely than fellow countrymen who became the prisoners of other powers, the focus on the Nazis and Soviets as captors also helped to reinforce the idea of postwar Italy as being firmly in the 'western' camp and distanced from both an Axis past and communist present.

In the same way, Giorgio Rochat has spoken of forty years of silence on the issues surrounding Italy's 600,000 servicemen in British, American and French captivity,[22] a silence engendered by the perceived need to show her as a partner of the western powers and not one of their erstwhile enemies. Thus only in recent years have Italian historians begun to give the experiences of these prisoners in the west greater attention. Prior to this, the only sources had been memoirs, but most of these had enjoyed only a limited circulation.[23] Nonetheless, they reflected the view that the trials and tribulations of these prisoners had been lost and forgotten in the process of constructing the collective Italian memory of the Second World War. One wrote, for example, of his years in India as a 'bitter martyrdom', and of how he and his comrades became a group apart – even from others who had fought in the armed forces – on account of their experiences in captivity.[24] Beyond the memoirs, there have been one or two attempts to produce comprehensive narratives on Italian prisoners in all the theatres of war, most notably by Luigi Pignatelli in 1969;[25] but the most comprehensive academic study on Italian prisoners in Allied hands to date is undoubtedly Flavio Giovanni Conti, *I prigionieri di guerra italiani 1940–1945*.[26] Published in 1986, this volume uses an extensive range of Italian and United States (but not British) archival and secondary sources to examine the various problems associated with prisoners-of-war in the Italian context before dealing with each captor power and the political divisions among the prisoners themselves. In addition, there is an extensive collection based on a conference held in Mantua in 1984, and edited by Romain Rainero. Here again, coverage was given to all the theatres in which Italians found themselves prisoners,[27] including important chapters on the French treatment of Italian prisoners and an insight into the captives' reaction to British propaganda carried out in India.[28] Beyond this, there have been a small number of journal articles which have added further to an understanding of the Italians in captivity, but much remains obscure.

This book is primarily an in-depth study of British policy towards the soldiers of her defeated Italian enemy during the Second World War, and an attempt to demonstrate the multitude of problems which the imperial authorities faced in dealing with captured enemy servicemen and how these problems were overcome. To that end, the narrative begins with a brief survey of British pre-war plans for dealing with prisoners, as in 1939 very little thought had been given to the treatment of enemy POWs by the responsible British authorities (primarily the War Office and Foreign Office). While policies and precedents existed from the First World War, the intervening 1929 Geneva Convention was as yet an untried piece of regulatory machinery. The first chapter demonstrates the extent and limitations of initial British plans, how they affected the small numbers of Italian captives in the first six months of hostilities and how the Foreign Office set up machinery for communication with the Fascist regime in Rome through a protecting power, and appropriate links with the International Committee of the Red Cross (ICRC).

From this follows a detailed examination of the treatment of the first large captures of Italian servicemen in the Middle Eastern and Abyssinian theatres in December 1940 and early 1941. This was the first real test for British plans and demonstrated that success on this scale created a whole range of difficulties for the military commanders in the field. These included the Italians as a drain on resources, as a security risk, as a hindrance to military operations by their sheer numbers, and as a danger to political stability in Egypt. What followed was a policy of dispersal and it is no exaggeration to say that Italian prisoners could be found in almost every corner of the British Empire at some time during or immediately after the war. However, the majority was concentrated in Britain, South Africa, East Africa, Australia and India. Chapter 2 charts the series of War Cabinet decisions that led to the movement of Italian prisoners from the Middle East to the United Kingdom. In May 1940, the British government had decided that, because of the security risks involved, German and later Italian civilians and POWs were too dangerous to be kept in the British Isles. This infamous policy of deportation to Canada and Australia became the norm and remained in force for German POWs until 1944. Yet by 1941, the parallel but unrelated imperatives of Wavell's need to move Italians from the Middle East, and labour shortages in the United Kingdom, prompted plans for the import of POWs to supplement the agricultural labour force. A small experimental group was followed almost immediately by larger numbers which swelled the total POW population to more than 150,000 by 1944. These prisoners were prized by various government departments as a docile but potentially invaluable source of labour, and this chapter examines their transhipment, arrival, and conditions once in Great Britain.

Dispersal elsewhere in the Empire required extensive negotiations between the various government departments in London and with the dominion and imperial authorities to bring this about. In addition, there were practical problems in executing this policy (which amounted to moving prisoners many thousands of miles from where they had been captured). These included the difficulties of provisioning, transporting and guarding en route, and arranging for an appropriate reception in the receiving country. Finally, there was also the impact which this dispersal to all parts of the globe had on the prisoners themselves, how they reacted, and how their government attempted to protect them. All these issues are examined in Chapter 3 in relation to Kenya and South Africa, and Chapter 4 in relation to Australia.

The interrogation of prisoners to gain military and political intelligence was a priority for all belligerent powers. In this respect, the British authorities used a variety of methods to extract information from their Italian prisoners. The information gleaned in the North African theatre provided an important element in shaping British perceptions of their Italian enemy. The first section of Chapter 5 looks at both the successes and failures of this process, focusing on the assessment and utilisation of the intelligence material obtained, and on the picture it gave about Italian morale in general, and about the views of the prisoners in particular. This, in turn, serves to highlight the comparisons noted by contemporaries about the differences between the German and Italian forces fighting in the North African theatre.

Chapter 5 also examines how Italian POWs were employed in the propaganda war waged against Fascist Italy by various British governmental and military agencies. In part this was a consequence of the British perception of Italian soldiers as uncommitted to the Axis cause. It fostered the belief that large numbers of captives would be open to political re-education and that this would facilitate the formation of anti-Fascist military and political organisations which could then be used to further the Allied cause during and after hostilities. These programmes were organised by the PWE, whose clandestine efforts to produce a Free Italy movement, while largely unsuccessful in themselves, did provide the experience for the planned re-education of German prisoners at the end of the war.

The Italian surrender in September 1943 represented not only a major breakthrough for the Allies in their war against the Axis, but also brought with it a whole array of additional problems. Not the least of these was the status of Italians captured during the previous three years of hostilities. By this time, the captives had been spread to all quarters of the globe and were proving to be extremely useful as a source of labour, especially in Britain, her Empire and several of her dominions. Chapter 6 examines the way in which the British authorities attempted to hold on to their Italian captives against the background of the wider negotiations about the future status of the post-surrender Italian state, the development of the concept of co-belligerency, and the postwar reconstruction of Anglo-Italian relations

Chapter 7 looks at the post-armistice history of the Italian prisoners in the United Kingdom, their increasing levels of freedom and the problems this created; for the authorities, the prisoners themselves and the public at large. After September 1943, these men continued to be perceived in many quarters as an essential element of the Home Front and the war effort. They were encouraged to become 'co-operators' who could be used on a much wider range of tasks than prisoners-of-war. However the inability of the authorities to provide sufficient incentive and the changing military situation both served to complicate matters as the war reached its end. Public opinion also had some bearing on the treatment and liberties accorded to prisoners and contemporary archive material sheds some light on the British attitudes to the enemy in its midst.

The dispersal throughout the Empire of tens of thousands of Italian captives, mainly to Australia, India, Kenya, Palestine and South Africa in 1941–2 may have relieved the strategic and logistical pressures posed by these prisoners on Middle Eastern Command, but it created different sets of problems in host countries which had initially been enthusiastic to offer their assistance to the mother-country in its hour of need. Although the colonial and dominion governments realised the labour potential of POWs, the social and racial structures of these territories made their efficient use problematic. For example, both dominion and colonial territories were woefully short of manpower, yet could not afford to use native militias or non-white troops of any description to act as guards for Axis Caucasians without seriously undermining the existing racial hierarchy. This problem took on a special significance in the fraught racial and political structures of South Africa. Therefore, Chapter 8 employs a comparative framework to explain the differences in treatment meted out by the detaining powers to Italian captives between 1940 and 1947.

Once hostilities in Europe had ended in May 1945, the British imperial authorities had finally to confront the need to repatriate all their Italian prisoners. How the captives responded to their continued incarceration and their slow repatriation in the years 1945–7 forms the basis for the final chapter. It seeks to explain British government decisions on the issue and to chronicle the last stages of the relationship between the British Empire and its Italian 'guests'. Yet even the final departures of Italian prisoners back to their homeland in the years 1945–7 do not really mark the end of the story. The experiences of these men sometimes led to their return to the country in which they had been held captive. Relationships forged with local women in the times when rules against fraternisation were relaxed or overlooked could often lead to marriage, and exposure to a different and potentially much better way of life could often also act as an incentive. Even if the prisoners themselves did not return, their stories would encourage members of their families to look for work in Britain or the dominions – an option facilitated by Britain's shortage of labour in the postwar era and the active encouragement of immigrant labour from continental Europe. While the postwar settlement of prisoners overseas cannot be said to have instigated new patterns of Italian migration (for example, there had been a visible Italian community in Britain from the nineteenth century and Italian migration to South Africa could be traced back several centuries), there is no doubt that they helped bolster and expand Italian communities throughout the British Empire and several of the dominions.

1
British Planning and Policy for Prisoners of War, 1939–41

When war with Germany was declared on 3 September 1939, the few British government plans for dealing with enemy civilians involved Home Office programmes for screening and the incarceration only of those who were perceived as a threat to security. This was based on the lessons learned during the First World War when wholesale internment programmes fuelled by anti-alien press campaigns and the notorious 'spy-fever' had led to violence and much unnecessary distress. Likewise, the War Office had earmarked only a small number of sites to be used as POW camps, as there was no expectation of large numbers being brought to Britain, and it was assumed that any fighting would take place on continental European soil. The period of the 'phoney war' bore out this prediction, with little or no fighting between Allied and German forces in the West and hostilities largely limited to the air and high seas. Thus in March 1940, it was reported to the House of Commons that there were no more than 257 German POWs being held in the country.[1] They were supplemented by a small number of captives from the Norwegian campaign and a contingent of some 1,200 Germans, mainly paratroopers, who had been captured by the Dutch and rapidly evacuated before that country's surrender on 15 May 1940.[2]

By this stage, as a result of the Norwegian debacle, the German invasion of France and the Low Countries and the supposed 'fifth column' threat, the Neville Chamberlain administration had fallen, to be replaced by a national government with Winston Churchill as prime minister. In the ensuing weeks, responsibility for security matters was vested in a new committee, the Home Defence (Security) Executive (HD(S)E) chaired by Viscount Swinton. Its deliberations took place in secret, and even members of the War Cabinet were not privy to its advice which was sent direct to the prime minister.[3] It was this committee which recommended the removal of all 'dangerous' enemy aliens to the dominions. In early June, the governments of Canada, Australia and South Africa were all approached to see if they were willing to accommodate those whom the Churchill cabinet wished to expel. While the Canadian and South African governments expressed some doubts about admitting internees because they had civilian internment problems of their own, all three were prepared to countenance the arrival of POWs. One can only surmise that prisoners were deemed less of a potential security risk than enemy civilians. In the event, Canada was persuaded to take all the initial deportees. It is now generally accepted that the 'fifth column' scare was wildly overestimated, and that the deportation policy was a panic measure for which there was no real justification.[4] At the time, however, it must have seemed an attractive proposition, to show that the new government was taking positive action at a time when military matters were going from bad to worse with the French about to sign an armistice with the Axis and the evacuation of British forces in disarray from Dunkirk.

The initial intention had been just to deport enemy aliens but sometime in May the programme was extended to include POWs as well. This prompted a good deal of protest from the Foreign Office, which was unrepresented on the HD(S)E, about the dubious legality of moving prisoners overseas.[5] While the British Empire might be considered as a single entity, moving enemy servicemen away from the theatre of war in which they were captured and exposing them to danger in a war zone, such as the North Atlantic, were both seen as potential breaches of the Convention. Nevertheless, Foreign Office objections were summarily overridden, thus demonstrating its weak position in these matters, and its legal department was forced to produce *ex post facto* justifications for what Churchill and the HD(S)E had decreed. As one Foreign Office official remarked, if the risk had to be taken, at least it could be said that 'we are sending them somewhere where they will be safe from air-raids'.[6] Nonetheless, this policy did set the precedent which was to be followed throughout the war and affect many hundreds of thousands of Axis servicemen: namely the practice of shipping them across the high seas to any part of the world deemed suitable for their incarceration.

In the first days of July 1940, several ships set sail for Canada, taking German prisoners, merchant seamen and civilians, together with members of the Italian community who had come under suspicion after Mussolini had belatedly brought Italy into the war on 10 June. Most of the servicemen were destined to spend the following six years in Canadian captivity while the civilians were gradually allowed to return after the scandal and mismanagement of internment were exposed. Several hundred of those deported were less fortunate, being on board the *Arandora Star* when she was sunk by a German U-Boat early in the morning of 2 July.[7] At this stage, the number of Italian prisoners in British hands was negligible. A few merchant seamen had been caught in British ports, but there were few if any servicemen taken into captivity in the weeks and months following the Italian entry into the war. At this stage, the United Kingdom had only two permanent prisoner of war camps, one at Grizedale in Cumberland for officers and a second at Glen Mill in Oldham, Lancashire for other ranks. For as long as the policy remained to deport all prisoners to Canada as soon as was practical, any increase in capacity was perceived as superfluous.[8] Further away from the immediate war zone, the colonial administrations and dominion governments also took steps to identify and intern German and Italian nationals and to secure any enemy service personnel who fell into their hands.

In the first year of war, the British authorities had to give little thought to POW problems. True, they had to abide by the terms of the 1929 Geneva Convention, but for the most part, the individual departments concerned relied on precedents set during the Great War. POWs were primarily the responsibility of the War Office and to expedite matters a Directorate of Prisoners of War (DPW) was created under the Adjutant-General's Department. It was run from its inception by Major-General Sir Alan Hunter (later succeeded in late 1941 by the 'first class administrator' Major-General E. C. Gepp) and its work included the administration and accommodation of prisoners in accordance with the Convention and other existing regulations. Inevitably, dealing with prisoners also involved contact with the enemy and therefore with protecting powers, neutrals and other non-governmental organisations such as the International Red Cross. This was the ambit of the Foreign Office, which dealt with most of these matters via the Consular (War) Department, an organisation which ultimately became the Prisoners of War Department (PWD).[9] Initially, both these organisations were often no more than one or two people or a 'desk' within another department. Only when problems started to increase did the scale of their operations and staffing also undergo a commensurate expansion.[10]

Until 1941, there was an *ad hoc* but nonetheless essential liaison between these organisations. A small committee had existed within the War Office which had representatives from other departments, but increasing public disquiet about the many thousands of British troops who were in enemy hands after June 1940 and the demands of dominion governments for a greater say in the fate of their men finally led to the establishment of a formal committee which included all the government departments concerned as well as the dominion High Commissioners. The committee, chaired by the Secretary of State for War, was the Imperial Prisoners of War Committee (IPOWC) which was formally announced in the House of Lords by the Secretary of State for Dominion Affairs, Viscount Cranborne, on 30 April 1941. Its purpose was to secure co-ordination of the action of the government in regard to matters relating to both Allied and enemy prisoners.[11] Ultimately, it was the DPW, War Office, and PWD working under the aegis of the IPOWC which were responsible for the treatment of Italian and other Axis prisoners, both during and beyond the war's end. However, as we will see, the Italians especially became the focus for plans from other government departments and agencies, both civilian and military. Indeed, the decision to deport the German prisoners, taken in May 1940, showed clearly that such actions, sanctioned at the highest level by Churchill and the War Cabinet on advice from the HD(S)E, could often conflict with what the individual ministries and later the IPOWC thought appropriate.

Negotiating with the enemy

As soon as war was declared, the relevant departments of British and Italian government began the process of creating the necessary machinery to oversee the workings of the Geneva Convention to which they were both signatories. The Foreign Office began by sending a *note verbale* to Rome on 5 July 1940 but had to wait more than five months for a response. Even then the Italian government wanted a further reply from London before it was prepared to regard the Convention as being in force.[12] While this tactic was easy to sustain when so few prisoners were involved, the situation changed quite radically when large numbers of Italians began surrendering in North Africa and Abyssinia. At that point, as the Admiralty observed, 'the Italians might well be interested in the welfare of Italian prisoners in the light of recent events'.[13] This prevarication over formal agreements did not prevent the United States taking up the mantle of protecting power for the British, and the Swiss an equivalent position for the Italians. There were few immediate problems, and over a period of time, additional matters outside the immediate scope of the Convention were also subject to bilateral agreements. Under Article 23 of the Prisoner of War Convention there were reciprocal arrangements for the pay of war correspondents and captured army nurses, and an agreed exchange rate of sterling–lira which was set at £ = 72 lira. In addition, under Article 24 measures were taken to enable the transfer of credits during capitivity, and under Article 23 the stoppage of pay for prisoners. There was also a reciprocal free issue of tobacco. Under Article 9 of the Sick and Wounded Convention, protected personnel were given special privileges and, within Article 12, there were agreements about their retention when required.[14] Other matters were left vague or not deemed worthy of a formal agreement – for example, the numbers of postcards prisoners were permitted to send, or whether they could receive (medicinal) drugs in parcels. Commenting on these and other marginal matters at the end of 1942, the Foreign Office noted that 'so far as [can be] seen, we have had no reply which is quite in accordance with Italian methods'.[15]

In the spring of 1941, the Admiralty produced more detailed figures for naval POWs. It recorded a total of 230 Italian officers and 2,432 ratings having been captured, a figure which included the personnel from at least one submarine. In addition, there were 151 merchant seamen who had all been apprehended in British ports when war was declared. This latter group was the subject of some discussion because their precise status was unclear. The Germans had treated captured British merchant seamen as POWs, imprisoning them alongside naval personnel in *Marlag* Xb, mainly because their own merchant mariners were considered to be state servants and an arm of the military.[16] This was something of an embarrassment to the British government as their merchant seamen were civilian employees with few employment rights and certainly no claim on the terms of the Geneva Convention. In August 1940, when the control of civilian internment camps had been transferred from the War Office to the Home Office, the German merchant seamen had been kept as prisoners in War Office hands while the few Italians had been transferred to Home Office camps as internees. This strange differentiation had grown up because the bulk of the 2,590 or more German merchant seamen[17] had been captured on the high seas, brought in by the Royal Navy and dealt with by the military authorities; while all the Italian merchant mariners had been arrested in British ports and thus dealt with by the police and local authorities.[18] The fact that such small numbers were involved made a rectification of this anomaly a low priority and the Italian merchant seamen appear to have remained in Home Office hands, interned with other civilians in camps on the Isle of Man. However, this discussion only related to merchant mariners captured and brought to the United Kingdom. It is evident, however, that those who were captured by British forces in other theatres or by dominion and colonial authorities (with one exception) were similarly treated as civilian internees until February 1942 when the British government decided on grounds of reciprocity and administrative convenience to reclassify merchant seamen as POWs.[19]

The problems of military success

The first real test of British policy came as a result of the unexpected scale of the early military successes against the Italians in Libya. On 9 September 1940, the Italian Tenth Army under the command of Marshal Rodolfo Graziani had attacked British positions on the Egyptian frontier. Despite its numerical superiority, the Italian offensive soon ground to a halt. Even before the attack, General Sir Archibald Wavell, British Commander-in-Chief, Middle Eastern forces, had formulated a counter-offensive to drive Graziani out of Egypt and capture the strategically important port of Tobruk. What began as a five-day raid quickly turned into a comprehensive British victory. By early February 1941, British and Commonwealth troops, who in the field had never numbered more than 30,000, had swept the Italians from Cyrenaica, advancing 550 miles and capturing 133,000 prisoners and vast quantities of war material. Churchill was delighted, noting that 'it looks as if these people were corn ripe for the sickle'.[20] Conversely on the Italian side, Count Ciano was stunned. The British attack had come like a 'thunderbolt' and, he recorded in his diary, 'something is the matter with our Army if five divisions allow themselves to be pulverised in two days'.[21] The Secretary of State for India, Leo Amery, was much more pointed in his assessment of British successes. When updating the Viceroy, Lord Linlithgow, on recent events, he remarked that while Germany was consolidating in Bulgaria, 'Wavell [was] mopping up the Wops in Africa'.[22]

The Italian collapse saw the destruction of four complete army corps, comprising nine divisions and part of a tenth. It was also a major surprise, even though British military and intelligence agencies were aware of certain problems that hampered their enemy's military proficiency and effectiveness. However, it was the huge number of prisoners that astonished British commanders and their political masters. One senior officer, General E. P. Nares, recalled that only two POW cages had been planned, each to hold 1,000 captives. 'In fact we thought that if we actually filled those cages we should have had a pretty successful party!'[23] This apparently resounding victory nevertheless posed immediate problems for the British in their attempts to process and despatch the prisoners from forward zones back to Egypt. Lieutenant-General Richard O'Connor, who commanded the Western Desert Force during Operation 'Compass', recalled that when 15,000 prisoners were brought in after operations on 12 December 1940, they 'added still further to our administrative difficulties'.[24]

On 7 January 1941, Wavell reported that recent captures had totalled around 59,000 (white) Italians and 14,000 (native) Libyans. The sheer numbers presented problems enough even when they had been evacuated to rear areas, with continuing difficulties in finding sufficient guards, accommodation and food for all of them. In addition, they were perceived as a military and political menace in a theatre of operations which would 'roll backwards and forwards [with] Egyptian sympathies veering at each stage'. Wavell believed that their continued presence adjacent to war zones would constitute a hindrance to future military operations. Moreover, he was also concerned about their potential impact on the political situation inside Egypt which was anything but secure. On these grounds, it was 'essential and urgent that [the] maximum possible number be evacuated from Egypt at the earliest date'.[25] Yet the problem continued to grow, as more and more Italians surrendered, and it was reported that the Tobruk cage held upwards of 20,000 men for periods during January.[26] Their removal was essential, not only to take them away from forward areas, but also because they were placing an intolerable strain on limited water resources, notably the wells around Buq Buq and Sidi Barrani. Finding guards was equally problematic and troops from the support group of the Western Desert Force had to be deployed in this role who would otherwise have been used in battle.[27] Yet very little transport was available and whole columns of prisoners were marched eastwards in Egypt with few, if any, guards.[28]

This situation was almost immediately compounded by similar successes in the Horn of Africa where 14,000 Italian and colonial troops had been captured in Somaliland by the end of February, and more than 50,000 in Abyssinia by British East African forces commanded by Lieutenant-General Sir Alan Cunningham operating from Kenya. To all intents and purposes, the war in Abyssinia had come to an end almost before it had begun, with a wholesale collapse of Italian military resistance. With the exceptions of the mountain fortress of Gondar in the north and General Pietro Gazzera's forces in the south-west, the whole of the country had been liberated by April. There are some uncertainties about the total numbers of prisoners taken in this theatre. Operational records show that for the period February to July 1941, there were 49,258 (European) Italian and 26,179 African prisoners; but at the end of May, Whitehall was being told that 58,000 Italians and 47,000 native colonial troops had been taken into captivity.[29] As in the North African theatre, the sheer numbers of prisoners stretched already limited resources, and a military report noted that 'the maintenance of such a number in the various [forward] locations furnished a really serious problem which, on certain occasions, was only overcome by the capture of large quantities of Italian food supplies'.[30] Thus not only were there military and security imperatives, but also crucial provisioning reasons for these men to be moved away from Abyssinia as soon as possible.

In an attempt to alleviate this crisis and to relieve troops from the burden of guarding large numbers of prisoners, Wavell had unilaterally sent some 5,000 Italian officers to India, but required Whitehall's sanction for any further movements. In the interim, he had also received permission to disarm and demobilise large numbers of Abyssinian, Eritrean and Somali colonial troops. (This in itself may help to explain some of the discrepancies in the numbers noted above.[31]) However, this could not be a solution for the rapidly expanding numbers of Italians being taken into captivity. Certainly a remedy was available. Shipping used to supply the Middle East theatre from the United Kingdom, India and the dominions was making return voyages empty, providing an obvious means of transport from Suez. Moreover, the governments of India and the dominions had agreed, during the dark days of June 1940, to provide space for internees expelled from Britain and Axis prisoners, but the situation demanded some immediate action and urgent enquiries were made in Australia, Canada, Ceylon, India, Jamaica, Kenya, Mauritius and South Africa.

The Indian government responded promptly, undertaking to accept 16,000 POWs by mid-January and more by the end of February 1941. South Africa offered to take 20,000 and expressed a willingness to increase the number if necessary. Ceylon agreed to take 2,000 but wanted guarantees that all expenditure including the requisition of land, erection of camps, recruitment of guards and costs of rations would be borne by the Imperial government. London replied that it was prepared to meet the costs of transport and maintenance.[32] Finally, Australia also agreed to receive 50,000 Germans and Italians. In the event, it was not accommodation, but transport which determined the rates at which prisoners were removed from the Middle East. The War Office had approved the use of troopships, such as the former luxury liner *Queen Elizabeth*, returning empty from Suez to Australia, as transport for Italians to India, Ceylon and the Antipodes, and convoy ships returning to South Africa from Egypt were also pressed into service. However, the capacity and the frequency of these ships was totally insufficient to meet Wavell's needs. Thus while the total number of prisoners in the Middle East had increased to 160,000 by the end of March 1941, only 30,000 had been removed to India and 10,000 to South Africa. Ostensibly, the problems of shipping made it difficult to send prisoners to other destinations. As a result, the Indian government were prevailed upon to increase their quota to 84,000 and the South Africans to 45,000. At that point, the Indian and Australian governments became alarmed by the situation in the Far East. Delhi, with a weather-eye on the gathering storm, claimed it could not receive any further prisoners, and the Australians wanted their quota cut to 16,000. As a result, South Africa was asked to increase its quota once again, this time to 60,000, a move sanctioned by Pretoria. While there were undoubtedly problems in moving prisoners away from Egypt, as General Sir Claude Auchinleck, Wavell's successor as C-in-C Middle East, reported in July 1941: 'Export business is brisk at present.'[33]

For the prisoners taken in East Africa, there was an alternative, and many thousands were sent by rail and sea to camps in Kenya. Indeed, Kenya proved to be doubly useful, not only for the permanent internment of East African prisoners, but also as a temporary location for prisoners from North Africa in transit to other destinations. By mid-April 1941 there were an estimated 17,822 Italian and colonial prisoners in Kenya and approximately 41,000 in the Sudan. However, the transfer to Kenya was far from easy because inadequate road and railway networks in Italian East Africa slowed down the movement of prisoners from the south of the country to the collection point at Nanyuki in central Kenya. The problem was further compounded by the large numbers of Italian civilians captured in Addis Ababa and other towns and cities. They too provided a drain on scarce resources. General Cunningham thought the best solution was the immediate repatriation of civilians, and he pleaded with Sir Henry Monck-Mason Moore, Governor of Kenya, for help. Moore sympathised with Cunningham's position, admitting that even though the Abyssinian campaign was 'fizzling out', they were going to have their 'hands full with prisoners of war and keeping supplies going' to the occupied territories. For the moment, however, he could do no more than offer moral support.

The inhospitable climate also exacerbated the transportation problems. When it rained, roads became quagmires and all but disappeared. In northern Abyssinia, prisoners were sent by sea to Kenya. Between Addis Ababa and the port of Berbera in British Somaliland, seven staging camps were constructed and a 'gradual process of evacuation ... by road and railway' was initiated. Yet even when this human cargo reached the coast to await embarkation for Mombasa, the whole process remained dependent on the availability of shipping. When this failed to materialise, the populations of all the staging camps became 'stationary'. Until shipping could be allocated, the camps became, in effect, permanent, and in April 1941 there were still 50,949 prisoners in forward camps in Abyssinia.[34]

However gratifying the large-scale capture of prisoners may have been to the British authorities and a boost to morale at home, it was self-evident that the sheer weight of numbers was putting enormous pressure on British resources. While the terms of the Geneva Convention allowed the capturing power to use prisoners as labour, there were a number of important restrictions, and while the matter had been discussed in Britain in the early months of the war, the small numbers involved and the security implications made the discussion almost academic. Only with the substantial captures in Libya and East Africa did the issue resurface. The prisoners did represent a potentially enormous pool of labour, but the initial impetus was to give them work to occupy their mental and physical energies in order to prevent boredom. During late December 1940 and early January 1941, Whitehall and Middle East Command discussed the issue. Under Articles 7, 9 and 31 of the Convention, prisoners were not permitted to work in combat zones and consequently their use was restricted to the rear echelons. The War Office suggested that prisoners be employed in labour companies but Cairo rejected the idea. It was argued that the only work available was in areas where there was abundant civilian labour. Rumours that prisoners were to be used had already led to outbreaks of labour unrest amongst the local population in Egypt. Wavell stressed that it was impossible to employ prisoners in the same places as civilians, and that it would prove difficult to find work that prisoners could undertake within the terms of the Convention which would not be better done by civilians.

The War Office disagreed, arguing that there had to be places outside combat zones where prisoners could be employed without conflicting with civilian labour or the terms of the Geneva Convention. It was suggested that Italians might be used on road, railway and pipeline maintenance in the Western Desert, or in unloading ships in Egyptian ports, or on salvaging equipment from the battlefield, or in the improvement of communications installations in the Sudan and East Africa. Similarly, the War Office could not understand why prisoners, whom they believed undoubtedly included personnel experienced in roadmaking, could not be used to replace Pioneer and Indian labour companies[35] – something which Wavell had dismissed as uneconomic except for certain technically skilled personnel.[36] The War Office did appreciate that the shortage of guards was a problem, but pointed out that steps were being taken to rectify matters. In the meantime, it was suggested that newly-arrived reinforcements or troops of lower combat ability might be utilised, supervised by Royal Engineers or communications units. It was stressed that there were three overriding concerns which made it vital for Middle Eastern Command to employ as many prisoners as possible. Firstly, it was essential to economise on British manpower requirements generally and the more prisoner labour which could be be employed the better, as this would free British troops for more important tasks. There was also a need to reduce demands on Indian manpower employed in the North African theatre as this was proving expensive for the Indian government to maintain. Finally, as the number of captives increased rapidly there was a real difficulty in finding accommodation for them outside Egypt and supplying shipping for their evacuation. Thus, if it was impossible to move them, it would be better that they were used constructively than left idle.

These arguments were relayed to Wavell with the injunction to reconsider the replacement of Pioneer companies by prisoners and a compromise of sorts was reached. The increasing demand for labour in Egypt coupled with the lack of outgoing shipping forced Wavell to create several prisoner labour companies. However, Cairo was able to side-step Whitehall's demands for large-scale mobilisation of Italian prisoners by employing captured Libyans in Cyrenaica. As one Colonial Office official admitted, no matter how many Italian prisoners were eventually placed in labour companies, it would 'not affect appreciably the urgent problem of removing as many as possible from Egypt quickly'.[37]

Some of Wavell's worst fears about housing Italian prisoners in Egypt were borne out in these first months of the campaign, but this seems to have been primarily due to the vast numbers involved rather than deliberate neglect or malice. When Dr G. Vaucher of the ICRC visited the Italian prisoners in Egypt in January 1941, he thought the British authorities were showing goodwill in carrying out the Geneva Convention, 'but are hampered by the unexpectedly large numbers to be dealt with'. The Foreign Office commented that Vaucher's report made interesting reading:

Captivity in British hands must be luxury compared to conditions in the Italian lines, where the men had become filthy. They have since been cleaned, and there are no serious complaints; the chief one relates to the bread ration, which is apparently low by Italian standards. Meat is said to contain an undue proportion of bone, and there were not enough palliasses some officers having to sleep on sand.

In fact, food was a prime topic of conversation in the early days of captivity. The British discovered that the Italians preferred more bread and less meat. 'They like a loose loaf rather than the denser tinned loaf, vegetable soups and macaroni as much as possible. Quantity rather than quality. They would eat bacon, jam and rice but would not miss them much if withdrawn and would only eat porridge if very hungry.' One War Office official requested that a more liberal diet of bread and vegetable soup be provided arguing that it would prove cheaper than the 'depot diet' laid down by military authorities.

The Italian perception of their situation was somewhat different. Prisoners taken in Abyssinia reported being force-marched to Addis Ababa where they were 'attacked with insults by the excited indigenous populace'. More alarmingly, physical attacks left one man dead and fifteen wounded. Prisoners taken in Libya were subjected to a similar 'exhibition' in the streets of Cairo.[38] This latter event was filmed by British Movietone News, which led to an extended debate in various Whitehall corridors about whether this contravened the Geneva Convention. Not surprisingly, it was Churchill who pushed the idea of parading captures through the streets as being 'highly beneficial'[39] as it would demonstrate the scale of the victories achieved. He also championed the idea of films which could then be shown more widely. Although Article 2 of the Convention dictated that prisoners should be protected from public curiosity, and the British and Italian governments had agreed that journalists would not be allowed access to prisoners, it was nonetheless decided that photographs and films taken outside the camps should not be prohibited, provided they were not derogatory to the prisoners. Certainly, it seems that the Convention was not going to be allowed to get in the way of a propaganda opportunity.[40]

There were also complaints about the ways in which the prisoners were treated. Their transport from one place to another, and from one continent to another was often traumatic.[41] Conditions were invariably cramped as the masses of Italians were moved away from the Middle East. Rainero describes the conditions endured by some prisoners as inhumane and responsible for losses of life which could not be accurately assessed. He also noted that many of the men suffered from serious malnutrition. Men sent to India were confined, 150 at a time, in a space 20 metres by 8 metres and were permitted only one hour of fresh air a day. For nourishment, they received a mug of tea in the morning, and then during the day they were given a slice of bread and a cup of warm water. Upon arrival, their belongings were hurled from on high onto the decks of a motor boat moored alongside the vessel. There were also quoted instances of British guards looting the possessions of their captives.[42]

At the time, the poor treatment meted out to the Italians was undoubtedly worthy of complaint, and it would be naive to think that some of their guards were not culpable in mistreating their charges. However, the complaints listed paled into insignificance when compared with events later in the war, and probably stemmed more from the unpreparedness of British Middle East Command in dealing with such huge numbers of prisoners than from any official policy of deliberate score-settling with the enemy. Shortages of accommodation and transport were a function of the sheer numbers involved. The perceived desperate need to remove these men from the area undoubtedly contributed to the overcrowding on ships chronicled by Rainero. Moreover, the shortages of food were exacerbated by the very different diets of the Italians when compared with their British counterparts and it took time for this to be recognised and then remedied. But finally, and perhaps most important of all, the prisoners were a long way down the list of priorities for Wavell and his staff attempting to eliminate the Italian threat to Egypt and North Africa.

The early campaigns in North Africa and Abyssinia set the tone for what was to follow in the remaining two and a half years of conflict between the two powers. The shifting fortunes of war saw many thousands of British, dominion and imperial troops fall into Italian hands, but they were dwarfed by the huge numbers of Italians captured in the various African theatres of war. The application of the Geneva Convention and the various supplementary agreements undoubtedly played a major role in the treatment of these men, but reciprocity was also a factor. Discussions within the IPOWC often centred on the equivalence of treatment between prisoners in Italian and Allied hands. Highlighted also in this early period were the many administrative, practical and security problems which these huge numbers created. The basis for the Italian diaspora throughout the British Empire was undoubtedly initially predicated on Wavell's perceived need to maintain security in Egypt and protect scarce resources. Later, other factors also played a role once the Italians came to be seen as a resource rather than just a liability to the British war effort.

2

The Essential Labour Supply: The Import of Italian POWs to the United Kingdom

As we have already seen, the Churchill government's policy on Axis prisoners-of-war captured in or near the United Kingdom was to hold them on the mainland for as short a time as possible before shipping them overseas to Canada. While the policy had been developed primarily to deal with the threat of a Nazi civilian 'fifth column', Italian civilians had also been included in the transports of supposedly dangerous enemy aliens to North America. At this stage, the nature of the war against Italy made it unlikely that more than a handful of her servicemen would be captured anywhere near North West Europe. While the policy of exporting 'dangerous' German prisoners to the dominions continued until 1944, the British government view of captured Italians underwent a complete change, resulting in the importing of Italians as a labour supply for the increasingly hard-pressed British war economy.

Consequently, at the time of the Italian surrender on 8 September 1943, there were 74,900 prisoners[1] in Britain, and by the end of hostilities in Europe this had increased to around 158,000.[2] The pattern of their dispersal also reflected the ways in which the British authorities' attitudes changed over time. Initially, it was intended that the prisoners should be sent to Scotland and the north of England, but even before the first drafts had arrived in late July 1941, new arrangements had been made for them to be distributed in the Midland counties.[3] Given that the need for agricultural labour was widespread, the decision to place them in more southerly parts of the kingdom could only imply that they were already being perceived by the authorities as less of a potential threat to security and public order. By 1945, Italians had been sent to camps in all corners of Britain, from St Columb in Cornwall and

27

Ashford in Kent to Dingwall near Inverness and Lamb Holm, one of the Orkney Islands.[4] They were also allowed increasing freedom of movement, to the point where several thousand were billeted on individual farms. Moreover, after the Italian surrender, their use was extended beyond the realms of agriculture to include all manner of tasks, some of which brought them into direct contact with the industrial and service sectors of the economy, and also with a much broader cross-section of the British people.

The importing of prisoners as a labour force

The possible use of enemy prisoners of war to offset labour shortages in the United Kingdom had been discussed since the early months of the conflict with Germany. The Ministries of Agriculture and Fisheries, and Supply (Forestry), both made representations to the Army Council and Ministry of Labour and National Service during October 1939 but found their requests refused. At that stage, it was felt that any such move would be widely resented as there was still widespread unskilled unemployment and that in any case there would be vehement opposition from the trade unions. However, Leslie Hore-Belisha, Secretary of State for War (1937–40), did not rule out changes and recommended an inter-departmental discussion on the issue. As one of his civil servants recorded:

> The Minister recognises ... that as the war proceeds unemployment will diminish and the labour of prisoners of war may be usefully turned to account and he sees no objection to preliminary plans being discussed departmentally in advance of such time on the understanding that there should be no (public) indication that the scheme is in contemplation.[5]

The discussions changed very little, not least because at that stage Britain had very few enemy prisoners-of-war. The only concession was made to the Forestry Commission which was told that it could use German prisoners held at Grizedale in Cumberland provided they were not removed from the camp.[6]

Thus when the Italians entered the war, there were no specific plans for prisoner use in the United Kingdom, and their small numbers in the early months of the conflict did not necessitate any changes of policy. As has been shown, this began to change rapidly as British successes in Libya and Abyssinia put pressure on Wavell and Middle East Command.

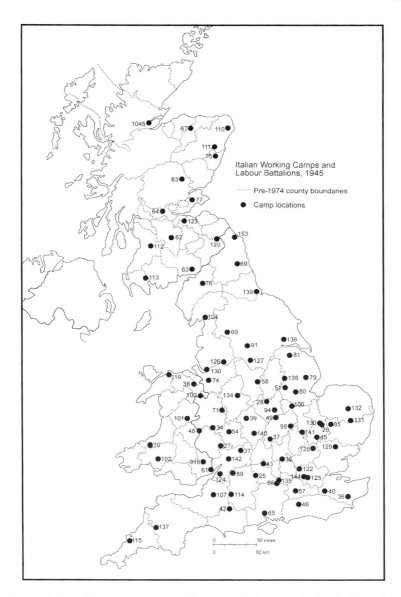

Map 1   Italian Working Camps and Labour Battalions in the United Kingdom, 1945

Source: Anthony J. Hellen, 'Temporary Settlements and Transient Populations: The Legacy of Britain's Prisoner of War Camps 1940–1948', *Erdkunde*, Band 53 (1999) pp. 191–291.

At the end of 1940, shortages were beginning to manifest themselves in the domestic labour market, just at the moment when the government was insisting on increased targets for agricultural production in general and food supplies in particular.[7] While the initial threat from the *Luftwaffe* had apparently been forestalled, the war for supplies in the Atlantic was beginning to bite. The 'happy time' of the German U-Boats (June–October 1940) had resulted in the sinking of more than 1.4 million tons of British shipping, and the total losses during 1940 stood at a staggering 4.7 million tons.[8]

These external and internal crises encouraged the Ministry of Agriculture and Fisheries to resubmit its request to the War Cabinet for prisoner labour, suggesting that 2,000–3,000 north Italian peasants be selected from amongst the prisoners taken in Libya to undertake essential drainage, ditching and reclamation work.[9] Given these new priorities, Captain David Margesson, the Secretary of State for War (1940–2) was agreeable 'provided that the prisoners [were] carefully selected so that they would not include any violent or Fascist types'.[10] The War Cabinet also gave the scheme a cautious welcome subject to the approval of the HD(S)E chaired by Lord Swinton,[11] which stipulated only that the prisoners be kept in large numbers to limit the number of guards required, and away from protected (military) areas. Certainly there were no great security objections except military ones: as a member of the HD(S)E observed, 'they are not even German'.[12] Subsequent to this decision being taken, discussions were held with the National Farmers' Union (NFU) and relevant trade unions to agree how the scheme might operate in practice. It was accepted that any work carried out by prisoners would have to be paid for at normal rates – to prevent their being perceived as cheap labour undermining minimum wage rates; and there was no intention that they should be employed on individual farms. It was agreed that employers would pay a sum equivalent to the 'wages' earned by the prisoners to the War Office which would help to offset the costs of feeding and housing the prisoners in camps.[13]

Inter-departmental discussions took place in February 1941 to discuss the practicalities of housing, clothing, guarding and employing the prisoners envisaged by the scheme. Even at this stage, only tented accommodation was being promised for the sites selected and no decisions were reached on the precise nature of the prisoners' uniforms.[14] The numbers requested were based not only on the presumed labour needs for drainage and reclamation work, but also on the numbers who might realistically be transported and accommodated in existing camp facilities. Certainly, the civil servants at the Ministry of Agriculture and Fisheries did not see a need for more than two or three thousand men, and it was only when requests were sent out to the various County War Agricultural Executive Committees that the true nature of the demand became apparent. These hard-pressed regional committees undoubtedly saw this new source of labour as a panacea for their problems and submitted bids for a total of 15,000 men. Furthermore, an inter-departmental meeting to discuss the terms of employment for the incoming Italians suggested that other civilian departments might also have uses for prisoner labour.[15] The military authorities were keen to extend the scheme too, suggesting that 15,000–20,000 prisoners 'of the type of good mechanic and workman fairly common among the Italians' might be used to conserve manpower resources at home.[16] The War Office could well have been influenced by intelligence reports emanating from Middle East Command. These indicated that many Italian Colonial Army prisoners thought the war unnecessary, were sympathetic to Britain and were virulently anti-German. Moreover, even the captured officers described themselves as 'Fascists by force' and resented the better pay and conditions given to the blackshirts who had made such a poor showing in battle.[17]

At this stage, Churchill was still worried about the possible security implications of such a step,[18] but he was soon to change his mind. In a memorandum to the War Cabinet Secretary, Sir Edward Bridges, on 29 May 1941, he outlined his reasons:

> It occurs to me that we must now consider using these Italian white prisoners in Great Britain. A plan was set on foot to bring 2,000 over here for the Ministry of Agriculture. I was not myself attracted by the idea, as it seemed to be on such a small scale but raising all kinds of novel complications. However, it might be better to use these Italian prisoners of war instead of bringing in disaffected Irish, over whom we have nothing like the same control. It would be worth while to make a plan for bringing in say 25,000 of these Italians, and employing them as an organised mobile body upon the land.[19]

His change of mind seems to have been prompted by increasing problems with recruiting Irish workers who had traditionally supplemented the British labour market. The Irish government had been anxious not to compromise its neutrality, and for security reasons Britain had placed restrictions on movement between the two countries after the fall of France. Moreover, the British authorities had been slow to realise that unskilled labour from the Irish Free State could be just as useful to the war economy as the skilled workers who were more obviously in short supply. As a result of all these factors, the movement of workers from southern Ireland to Britain had slowed to a trickle.[20] An even more pertinent problem was that of Northern Ireland. The scarcity of flax supplies had led to high levels of unemployment among linen workers there, but little movement of labour to the mainland. Moreover, even those who could be persuaded to move proved difficult to retain. Herbert Morrison, the Home Secretary, was scathing about them, claiming that they 'often returned [home] if bombed [although] less so since Belfast became a target'.[21] With the Irish Free State and Northern Ireland as just about the only large-scale sources of additional labour for the British war effort in 1940 and early 1941, it is easy to see why Italian prisoners began to be seen as such an attractive prospect.[22] Put another way, it seems that the impetus for the large-scale importation of prisoners into Britain arose directly out of the crisis in the labour market and the partial breakdown of traditional links with southern Ireland.

As the principle of bringing Italian prisoners to the United Kingdom as a labour force had already been established and many of the political, military and security details had been addressed and organised, it was not long before Churchill's idea of increasing the numbers of prisoners was put to the War Cabinet, in the form of a paper from the Lord President, Sir John Anderson.[23] The proposal suggested a new draft of 25,000 men, to be brought in on unescorted transports at the rate of 5,000 per month. This was determined by the likely availability of shipping and guards from the Middle East theatre, and the difficulties of finding space for guards making return journeys. Any diminution of space on outgoing ships would deny Middle East command reinforcements which had already been incorporated into military calculations. The suggestion was to minimise this potential loss by reducing the normal scale of one guard for every ten prisoners, and providing extra guards at any ports where the ships carrying them put in. Whether this calculation was based primarily on the supposed docility of the Italians or was merely a pragmatic response to an otherwise insoluble problem remains unclear. It was concluded that the C-in-C Middle East was to have the final say in whether he was prepared to sacrifice some reinforcements in exchange for the removal of prisoners from his theatre of operations. The War Office had estimated that guarding and administering these prisoners in the United Kingdom would require between six and seven thousand men, but this was to be circumvented by allocating men from the Pioneer Corps as guards, whose current work would then be done by the prisoners. This, in turn, would minimise the War Office's loss of effective manpower. This did, however, create some potential difficulties in the sense that the Pioneer Corps were engaged largely in low-level military work which, it could be argued, was forbidden by the terms of the Geneva Convention. However, at this stage, it was seen as an appropriate solution to the problem and the measure was approved by Cabinet.[24]

Detailed discussions at the end of June 1941 attempted to solve the more detailed technical problems of making the scheme a reality. It was hoped that numbers of skilled tradesmen could be found among the prisoners as well as those proficient in agriculture. However, it was made clear that projects employing fewer than 500 men would be impractical as the manpower costs of guarding and accommodating them would be too great. Location was also problematic. Prisoners would have to be kept away from military installations and centres of population. Moreover, the Foreign Office insisted that they should be housed in proper accommodation lest the Italians saw this as a violation of the Geneva Convention. This meeting also received a demand for 2,900 men from the Admiralty for work in the Orkneys, although even its representative was not sure if the work projected was classed as operational or defensive (the former being forbidden by the Convention).[25] Other ministries and government agencies were also given leave to bid for a proportion of this new labour force.

The first Italians to be brought from the Middle East arrived in the United Kingdom on 26 July 1941.[26] Before this, in April 1941, Major-General Sir Alan Hunter, head of the War Office Directorate for Prisoners of War and a member of the HD(S)E, had already suggested that guards might be dispensed with altogether as 'those being selected would be North Italians (not blackshirt battalions) who would be only too glad to work in agriculture and whose hearts were not in the war'.[27] At this stage, there was no direct experience of prisoners in the United Kingdom to justify this decision, but early reports of the first batch of prisoners undoubtedly bore out Hunter's confidence. Most were under 30 years of age, and were described as 'excellent' and 'containing some very good material', of good physique and having a willingness to work. Some were 'adept with sickle and scythe', while others were singled out for their adroit skills in ditching and drainage work. Although many had experience ploughing with horses and oxen, few had experience of tractors or threshing machines. Within weeks of their arrival, the HD(S)E, which had been so keen to deport German prisoners at the earliest opportunity, was prepared to relax the conditions for Italian prisoners working in agriculture still further, to the point of allowing small parties of two or three men to work without escorts.[28] This led the Ministry of Agriculture to ask if Italians could be billeted on individual farms. In effect, the ministry had been given access to exactly what it wanted, a compliant and flexible labour force which could be used more or less anywhere in the country with minimal restrictions.

This should not, however, suggest that all the administrative problems had been solved. It was recognised by all concerned that even if there were few security difficulties, the billeting of prisoners with farmers created all manner of other problems, not least linguistic ones. As an interim measure, the HD(S)E suggested that 'as an experiment', 500 prisoners be accommodated in hostels as a form of intermediate stage before their placement on individual farms. As the Ministry of Agriculture noted, this would also allow the farmers to get used to the idea.[29] The War Office raised objections both on the grounds that it would reduce controls over the prisoners, and because it would have to find the manpower for additional guards. It even went so far as to suggest that the hostels be entirely unguarded.[30] This was rejected and the War Office expressed itself willing to proceed with the experiment, in spite of its reservations, in the light of the pressing need for manpower at home. The War Office also succeeded in obtaining an assurance from the Cabinet that the Secretary of State for War would not be held responsible for any escapes.[31] Agreement on this scheme did not iron out all the problems, and discussions about the nature of the guard to be mounted over these hostels, whether it should be limited to night time, and how men were to be monitored on their rest-days continued until the end of the year.[32]

No sooner had this scheme come into force than attention was focused on the billeting of prisoners with farmers. When this had first been suggested, even the civil servants at the Ministry of Agriculture had wondered if the time was right for such a step.[33] At the end of December 1941, the ministry drafted a press release announcing the introduction of the new scheme. It was not expected to attract much attention except in the farming press. However, *The Times* and other papers reported it and the *Daily Express* even carried some comment, quoting apparent widespread discontent among the farmers and rural communities in general.[34] At this stage, the hostel scheme was barely in operation. Because of the changes made to the regulations regarding the guarding of prisoners and changes in the location of hostels, H. J. Johns at the Ministry of Agriculture reported that on 19 January 1942, only two had been filled, and even these two had only been occupied for a week.[35] By February it was reported that 438 men were accommodated in hostels where the security arrangements were 'considerably relaxed',[36] and a further 143 had been billeted on individual farms.[37] The location of hostels also occasionally created problems as GHQ (Home Forces) could not indicate on a map where prisoners and hostels should be excluded as this would betray security information. Thus, each request had to be dealt with on its merits.[38]

It was estimated that by the end of 1941 some 7,000 Italians would have arrived in the United Kingdom, and that the remainder of the sanctioned 28,000 would arrive early in 1942.[39] There had been an initial agreement that the majority of the prisoners would be allocated to agricultural work, with the War Department taking 9,000 to offset manpower losses created by the need to provide guards, and a small group of 600 being allocated to the Admiralty for work on the Orkney Islands. The success of the first drafts and the relaxation of the regulations encouraged other government departments to stake claims for this new and valuable supply of labour. Certainly, the Ministry of Labour felt that large numbers of men could be employed in gangs and away from population centres on timber production and civil engineering projects.[40] This led to disputes as each ministry guarded its quota jealously while others vied for allocations of their own. Requests came in from all quarters. The GPO wanted between 500 and 1,500 prisoners to dig cable trenches and the Board of Trade saw their potential for laying gas mains.[41] Adamant that it needed every available man, even the Ministry of Agriculture which had by far the lion's share of the prisoner labour, was forced to concede that some flexibility in initial allocation was required. Without the provision of proper accommodation, the movement of Italians to Britain would have to be slowed, to everyone's disadvantage.[42] The Foreign Office expressed concerns about potential complaints to the Protecting Powers and advised delay until work on camps was completed and shipping could be assured. However the non-arrival of promised drafts of prisoners actually served to exacerbate the situation by preventing the completion of the camps on schedule.[43] Thus while the Ministry of Agriculture felt it had prior claim through being the instigators of the original scheme and being under extreme pressure to meet food production targets,[44] some concessions were grudgingly made to the Ministries of Supply, and Works and Buildings in early 1942 to speed up the camp building programme. However, even this 'poaching' did not provide an automatic solution to the problem as, at this stage, prisoners were only being screened for their abilities in agriculture and not for other skilled occupations. Agriculturalists could not be transformed into skilled craftsmen overnight and further reallocations of manpower had to be effected to make the system work. In spite of this agreement, the squabbles between ministries over allocations continued and were dealt with by Sir John Anderson who had been nominated by the War Cabinet as adjudicator.[45]

Ironically, just as government ministries in the United Kingdom began to realise the prisoners' potential as a source of labour, the supply showed signs of drying up. In August 1941, Wavell's successor as C-in-C Middle East, Lieutenant-General Sir Claude Auchinleck, asked if London still wanted the prisoners as it was 'not now essential to send [them]'.[46] The War Office responded immediately, that the prisoners were 'definitely required' and that the 'best possible selection' of skilled men be retained in the Middle East until accommodation in the United Kingdom became available.[47] However, from being adamant about the need to remove prisoners from Egypt, by early September Auchinleck had completely changed his mind. He cabled the War Office to say that he intended to keep all skilled labour in Egypt; no doubt, in part, to help with the preparations for the forthcoming 'Crusader' offensive.[48] Seen initially as a threat to the British war effort in the Middle East, in the space of a few months prisoners had become the most sought-after of resources and the War Office insisted that the War Cabinet decision to bring prisoners to the United Kingdom be upheld.[49]

Such was the desire to exploit this new source of labour that the War Office also cabled Pretoria in September 1941. 'Problem of finding adequate numbers of skilled tradesmen of politically harmless character in Mideast. Consideration being given to effecting transfer of numbers to complete 28,000 required here from prisoners of this description in your hands.'[50] When the detailed demand for types of skilled men arrived it included a whole hosts of trades, including bricklayers, drivers, plumbers, electricians and carpenters.[51] Clearly the priority was to try and find men who could help solve the problem of camp construction in the United Kingdom.

The Italians at work

In spite of these problems, the utility of prisoners to overcome chronic labour shortages was now evident to all concerned. By the end of 1941, some 9,015 Italians (2,000 more than expected) were already being employed: 1,200 for the War Office; 600 for the Admiralty; 500 in Timber Supply; 4,700 in Agriculture; and the remaining 2,015 were available to help build the 40 new camps still required to house the expected 28,000.[52] It was estimated that 8,000 men would be needed to complete all the camps by 1 October 1942, at which point they would be transferred to agricultural and timber work.[53] Yet in spite of these pressing accommodation problems, in November 1941 the Cabinet was asked to extend the scheme to bring a further 50,000 Italians to Britain during 1942. Even with minimal guard requirements, this was a substantial increase which would require even more encampments than were planned. In reality, the problem of building accommodation could not be solved so easily. The request for skilled tradesmen from the South African drafts had had little result, in part because of stiff resistance by South African authorities who wanted to keep these skilled artisans for themselves. To make matters worse, of the 10,000 men promised by the Ministry of Labour to assist the construction work, by October 1941 only 100 had actually appeared.[54] However, the schemes established for hostels and billeting provided a potential solution. Not only could this official relaxation provide a means of using the planned increase in prisoners far more effectively and efficiently, but it also reduced the numbers of guards needed from Pioneer Corps units.

The first permanent camps for Italian prisoners were scattered across central England, their location being determined by the need for large quantities of labour in specific places, but limited by restrictions on the siting of camps.[55] Each camp was expected to supply approximately sixteen working parties for agricultural or drainage projects except Royston in Hertfordshire which was limited to ten. In addition to these camps in England, one further small camp was created in Wales – No.32 (Glan Morfa, Anglesey) was established to house prisoners in order to carry out a specific drainage project on the island under the auspices of the Ministry of Agriculture. The County War Agricultural Executive Committees were given specific instructions on how prisoners were to be used. In the first instance, they were to be employed mainly on drainage and reclamation work, in parties of 25 and under armed guard. Committees were responsible for providing transport, tools and gumboots for the prisoners, while other clothing remained the responsibility of the War Office. The same office also undertook to provide one official interpreter for each camp, but interestingly took the view 'that many of the Italian NCOs will know enough English to be able to understand instructions and make themselves understood'.[56]

These early drafts of prisoners, while largely compliant, did occasionally make their feelings known. Thus in April 1942 there was a disturbance at Camp No.26 (Ely/Soham), when the inmates discovered that the *Daily Herald* had described them as 'volunteer' prisoners of war. Moreover, when some of their number were transferred to Newmarket, they refused to erect tents for their accommodation on the grounds of the camp's proximity to an airfield.[57] These collective protests aside, by early 1942 the Home Office could only report two cases of prisoners misbehaving. One complaint centred on a supervisor who had allowed his charges to engage in prohibited activities and to mistreat a swan; while the second involved a prisoner employed in forestry who had 'wandered away a mile or two from his guard and indecently exposed himself to a lady'.[58] However, the fact that these are almost the only incidents relating to imported Italian prisoners deemed sufficiently serious to be minuted by the IPOWC suggests that they were the exception rather than the rule. Later in the year, the press did begin to report an increasing number of escapes. Ten men were reported to have escaped from a camp in the Midlands on 10 May, but these were all navy or airmen, suggesting that they had not arrived in Britain as part of a labour force, but had been captured by ships en route to home waters or brought to the United Kingdom for intelligence purposes. All were recaptured within three days.[59] Three others who escaped from a camp in the West Country were found in a nearby wood by police within forty-eight hours. Finally, there were two Italians who, with a German comrade, had escaped from a hospital in the west of Scotland and had tramped more than twenty miles, before eventually giving themselves up to the authorities, exhausted.[60]

In early 1942, British public reaction to the presence of Italian prisoners in its midst was mixed. In January, the *Daily Express* had reported the hostel scheme under the headline 'Farmers won't have prisoners. Why should our wives look after Italians'. Trawling for comment in an area of Buckinghamshire where prisoners had been employed, their correspondent, Hilde Marchant, cited testimony to their laziness and surliness. Elsewhere, she found more equivocal comment; that some were quite good and others very bad.[61] A day later, the same newspaper carried a report from a member of the NFU Council insisting that the authorities were too soft-hearted and 'not getting the work out of [the prisoners] that the seriousness of the situation require[d]'.[62] A more measured response on the hostel scheme came from the Ministry of Agriculture:

Considerably more prisoners are employed by individual farmers in twos and threes than in gangs. Comments on the prisoners' work are favourable. It is thought that farmers will continue to ask for prisoner of war labour, though that by no means all ... are thought likely to want the prisoners to live in. Most places have taken kindly to the prisoners, though at Chippenham, Northleach and Ampthill people are inclined to ask why they should be better housed than soldiers in the neighbourhood.[63]

Certainly, neither press comment nor public opinion had any noticeable effects on the plans to import more prisoner labour. Farmers were under no obligation to employ Italians and indeed had to apply to do so. Those that did clearly found plenty of work for their charges, in one or two cases apparently forgetting the nature of their new labour force. Thus the HD(S)E received two complaints about Italians walking around with shotguns, having been given these by the farmer to shoot rabbits. Steps were hurriedly taken to have this practice stopped.[64] Other conditions were, however, relaxed. By September 1942, it had been established that Italians could drive tractors on farms, as long as they did not 'infringe on the public road'; and it was also agreed that they could be put to work in mines, 'provided the work was not unhealthy or dangerous, and that prisoners were suited to such work'.[65]

As more and more Italians were brought into the United Kingdom during the course of 1942, so the demand for their labour also increased. Thus an inter-departmental meeting at the beginning of December drafted plans for a further 36,000 to be imported during 1943.[66] Yet even this was not enough to assuage the projected demand, which was estimated at the same meeting to stand at 44,348 men.[67] The main constraints on the programme were still those imposed by the provision of accommodation. To expedite matters, the Ministry of Agriculture agreed to the temporary release of some 4,000 men to be employed in building camps, their numbers to be replenished by newcomers from the Middle East or South Africa. The supply of prisoners was not perceived as a problem, but transport and guards remained a headache. The question of guards was partially overcome by reducing the required ratios; but transportation was hampered by an Admiralty ruling that no more than 500 prisoners should be carried on any one vessel. The restriction had been prompted by the sinking of ships carrying prisoners, including the loss through submarine action of 1,800 men on a single vessel, HMT *Laconia*, in October 1942.[68] However, the need for labour in Britain was seen as 'so urgent that there was a *prima facie* case for bringing ... all the prisoners who could be accommodated in the available shipping space'.[69] Yet even if the Admiralty waived its stipulation, the provision of accommodation still served to limit the actual numbers disembarking on British soil. The 1943 programme alone involved the construction of 33 new camps, 219 hostels (each housing 70 men) and fifteen camp extensions.[70] While the scheme envisaged a rate of 5,000 arrivals per month, the system was unlikely to deliver more than 2,000 per month and the camp construction programme could only be met through the use of some British civilian labour. Moreover, there were still restrictions on the siting of camps. HD(S)E had insisted that they should be prohibited fewer than ten miles from the coast in certain areas and in places fewer than three miles from aerodromes. While the former provision was considered eminently sensible, the latter was not, given that 'owing to the recent increase in the numbers of aerodromes ... there were virtually no sites on which camps could be constructed'.[71] Again, those most anxious to use prisoner labour looked to the HD(S)E to relax restrictions in their favour.[72]

Some compromises had already been made. In the summer of 1942, attempts were made to increase the value of existing accommodation by reducing the allocation of space for each man from 45 to 30 square feet, and then by allowing them to cycle up to seven miles from camp or hostel to work each day.[73] This allowed more men to be packed into the camps, and International Red Cross reports for 1942 often indicated that camp populations exceeded the stated maxima. For example, an ICRC report on a camp near Leominister in Herefordshire noted that its capacity was given as 400, but that in August 1942 it contained two officers and 574 NCOs and men, 170 of whom were being accommodated in tents.[74] While the ICRC delegate made no great issue of this at the time, presumably because it was in high summer, his reaction would doubtless have been different if this had been in the depths of winter. A similar report for the same month on Camp No.2 (Glen Mill, Oldham), noted that the camp also held 75 men more than the stated capacity.[75] Moreover, by permitting prisoners to travel further afield, the British authorities were able to use their charges more widely – on additional farms and more far-flung projects.

The increasing relaxation of the restrictions on Italian prisoners in the United Kingdom meant that they were rapidly distributed to almost all parts of the country. The map showing all the camps on the British Isles scarcely does justice to the Italian diaspora which took place in the years after 1941. Prisoners were increasingly billeted in hostels, individual farms and even commercial premises. Moreover, the travel and curfew arrangements meant that they were often in regular contact with local people, even if the nature of these contacts was still severely restrained by government edict. Early on, the authorities acted swiftly against any form of fraternisation. Thus the *News Chronicle* on 8 July 1942 reported two cases: one where a woman in Derbyshire had been fined £5 for giving cigarettes to Italian prisoners, having been previously warned about her conduct; and the other of a farmer's daughter who had been writing to a prisoner who had subsequently escaped. The authorities took a dim view of her conduct but, although liable to a maximum fine of £100 or three months' imprisonment, she was fined only £3.[76] Others incurred the displeasure of the courts for associating with prisoners, acting as intermediaries for letters,[77] selling food to the prisoners for money, or for jeering and trying to provoke them.[78] These prosecutions had taken place mainly under the Prisoners of War and Internees (Access and Communications) Order of 1940 but it was discovered that amendments would have to be made to Defence Regulation 18C (2)(a) if members of the public were to be prosecuted for interfering with the discipline of the prisoners away from their places of detention.[79]

One feature of the Italian prisoners brought to the United Kingdom was that they were nearly all NCOs and other ranks. This was entirely a function of their intended use. Officers could not be required to work, and were only likely to create problems. Thus there were only 22 officers among the first drafts of 6,464 men sent to Britain in the summer of 1941.[80] Most, if not all of these officers were protected personnel. For example, the roll for Camp No.34 records a single medical officer and a lieutenant chaplain responsible for the physical and spiritual health of more than 500 men.[81] In spite of their minuscule numbers, it was the officers who seemed to give rise to the greatest security concern. It appears that medical officers and chaplains were given limited parole,[82] but this led to their being noticed by the police who had not been informed of this privilege. Thus, in September 1942, a medical officer from Camp No.57 (Guildford) was reported to have engaged in a conversation with a member of the public. This turned out to be the officer, who spoke no real English, exchanging a 'Good Morning' with a woman and her dog whom he encountered regularly on his daily constitutional. In other words, no more than a storm in a teacup.[83] Subsequent wider dissemination of the rules for unescorted prisoners appears to have had only a limited effect, as ten months later another Italian medical officer found himself court-martialled for a similar offence.[84]

In spite of the reports of those actually employed on the land, not all the prisoners brought to the United Kingdom were in good physical health. An ICRC report on No.4 General Hospital (Italian Prisoners) on 19 November 1941 noted that there were 4 officers and 121 other ranks as patients. They had been transferred from the Middle East as part of the labour draft, but 'their journey took several weeks and took them through varied climates. A great number of those sick are suffering from dysentery and they arrived here in a destitute condition.'[85] On the assumption that the men had contracted dysentery before they had left the Middle East, it may be that the symptoms did not begin to show until they were on board ship. However, the suspicion remains that those carrying out the screening may have been more concerned with the agricultural backgrounds of the prisoners than their physical health, or anxious to remove them from the Middle East theatre at all costs. Certainly the Red Cross delegate was less than impressed. 'The prisoners arriving from the Middle East were lacking in practically everything and this situation particularly affected the sick, unable to earn money with their fellows in agricultural camps.'[86] To try and ameliorate matters, he arranged for his organisation to send £30 to help these unfortunates.

However, it would be wrong to see this as the norm. Surviving Red Cross reports indicate the general pattern of reception and treatment:

> On arrival, the prisoners, who have usually come from South Africa, are assembled in a large room [in this case, the floor of a cotton mill] and searched. Their clothes are sent for disinfecting and a new distribution of clothes made ... They take a bath ... and are given a medical check. Those who are ill are conveyed either to the [camp] infirmary or to a nearby hospital, depending on their needs. During this time, the Italian cooks [some of the 43 prisoners permanently held at the camp] prepare a meal for the new arrivals ... The beds are of standard army design (made from wood or wire) and each prisoner receives a paillasse [straw mattress] and three blankets – in summer.[87]

This report noted that most of the men had been in the camp for fourteen days, but that the orders for their distribution to work camps and hostels had arrived on the evening of the ICRC visit. Praise was given to the camp commandant by the prisoners but they did have some complaints – the most pressing being that food was distributed according to regulations, but this did not take account of the long journeys made by the prisoners and the possibility that sea-sickness might have taken a toll on their general health. It was requested that some food be stockpiled to provide extra nourishment for those who needed it on the first days of their arrival at the camp.[88]

The problems associated with transport and accommodation also remained partially unsolved. In January 1942 it was reported that shipping of prisoners from the Middle East to the United Kingdom could not be expedited at the rate of more than 2,000 per month. However, there were already 19,000 Italians being held in South Africa who could be more easily removed to the British Isles.[89] This may help to explain the poor condition of some prisoners. Having been captured in the North African desert, they were then removed from the Middle East to South Africa by sea, and subsequently re-embarked on vessels which would take them to Britain. Often they had been captured with only the clothes on their backs, and in the desert this probably did not amount to very much. While some further kit may have been found for them, they were then consigned to ocean-going ships, sometimes as deck 'passengers', for long journeys through major climatic changes from the northern to the southern hemisphere and back. Certainly, it appears that this globe-trotting did little to improve the prisoners' health, and in December 1942, 1,316 Italians were sent to the United States as they were deemed either 'permanently sick, redundant or useless for labour purposes'.[90] However, whether this was due to their passage to, or conditions in, the United Kingdom, or the result of a lax screening process, it is impossible to determine.

The end of 1942 and beginning of 1943 saw the numbers of captured Italian servicemen break all records. There was no shortage of potential employment, but some qualms about their uses in the United Kingdom remained. In March 1943, the IPOWC restated the view that the employment of enemy prisoners was 'a factor in determining the conditions under which British prisoners were employed by enemy governments'; but that in view of manpower shortages, 'the fullest use (within the limits of the Convention) must be made of prisoner of war labour, thus obtaining maximum benefit from their capture'.[91] At this stage, there was also some discussion about other uses which prisoners in the United Kingdom might have. The Foreign Office suggested that, suitably screened, they could be incorporated into labour detachments, a step which might ultimately allow them to be converted into anti-Fascist fighting units. In addition, the PWE saw them as a potential propaganda tool in the battle for Italian hearts and minds and pressed for access to the camps to begin screening for re-education programmes. While there were all manner of practical objections to these various schemes, it was the Ministry of Agriculture which ensured their rejection, on the grounds that the 'Italian prisoners [were] already being used for work of national importance'.[92] For the time being, therefore, the Italians in Britain remained unaffected by these plans. Their desirability as a supply of labour was undiminished and there was every expectation that they would continue to contribute to the British war effort until the defeat of the Axis powers.

3
Italian POWs in Africa, 1940–3

The road to Kenya

The first few months of 1941 saw the British authorities establish the pattern for accommodating their Italian prisoners across the Empire. The immense numbers captured in Italian East Africa were eventually despatched by rail and by sea to camps in Kenya. As had been the case in Libya and Egypt, it was deemed urgent for strategic reasons to evacuate the prisoners from Abyssinia as soon as possible. However, the transfer of prisoners to Kenya was far from easy. Logistical problems combined with the now familiar delays due to a shortage of shipping prevented British military authorities from sending large numbers to Kenya after the completion in April 1941 of the first stage of operations in Italian East Africa. Nevertheless, the delay proved to be a small blessing for it allowed time for the Kenyan authorities to build twelve permanent camps that would house 50,000 European captives.[1] In the Sudan a similar system of twelve semi-permanent camps was built to accommodate a population which had grown to 79,000 POWs by July 1941. The camps were divided into three administrative regions located along the Nile valley between Khartoum and Atbara, in the Red Sea hills near Port Sudan and in Eritrea outside the port of Massawa. Once at the Sudanese and Eritrean coasts, the POWs were transported to India, Kenya and South Africa when shipping could be found.[2] However gratifying the capture of tens of thousands of Italian and colonial troops, it was self-evident that the sheer weight of numbers was putting enormous pressures on British resources.

The use of POW labour in Kenya, as opposed to the United Kingdom, was in some ways much more controversial for two distinct but associated reasons; and the ensuing debate over the use of this labour also

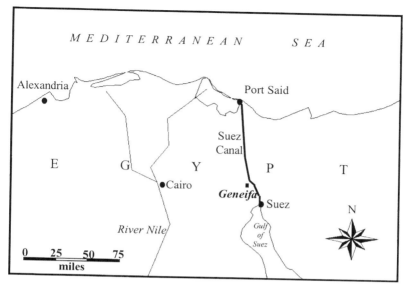

Map 2   Prisoner of War Camps for Italians in Egypt, 1941–3

highlighted the strong differences of opinion held by officials in London and Nairobi. The shortage of white troops to guard European captives meant that black soldiers would have to be employed for garrison duties. Metropolitan administrators feared that this would be resented by some POWs and initiate stern protests from the Fascist authorities in Rome, while others felt that 'there [might] be some objection under the terms of the Convention to employing white Italians on work in East Africa which Europeans are not ordinarily called upon to do'. This in turn might spark threats of reprisals against British and Commonwealth POWs held by the Italian government.[3]

Protests were indeed made by some hard-line Fascists about the racial origin of their guards. As one Middle Eastern POW censorship summary noted in August 1941, '[n]ot for the first time [did Italian POWs] express their dislike of Indian and Egyptian guards'.[4] Similar findings were recorded in the Sudan where several Italian officers considered that they had been 'insulted' by the fact that their guards were Sudanese. 'This they consider the final touch of humiliation added to their lot.'[5] Again, in East Africa, there were strongly worded complaints about the skin pigmentation of the camp guards. In part, some of these claims reflected the deep-seated racism and genuine contempt with which some Italian

POWs viewed their black and brown captors. For others, it was a way of making trouble or mischief. It also reflected the growing frustration among Italian POWs, especially the officers, who, guarded by Indian soldiers, could not make any impression at all on their guards 'who appear to be deaf to their blandishments and cajoleries'.[6]

Racial prejudice was not confined to the Italians. Lord Lloyd (Secretary of State for the Colonies, 1940–1) noted that the prejudices of some elements within Kenya's settler community against employing Europeans in manual labour might be another obstacle to the utilisation of POW manpower. These difficulties, he argued, would be greatly reduced if Libyan natives instead of white Italians were employed. Governor Moore disagreed. Doubting that there were any strong political objections in Kenya to the employment of white Italian prisoners, he nevertheless endorsed the use of Libyan or Italian native levies in the colony because they were cheaper to maintain than their European counterparts. One Whitehall official mooted that it was preferable to leave the Italians in Egypt and instead employ Kenyan labour in the colony thereby avoiding unnecessary travel and maintenance costs. However, if Italian labour was to be employed in the colony, any suggestion of putting Italian POWs in charge of native labour was most undesirable and out of the question. Not only would it be deeply resented by the natives themselves, but they would also 'quite fail to understand why they should have to obey the orders of Italians who had been beaten up and taken prisoner by their own brothers'.[7]

For the first six months of 1941, Colonial and War Office officials eagerly debated the pros and cons of employing Italian POW labour with the Kenyan government. Some white settlers were attracted to the idea of using POWs on anti-erosion schemes and irrigation projects. The South African Prime Minister, Jan Smuts, suggested that they also be utilised in repairing the Great North Road; a dirt-track which 'was "great" and "road" in name only'.[8] Nonetheless, it was the only overland supply line, which linked Britain's central and east African colonial dependencies, and hence was of vital strategic importance. The chance to make it an all-weather road using POW labour was an opportunity some colonial administrators could not ignore. Besides, 'Italians are noted as road makers', reported W. C. Huggard, the Acting British High Commissioner in Pretoria (1940–1 and 1944), 'and might volunteer for this service at the small wage to which they are accustomed in Italy'. Churchill, echoing similar War Office observations, endorsed this and thought it 'a good idea'.[9]

Inevitably, the question of guarding captives employed on work details was raised, as were the rates of pay for POW labour, accommodation, rationing, transportation and medical care. Equally important, who was to pay for their upkeep and maintenance, the military or the colonial government? Cunningham, GOC-in-C East Africa, complained he had no troops in Kenya available for garrison duty. If POW work parties were to be 'strung out' along the entire length of the Great North Road in Kenya, it would involve building seventy camps and the provision of 300 officers and non-commissioned officers (NCOs), 150 medical personnel and 2,150 armed African soldiers. Permanent camps were being built, but in the meantime officials complained that they could not even provide temporary shelter during the construction of the camps as they had no tents. Supplies would have to be despatched by road from the railheads near to work camps using 250 lorries with 350 drivers including maintenance personnel. Medical stores, equipment and arms would have to come from sources outside the colony as present stocks were inadequate. One suggestion put forward was that the Northern Rhodesian Brigade could be allocated for garrison duty until the necessary white personnel were raised to officer new garrison battalions. Sir John Maybin, Governor of Northern Rhodesia, however, relied on this unit for internal security; and even if permission was granted for its transfer it was untrained, inexperienced and not fully armed.[10]

The threats posed by guarding such large numbers of POWs stretched along hundreds of miles of road can best be illustrated by the reminiscences of Colonel J. H. S. Martin, who commanded a garrison company from the Northern Rhodesian Regiment. In 1942 Martin and his 100 African soldiers or askaris were responsible for guarding between ten and twelve POW work camps along eighty miles of the Great North Road. Established at POW Camp No. 361 near Kajiado, sixty miles from Nairobi, Martin recalled:

> I was told that we would be doing Garrison duties at Italian Prisoner of War Camps. My heart sank on hearing this piece of information. Garrison work is a whole time job and gives one very little opportunity for training and the monotony of continual guard[ing] destroys the enthusiasm of even the best Askaris.

To emphasise the chronic shortage of equipment, he recorded that his men were dressed in 'every type of worn out Army clothing, some in slouch hats some in round pioneers hats. They looked ill disciplined and untrained, and my depression was deepened. They were in possession of 117 old Italian rifles' of 1897 vintage. These Italian 'blunderbusses' were

eventually swapped for .303 rifles but only when the unit was transferred to guard duty at Command Headquarters later in the year.[11]

In February 1941 the War Office complained that the numbers and
types of projects for which the Italian POWs were being earmarked had
'merged into a rather untidy jungle'.[12] Governor Moore stressed that the
most useful and economically effective way of employing the largest
number of POWs was to put them to work on road construction and
maintenance. The Colonial Office agreed, as many roads in the colony
were rapidly deteriorating under the weight of military traffic. Apart
from ordinary maintenance on the existing road network, it was decided
that the 1,535-mile stretch of the Great North Road between Broken Hill
in Northern Rhodesia and Nairobi should receive the utmost priority.
The proposed anti-erosion projects were deemed unfeasible and quietly
dropped.[13] However, the stereotype that Italians were willing and natural roadmakers was challenged by a medical officer attached to one of the
POW work camps. Writing to a relative in Canada, Captain F. M. Fraser,
Royal Army Medical Corps, wrote: 'We have a great number of "Wop"
prisoners here abouts, living on the fat of the land – they were set to
work building a decent road about a year ago'. Despite good wages,
Fraser complained that in his district not one quarter of a mile had been
completed to date. 'This in spite of the fact that every day after the rain
scores of army vehicles become bogged for hours on end. The "Wops"
also go on strike every once in a while for various reasons and appease-
ment is the order of the day – at the expense of the British people'.[14]

Initially, 12,000 Italian POWs were assigned to the Great North Road
project. A total of twenty-nine camps were built at regular intervals with
three in Kenya and thirteen each in Northern Rhodesia and Tanganyika.
Each camp contained approximately 400 prisoners. As this was a military
project, sole financial responsibility rested with the War Office. Although
the financial lines of demarcation between the military authorities
and the colonial government were made crystal clear, tensions between
the two mounted. Arguments arose between the military and colonial
authorities over the responsibility for the upkeep of the surplus POW
labour in Kenya, which in September 1941 comprised 10,967 Italians
and 5,070 natives. Governor Moore complained bitterly that the military authorities in Kenya were trying to saddle the colonial government
with all the responsibility for the large numbers of 'idle mouths we are
feeding at present'.[15]

With the cessation of hostilities in Abyssinia in November 1941,
Moore realised that Kenya would now be called upon to play a more 'passive role' in the war effort. The new challenge was to make the colony

self-supporting in all essential foodstuffs, the prime task being to increase maize and wheat production. The catch, however, was to secure not only the much needed native labour, but also the requisite white personnel to act as overseers and managers. The case for the legal compulsion of native labour was thus made stronger, but Moore questioned whether London possessed the determination to help him obtain the release of white Kenyan farmers from the army who were essential if production was to increase. He appreciated that both the army and the white settler community were competing for the same Europeans, but he wanted to know 'whether it [was] more important to release a farmer to grow some more wheat, or leave him in the Army to guard Italian prisoners here or in Abyssinia and lead what would be for him a more gentlemanly life'.[16] Although he recognised that many whites would not want to abandon the uniform because of the higher military pay, Governor Moore reiterated that many white farmers who had enlisted for combat now wanted to return to their farms. These requests were not made simply to escape the lonely tedium of garrison duty. The concern was real and stemmed from the fact that wives of these absentee husbands were single-handedly carrying on the day-to-day management of their farms under very trying circumstances.[17]

In December 1942 the number of Italian POWs in Kenya exceeded 58,000. The colony was also experiencing a severe food shortage. This inevitably affected the supplies available to the camp canteens and made it difficult for camp authorities to guarantee the existing ration scale indefinitely. There was also London's dissatisfaction over what, it claimed, were too many idle prisoners in the base camps; a sentiment echoed by a member of the Army Council, Duncan Sandys MP, during a visit to the East African Command in December 1942. If more POW labour could be utilised, especially by white farmers, not only would this help relieve the overall food shortage, but also ensure that the POWs would not suffer severe privations. As a result, the military conducted a review of POW labour requirements.[18]

One problem was that POW labour was more expensive to employ than native labour. The Colonial Office pointed out that if Italian POWs were paid at approximately British pioneer rates of between 2s and 2s 6d per day the cost would exceed considerably that of African labour. Neither the Kenyan government nor the white settlers, it was argued, would employ prisoners unless African labour was unobtainable. 'If the supply of native labour were to dry up', commented one official, 'the position would be different, but even then, unless the work on which the prisoners were to be employed was essential and urgent, it would still be uneconomical to employ them so far as the local governments are concerned.' Rates of pay, which were eventually fixed by the War Office in early 1942, clearly demonstrate the inequalities in daily pay between the Italian POWs and African labour. A maximum of six pence per day was set for an unskilled POW and one shilling per day for a skilled man, as opposed to three pence a day for an African labourer.[19]

Nevertheless, the under-utilisation of prisoner labour remained a problem. In October 1941, a parole scheme was established to encourage private enterprise to use more POW labour. Individuals or small parties of artisans were selected and hired out to commercial interests or civilian authorities. No guards were required as the responsibility for supervision and discipline was given to the employer. To a degree, this circumvented the provision of guards that were always in short supply. Pleased with the results in the urban areas, pressure was applied to expand the scheme and send work detachments of up to twenty-five POWs into the rural areas to help with harvesting work. The attraction was that more POWs would be kept busy and make a valuable contribution to food production. Governor Moore supported the parole system, but warned London that opinion varied from district to district.

The scheme's detractors were apprehensive lest the employment of POWs should disturb the normal work patterns and relationships between the white farmer and his African labourers. If large numbers of POWs were employed 'it would be increasingly difficult for the native labour[er] not to be put to some extent in charge of the Italians'.[20] Indeed, this was abhorrent to some elements of the settler community, as was the idea that Italians could be put in charge of native labour or even work side by side with them. There were also difficulties in the provision of housing and food while on site. Although the POWs received Army rations, their civilian employers were expected to provide them with a certain amount of fresh meat and vegetables. The pressing food shortage made this problematic. Large-scale expansion was therefore fraught with difficulties. The parole scheme, which involved 1,385 POWs by mid-March 1943, did little to offset their under-utilisation. Statistics show that of the 19,091 POWs employed in Kenya, 10,806 were used by the military within POW camps, and a further 3,367 outside on day release but guarded in camp at night. This left 4,918 employed by civilians of which 3,533 were under guard.[21]

In addition, some Kenyan officials argued that the relaxation of security precautions, which an expanded parole system implied, might lead to an increase in sabotage, mass escapes and the leakage of intelligence information to the enemy. Most importantly, it might endanger the safety of the civil population. It was this final point which was of para-mount importance, especially in the rural areas. For example, what about the safety of lone women on farms which employed POWs? Fears of molestation were raised, but Governor Moore did not think that there was a general consensus on this issue.[22] Mass escapes posed their own problems, but once again there were conflicting views. Colonel R. J. Brett, a POW liaison officer, remained sanguine over potential security problems. 'The majority of Italian POW[s] have little desire to escape, while the nature of the country presents a hazardous problem to would-be escapees.' Yet, in almost the same breath, he admitted that there was 'really little to stop men determined to escape'.[23]

Take for example the three Italians who escaped from POW Camp No. 354 at Nanyuki. Built in the shadow of the 17,000-foot-high Mount Kenya, the Nanyuki camp was one of the largest of the fourteen POW camps in the colony. Bored with the monotony of camp life, the three, who were keen mountaineers, could not let such a temptation go unchallenged. In late January 1943 they escaped, leaving a note for the camp commandant, which did not disclose their intentions but assured him that they would return. As promised, they returned in early February after the near completion of their epic climb with home-made equipment. According to *The Times*, an Italian flag had been discovered hoisted upside down at over 16,000 feet on Point Lenana. In nearby snow was a half-buried bottle, which contained a note 'expressing faith in a Fascist victory and hopes of an early restoration to freedom'.[24]

Colonel Brett's review of the POW situation in Kenya in mid-1942 gave the local authorities a clean bill of health over camp conditions and the maintenance of the Italians in their care. The only criticism was the under-utilisation of POW labour. By the end of 1943 the Kenyan authorities had worked diligently to rectify this predicament, and 34,000 of the 49,000 Italian POWs in Kenya were by then employed in camp maintenance, agriculture, building and construction, quarrying and roadwork. The largest employer remained the various branches of the armed services. The surplus 15,000 were designated to start work in the United Kingdom in early 1944.[25]

South Africa: the camp at Zonderwater

The South African authorities encountered similar problems over the incarceration, employment and security of their substantial Italian POW population. Again, the issue of race was an especially sensitive issue; but it was much more problematic here than in Kenya because of the rigid state-enacted policies of racial segregation initiated by the Union government after 1910. This, combined with a fervent pro-German and staunchly anti-British sentiment within a large element of South Africa's Afrikaner community, threatened to undermine the government of Prime Minister Smuts between 1940 and 1942. Domestic political issues therefore invariably impinged on what, at one level, were simple matters of imperial military co-operation.

The first inkling that the use of South Africa as a detention centre would be a contentious issue occurred before Italy had joined the war. As in Britain and the dominions, the fear of fifth-columnists, compounded by xenophobia, saw the introduction of an internment policy. The presence of a large German-speaking population in the mandate territory of South West Africa (Namibia) provided one of the largest sources of enemy aliens who were deemed a serious threat to internal security. German merchant seamen and other Germans resident in the Union were also rounded up and interned in a series of camps established in the Transvaal and Orange Free State. Security was provided by the newly formed South African Internment Battalion, which was a full-time unit of the Active Citizen Force (ACF). Soon after its establishment, further restructuring by Defence Headquarters redesignated this unit as the 6th Battalion, 1st Reserve Brigade.[26] The number of detainees continued to grow. In 1940 South Africa agreed to receive German civilians detained throughout the rest of British colonial Africa, most of who came from East Africa.[27] With the fall of France in June 1940 and the threatened invasion of England that summer, London was keen to 'export', on grounds of national security, more than 5,000 civilian internees. Although Canada agreed to take 4,000, the Dominions Office requested that South Africa take some of these enemy aliens. Smuts replied that the Union government could not accede to the proposal because of the already large German population in South and South West Africa, which had been bolstered by those from neighbouring British territories and captured enemy ships. Mindful that many die-hard Afrikaners were also pro-Nazi and sympathetic to the Axis cause, and therefore potential candidates for internment, he reminded London that: 'The local political situation has also to be borne in mind.' Therefore, because of domestic reasons Pretoria preferred to see these British-held internees transported to distant colonies or dominions, which were 'free from German or Nazi troubles'.[28]

Italian POWs were an entirely different matter. Like their British counterparts, South African ministers did not believe that Italians were driven by or deeply committed to Fascism. Rather, they had been duped by

53

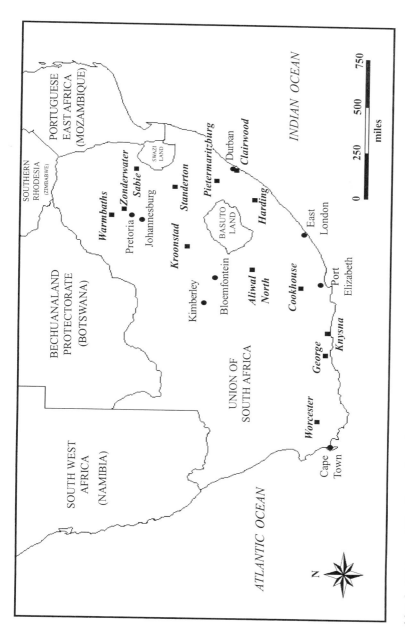

Map 3 Prisoner of War Camps for Italians in South Africa, 1941–7

Mussolini. Moreover, the Italian population in South Africa was insignificant and did not pose a serious security threat, unlike the German connection that had a long history. Therefore, when the British urgently requested imperial assistance in early January 1941 to relieve Wavell's beleaguered Middle Eastern Command of its captives, the Union government did not hesitate to take 20,000. Self-interest also played a role in Pretoria's unflinching decision to take so many prisoners; these men would offset a growing labour shortage. Thus, it was no coincidence that out of the first batch of POWs, 90 per cent were prioritised for road building and agricultural labour.[29]

The first instalment of 7,593 POWs embarked in Egypt on three ships in late March 1941 and were guarded by units of the Cape Town Highlanders, who had been transferred to the Middle East that February for escort duty. The twenty Italian officers and 7,573 other ranks arrived in early April. By the end of that month there were 10,000 Italian POWs in the dominion.[30] The *Cape Argus* reported that those who saw the prisoners land were surprised to find that most of them 'were little more than boys. Here and there were some men with Great War ribbons, but the majority were either in their late teens or early twenties. They stumbled down the gangways to the waiting trucks in silence. Their faces were expressionless, but some smiled nervously as the guards shouted "Presto" – or in plain English "Get a move on".'[31] Headlines in the *Cape Times* and the *Rand Daily Mail* announced 'Italian Prisoners Happy in Union' and 'Italians Happy in Prison Camp'.[32] Nonetheless, their arrival in South Africa was not without incident. In May, two train-loads of Italian POWs arrived at Pretoria station. As they were detraining, a number of men from the nearby railway workshops gathered round for a closer look. According to one eyewitness, several of the railwaymen greeted the prisoners with the Nazi salute, which was returned by the prisoners! 'This barefaced exhibition of sympathy with the enemy' reported one intelligence officer, 'caused feelings to run high among the loyal workers and there was talk of "downing tools" until the Fifth Columnists were removed.'[33]

By late April 1941, POW congestion in Egypt had become acute. There were now an estimated 145,000 Italian POWs in the Middle East, including Abyssinia and Eritrea. Evacuation to India and Australia had been slower than expected due to shipping shortages. In light of the emergency, Clement Attlee, the Secretary of State for the Dominions, asked the UK High Commissioner in South Africa to approach Smuts about increasing the quota by an additional 25,000 POWs to be transported over a six-month period starting in May. The request was immediately sanctioned by the South African government which despatched another battalion to the Middle East for escort duty.[34]

Meanwhile, on 24 January 1941, Prime Minister Smuts appointed a committee headed by Colonel P. I. Hoogenhout, chairman of the National Roads Board (NRB), to consider steps for the accommodation and employment of its Italian charges. Members included the Secretary for Defence, Brigadier C. H. Blaine and Colonel L. Strickland, Director of Internment, as well as the NRB's technical advisor and representatives from the Public Works Department and the South African Railways and Harbours (SAR&H) authority. At its first meeting three days later, the committee allocated responsibility for the control of South Africa's POW camps to the Department of the Interior, which already had the authority for the administration of the country's civilian internment facilities. It was acknowledged that tentage was available for 18,000 POWs. In addition, immediate construction of a reception camp for 5,000 prisoners at Clairwood, near Durban in Natal, was approved. More significantly, the NRB stated that it was interested in employing 4,000 POWs to improve the mountain pass network in the Cape: in particular, at Du Toit's Kloof, to better communications between Cape Town and Worcester; and the construction of a new road through Montague Pass. Telegrams were also received from several local authorities in the Orange Free State urging the committee to employ POWs to accelerate the National Roads programme in their areas. Not to be outdone, the SAR&H representative informed the Hoogenhout committee at its second meeting in early February that his department contemplated utilising between 7,000 and 10,000 POWs. Indeed, because of the severe shortage of skilled fitters, turners and precision engineering personnel, the Director-General of Technical Production, J. Dickson, made the extraordinary plea to Brigadier O. J. Hansen, Director-General of Technical Services, whether captured Italians skilled in these professions could be employed on armament manufacturing in specially designed and supervised workshops![35]

The overarching question however was where these prisoners were to be incarcerated? Two enterprising officials in South West Africa suggested that POW camps could be sited in the territory. The magistrate and Native Commissioner for the Caprivi Strip, Captain L. F. W. Trollope, believed that 1,000 prisoners could be housed and employed in his district. From Windhoek, the secretary to the Administrator for South West Africa informed his superiors in Cape Town that during debates in the House of Assembly several speakers also raised the question of establishing an Italian POW camp near Tsumeb. Drought was ravaging the territory, depressing prices for agricultural products, in particular livestock. Siting a camp in the region would not only create additional demand for the territory's primary produce, but it would also provide badly needed markets for the ailing livestock industry. The climate was reportedly healthy, and in spite of the drought, the water supplies at the proposed site were plentiful. Furthermore, the proximity of a local abandoned copper mine and its existing buildings would provide initial shelter for the POWs or their guards while new accommodation was being built.[36]

Smuts, who was also Minister of Defence, had other ideas. In mid-February, security considerations dictated that the Department of Defence would have sole responsibility for the welfare of all POWs in Union custody. It was also decided on grounds of efficiency and economy to concentrate all the Italians at the Premier Mine complex near Zonderwater, forty-five miles north-east of Pretoria. This location was then occupied by the 2nd South African Division, which was completing its training before embarkation to North Africa in mid-June. Space was available for 5,000–6,000 POWs, but once the division had vacated the camp a total of 15,000 could be housed. However, hutted accommodation was at a premium. Until new buildings could be erected, only 25 per cent of the inmate population could be housed in timber-frame buildings; the remainder would have to be put under canvas. This worried Blaine, for according to Article 10 of the 1929 Geneva Convention, tents were only permissible except as a 'purely temporary measure'.[37] Smuts was less concerned, remarking that the POWs should consider themselves lucky to get tents.[38] With regard to sending POWs to isolated regions like the Caprivi Strip, however attractive the idea it was rejected in favour of centralisation. The area had been declared a Native Reserve, and was therefore out-of-bounds to white settlement. Moreover, it was a notorious fever region, which the Union government deemed unsuitable for Europeans.[39]

With the expected 'rush' of prisoners from the Middle East and East Africa, the authorities discussed the type, quantity and supply of POW rations. Using a tendering process, all supplies were to be requisitioned through the Quartermaster-General. A daily ration schedule per man, based on the increased quota of 45,000 prisoners announced in May was then calculated. Dietary requirements included bread, meat, potatoes, fresh milk, fruit and vegetables, butter, macaroni, sugar, tea, salt, mealie meal (samp) and rice. Additional items such as dried fruit, coffee, pepper, mustard, cottonseed oil, cigarettes and tobacco were factored in, as well as more luxurious items like jam and cheese. To feed this number of prisoners over an eleven-month period (May 1941–March 1942) was estimated to cost just over £608,000.[40]

However, there were problems with the availability of some of these commodities. The Food Supplies Committee, which was appointed in 1940 to monitor food stocks in the Union, was deeply concerned about the 'liberal' ration proposed in respect to wheat products (such as bread, biscuits and macaroni) and potatoes. The Secretary for Agriculture and Forestry, P. R. Viljoen, warned Brigadier Blaine that current South African wheat supplies would have to be augmented by the importation of 1 million bags in 1941. As freight was 'almost unprocurable', there was no prospect of getting such a large consignment. Thus, steps were taken to introduce a standard loaf of a less refined meal. Potatoes were a problem too. Although the supply position was not acute, prices were rising steadily, signalling the development of a serious shortage. Viljoen urged Blaine to consider keeping these products to a minimum and suggested that more maize be introduced into the prisoners' diet.[41] To relieve the food supply problem further, he also recommended that POWs be encouraged to grow their own vegetables. Finally, it was proposed that a dry wine with a low alcohol content should be included in the ration. The directors of the Koöperatieve Wijnbouwers Vereniging van Zuid-Afrika (KWV) in the Paarl region of the Western Cape had approached the Department of Agriculture with the suggestion. The war had stopped their exports of wine and brandy to the United Kingdom. Like the livestock producers in South West Africa, Cape wine producers saw the POWs as an alternate but lucrative outlet. Blaine nonetheless rejected this amusing request. Union troops encamped in South Africa were not issued with wine or brandy and 'any discrimination will inevitably lead to serious dissatisfaction'.[42]

In July 1941, London requested that South Africa take an additional 15,000 POWs bringing the aggregate to 60,000. A lack of shipping to Australia had forced the Middle Eastern authorities to reassess their evacuation schedule, once again imposing on Smuts's government, which in turn was stridently confident that South Africa could absorb as many as 100,000 POWs. Without hesitation, he agreed to the request and immediately sanctioned the construction of extra accommodation at Zonderwater.[43] Inevitably, the sheer numbers of POWs now arriving in South Africa began to stretch South African resources. Moreover, the prisoners began to lodge complaints against the camp authorities. Brazil had been entrusted with looking after the interests of Italian POWs in South Africa as the Protecting Power. The Consul-General, Julio Diogo, presented the Department of External Affairs with a list of complaints. First, the men were not satisfied with the rations and requested that they be allowed to buy extra food and provisions for themselves. They also complained about improper sanitation and demanded that hot showers be provided in the officers' quarters. Delays in the forwarding of mail from Egypt was another problem, as was the more petty request that men of the Union Defence Force (UDF) inferior in rank to Italian officers be compelled to salute them.[44]

Apart from food and accommodation, sanitation and camp hygiene were the most important issues that Pretoria had to tackle during these initial stages. The overloading of Zonderwater had put enormous strain on the woefully inadequate latrines. Apart from the facilities which had existed while the 2nd South African division was quartered there, only two sets of additional latrines containing thirty-eight toilets each had been completed in just one of the new but hastily constructed blocks which was to hold 5,000 prisoners. The severe shortage of building materials was cited as one of the main reasons for the inadequate sanitary arrangements. It was now a matter of extreme urgency that more facilities be built and quickly if epidemics like enteric fever or amoebic dysentery were to be avoided. Fearful that a number of POWs had contracted these diseases in the Middle East before their transportation to South Africa, the authorities realised that it was imperative that cases be diagnosed and isolated, and countermeasures taken as a matter of urgency. But containment could only be assured if an isolation ward and new latrines were built forthwith.[45]

The need to improve camp hygiene and sanitation was continually on the agenda at weekly POW staff conferences throughout the remainder of 1941 and early 1942. The cost of building water-borne sewerage was estimated to be £200,000–£250,000. Moreover, the Director-General of Medical Services, Brigadier E. N. Thornton, reiterated the danger of a serious health risk if the existing situation at Zonderwater continued. The weight of the Chief of the South African General Staff, Lieutenant-General Sir Pierre van Ryneveld, was thrown into the fray when he insisted that a long-term solution had to be found in order to protect the health of not just the prisoners but also UDF personnel.[46] The prisoners themselves did not help the situation. Materials were being stolen by the inmates, including seats from the latrines which were fashioned into curios and then sold to the public. Even the fire buckets had to be removed from the compounds as they too were being sold on to civilian consumers by enterprising POWs.[47]

Despite urgent requests for action from the highest military authorities and promises from Brigadier J. Mitchell-Baker, the Quartermaster-General (QMG), to speed up construction, it was obvious that by January 1942 very little had been accomplished. In mid-January, the camp commandant pleaded with the QMG by pointing out that unless the hospital extension and latrine programme were 'tackled seriously and vigorously' it would be impossible to cope with any epidemic which might break out. To prove his point, he added that an outbreak of dysentery had already occurred at Zonderwater. At a conference held on 30 January, representations were made by the Chief of the General Staff (CGS) for the need to expand the camp hospital to 2,000 beds. The isolation block, complete with separate latrines, kitchens and messing shelters – which the Director of Works said would be ready in twelve days – took twelve weeks to build. The last latrine in the isolation block was completed in late May 1942! Congestion within the hospital was still a problem. Although new accommodation had been built, there were still a considerable number of tents pitched between the rows of huts. Consequently, sanitary facilities could not cope.[48]

Improvements were promised by the QMG who stated he would intervene personally if need be. By mid-February 1942 nothing had materialised. This prompted the Adjutant-General (AG), Brigadier Len Beyers, to propose that either a private contractor be employed to expedite the situation or that the camp commandant be vested with the responsibility to complete the work. Growing impatient with the poor co-ordination, lack of co-operation and bald-face excuses rampant in the QMG's office, Beyers reminded his colleagues that it was his office that was responsible for South Africa's adherence to the provisions of the Geneva Convention. Any failure in any particular exposed South Africa to an adverse report to the Axis both by the Protecting Power and the delegates of the ICRC. The crux of the matter was the all-important principle of reciprocity. Beyers was adamant that proper compliance to the terms of the Convention were essential 'in the interests of our own prisoners of war against whom reprisals may be taken by the [enemy] for breaches of the Convention by us'.[49]

London was equally anxious about the conditions at Zonderwater for the same reasons. The South African High Commissioner in London cabled Pretoria stating that British authorities feared that unless the situation within the camp was altered radically and quickly the Italian government would undoubtedly lodge protests with the Foreign Office claiming that the Geneva Convention was being contravened. Moreover, like Beyers, Whitehall feared repercussions in the treatment of British and Commonwealth POWs in Italian hands. Alarmed by the camp reports submitted by the British Military Mission in Pretoria and the camp commandant at Zonderwater in January 1942, the War Office suggested that Colonel Brett, who was due to visit the Union in April, might be of some assistance.[50]

Brett made two inspections of the camp at the end of April. He stated that although there was some cause for concern, especially in terms of sanitation, diet and hospital accommodation, the South African authorities had coped remarkably well under very trying circumstances. Indeed, conditions were improving, especially in the area of hygiene. The camp's medical staff under the command of Major L. Blumberg, the Senior Medical Officer, were singled out for their energy, motivation and professionalism.[51] However, continued failure by Mitchell-Baker's department to meet its responsibilities was to be tolerated no longer. Beyers charged that the QMG was 'guided entirely by his subordinates'. Even more damning was Beyer's claim that the QMG had only made his first visit to Zonderwater in mid-May 1942, over a year after its inception as a POW facility. In June, and with Smuts's backing, the QMG lost the responsibility for POW camp maintenance and construction. All future building and maintenance work undertaken at South African POW camps was hereafter vested with the Adjutant-General, who would requisition tools and material from the QMG. Labour would be provided from the inmate population.[52]

Beyond the camp: employment in farming and forestry

When it was announced in early 1941 that South Africa would receive large numbers of Italian captives, their potential as an alternative source of cheap labour was quickly realised by private employers. W. A. Edmonds, secretary of the Queenstown Farmers Association, requested on behalf of his members that the government explore the use of Italian POWs to enhance the agricultural development of the Union. Suggested tasks included anti-erosion work and the construction of storage dams, work usually confined to native labour.[53] Trades unions, however, saw prisoner labour as a direct threat to their members' working conditions. In February 1941 the Cape African Congress passed a motion requesting that Pretoria guarantee that no enemy POWs be employed on existing public services or those to be undertaken in the future. In addition, it sought assurances that if POW labour was to be used that it be diverted into channels which would not bring them into 'competition with loyal African free labour'. Blaine replied to the Native Affairs Department that no decision had yet been taken whether Italian POWs were to be employed, 'nor where and how, if employed at all'.[54]

Nonetheless, once the government had established the Zonderwater facility, it began to investigate the possibility of establishing a series of 'detached' camps which would allow prisoners to undertake work on government-sponsored projects, like road building or tree felling, or private ventures as suggested by Edmonds. Lord Harlech, the UK High Commissioner in South Africa (1941–4), reported to London in September 1941 that Marcel Junod, the Swiss representative of the ICRC in South Africa, noted that the present system whereby most of the prisoners had no work to do was 'breeding degradation and slow demoralisation. The prisoners – many of them peasantry, artisans, road makers etc. – are crying out for work.'[55] Fearing trouble, and despite the Defence Department's refusal of the Queenstown Farmers Association's request for paroled POW labour, preliminary discussions had already taken place between the Adjutant-General's department and the CGS about employing Italian POWs on outside contracts. Tentative proposals were drafted in September 1941. Prisoners were to be paroled to farmers and put into small batches of between 5 and 10 per group. Rates of pay were to be kept as low as possible. If POWs were employed on railway maintenance, the condition was that an equal number of men would be released for service with the UDF as a quid pro quo. In late October, a more detailed set of conditions for outside employment was formulated which included rates of pay, clothing allowances, accommodation, rations, medical attention, transport arrangements and general conditions of treatment while outside. By mid-December, the necessary employment forms had been printed outlining in great detail the employer's responsibilities to his charges. Of note was Smuts's anxiety that POWs should not get into the wrong hands. In other words, employers had to be carefully vetted to ensure that their political leanings did not match those of their prisoners.[56]

With the introduction of the parole system and the contracting out of POW labour to private individuals, one of the key problems – which bedevilled South African authorities through out the war – was security. In December 1941, the Director of Forestry broached with the Adjutant-General the subject of employing Italian POWs on the Weza forestry plantation in the Natal Midlands. The AG thought this an excellent opportunity for hand-picking men who represented 'a very superior type'. No trouble was anticipated from the first batch of 100 POWs. The only uncertainty expressed by officials, however, was the danger to women in the areas surrounding the work camps.[57] In June–July, near Harding, the government's worst fears were realised. The Division of Forestry discovered that prisoners had been regularly violating their parole, trespassing on the nearby Weza reserve and allegedly molesting native women. The Native Commissioner in Harding informed his superiors in Pietermaritzburg that an ugly incident had narrowly been avoided by the timely intervention of the head induna, Bukwana. Angered by the constant harassment of their women, the men in the reserve had vowed that if the interference by the POWs continued they would not hesitate to 'take steps to stop it with assegais'. When three prisoners continued to make 'indecent overtures' to the women and 'tendered them with money to satisfy their lusts', the African menfolk became enraged, threatening to attack and kill the culprits. Only after the entreaties of Bukwana and the local magistrate and their promise that these incidents would receive immediate investigation by the authorities did the men reluctantly agree not to take the law into their own hands.[58] As the Commissioner of the South African Police was warned by the Deputy Police Commissioner of Natal, Rost A. Meston, the Africans in the Harding area were a 'fearless and obstinate tribe' who would not hesitate to resort to the assegais if the Italians again accosted their women. 'We are all aware of the Italians' low social status [and] of their cunning', he warned. 'I personally think it is undesirable for prisoners of war to be permitted to work in a forest where the careless (??) discarding of a cigarette end may result in a conflagration worth millions of pounds.'[59] Evidently, further forays by sex-starved prisoners were halted, but only after the tightening of camp security, an increase in the number of forestry guards and the deportation to Zonderwater of the offending POWs.

An equally serious problem in the Eastern Transvaal eventually forced the closure of the Ceylon POW forestry camp near Sabie. Established in late 1942 as one of a network of forestry camps employing a total of 1,500 POWs, there was apparently little or no control over the movements of the 300 prisoners who roamed about 'indiscriminately in the town day and evening'. Prisoners were using the local baths and reading rooms without permission, and complaints were made that these men were also frequenting the nearby native compound – 'miscegenation the motive'. The lack of control was attributed directly to the District Forestry Officer and his three juniors at Ceylon, who, it was claimed, were anti-government supporters, although there was no evidence to link them to the *Ossewabrandwag* an avidly pro-Nazi, paramilitary Afrikaner organisation. At several concerts hosted by the POWs, at which local townsfolk were present, some women were seen in Voortrekker costume! Closer supervision and the imposition of tighter discipline were recommended. However, because of the camp's proximity to neutral Portuguese East Africa, too many prisoners were attempting to escape. The camp was closed in March 1943 and its inmates redistributed to more secure tree felling facilities at George and Knysna in the Western Cape.[60]

However unpleasant or embarrassing these events were, and despite fears that such incidents might occur elsewhere in the future, they did not prevent the South African government from expanding its outside employment programme. The need to alleviate the chronic shortage of labour in the dominion overruled private fears about molestation and miscegenation. By January 1943, 5,874 POWs were employed on outside contracts in work camps dotted throughout the Union; a figure which would triple by August 1944. Apart from the utilisation of 300 POWs by the Department of Lands for the construction of settlements for returning South African veterans, 800 POWs for afforestation work and 25 POW potters deployed in four potteries, most of the captives were employed as farm labourers either on fixed term contracts with individual farmers, or as casual labour to meet varying seasonal demands. Indeed, one of the biggest and most important casual labour camps was located in the Western Cape at Worcester where prisoners were contracted out for planting, weeding and harvesting.[61]

Guarding prisoners in the racial state

As camp conditions at Zonderwater began to improve, more contentious and highly sensitive problems came to the fore: camp security, the provision of garrison troops and POW employment. Harlech informed London in November 1941 that the more Italian POWs it could transfer from South Africa to Great Britain for employment, the better:

> The problems of guarding them here are acute and employing them runs the South African Government up against not only the white trades unions and labour party here, but against the 'colour' question of employing Europeans on 'Kaffirs work'. If we get a new haul in the Western desert I see the greatest difficulties disposing of further batches of prisoners.[62]

Harlech's anxieties stemmed partly from the strain the war effort had placed on South African manpower and resources. Hard-pressed to find adequate numbers of troops for its overseas commitments, internal security and POW garrison duties, South Africa was forced in late 1941 to revise downwards the number of POWs it could accommodate. The real problem, as recognised by the High Commissioner, originated with the *Ossewabrandwag*, that orchestrated a determined anti-war campaign in South Africa. It was this perceived challenge to South Africa's internal security between 1940 and 1942, which prompted Harlech's plea for the transfer of the POWs to Britain, which would then enable South Africa to concentrate its resources on the internal threat. Undoubtedly, this domestic crisis had cooled Smuts's initial enthusiasm to accommodate a projected 100,000 Italian POWs, but by the end of 1941 almost 60,000 were already incarcerated in the Union.[63]

As in Kenya, officials in Pretoria were equally apprehensive of the political fallout from the utilisation of Africans to guard European prisoners and the subsequent employment of these prisoners on work traditionally reserved for Africans. As Louis Grundlingh has pointed out: 'Traditional government policy in South Africa was that only whites should serve in combatant roles in the armed forces. The spectre of blacks trained to use firearms roused white fears about the security of the racially organised state.'[64] Lord Harlech graphically illustrated this point when he confessed to Governor Moore of Kenya that it was not only the parliamentary opposition 'to whom the idea of armed natives is anathema – a good many Afrikaner *and* English supporters of the Government are no doubt equally sensitive on this issue. In Natal, for example, any idea of arming Zulus creates the most violent outcry.'[65]

Frustrated by South African negrophobia and 'aghast at the depth and bitterness of the "colour" feeling' in the dominion, Harlech conceded, albeit reluctantly, that this was strictly a domestic issue.[66] As a result, African soldiers were confined to non-combatant roles and organised into pioneer battalions to perform essential tasks involving heavy manual labour. For those involved in garrison duties or the guarding of Italian POWs in the permanent camps in the interior or German POWs in the trans-shipment camp in Natal, the only concession granted by the white government on the issue of arming its African soldiers was that they be allowed to carry traditional weapons such as the assegai or knobkerrie. Once again, domestic political considerations and the perceived threat of the *Ossewabrandwag* had to be taken into account.

Although African soldiers were not armed with modern weaponry, concessions had to be made to the Cape (Coloured) Corps battalions, which by mid-1942 provided the bulk of South Africa's guard troops. The issue was the chronic shortage of European manpower for frontline duties and the poor quality of some of the European detachments initially assigned to guard the burgeoning number of POWs. In April 1942 General Beyers reported to Secretary for Defence Blaine that two

European Guard battalions attached to Zonderwater were proving problematic. Both units consisted of low category material classified as C1, 2, and 3. Most were over fifty-years-old. Their advanced age and poor physical fitness, combined with a shortage of hutted accommodation, meant that most of the men were living in tents, which was slowly sapping their will to carry out their duties. Owing to these unsatisfactory conditions 275 out of a total of 590 men from the 1st National Reserve Volunteer battalion had resigned. European guards, always in short supply at Zonderwater, were now at desperately low levels.[67]

At a staff conference in June 1942, the CGS alluded to the necessity of releasing as many full-time European troops as possible from guarding and escorting enemy POWs. Described as 'handy-men' by General van Ryneveld, Smuts approved the arming of Cape Coloured personnel for this specific function. By the end of June, two battalions of European troops from the 1st Reserve Brigade had already been relieved from POW duties by two Cape Corps battalions. In all, six – later eight – Cape Corps battalions were established on a full-time basis for POW work.[68] The initiative, largely born out of expediency, was to prove a mixed blessing.

Fears about the presence of armed non-whites were not confined to the domestic scene alone. Serious objections were also raised by high-ranking officers in the South African defence establishment about visits by armed non-white Allied troops to the Union while in transit or as POW escort troops.[69] Here too, domestic political and racial issues were about to clash with military necessity. As we have seen, the Axis counter-offensive in North Africa in April 1941 added renewed urgency to the problem of ridding Middle Eastern Command of as many POWs as possible. It also highlighted the problem of having to rely on Indian drafts for POW escort duty. Apart from the small numbers of British and UDF personnel travelling to the Union on leave, European guards on POW ships were in short supply. In order to release frontline troops hitherto tied up on guard duty, in May 1941 Wavell was forced to employ Indian infantry as escorts for POWs being evacuated from Egypt and the Sudan to South Africa. Aware that this was highly undesirable from the Union government's point of view, there was little he could do except impose on South African goodwill.[70]

Prime Minister Smuts responded positively. First, he instructed his defence chiefs to treat the Indian soldiers well during their stay in Durban. Second, and to counter adverse domestic criticism, the Defence Department had to explain to the public that these sepoys were providing an invaluable service to the Allied war effort. Meanwhile, to prevent 'local malcontents' from trying to incite violence when the Indian soldiers were on shore, they had to be 'shepherded' by their own patrols which would be accompanied by detachments of municipal or South African Police. The municipality was also instructed to provide police escorts to Indian commissioned officers when they were on furlough in Durban.[71]

The India Office was encouraged by the positive response they received from the South African authorities when the first contingent of Indian escorts arrived in Natal in May 1941. 'Durban has been behaving very well indeed to the Indian contingent', reported the Assistant Secretary (Military), J. A. Simpson, '[with] hotels, cinemas, clubs, ... having been thrown open to them. I half expected this since Durban is essentially a British city, and it is the Afrikaners who cause most of the mischief.'[72] However, the India Office was reminded by the British High Commission in South Africa that there was no guarantee that racial incidents would not occur. As a result of this concern, Wavell was reminded of the delicacy of the race issue in the Union. However, Simpson was quick to point out that military considerations 'must override any domestic sensitivities'. The War Office did not share such naivety. More attuned to the domestic political impact of their request, the War Office had sought to avoid sending Indian escorts to South Africa. Concerned about military discipline and morale, it nevertheless was forced to concede that the current military crisis in the Middle East demanded exceptional measures to expedite quickly the POW problem in Egypt.[73]

Inevitably, complaints were made by Italian POWs in South Africa about their non-European guards. In February 1943 Giovanni Fanciullo, aged 22, alleged that he and twenty-six fellow prisoners were mistreated by their Cape Coloured guards while travelling on a train from Worcester, where they had been working as farm labourers. Several of the escorts, who were armed with rifles and bayonets, asked the POWs for cigarettes. They replied that they had none. At that point, the POWs claimed that they had been assaulted by the guards who stabbed and pushed them with rifles and bayonets. A little later, when the POWs asked for drinking water they were refused and driven back from the lavatories with fixed bayonets. One POW was allegedly stabbed through the arm. Although these incidents were reported to the European officer in charge, nothing was done. 'We also had to sleep in the same compartments with the coloured soldiers which was very inconvenient as a consequence of the smell of their feet.' Rather than return to Zonderwater, Fanciullo had had enough and jumped off the train in an unsuccessful bid to escape back to Worcester.[74]

The stereotype of the Italian POW as a cheerful, contented individual held great sway amongst many British military and colonial officials. In many respects, this was why British authorities valued Italian POWs more highly than their German counterparts because, with the exception of hard-line Fascists, the Italians were seen as a source of malleable labour who, with a modicum of effort, would willingly work for their captors. The use of Italian POWs in South Africa and the problems the dominion authorities faced will be discussed in greater detail in a subsequent chapter. However, it is important to emphasise that not all prisoners were the docile and co-operative guests their imperial hosts would have preferred. Far from it. Escapes were commonplace, especially when the POWs were detailed for work outside the camp or billeted to farmers.[75] Moreover, there were outbreaks of violent POW unrest, ill-discipline and non-co-operation throughout Africa, especially after the Italian surrender in September 1943. In some cases, however, outbreaks of unrest were the result of the poor quality of troops sent to guard the POWs, insufficient training and the inadequate supervision by the imperial authorities themselves.

It was clear that by the end of 1941, the South African government was finding it difficult to cope with the number of prisoners. One European guard told a relative in New Zealand that in October several escapes had been attempted by the POWs at Zonderwater. Whenever there was a heavy thunderstorm at night, the lights would invariably go out throughout the camp, providing would-be escapers with an excellent opportunity to climb the security fences. As a result, every available man was turned out to guard the perimeter until the lights were repaired. As a result, 'a good many have been shot and stabbed by the Native guards'.[76] In February 1943 Celestino Faraone was shot and killed at Zonderwater by a 21-year-old Cape Coloured guard called Barend Schoeman. Charged with culpable homicide, Schoeman had also wounded two other prisoners. He alleged that the POWs were throwing stones at him. Thinking his life was in danger he opened fire. Reported as 'perfectly sober' by the Camp Security Officer, Captain Frank Heywood, he informed the camp commandant that Schoeman had given his full co-operation during the investigation. The young soldier pleaded not guilty, but the enquiry found him guilty and he was given seven days' imprisonment with hard labour. Compensation was sought by Faraone's family, but the case was deferred until the end of hostilities.[77] As we have seen, this tragic event was not an isolated incident. As the senior staff officer at Zonderwater commented, 'There is far too much shooting going on.'[78]

One of the most notorious examples of ill-discipline on behalf of the guard detachments occurred at Zonderwater on New Year's Eve 1942. A number of men of the 4th Cape (Coloured) Corps looted a 'wet' canteen in one of the camp blocks, became intoxicated and grew increasingly threatening. The European officers and a 200-strong detachment of South African Military Police attempted to quell the disturbance which threatened to spread to several other Cape Corps guard battalions posted nearby. Shots were fired from the Cape Corps camp, including automatic fire from a Bren gun in the possession of one of the drunken soldiers. As the European officers and military police tried to expel the rioters, they were also met by a heavy barrage of stones, bricks, broken bottles and other missiles from the nearby Cape Corps barracks.[79]

It was also alleged that a small number of Cape Corps guard troops entered the POW camp and that a serious brawl ensued with the inmates. Armed soldiers were despatched to eject the rampaging guards and in the course of the struggle between fifteen and twenty-six Italian officers and men sustained minor injuries, 'chiefly bruises and abrasions' suffered as a result of their efforts to assist in the removal of the guards responsible for the incident.[80] Two Italian POW officers were also reported to have suffered gunshot wounds but they were described as being of a 'trivial' nature.[81] This was an extreme example of the all too frequent breaches of South African discipline about which British military officials often complained. However, it was also indicative of the security problems faced by all combatant nations responsible for large concentrations of POWs. Ironically, it was with the help of some of the POWs themselves that the rioters were eventually contained. Indeed, the camp commandant, Colonel D. W. de Wet, recorded that all was quiet in the POW blocks during the disturbances and that the behaviour of the POWs throughout the night had been 'exemplary', despite the trepidation they must have experienced.[82] Smuts was also quick to praise the Italian POWs for their valuable 'support given freely and voluntarily [and] whose conduct appears to have been most commendable' during the riot. Fearing adverse publicity, and perhaps reprisals against South African prisoners in Axis hands, the prime minister was quick to report the incident to the Swiss Consul General in South Africa, C. Diethelm, whose nation had replaced Brazil as the Protecting Power in the dominion.[83]

Embarrassed by the mob violence displayed by its troops, Pretoria immediately sought to implement the recommendations outlined in two reports, ironically tabled three weeks before the disturbances at Zonderwater. Both Colonel Brett, the War Office POW liaison officer, and

Colonel R. D. Pilkington-Jordan of the South African Adjutant-General's office reported that the administrative channels of communication between the various departments responsible for POW affairs were woefully inadequate. In light of the trouble at Zonderwater, procedures were deemed either slow or inappropriate. The AG recommended a new POW directorate. Although challenged by the CGS, it was abundantly clear that one central authority had to be made responsible for POW issues. Furthermore, greater care and co-ordination had to be fostered on issues like guarding, security and logistics.[84] 'It is a most distressing document', lamented Smuts to van Ryneveld, 'gravely reflecting on the camp administration. I expect we shall hear more about this from responsible quarters. You should take steps, drastic steps, to have this situation reformed immediately.'[85]

The replacement of de Wet and the installation of his adroit second-in-command, Colonel H. F. Prinsloo, as camp commandant, was a positive step forward. Smuts also agreed to appoint a senior officer from within the AG, together with the necessary staff, to co-ordinate and administer all POW functions in the Union. Sir Roger Wilson, who used to sit with Lord Harlech on the Committee of Imperial Defence (1936–7) and was a former AG in India, was chosen as the Deputy Adjutant-General (POW).[86] His first two progress reports on the conditions at Zonderwater made for depressing reading. Approximately 25 per cent of the POWs inspected in February 1943 lacked the necessary basics in clothing such as boots, shirts and trousers. Wilson revealed that many prisoners were 'clad in rags, whilst their boots consist of uppers only, and are beyond repair'. Even more worrying, he recorded that too many POWs were still housed in tents which would not survive another winter. 'Not an altogether happy record of past achievement', minuted one Defence Department official.[87]

Although the new administration attempted to rectify past shortcomings, an ICRC delegation visited the camp at the end of February before many of the reforms had been completed. When Wilson returned in mid-March he noted that the visit had taken place before the arrival of considerable stocks of clothing and boots. Despite Prinsloo's assurances that supplies were on their way, they carried very little weight with the ICRC delegation. According to Wilson, as far as clothing and accommodation were concerned, the only visible change had been for the worse. Fortunately for Pretoria, the visit by the ICRC delegates had taken place a week before a period of heavy rainfall which would have dramatically shown how unwaterproof the tents had become. POWs, who were lying on the ground in leaking tents, had become 'intensely miserable' during this bad weather. So too had the camp staff who were growing impatient for the lack of results. One consolation was that the general health of the inmates was good, although there were a high number of mental and tubercular cases. The camp hospital now contained 2,500 beds of which 1,200 were occupied, including some who were due for repatriation on medical grounds.[88]

Conditions and morale appeared to be on the mend. Unfortunately for Pretoria, circumstances intervened which marred the progress made since March. In June 1943, another disturbance at Zonderwater, this time by the 2nd Cape Corps battalion, embarrassed and alarmed South African and British officials alike. The events need not concern us except as an illustration of how problematic it was becoming for the Union government to find the requisite number of reliable troops for POW guard duty. Described as a 'strike', the rioting on 13–14 June was sparked by grievances over working practices. Many in the battalion were 'fed-up' with the monotony of guard duties that arose out of their lengthy posting to Zonderwater. As a result, idleness was rife, reported Zonderwater's information officer, Lieutenant Arthur E. Hammond. Discipline was very poor, continued Hammond, as the NCOs and other ranks 'still fraternise freely in such malpractices as Gambling and Dagga Smoking'. In addition, there was a distinct lack of social amenities in the adjacent towns, especially for those who wanted to take advantage of weekend leave which averaged one weekend every six months! For those wanting to entertain family, friends and visitors at the camp on the weekend, no such facilities existed for non-European troops. Finally, complaints were also levied by the men against many of their European officers who had no interest or experience in commanding non-European soldiers. This last point prompted calls for the disbandment of the battalion so that these said officers, who were apparently not up to scratch, could be released. Fortunately, the rioting and violence was confined to the Cape Corps barracks; Italian POWs were apparently not involved nor had they been targeted by the mob.[89]

However regrettable these breaches of discipline by South African POW guard units were, the fact remained that it was a price Pretoria was willing to pay in order to increase wartime agricultural production; pressures which would increase between 1943 and 1945. In the end, the British and South African response to the challenges of housing, feeding, administering, transporting and guarding thousands of Italian prisoners in Africa between 1940 and 1943, especially during the 'flood' of early 1941, was relatively swift, effective and humane. Admittedly, there were problems. These shortfalls, however, had more to do with the unpreparedness brought about by the overwhelming number of captives which stretched what limited resources were available to Britain and her colonial partners during the initial stages of these campaigns. As we have seen, the Imperial authorities worked diligently to ensure that there was a uniformity of treatment for all Italian POWs whatever part of Africa they were located in. Even the delicate issue of race vis-à-vis the employment of white prisoner labour in a colonial setting and the use of non-European soldiers to guard white enemy prisoners was, with several exceptions, mindfully handled. Failure to do so meant that the Axis authorities might retaliate against Allied POWs in their custody; a fear, which continually haunted civil and military planners alike. Therefore, reciprocity rather than the 1929 Geneva Convention underpinned British and Commonwealth POW policy.

The eviction of the Axis from North Africa in April 1943 and the Allied invasion of Italy in July were important turning points during the war. This was followed soon after by Italy's surrender in September and the granting of co-belligerent status to this one-time foe which, in turn, had potentially significant implications for the Allied treatment of its Italian prisoners. These issues will be discussed in Chapter 6. It must be remembered, however, that beneath the veneer of humanitarianism lay the cold political reality that POWs continued to be a highly prized and exploitable resource; and that from 1943 onwards the British and Commonwealth governments continued to marshal Italian POW manpower for work in their respective countries. Co-belligerency also raised a number of key diplomatic and moral issues regarding the future treatment of these captives. New problems, especially concerning security, were encountered as more POWs were paroled to provide much needed labour for war work, especially food production. The increased contact between prisoners and the local community in a much more relaxed environment after 1943 also raised new tensions concerning appropriate behaviour in the ever-changing relationship between Italian prisoners and their captors.

4

'Farming Down Under': Italian POWs in Australia, 1941–3

A contribution to the imperial war effort

For the most part, the experiences of the 18,432 Italian POWs held in Australia between 1941 and 1947 mirrored those of their comrades incarcerated in Britain, the Middle East, India, Kenya and South Africa.[1] One specialist on Australian internment policy, Kay Saunders, argues that the story of the Italian POWs in Australia 'is neither eventful nor horrific. There are no inspiring tales of self-sacrifice or heroism'; and that the entire process was 'marked by an orderly adherence' to the regulations as outlined by the 1929 Geneva Convention which were dutifully followed by the Australian Army and the Director-General of Manpower.[2] This contention is supported by the unfootnoted work of the former journalist and amateur historian, Alan Fitzgerald. Although there were isolated incidents of racial bigotry and complaints from Australian trades unions that 'cheap' POW labour was undermining their members' rights, in general the Italian POWs in Australia were well treated and respected by the local populace.[3]

On the surface there is a great deal of truth to these observations. The time spent in Australia by many of these men was relatively carefree and uneventful. However, with the release of new archival sources, in particular internal security documents, a more detailed picture emerges which highlights the deep ideological divisions between the prisoners themselves.[4] This factionalism between Fascists and anti-Fascists (also known as Royalists) not only affected morale and discipline within the extensive camp system, but also helped shape the Commonwealth of Australia's POW policy. In other words, a much more complex picture has now emerged about the Italian POW experience in Australia which suggests it was not as idyllic as previously portrayed.

When Italy declared war in June 1940, Australia, like Britain and her sister dominions, reacted swiftly by interning elements of its Italian community. By late September 1940, 1,789 'locals' had been rounded up, detained and transported to internment camps where over 3,000 German internees had been housed since September 1939. Of the Italians, the largest numbers were aliens resident in Australia, but the statistics also included naturalised British subjects and a handful of natural-born Australians of Italian descent. These numbers were bolstered with the addition of 245 Italian civilian internees from overseas who, for security reasons, were transported to Australia from the United Kingdom and Singapore. The largest concentrations of Italians were found in Queensland, Western Australia and New South Wales. Of the estimated 33,000 Italian-born immigrants in Australia at the end of 1939, a total of 4,727 were interned at one time or another during the war; a number which peaked at 3,836 in December 1943. The exact total of Italian internees who were either naturalised British subjects or natural-born Australians stood at 1,009, or 20 per cent (62 natural-born and 947 naturalised British subjects). Interned Italians from overseas reached 425 and included people from as far away as Palestine, New Caledonia and the New Hebrides.[5]

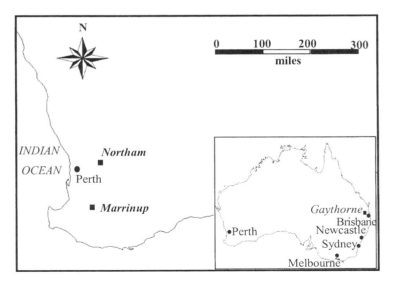

Map 4   Prisoner of War Camps for Italians in Western Australia, 1941–7

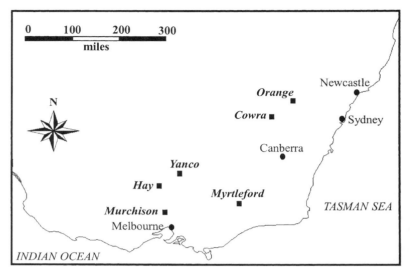

Map 5   Prisoner of War Camps for Italians in New South Wales and Victoria, 1941–7

During the initial stages of the war, the Allies treated merchant seamen as civilian internees. In February 1942, however, Britain advised the dominions that because the Axis powers treated all merchant seamen as POWs, Allied policy would be brought into line with that of the enemy. As a result, 268 Italian merchant seamen were transferred from being internees to POWs overnight.[6] Therefore, technically, the first Italian POWs captured by the Australians were in fact merchant seamen from two Italian merchant ships, the MV *Remo* and MV *Romolo*. On 11 June 1940, the *Remo*, which had been deliberately delayed from sailing by the port authorities, was seized at Fremantle; its 125 passengers and crew being interned in Western Australia. The *Romolo*, which had sailed from Brisbane on 5 June, was intercepted by the Royal Australian Navy (RAN) seven days later. However, the crew was able to scuttle the ship by setting her on fire before it was taken as a naval prize. All on board were picked up, taken to Townsville and interned in Queensland.[7] When the decision was taken to upgrade these merchant seamen to POW status they were relocated to appropriate POW facilities.

It was in March 1941 that the Dominions Office passed on the request from the War Office for dominion assistance in urgently relocating Italian POWs from Egypt. Referring to earlier communications made in

July 1940 and February 1941, where Canberra had agreed to take 6,000 civilian internees, London noted that as only 3,792 internees had so far been accommodated the imperial authorities wondered instead if accommodation could be provided for 2,200 Italian POWs from the Middle East. On 2 April, the Australian Department of the Army recommended the transfer of 2,000 Italian captives, subject to inter-governmental financial arrangements similar to those negotiated in relation to the custody of civilian internees sent from the United Kingdom during the previous year. That is, under the agency principle, Britain would offset the costs of camp construction and upkeep. This proposal was submitted and approved by the Australian War Cabinet the same day.[8]

Three weeks later and on the heels of General Erwin Rommel's dramatic counterstroke in the North African desert, Canberra received another urgent plea from London to accept an additional 2,000 prisoners in May and 1,000 per month for the next five months beginning in June 1941. The Secretary of State for Dominion Affairs, Clement Attlee, suggested that if large-scale movements of prisoners became possible, could the Commonwealth government house a total of 50,000 German and Italian POWs in the next six months? In his submission to the War Cabinet, the Minister for the Army, Percy Spender, noted that if Australia agreed to accept the 7,000 extra Axis prisoners an additional £450,000 would be required to build new and secure accommodation. Moreover, these figures did not include money necessary for raising and maintaining the necessary guards and hospital facilities. The second point he raised concerned the British request for the Commonwealth government to take up to 50,000 captives over six months. Despite the provision of a large security force and the construction of an extensive POW camp system, the Military Board was optimistic that these requirements could be met provided early warning was given as to the time-frame and programme of shipments. Spender also believed that a large proportion of these men would be colonial troops. Surprisingly, in a country so determined to maintain its 'White' Australia policy, the inclusion of African troops was not a problem, according to Spender. Most telling was the Board's conclusion 'that the national benefits to be derived from the acceptance by the Commonwealth Government of these prisoners of war are considerable'.[9]

Therefore, almost from the beginning, Australian ministers were keenly aware of the wartime labour potential POWs could provide. This destroys the contention, advocated by Kay Saunders, that Australia's decision to take civilian internees, political refugees and POWs was hardly the act of an independent or sovereign nation, but rather a form of contrition reminiscent of her convict past. 'Australia constituted itself as a dependent colonial outpost ready to accept more powerful Allies' problems.'[10] This is nonsense. Australia could have refused to accept any or all of the civilian internees and POWs it was asked to take. Furthermore, in the case of Axis POWs, it was victorious Australian forces that had bagged thousands of prisoners – over 25,000 at Bardia alone – in the early stages of the North African campaign. Capturing a large number of human trophies was not only a potent reminder to those at home of the might and skill of Australian arms, but having Axis POWs in Australia was also a useful reminder to the belligerent powers to take good care of those Australians who had fallen into their hands. Although left unspoken, POWs were useful bargaining chips in the age of total war. In the end, the issue of reciprocity and fears of reprisal were not far from the surface when Canberra decided to assist its beleaguered ally.

On 30 April, the Australian War Cabinet approved the British request for the transportation of the additional 7,000 POWs. Canberra insisted that only a small number of Germans be sent. The bulk, therefore, would be Italian. Crucial to understanding this insistence was security: 'that accommodation for Italians could be on a simpler scale than for the Germans'. As a result, the evacuation of the Italian prisoners could be more easily facilitated because they could, in the first instance, be sheltered under canvas while hutted accommodation was being built. The Australian authorities, like their allies, seemed to be influenced by the now well-entrenched stereotype that Italian POWs were docile, less demanding than their more ideologically driven German allies and either possessed simpler tastes or had lower expectations while in captivity. Nevertheless, fearful of reprisals by the Axis, the Australian War Cabinet was equally apprehensive about the need to provide the minimum standard necessary and equal to what British and Australian POWs in Italian hands were receiving. Shortfalls in providing essential services for maintaining basic hygiene and comfort for Italians in Australia were unacceptable if this exposed Australian captives to ill-treatment. The Australian War Cabinet was adamant, despite Spender's earlier optimism about taking colonial prisoners, that importing African captives was, for political (and racially xenophobic) reasons unfeasible and therefore was rejected.[11]

While the first batch of prisoners was in transit, preliminary discussions about their utilisation were under way. One suggestion was that they be employed on the construction of strategic roads or railways. 'Idle men are generally discontented men', commented the Board of Business Administration after the submission of a full report by the Chief Inspector of POW and Internment camps. One Queensland politician, who was resolute that Axis POWs must not be allowed to 'loaf', reached the same conclusion. Work would not only combat idleness, but would also help offset increased state expenditure for the upkeep of the burgeoning number of internees and POWs. Costs would be recouped and POW labour would provide positive benefits to an already overstretched war economy. The Acting Chief of the Naval Staff concurred. Complaining that the employment of defence personnel for the construction and maintenance of harbour defences in Darwin was seriously interfering with their training, he suggested that 200–300 prisoners be employed on 'purely pick and shovel work' building breakwater extensions on the port's boom defences and on the excavation for a new magazine.[12]

In early July, the War Cabinet met to discuss these and other proposals. It quickly emerged that Article 31 of the Geneva Convention, which prohibited the use of POWs on work directly connected with wartime operations (as suggested by the RAN in Darwin), imposed serious limitations on their deployment. For the immediate future, prisoners were confined to the following types of work: camp fatigues and normal day-to-day maintenance; work on the construction, improvement and renovation of the POW camps and their essential services; and employment on government and private enterprises such as road work, reforestation, irrigation, timber cutting for firewood, charcoal and pulp wood, fruit picking, harvesting and other non-war work.[13] Under Article 34, prisoners would not be paid for work carried out as part of their normal camp duties. However, as we have seen, uniform rates were applied throughout the Empire for work conducted in the construction, improvement or repair of the camps. Men would be paid $7\frac{1}{2}$ (Australian) per day for unskilled work and is 1s 3d (Australian) per day for skilled work. Rates of pay for outside contracts both state and private were set at local wage levels, subject to the usual deductions for food and accommodation where provided by the employer. POWs quickly lost their appeal as a source of cheap labour when many prospective employers discovered that while the prisoner received a minimal wage, the employer had to pay full market rates.[14] Another fly in the ointment was security. If, according to the Geneva Convention, it meant employing one guard for every POW on outside contracts the burden on military manpower and the additional security costs this entailed would not only seriously curtail the use of POW labour, but also eliminate the obvious benefits of using it in the first place.

Meanwhile, the first shipload of 512 Italian POWs, which included five medical officers, had disembarked in Sydney in late May. Still wearing the tattered remnants of their uniforms, many prisoners were still in shorts. One Sydney newspaper recorded:

> They wore towels, rags, cotton waste, crochet lace, and white stockings as neck scarves. Headwear included bowlers, sun helmets, felt hats, berets, forage caps in green and khaki, birettas of hessian, and canvas and tight-fitting skull caps. Types of footwear were mud-caked patched military boots, sandals, sand-shoes, and felt and leather slippers.[15]

Apparently, because of their good conduct onboard during the earlier stages of the trip, the prisoners were given the run of the ship. Many 'who had been café proprietors and waiters in private life', noted the reporter, 'were allowed to become ship's stewards'. The article boldly reported that none of the prisoners were Fascists, but were all 'King's Men' who supported Italy's monarch, King Victor Emmanuel III. Nonetheless, the landing authorities took no chances. Military police assigned to escort the new arrivals while disembarking from the harbour ferries were armed with rifles and revolvers. When the prisoners came ashore at Pyrmont they were marched through a double line of soldiers with fixed bayonets. Before they were entrained, each POW was issued a burgundy-coloured greatcoat (to denote his POW status) and a tin pannikin. One Anzac guard, who had been a veteran of the Great War, described the prisoners as a 'docile bunch. They are only a lot of boys … like the lot we used to bring down from the Somme.'[16]

Owing to the uncertainty of available shipping, only 2,000 Italian POWs had arrived in Australia by mid-July 1941. Nevertheless, plans had been drafted to provide accommodation for 12 group camps able to hold 4,000 prisoners each, together with a smaller camp for officers. A garrison force of 7,500 men was also established. The newly-built facilities at Hay in New South Wales, where the first batches of prisoners had been incarcerated, were initially designed to hold 3,000 men. Work on camps to hold equal numbers of prisoners had begun in Victoria at Murchison, and Loveday in South Australia. A similar facility to hold 2,000 prisoners was also under construction at Cowra in New South Wales. More sites were contemplated. It was noted that although security, and availability of water, electricity and sewerage, were of fundamental importance when locating these camps, it was recognised that at a later stage, future sites would be built with an eye to the utilisation of the inmates for labour. On 23 July, the Australian War Cabinet approved the expansion of its POW camp network. The total cost to the British Exchequer to house 50,000 at £50 (Australian) per head was estimated to be £2.5 million.[17]

The chronic shortage of shipping throughout 1941 played havoc with Middle East Command's desire to unburden itself of as many of its POWs as it could to Australia. However, it was the launch of the Japanese offensive in December 1941 which led to the immediate suspension of the POW relocation scheme. Apart from the first contingent that was landed in May, only five more batches were sent to the dominion that year: two in August, two in October and one in December. Several groups were shipped from Suez on the luxury liners SS *Queen Mary* and *Queen Elizabeth*. A total of 4,957 Italian POWs arrived from Egypt that year, comprising 561 officers and 4,396 other ranks.[18] Nevertheless, the shipping problem and Japan's entry into the war proved a blessing for Australian POW authorities. Unlike Kenya, South Africa and India, there was no sudden deluge of prisoners that made it difficult for the camp authorities to cope with the volume. The steady stream of prisoners over an eight-month period allowed the Commonwealth government, first, to allocate resources to an ever-expanding camp system, and second, to secure the amenities its 'guests' were entitled to under the Geneva Convention before they had arrived. In part, the Australians benefited from a pre-existing system established to process and handle civilian internees. With a basic administrative structure already in place possessing clear delineation between national agencies and regional commands, combined with regular shipping intervals, the desperate situation which confronted African and Indian authorities in 1941 failed to materialise in Australia.

So who were these men? The leading occupation amongst the rank-and-file soldiers was unskilled labourer. For example, of the 306 other ranks that made up one of the two August shipments, 132 were classified as labourers. The building and automotive trades were next, with bricklayers, carpenters and mechanics comprising the second and third largest occupational categories respectively. Scattered amongst the remainder were bakers, barbers, blacksmiths, butchers, clerical workers, farmers, gardeners, painters, students and tailors. In another batch of 509 men of whom 403 were officers, the professions that predominated were clerical work, engineering, journalism, law and teaching.[19] The Italian Army's reliance on the illiterate peasant and labouring classes was also reflected in those Italian migrants who had made Australia their home prior to the war. According to one Australian intelligence officer, the great bulk of the Italian community in the dominion consisted of cane cutters, general labourers, fruit vendors or market gardeners who had migrated from Naples, Sicily and destinations in between.[20] Many Australian officers who were in close contact with them concluded that because the majority of the rank-and-file prisoners were from peasant or labouring backgrounds, and showed a willingness to work, they could be weaned off Fascism and be exploited for labour purposes. As we shall see, this assessment was over-simplistic.

According to Dr G. Morel, the Swiss representative of the ICRC who made his first POW inspection at Hay in August 1941, the treatment of prisoners, and the conditions, were 'excellent'. He observed that a good rapport existed between the prisoners and their guards. No escape attempts had been made since the camp was established on 3 June. A total of 42 punishments had been meted out to the men: 32 in Camp 7 and 10 in Camp 8. Offences ranged from insubordination, stealing and being absent during roll call, to abusive language and assault. Detention varied depending upon the severity of the case and ranged from one day to 28 days. The food was deemed excellent and the rations were copious. Health was good and the medical facilities were fine with very few hospital cases. Complaints were few and of a minor nature, consisting of the need for more tools in the workshops, no money to purchase tobacco, a lack of reading material and the need for a larger quantity of games.[21]

One danger that the Australian medical authorities were determined to avoid was an outbreak of tropical disease such as dysentery. In mid-October 1941 an investigation at Hay by the Deputy Director of Medical Services, Eastern Command, Colonel A. M. McIntosh, revealed that of 1,000 POWs examined 82 (or 8.2 per cent) had tested positive for amoebic dysentery. Of the 100-strong garrison, two had contracted the disease.[22] Almost from the beginning of the POW transfer programme, the medical authorities had taken great pains to establish the proper medical procedures and quarantine facilities at the ports of disembarkation and within the camps to ensure that these imported diseases did not become a serious public health risk. Procedures were drafted and approved by the military authorities in conjunction with the Director-General of Health in Canberra. Special arrangements were made in respect of sanitation and camp hygiene; in particular, the urgent completion of water-borne sewage facilities at Hay. A mobile bacteriological laboratory was stationed at Hay to monitor the camp's medical progress, while a permanent laboratory was being installed at Cowra. The School of Public Health and Tropical Medicine in Sydney was invited to participate and given the all-important task of conducting bacteriological and pathological investigations of incoming prisoners, internees and returning Australian veterans.[23] As a result of these safeguards, no serious outbreaks of enteric fever were recorded; unlike South Africa, where camp authorities at Zonderwater had a potential epidemic on their hands during the early stages of captivity.

By November 1941 it was realised that the Commonwealth would fall far short of reaching its POW quota of 50,000. For the remainder of 1941 and all of 1942 the 5,000 Italian prisoners were largely confined to camp fatigues, working in closely supervised detachments within a 10-mile radius of the camp, or based in remote areas deep in the interior of the Australian outback. As noted above, failure to meet the original quota was probably a temporary blessing in disguise. The fear of a Japanese invasion necessitated that all governmental energies be expended on mobilising manpower resources for home defence. To initiate a large-scale system of outside contract work at a time of national crisis – a programme which required extensive garrison forces to act as escort – was an unnecessary drain on precious manpower resources which the Australian Military Forces (AMF) could ill afford.

Medical considerations also influenced Canberra's reluctance to exploit this resource on outside work. It was decided that no POWs would be employed on work away from their camps until six months after their disembarkation in Australia. This observation period not only allowed medical authorities to monitor and treat those prisoners who had contracted tropical diseases, but it also allowed those prisoners not afflicted to acclimatise to their new environment before being transported deeper into the interior. The prisoners were nevertheless kept busy. The ongoing programme of camp development, combined with market gardening and firewood cutting in the immediate vicinity of their camps preoccupied many POWs who were mostly manual workers or agricultural labourers. There were also a number of discussions with London to agree the rates of pay prisoners would receive for their work. Keen to comply with the provisions of the 1929 Geneva Convention and to observe a uniform wage policy, the Military Board was eager to avoid setting up differences of treatment between Britain and the dominions that could be exploited by the Axis powers. The simple fear was that a disjoint allied policy 'might lead to retaliatory action against British (or Dominion) POWs held by the enemy'.[24]

In January 1942, governmental approval was given for the employment of POWs generally on work other than that connected with camp upkeep. A detailed survey conducted by senior officials in March–April noted that of the 6,366 POWs then held in the dominion, 3,300 could not be regarded as available for general employment. Nonetheless, for the remaining 3,000 the survey recommended a variety of outdoor relief, mainly agricultural and forestry, in close proximity to each camp. As the type of land and farming practices differed from camp to camp, the authorities explored ways to maximise the labour potential available to them. The Chief Inspector strongly recommended that detailed planning and definite allocation of work to a camp be carried out according to the suitability for the particular type of primary production. Concerns about security cover for these outside projects nevertheless imposed certain limitations upon the scope of employment. The Department of the Army reminded those agencies involved that fewer escorts were needed for larger groups of prisoners. The division of POWs into small working parties would necessitate the deployment of a larger number of escort troops, which the existing war establishment could not provide.[25]

By July 1942, the Australian government had taken limited steps to employ its POW and civilian internee population. At Hay in New South Wales there were 2,000 Italian POWs, 1,500 of whom were available for work projects. One work detachment comprised of 300 prisoners was relocated to nearby Yanco to grow vegetables for the AMF through the supervision of the Department of Supply and Development. Another detachment of 300 had been sent to South Australia and dispersed in a series of six work camps on a 280-mile section of the trans-Australian railway 525 miles from Port Pirie Junction. The remainder, which included a smattering of civilian internee volunteers, was employed on a government-sponsored 250-acre market garden irrigation project. Another 600 acres was being developed for mixed farming that involved the raising of poultry, pigs and dairy cattle. The underlying principle was to expand the programme in order to absorb all available labour and make the camp self-supporting. Officials estimated that a turnover of £78,000 in farm income could be produced that year by an immediate outlay of £9,000 on essential seed, fertilisers, sheds, drainage and implements. Several criticisms were made that the projected revenues were over-optimistic. Nonetheless, there was a consensus between the military and agricultural authorities that the forthcoming year would generate a welcome surplus. Encouraged that the employment projects at Hay were 'on a sound basis and [were] being energetically conducted', the necessary funds were approved. Irrigable cultivation was to be expanded to 550 acres, which included a 50-acre test plot for cotton cultivation.[26]

Despite the initial strides made at Hay and plans to expand operations at Cowra and Murchison, 1942 witnessed an under-utilisation of POW labour. For the time being, the medical and security risks appeared too high for large-scale expansion. There were also problems with the prisoners themselves. At Hay, it was observed that most of the trench-digging parties were doing practically no work 'notwithstanding that an armed escort was standing over them'. A definite 'go slow' attitude was clearly evident amongst these men, reported one inspector, despite the fact that this was paid work. The work of these POWs was so 'unimpressive' that the Group Commandant suggested introducing a 'No work – No pay' policy. Although this industrial action involved a small group of POWs, this determined and obviously organised resistance to Australian authority was not an isolated incident.[27] By the end of the year, however, chronic manpower shortages and an overstretched wartime economy forced Canberra to re-examine the entire POW labour issue.

Security and the screening of POWs

Another hitherto neglected factor which facilitated a smoother administration of Italian POWs in Australia – and hence the identification and removal of potential troublemakers – was the success of Australian intelligence agencies in the monitoring, screening and assessment of its captives. To say, as Saunders and Fitzgerald do, that the Italians did not give the authorities much trouble, that they were not ideologically driven and that for the vast majority of POWs their time in Australia was uneventful, is somewhat misleading. If it had not been for the vigilance of the Australian security services and the methods they employed against Fascist cells in the camps it might have been a different story. Nevertheless, Canberra had an important advantage over its imperial associates which made this task more manageable. It had the smallest inmate population of all its allies which made it easier for the Australian POW authorities to monitor and marshal its prisoners.

As we have seen, the fluid nature of the fighting in North Africa prevented Middle East Command from embarking upon the systematic segregation of its Italian captives. The strategic necessity of extracting as many as possible from the war zone in 1941 and the speed with which many were shipped from the Middle East to their new homes in Britain and its empire impeded these processes even further. Despite the urgent pleading by the Political Warfare Executive (PWE) for proper screening, many Fascist POWs were despatched to Australia in 1941 which posed a potential security risk for the Australian authorities. Combined with this was the racial stereotyping which occurred regarding their Italian foe. Like their British comrades, Australian soldiers mocked the abilities and performance in battle of the Italian armed forces. For many Australians the real enemies were the Germans and the Japanese. The Italians, it was alleged, did not have the stomach for a fight, they were ill-trained, lacked discipline, were ill-kept, lived in squalid conditions on the battlefield and cowered in the face of a determined foe. Upon capture, they were submissive and malleable. Once the shock of capture had worn off, they appeared very relieved to be out of the contest and seemed only too eager to help their captors in any capacity.[28] This stereotype was not confined to front-line soldiers and their commanders. Many Australian civilians and government officials held similar prejudices in the initial stages of the war, and these had to be overcome if the maintenance of camp security was to be safeguarded.

The monitoring and synthesis of camp intelligence information by the Australian security agencies provided an important service to the Commonwealth authorities. Quite simply, without the development of a thorough and sophisticated intelligence branch within the POW and internment administration, Canberra would not have been able to take the decisions it did regarding the employment of Italian POWs with or without guards on outside contract work. In other words, the careful accumulation and interpretation of camp intelligence obtained by a number of means informed the relaxation of security regulations regarding the employment of POWs by private citizens. The constant vigilance by the military intelligence officers provided invaluable information on camp morale, the strength and organisation of Fascist cells and the activities of potential troublemakers. This information, in turn, helped camp authorities to thwart escape attempts, and curb a resurgence of Fascist resistance, in particular as new drafts arrived in Australia from India from 1943 onwards. Moreover, it allowed the Commonwealth government to take informed decisions about the selection and deployment of its Italian charges when chronic domestic labour shortages threatened to undermine the production of foodstuffs between 1943 and 1945.

The decision to give the military responsibility for internal security was sanctioned shortly after Adolf Hitler came to power. In 1934 a system of military reporting was established throughout the Commonwealth which covered all rural districts and communities. The establishment of a new internal security network included the appointment of a Director of Military Intelligence who reported directly to the Australian Chief of the General Staff. The creation of this new agency was not without its problems; not least of which was the rivalry between itself and the Commonwealth Investigation Branch (CIB) which until 1934, and under the auspices of the Attorney-General's Department, had been responsible for co-ordinating and safeguarding federal security. The twists and turns involved in the reorganisation of Australia's internal security network between 1934 and 1939 need not concern us here, except to note that by the time of the Munich crisis in 1938, the Australian army had triumphed to become the chief agency responsible for internal security; all other agencies, both state and federal, were now obliged to hand over their security material to military intelligence.[29] The creation of a network of Military Reporting Officers throughout rural Australia allowed military intelligence to keep tabs on anti-war activists, anarchists, pacifists, and communists, trades unionists, foreigners and the unemployed. Of particular interest were the political and economic activities of Japanese, Italian and German nationals, and links with their respective communities already resident in Australia. From 1934 onwards, the military intelligence diaries and summaries included an additional section on internal security which was now covered in the monthly intelligence notes.[30] The establishment of such an extensive internal surveillance network meant that when war broke out in Europe, the internment of German aliens and their sympathisers, followed in June 1940 by the internment of many Italians resident in Australia, was swift and comprehensive.

Many of the intelligence procedures and mechanisms designed to handle civilian internees, including the establishment of small teams of intelligence officers at each camp compound, were therefore well established before the first shipments of POWs arrived in Australia in mid-1941. This administrative framework was bolstered in August, when Canberra drafted a series of national security (POW) regulations and camp orders specifically governing the administration of enemy POWs in the dominion. These included procedural rules for the trials of POWs and POW correspondence orders.[31] In late November a three-day conference was held at Army Headquarters (AHQ), Melbourne, to discuss POW and internment camp administration. Chaired by Colonel McMahon and attended by senior AHQ staff and all the camp commandants, one of the key observations made was that the numbers of intelligence or 'I' personnel at all the POW groups were far below the recommended establishment. The Deputy Director of Military Intelligence promised to investigate, but commented that there was a shortage of personnel with suitable qualifications for this type of specialised work.[32]

Despite the availability of a system, it was obvious by October 1942 that very little information from the camps was being fed to the security services. Japan's entry into the war and Australia's preoccupation with home defence in the first six months of 1942 undoubtedly interfered with a systematic synthesis of camp intelligence. The need for trained intelligence personnel in the Middle East and in the various Australian Commands must also have contributed to the procedural lapses within the domestic intelligence network which, as we have noted above, were already understaffed. The threatened invasion by Japan also put enormous strains on internal security services, as a xenophobic public demanded large round-ups of those foreign-born nationals who had so far evaded internment. With such internal and external pressures, combined with operational priorities, it is not difficult to see why the channels of communication and the transmission of information between the camps and AHQ were not working effectively.

However, the real problem lay in the poor communications and strained working relationships which existed between those agencies responsible for internal security. A remedy was soon found. In March 1942 Lieutenant-General Sir Thomas Blamey was appointed Commander-in-Chief of the AMF. Although most of his attention was spent on the defence of Australia and the training and deployment of Australian forces for upcoming operations in the South West Pacific, he made enormous contributions in the reorganisation of Australia's intelligence and security services. The greatest strides were made in signals intelligence and special operations which included a complete overhaul in the areas of intelligence gathering, inter-service and inter-Allied intelligence co-operation and propaganda.[33] Domestic security did not escape his attention either.

The jurisdictional rivalry between the Army and CIB on internal security matters had failed to dissipate after the reforms of 1938, when military intelligence had been given the central role of co-ordinating internal security. Jealous of military control, the CIB resisted by not co-operating fully in the sharing of security information with its military counterpart. Tired of this internecine warfare, at long last Canberra decided in March 1942 to create a new Commonwealth Security Service, first mooted in February 1939. Under the direct authority of the Attorney-General's department, this new agency, commanded for the first six months by W. J. MacKay, the Commissioner of the New South Wales Police, would have sweeping powers.[34] Blamey was eager to co-operate, but as most of the experienced security personnel were employed in military intelligence he was wary of his men being seconded and placed under civilian control. The appointment in September 1942 of Brigadier W. B. Simpson (Blamey's Judge Advocate General when he was Deputy C-in-C Middle East) as Director-General of Security temporarily alleviated Blamey's anxieties,[35] as his energetic approach injected a renewed sense of urgency and purpose into intelligence gathering in the POW camps throughout Australia.

One of Simpson's first tasks was to improve the working relations between military intelligence and the new security service. Simpson informed the Director of Military Intelligence, Brigadier J. D. Rogers, that he was 'very keen to have his part of our joint responsibility in P[O]W camps working smoothly and efficiently'. He suggested that one of his officers tour all the POW and internment camps to ascertain if the intelligence officers in each camp were doing the jobs that were intended. Of fundamental importance was to investigate if these men were 'getting from the camps, and from people in camp areas who are in communication with internees [and POWs], such information as will help [the] Security Services carry out their task'.[36]

During the last two months of 1942 the Military Intelligence Supervisor for Australia's POW and internment camps, Lieutenant-Colonel J. U. Leask, toured most of the Commonwealth's POW and internment facilities. Prior to his tour, his preliminary investigations of existing practices confirmed that the biggest problem facing all staffs at both the POW and internment camps was the lack of basic information concerning the prisoners in their care. Arriving batches of prisoners were received without any indication as to those who were 'potential escapees or trouble makers'. This could be easily overcome by arranging for the Security Service to supply camp intelligence officers with a full précis of prisoner dossiers, which included extracts from overseas intelligence reports. Admittedly, there was a shortage of trained personnel in Canberra to tackle this huge but vital task. Nevertheless, steps were taken to alleviate this staff shortfall and provide specialist training for the burgeoning number of camp intelligence officers. The real key, as Leask saw it, was the sharing and free-flow of information both upwards and downwards within Army channels and between them and the Security Services.[37]

These practical administrative proposals were supplemented by a series of suggestions designed to enhance existing facilities. Leask endorsed the use of stool pigeons, hidden microphones and other clandestine operations, first pioneered in Britain and the Middle East. 'Searches should be frequent and at irregular times,' he continued. The drafting in of expert searchers, such as specialised customs or police personnel, to instruct camp staffs during their initial stages of training was also recommended. For the time being existing censorship channels were deemed adequate, but Leask advised continued vigilance and instructed camp personnel to 'watch carefully for any writing in unorthodox places, and for any evidence of codes or of invisible inks'. Of crucial importance was the immediate despatch of all information from censorship channels to camp intelligence officers for noting in the personal dossiers.[38]

The first POW camp to be inspected by Leask was at Myrtleford in Victoria where 801 Italians, including 589 officers, were held. His three-day inspection revealed that the camp was capably staffed, and he was impressed with the 'well organised, well commanded and well equipped' facility. The personal dossiers came in for particular praise. Each was updated on a regular basis, and the filing system had been carefully planned and well kept. Information within the dossiers was obtained largely from POW mail, captured documents and diaries. No items of possible source information were overlooked, which meant that the 'dossiers were steadily building up into a valuable and useful record'. Searches, which were frequent, were also conducted whenever the slightest suspicion had been aroused. Leask was also pleased with the commandant's success in weeding out doubtful or unsatisfactory garrison personnel.[39]

A visit to the Murchison complex in early November, which housed 1,562 German and 1,392 Italian POWs, was equally successful. Leask reported that the administration was 'well organised and efficiently handled', although he recommended a more systematic approach in compiling the POW dossiers. There was a different story at Cowra in New South Wales which housed 1,024 Italian POWs and 920 Italian internees. The working relationship between the camp staff and the intelligence section was poor, despite claims at HQ New South Wales to the contrary. Intelligence NCOs frequently heard themselves described by the garrison troops as the 'Gestapo' and knew that they had been pointed out to the prisoners as such. The worst offenders were apparently the camp interpreters, but some senior staff officers in the camp also possessed a deep misconception about the role of the intelligence section at Cowra. Leask noted that positive steps had been taken to clear up any misunderstandings between the two groups and improve the working relationship between them. Heartened by the enthusiasm and high quality of the intelligence team, Leask commented that the shortage of basic office equipment had prevented the establishment and collation of proper intelligence records. More ominously, he noted that the 22nd Garrison Battalion was barely sufficient to maintain a two-guard strength, and escorts for working parties were necessarily light with most soldiers being armed with single shot rifles.[40]

For Hay, where there were 1,354 POWs, and Yanco with its 348-strong labour detachment, there was nothing but praise. The Hay–Yanco complex was described as 'outstanding for the diversity and extent of its works projects'. POW activities included vegetable growing, dairying, pig and poultry raising, brick and soap making and timber cutting. From an intelligence viewpoint, these all-important duties had a positive effect on POW morale and 'general contentment'. Moreover, according to Leask, they provided his officers with excellent opportunities for obtaining information on compound activities, personalities and camp politics.[41]

However, the camp did have its problems. At Yanco, only the tree felling was under military control. Eighteen civilian overseers from the NSW Department of Agriculture supervised all farming activities on the 1,000-acre site, garrison personnel acting merely as escorts. The POWs grew resentful of being ordered around by civilians and there was criticism from the camp authorities that the entire scheme should be under military control. Added to this was the disturbing problem of security. The civilian overseers were tolerated, but the military authorities objected to their being accompanied by their wives and children. Nevertheless, unlike Cowra, there was a genuine attempt by the intelligence section and the Camp Commandant and his staff to earn each other's respect. Admittedly, there were a few misconceptions as to the proper function of an intelligence unit in the camp. And it was true that some of the intelligence staff lacked training in the fundamentals of intelligence work. Nevertheless, Leask reported that there were no serious obstacles to overcome in developing and maintaining a good working relationship between his staff and the camp authorities.[42]

While the Australian War Cabinet debated the pros and cons of extending the outside employment scheme to private individuals during the first few months of 1943, Leask undertook a second tour of the camps in February–March. The Myrtleford intelligence section was once again praised for its organisation and smooth operation; especially its record-keeping which was second to none. The guard officers were still expressing a residual amount of antagonism towards the intelligence officers, but Leask admitted that the full co-operation of the latter in security matters could not be ordered. It could only be developed by the 'exercise of much tact and diplomacy' on the part of the intelligence officers themselves. Herein lay the tension between intelligence officers and the Commandant's staff on security matters. The intelligence section was responsible for reporting and advising on camp security, but it was the Commandant who had the ultimate authority to decide the appropriate action. The problem was that if an intelligence officer continued 'forcibly' to present security matters to guard officers whom he considered lax, the inevitable consequence was that it would close important channels of compound information.[43] The one criticism lodged by Leask was that the weekly intelligence reports, despite an excellent dossier system lacked essential information on the personalities and politics in the compound. In future, when commenting on incidents such as escape attempts or camp quarrels it was vital for camp intelligence sections to provide brief notes on the individuals involved.

These notes make for interesting reading. In late March 1943 fresh earth was discovered in large quantities on the south side of the compound at

Myrtleford. Investigations revealed that several POWs had been scavenging bricks and timber from a new recreation hut, which was then under construction. These materials were being used for 'home' improvements in one of the huts. The material was confiscated and the two prisoners sentenced to five and seven days in the cells respectively.[44] Snap searches also revealed that several POWs who had just been transferred from Cowra had been communicating through the post with registered enemy aliens resident in Australia, some of whom had recently been interned. A passive resistance campaign had also been orchestrated by a handful of POW officers. These men had been absenting themselves from parades, claiming sickness as the reason. All the participants were warned that exemption from parade duties would in future be granted only with proper certification from the camp medical officer.[45]

Indeed, the efforts by the Fascists to maintain their party structure posed an immediate challenge to the POW authorities at Myrtleford. Nevertheless, it also provided an opportunity for the camp authorities to test the effectiveness of their intelligence gathering network and gauge the success of their countermeasures. For example, an unsigned letter had been removed from a junior medical officer who had been transferred to Myrtleford from Hay. It was revealed that the young lieutenant had been removed from his post as medical officer at Hay because of his Fascist activities. The letter spoke of a plan to distribute propaganda amongst the Australians, presumably the garrison force. The 'New Order' would be printed in English, contain simple but punchy messages and 'wake up' Australia to the benefits of Fascism. Information received from one of the POW compound leaders, Lieutenant-Colonel Tocco, indicated that it was not just the officers who were trying to disrupt camp routines. He reported the refusal of POW rank-and-filers to carry out their daily camp duties. Claiming that they were members of the Fascist Militia, Tocco had nothing but contempt for these men who, he claimed, were ill-disciplined cowards. On another occasion, it was noted by a guard that a Captain had saluted a Lieutenant. The explanation given was that the junior officer was one of the Fascist leaders in the camp and that his seniority in the camp's Fascist organisation had overridden the military seniority of the Captain.[46]

In New South Wales, a search revealed that two Italian POWs recently transferred to the labour detachment at Yanco from Hay were used as couriers by the camp Fascists. It was disclosed that fifteen notes had been hidden in the men's boots and socks. Not only did this find emphasise the use made of POW transfers as messengers between camps, but it also alerted the military authorities to the need to maintain constant vigilance. A further search of two other POWs uncovered in addition to concealed letters a 'small bottle of spirit, 2/- cash in a tin of Fruit Salts, a dagger-pointed table knife and a home made screw-driver'. The letters were found in boots, a service cap and packets of tobacco. There was also incontrovertible proof that the Fascists were attempting to revive their organisation at Hay. A Fascist membership card dated 30 January 1943 was confiscated from one POW which had been counter-signed by a medical officer who had recently been transferred to Cowra. The military authorities immediately convened an investigation into the extent of Fascist activities at the Hay complex.[47] Similar political activities were reported in Cowra. Intelligence officers reported that the ringleader was the camp chaplain, Padre Faustino Lenti. Claims were made that he was protected by a bodyguard of Fascist NCOs who worked under his orders intimidating prisoners and fermenting hatred of Australia. Lenti, like some of his brethren in South Africa, also used the altar to threaten suspected anti-Fascists and point an accusing finger at those the Fascists deemed enemies of *Il Duce.*[48]

These early examples of intelligence surveillance demonstrate several key points about the approach used by Australian military authorities in their ever-expanding POW system. Right from the beginning, Canberra was determined to construct a highly efficient intelligence gathering network in the camps, possessing clear lines of communication between the intelligence sections, garrison personnel and the Security Services. True, there were problems of jurisdiction, communication, training and administration. However, this was matched by a fervent determination to solve any difficulties which were bound to arise as quickly and as painlessly as possible.[49] The enthusiasm of the young camp intelligence officers, combined with the experience Australian intelligence officers had gained while serving in the Middle East, gave Canberra a real advantage over its POW charges very early on during their incarceration. Moreover, the deep divisions between Fascists and Royalists within several camps, although a worry, provided the intelligence agencies with an excellent opportunity to monitor the success of their counter-intelligence methods. As we shall see, this experience would prove invaluable as Australia paroled an increasing number of captives into the wider community after April 1943.

5
Intelligence, Propaganda and Political Warfare

Sir Harry Hinsley stated that from the outset of the Second World War, POWs were considered important sources of political and military intelligence, although it was not until 1942 that the various British military intelligence branches classified POW interrogations as among their more reliable sources of information. Indeed, according to Lieutenant-Colonel G. L. Harrison, a former commander of the Combined Services Detailed Interrogation Centre (CSDIC) in Egypt, at least 40 per cent of British intelligence had been obtained from POW interrogations, 'while most essential confirmation of that obtained from other sources' had also been acquired from this source.[1] With the release over the last decade of voluminous amounts of intelligence material in British and overseas archives a more complete picture has emerged regarding the utilisation of material gleaned from POW interrogations. New research not only confirms Hinsley's earlier contentions, but has also provided scholars with fresh and exciting avenues with which to demonstrate how useful POW intelligence was to the Allies in defeating the Axis powers.[2]

The significance of British efforts in extracting, collating and distilling material painstakingly collected from Italian POWs during the war is three-fold. First and foremost, Italian POWs were the largest single source of captives held by the British and her imperial partners between 1940 and 1943. As we have seen, the incarceration by mid-September 1943 of almost 500,000 Italian service personnel – 316,000 of whom were in British hands – provided the Allies with a seemingly inexhaustible supply of potentially useful information on a myriad operational, strategic and political matters. Secondly, it was the policies and procedures developed to cope with this large intake of Italians which provided the basis for a more systematic approach to processing intelligence material garnered from POW interrogations. This is especially true in the area of political 're-education'. While historians have written extensively about the de-Nazification of Germany and its military after the Second World War, the 'de-Fascisation' of Italy's armed forces has been woefully neglected. Nonetheless, it was the pioneering work involving the 're-education' of these Italian captives which pre-dates those schemes subsequently directed by the Allies against their German prisoners later in the war.[3] Finally, and running in parallel with political reindoctrination, it was the Italian POWs who first provided the raw material for British propaganda and psychological warfare experts to develop and sharpen their black arts in the all-important battle for hearts and minds. However, before an analysis of the specific procedures and problems can be undertaken, it is first necessary to sketch briefly the administrative structures which were established by each of the three British armed services to deal with the acquisition and integration of intelligence material obtained from Axis, in particular Italian, POWs in the formative years between September 1939 and the end of 1942.

The machinery for screening and intelligence gathering

It was not until the latter stages of the First World War that senior British intelligence experts realised the necessity of developing a long-term strategy for the screening and detailed interrogation of selected enemy captives. Although it had been understood by some British field commanders that POWs were a potential source of limitless but as yet untapped information on a whole range of technical and military subjects – information which they employed in their individual sectors of the Western Front[4] – it was not until 1917, with the creation by the War Office of a small organisation in Cromwell Road, London, that the real general intelligence potential of enemy POWs was fully recognised.

The Royal Navy and British Army at first jointly operated the new sub-branch of the War Office's intelligence directorate, designated MI1(a). Its primary task was to secure from those German POWs relocated to camps in the United Kingdom specialist knowledge which had not been revealed during their initial interrogations in France. Keen attention was paid to captured submariners and aircrew who possessed vital and complex technical knowledge.[5] With the establishment of the Royal Air Force (RAF) in April 1918, bombing target intelligence became of 'paramount' importance. As MI1(a) extended its activities and consolidated its inter-service basis, new quarters were obtained in Wimbledon, complete with special listening devices, in order to deal with its increasing obligations. The formal opening of these facilities was scheduled for 11 November 1918. Consequently it never housed a POW.[6]

With the Armistice, this rudimentary organisation lapsed. Although the First World War had highlighted the value of POWs as a source of intelligence, no specific technique of interrogation or processing had been formulated.[7] The result was that this type of intelligence gathering was given a low priority by the British military establishment. Only when war clouds once again loomed menacingly on the European horizon in 1938 did the War Office begin to respond to the whole issue of the treatment, administration and use of POWs for intelligence purposes. In August 1938, the Committee of Imperial Defence (CID) approved a series of policies concerning the movement, guarding and administration of all POWs, irrespective of the service to which they belonged or of their captors. These responsibilities were assigned to the War Office.[8]

The second development initiated in November 1938 by two staff officers located in separate branches of the War Office, both unknown to each other and working independently of each other, were plans for the resurrection of the defunct MI1(a). One of them, Captain A. R. Rawlinson, had served as an intelligence officer in the original branch in 1917–18. The other, Captain J. C. F. Holland, worked in the obscure section of Military Intelligence Research (MIR) where he was exploring and developing his ideas on sabotage, deception and subversion. Some of this work was to become the stock-in-trade for clandestine organisations such as the British commandos and the Special Operations Executive (the latter founded by Prime Minister Winston Churchill in June 1940).[9]

The initiatives undertaken by these officers did not go unnoticed during the winter of 1938–9. A conference held at the War Office in March 1939, attended by representatives of the War Office, Admiralty, Air Ministry, Home Office and MI5, decided that an intelligence organisation charged with the interrogation of POWs should be created. Between May and July, further discussions were held which confirmed an inter-service bases for the revamped MI1. Most important, it was agreed that within 24 hours of the outbreak of war, a fully operational interrogation centre would be established within the cramped precincts of the Tower of London. Preliminary arrangements were also made with the Post Office and the private communications firm RCA for the supply of listening or 'M' equipment.[10]

When the original charter for outlining departmental responsibility for POWs was drafted, the custody and transport of all POWs was given into the hands of the British Army. This included escorting enemy captives who were being transferred to the inter-service interrogation centre in

London. The War Office's responsibility for the physical requirements associated with POWs, including the construction and administration of all POW camps in the United Kingdom and in overseas theatres under British control, was also reaffirmed. The assumption made was that during the initial stages of the war, the largest number of enemy POWs would be soldiers. The allocation of responsibility for co-ordinating POW matters fell to the War Office's Directorate of Prisoners of War (DPW).

In fulfilment of the provisions agreed six months earlier, within 24 hours of the outbreak of hostilities, the nucleus of a combined services detailed interrogation centre was situated in the newly vacated married quarters of the Tower of London. One naval, two RAF and three army officers were established in their new accommodation, complete with two rooms installed with eavesdropping equipment. However, the war followed a different pattern from that envisaged by the pre-war planners. It was the RAF and the Royal Navy, not the British Army, which acquired a steady stream of prisoners during the first 22 months of the war. By the summer of 1940 and before their hurried departure to Canada, several thousand German captives, mainly *Luftwaffe* and U-boat crew, had already been processed by CSDIC(UK).

The Tower of London very quickly proved unsuitable for CSDIC(UK). In response to Admiralty pressure, more appropriate premises were found north-east of London at Cockfosters Camp in Trent Park, where on 12 December 1939 the new interrogation centre was established. Plans were also drafted for the construction of two detention camps specifically designed for interrogation work at Latimer and Wilton Park, near Beaconsfield in Buckinghamshire. But it was not until July 1942 that Latimer was fully operational. Its work was confined largely to extracting information from German captives. Five months later, Wilton Park was opened primarily for the interrogation of Italian prisoners.

The War Office's Prisoner of War Interrogation Service, PWIS (Home), supplemented the work carried out by CSDIC(UK). Established in July 1940, the unit was commanded from its London headquarters in Kensington by Lieutenant-Colonel A. P. Scotland. Better known as the London District Cage, this facility acquired a fierce reputation amongst Axis POWs who had been sent there for debriefing, many of whom found the experience intense and highly traumatic. Scotland, who had been a POW in German South West Africa during the First World War, knew from bitter experience how far a person could be pushed under an interrogation, what strengths were needed to resist successfully the blandishments of one's interrogators, and the tell-tale signs of a prisoner close to breaking point. Such personal insight was indispensable when choosing and training prospective interrogators. Apart from the London cage, over the summer of 1940 PWIS (Home) also created a network of regional detachments. Twenty officers were posted to several territorial commands throughout the country to undertake the selection and preparatory interrogations of German and Italian captives who had been trans-shipped from overseas and were now billeted in POW facilities within their respective command's jurisdiction. After this initial sifting, if a POW was deemed to have important additional information, he was sent to London where Scotland's interrogation teams went to work unlocking more secrets.[11]

A vital supplement to POW interrogations was the censorship of POW mail, both British and Axis. Prior to May 1940, censorship control of POW mail was primarily a War Office responsibility. However, it was assumed that greater efficiency in censorship matters could be effected using the extensive knowledge and experience of the Postal and Telegraph Censorship Department housed at Edge Lane, Liverpool. When these tasks were transferred to the department's Liverpool facilities, at first, the processing of POW mail was a comparatively small and manageable task. Priority had been given to civilian mail, especially the correspondence sent and received by interned enemy aliens and suspected fifth-columnists. As the war intensified, so too did the volume of POW mail and pressures for additional premises to handle it. Another office in Liverpool at Newsham Park was opened; and by November 1941 the number of examiners employed here analysing POW mail alone had reached over 350. More capacity was badly needed, however, and it was proposed to shift the work specifically dealing with British POW mail to the censorship branch in Manchester where it was claimed that as many as 800 examiners could be accommodated in the first instance.[12]

Apart from the problems with space and the sheer volume of mail needing examination, the shortage of qualified linguists with a knowledge of German and Italian plagued the postal censorship department's POW branch throughout 1941–2. In early 1941, the weekly number of letters available for censorship both to and from Italian POWs averaged 100. One year later between 25,000 and 30,000 items were arriving or being despatched weekly. Mail to and from German POWs had also increased, but was not on the same scale as the consignments of Italian POW mail. In 1941 the weekly average was between 3,000 and 3,500 letters; a year later it had increased to between 9,000 and 9,500 items per week. To meet these demands, further reorganisation was undertaken in March 1942 whereby all enemy POW mail, including that of enemy aliens and captured merchant seamen, was channelled through Liverpool. As a result, most of the Italian and German linguists were concentrated on Merseyside. To help relieve the burden on the Edge Lane office, the Manchester censorship branch was finally given exclusive control over British POW mail.[13]

Although the War Office had relinquished its control over the censorship of POW mail, it nevertheless maintained its pivotal function as an information exchange on intelligence matters. Co-ordinatory authority was handed to MI12, which acted as liaison between the Directorate of Military Intelligence (DMI) and all military and civilian branches of the government involved in processing and disseminating censored material. In February 1941, a sub-section of MI12 was established to act as the intermediary between the military authorities and the POW branch of the postal censorship department on all questions touching upon British and enemy POWs. Designated MI12(PW), its key roles were to obtain from the postal censors information on Axis POW morale and welfare, to report any breaches of camp regulations, to record complaints addressed to the Protecting Power by these prisoners, and finally, to note any details of general interest. In addition, MI12 was to liase between the POW censorship stations in the United Kingdom and the empire; distribute material derived from these stations to the War Office's intelligence and POW sections; and communicate these findings to the other service intelligence agencies discussed below.[14]

Interrogating the Italian enemy

Contained within the Trent Park facilities were the three service branches which constituted CSDIC(UK). The Army's section was first known as MI1(h). This was later changed in March 1940 to MI9(h) under its controlling War Office branch MI9(a). With the establishment of the Deputy Director of Military Intelligence (PW) on 1 January 1942, MI9(a) became the more familiar MI19.[15] One week later this section ceased to be a branch of the War Office and assumed the title of the combined centre, CSDIC. In early 1940, the naval section became an Admiralty department and was designated NID11 (Naval Intelligence Division). In January 1942 it was divided into NID1 (PW) and NID3 (PW) to handle German and Italian prisoners respectively.[16] According to Group Captain S. D. Felkin, who commanded the RAF interrogation section for all but the first four months of the war, it 'took on its own individuality', and became an Air Ministry section, AI1(k). A 'brilliant' interrogator, and man of tremendous energy and drive, Felkin stamped his personal authority on this section. According to one senior officer, by early 1945 Felkin had by 'sheer force of personality and professional competence, built up a position which, for an officer of his rank, [was] perhaps almost unique on the Intelligence side'.[17]

During the first few months of the war it emerged that there were fundamental differences in method between the British Army on the one hand, and the RAF and Royal Navy on the other. Officers within MI1(h) dealt solely with the detailed interrogation of enemy prisoners. Field interrogations were conducted by general staff intelligence officers operating within army formations as far down as division level. This decentralised approach was in stark contrast to the highly centralised strategy employed by the other two services; for there was no provision for interrogation officers with lower formations in the RAF and Royal Navy. Therefore all interrogation, both preliminary and detailed, was aggregated and co-ordinated at the Admiralty and Air Ministry level. Differences in working procedures were also reflected in the way in which captured documents were examined and collated. All *Luftwaffe* documents, whether taken from POWs or from airfields and headquarters, were centralised in AI1(k), later redesignated AI(K) in July 1942. Military documents were handled by MIR – an organisation entirely unconnected with the British Army's interrogation service.[18]

The fact that the RAF and Royal Navy conducted virtually all of the detailed interrogations for the first three-and-a-half years of the war did not mean that the Army's role in CSDIC(UK) was redundant or unappreciated. On the contrary, this allowed the Army personnel to concentrate on the production of special reports for all three services and on general administration. As one in-house observer commented, since both naval and air intelligence were solely concerned with operational intelligence throughout 1940–1, this allowed the army to concentrate its efforts on the equally valuable task of accumulating non-operational intelligence concerning political and economic issues of interest to the Foreign Office, Ministry of Economic Warfare and the Political Warfare Executive (PWE). The success of this unforeseen demarcation was highlighted in March 1944, when it was revealed that the Army had issued 5,080 reports for the RAF, 3,144 for the Royal Navy and 495 for itself.[19] Although volume is not necessarily an indication of worth, it at least signifies that a pool of *potentially* useful knowledge and insight was being made available to a variety of civil and military agencies. Moreover, it was in North Africa, where over 160,000 Italians were captured during the British offensives of December 1940–March 1941, that Army authorities deployed its POW interrogators in greatest number and, as a result, reaped substantial benefits.[20]

The central importance of the Middle East to British political and military strategy prompted the Joint Intelligence Committee (JIC), with the full support of the British Chiefs of Staff (COS), to explore in February 1939 an amalgamation of all intelligence gathering facilities in the region under one authority. Hitherto, the tendency had been for government departments to pay strict attention to those areas and sources which were of their direct responsibility to the exclusion of information from elsewhere. Failure to share or integrate intelligence often led to misleading if not potentially dangerous situations for those concerned with Middle Eastern security because no complete or comprehensive intelligence picture was readily available. To continue to view the situation in 'penny packets' was deemed unacceptable. So, in May 1939, the formation of a combined intelligence bureau was discussed and endorsed by the CID. On 1 August 1939 the Middle East Intelligence Centre was established.[21]

As part of the ongoing intelligence review, and in recognition of good work already being accomplished at Cockfosters, it was decided in August 1940 to augment British intelligence capabilities and organise a CSDIC in the Middle East based at Cairo. By December an interrogation facility had been established at Maadi near GHQ, Middle East Command, where as many as sixty prisoners per day could be processed. The information collected in the rear echelons had little operational value, however, because the POWs had been removed from the battlefield. Instead, questions were in the main directed at acquiring material that could be used in the long-term for propaganda, psychological warfare and political re-education. In order to expedite these functions a holding camp for 800 POWs was built where prisoners were segregated into compounds according to intelligence priorities and requirements. Prisoner segregation, a recurrent problem throughout the war, proved essential, not only to separate POWs who were awaiting interrogation from those who had been processed but, equally important, to allow British intelligence officers to identify war criminals, propagandists, friendly POWs and enemy agents.[22] The PWE, created in July–August 1941, also worked closely with CSDIC(ME). It was given the monumental task of developing and orchestrating a long-term propaganda campaign against Fascist Italy in addition to a political re-education programme amongst the burgeoning numbers of POWs.[23]

Operational intelligence from POWs in North Africa proved problematic during these early days. The rapid successes scored by British arms in North Africa, coupled with the shortage of CSDIC personnel who had been concentrated in Cairo, forced the War Office to post officers from the United Kingdom to work with the forward divisions. This worked well, provided that the forward units, British Army HQ and CSDIC (ME) could keep in constant communication. However, the emphasis on mobility and the seesaw nature of the fighting in North Africa, exacerbated by the problems of distance between the various intelligence sections, raised new problems. The essential demand for rapid, detailed interrogations at Army HQ – information which could not be immediately supplied from Cairo because of the time interval – forced the establishment of mobile CSDIC units. In spite of Army HQ reluctance, five such units were successfully operating in the field throughout the Middle Eastern theatre by May 1942.[24] POWs and captured documents processed at the divisional level and enhanced by the work of the mobile units at the advanced headquarters played their part in revealing the enemy's order of battle, equipment, logistics, defences and morale.[25]

There were three techniques adopted by British interrogators to reveal information: direct interrogation, eavesdropping using hidden microphones, and the introduction of stool pigeons.[26] Direct interrogations were the most effective means of accumulating a bank of information providing the subject was willing or could be induced to co-operate. Success, however, depended upon the skill and experience of the interrogating officer, the nature of his brief and the rapport he was able to establish with his prisoner. Debriefings contained information about the prisoner's personal and service histories; his unit, its strength, and command structure, as well as details concerning tactics, callsigns, weaponry, training, previous missions and new technology. In addition, prisoners were probed about their political beliefs, the course of the war and their attitude towards not only their own officers and political leaders but also their Axis partners.

An absorbing means of gathering intelligence from enemy POWs was the use of concealed microphones in specially-built 'M' rooms. These operations were first carried out in the Tower of London and at Trent Park, where 12 specially 'miked' rooms had been fitted. Inadequate space prompted the relocation to Latimer and Wilton Park, where in July 1942, 30 purpose-built listening rooms and six 'miked' interrogation rooms were provided in each camp. Not more than three (but preferably two) POWs were allocated to each room. Prisoners were not allowed out of these rooms for long periods other than was absolutely necessary – such as visits to the lavatory and a daily 30-minute exercise period. This prevented conversations from taking place out of range of the microphone. A minimum amount of literature was provided because the interrogators wanted the prisoners to talk rather than read. However, one newspaper per day was found useful for it could stimulate conversation along desirable lines.

'M'-room staffs were to listen in to, and where necessary 'cut', records of the conversations of selected POWs. These listening reports (designated SRs) were then circulated to those intelligence services which cross-checked the information with that obtained from direct interrogations and stool pigeons. In 1942, for example, 700 German and 164 Italian POWs were processed at CSDIC(UK); over 9,000 records were 'cut' and a grand total of 3,374 reports were compiled and circulated. By the end of 1944 a total of 17,746 SRs had been produced involving 8,606 POWs. These records, including complete sets of daily prisoners' reports, were also sent to the Government Code and Cypher School housed at Bletchley Park where British codebreakers used this information to fill in the picture provided by intercepted signals communications.[27]

Selected rooms were monitored around the clock, either because a particular batch of prisoners was deemed to possess vital information which had not yet been divulged, or because a particular subject or range of subjects were being scrutinised in order to provide detailed profiles for long-term projects involving propaganda and psychological warfare. Clearly, an advantage of eavesdropping was that, unlike direct interrogation which might uncover valuable operational information, secret microphoning provided the interrogators with further insight into a prisoner's mind, his likes and dislikes, ambitions and fears. Listening personnel were divided into squads of approximately twelve operators, with each squad divided into two shifts. It was vital that the utmost concentration be maintained at all times. Thus, shorthand notes were discouraged as this distracted the operator. In addition, the operator covering the room knew what questions the prisoner had been asked during the preliminary interrogations and was therefore primed for the reactions he was to expect from the POW once he had returned to his quarters. This procedure provided 'a most valuable check on the accuracy or otherwise of [POW] statements made under interrogation'.[28]

These intelligence gathering procedures were intensive, and extremely demanding, but, as we have already discovered, very rewarding for Britain and her allies. Nonetheless, these procedures were not without their problems. There were never sufficient numbers of suitable British officers with the requisite knowledge of colloquial Italian or German. 'Very frequently it was found that Englishmen with a perfect academic knowledge of German and even some aliens with a native knowledge of the language were quite unsuited for "M" work', declared one report. As well as being mentally alert and adaptable, operators had to have extensive knowledge of service slang and technological jargon. It took time to train these men. Shortages of trained linguists however meant that at the end of 1942 German and Austrian refugees, many of whom were Jewish, were selected and employed as NCO operators. This helped the monitoring of German prisoners but did little to solve the shortage of Italian linguists. Nonetheless, by 1944 the total number of 'M' staff had reached 100.[29]

Information from stool pigeons – designated 'Z' officers – provided important supplementary material, which was used to corroborate that gleaned from interrogations and microphoning. Primed with knowledge obtained from earlier interrogations, stool pigeons were sometimes deployed in the 'M' rooms to assist interrogators and verify information. RAF and Royal Navy interrogators favoured the use of stool pigeons because their captives were deemed to be more security conscious; and hence less forthcoming during the interrogation processes. By the end of 1940, four stool pigeons had been selected from 93 civilian candidates, all of whom were German or Austrian refugees; but during the course of the war, 49 POWs were also selected to augment these 'professionals' to act as stool pigeons. Some were deserters, but a few were ordinary prisoners 'who from motives ranging from a desire for their own comfort to genuine idealism' willingly undertook these duties. Each stool pigeon was assigned to a specially chosen Army officer who looked after the mental and physical welfare of his charge. The methods by which the stool pigeon obtained information from his prisoner depended largely upon the ability and initiative of the stool pigeon himself, 'who had to maintain an air of genuineness and possess the versatility of an actor'. A special fund was instituted to help CSDIC(UK) finance these operations. Apart from the salaries paid to the professional stool pigeons, the POW operatives were also paid a working wage and given additional comforts from the canteen such as extra cigarettes and occasionally beer. Preferential treatment also included regular outings and better quarters, such as a cottage in a secluded part of the camp.[30]

Such risky work was not without its occupational hazards. Felkin reported that the continual strain and extreme nervous tension under which they worked 'caused them to be subject to severe stomach disorders'.[31] The strain of the work imposed on stool pigeons at CSDIC (ME) was also fully recognised, to the extent that part of one of the specially designed interrogation huts was given over to these men so that they could relax and rest while off-duty. The rooms were made cosy and various privileges were granted, including a £2 weekly bonus, which could be spent in the canteen to procure certain luxuries as a reward for their hard work. Another difficulty with this form of intelligence gathering was the disposal of the POW stool pigeons once their cover had been blown or they had become too stale.[32] Beatings and untimely or unexplained deaths in several POW camps were usually the result of reprisals carried out against prisoners by former comrades who suspected them of being stool pigeons. The sensitive and extremely dangerous work of stool-pigeon activity needed constant monitoring as well. Occasional security checks using microphoned material called 'X' files revealed in CSDIC(Mediterranean or (MED)), for example, that on several occasions stool pigeons worked as double agents. On the other hand, stool pigeons performed vital work during security investigations. Two of CSDIC(MED)'s most effective interrogators were former enemy agents. Ultimately, between 1940 and 1945 a total of 1,506 Axis POWs were unknowingly manipulated by British-handled stool pigeons.[33]

The types of information divulged by Britain's Italian captives were many and varied. Operational information which could be deployed immediately was in the first instance, and despite initial scepticism, the most valuable to British field commanders. Nevertheless, to trace information obtained from POW interrogations and follow it through to its direct application on the battlefield has proved illusive. In part, this is due to the dearth of surviving individual POW interrogation files. Any information of immediate tactical or operational use would have been forwarded without delay to battalion and divisional HQs for further analysis. How this information was interpreted and acted upon at the higher echelons, if at all, is difficult to ascertain. This is not helped by the fact that the vast majority of unit war diaries are notorious for their blandness and lack of information on this matter. The private papers of leading general officers available to the public make no or only passing reference to intelligence matters; and even this is of an innocuous or fleeting kind. Odd references appear in despatches, usually in conjunction with information obtained from other sources such as captured documents or enemy wireless intercepts. Furthermore, when such scraps of operational intelligence obtained from POWs have been unearthed, it is usually written as a postscript to events which happened days or weeks earlier. Therefore despite the abundance of wartime intelligence information obtained from POW interrogations, the vast majority of references deal with the processes and procedures for extracting, collating and interpreting this material which was later used for long-term strategic or political purposes rather than its day-to-day usage.

An analysis of several POW interrogations conducted in the early phases of the Abyssinian campaign help illustrate the above points. In early February 1941 five crewmen from two Italian Caproni light bombers shot down during operations over Digh Merer on the Kenya–Italian

Somaliland frontier were transported to and interrogated in Nairobi ten days after their capture. The Air Intelligence Officers (AIOs) concentrated their attention on a number of key issues: the particulars of the other crews in the flight; enemy operational instructions; Italian photographic reconnaissance; priority and details of individual targets; reasons for forced landing and/or abandonment of aircraft; enemy landing grounds; fuel stocks; enemy arms and logistics; means of communication; enemy air strengths, locations and movement; enemy ground strengths; and finally, the state of Italian morale.[34] In other words, the topics selected were designed to assist British planners in the compilation of a portfolio of information which could be deployed in forthcoming operations.

These categories comprised the backbone of most POW interrogation reports, although each service had specific categories unique to itself, particularly if they involved highly technical issues, the introduction of new equipment by the enemy, or specifics about air and harbour defences. In the case of the Royal Navy, keen interest was demonstrated in Italian special assault units – such as the X Flotilla MAS, the exploding motor torpedo boats (MTMs) and the two-man 'human-torpedo' units which throughout 1940–2 launched, with mixed success, daring attacks against British shipping in Gibraltar, Malta and Alexandria.[35] This information would be cross-referenced with that obtained from other interrogations and intelligence sources. Slowly, a picture would emerge of the enemy's order of battle, strength, training, deployment, fighting efficiency and morale. In January 1941, for example, a POW interrogation confirmed what many senior British officers had long-suspected about some aspects of the relationship between the Italians and their native conscripts in Africa. The Italian POW described the native soldier as 'quite good if properly handled, i.e. with one hand full of money and the other armed with a heavy whip'. He added: 'They were hardy on the whole and could cover remarkable distances on foot at the double.' Food was not as important to them as water; and 'if they lacked their tea they gave up instantly. Their behaviour under rifle fire was excellent, but the sight of planes, tanks and even armoured cars broke their morale instantly.' This prompted the war diarist to remark: 'This must be bitter news for the enemy in I[talian] E[ast] A[frica] who is known to be short of material and must feel more than ever isolated'.[36] It also confirmed that British propaganda might be able to exploit further the obvious racial and cultural tensions which existed between the hard-pressed native conscripts and their heavy-handed Italian masters by 'raising the tribes' against the enemy in Abyssinia (a policy which the British had been examining since 1938).[37]

It also emerged that most Italian captives were not well trained in security. There were exceptions however. In the early stages of the North African and Abyssinian campaigns some Italian officers were more conscious of the need not to divulge too much to their interrogators. One captured naval officer, 2nd Lieutenant Antonio Metallo, who had been shot down while acting as an air observer during the Battle of Matapan in late June 1941, was forthcoming on questions regarding his mission and actions during the engagement. However, when pressed for further details on previous patrols, order of battle and unit strength he refused to answer stating that neither he nor his brother officers would disclose such information. When pressed further he simply invented stories. Others would refuse to talk or would pretend they knew nothing.[38] Several were forthright but apologetic in not divulging any information. One pilot, Sergeant-Major Lambert Molinelli, did not want to seem disrespectful to his interrogators, but freely admitted that he had no intention of giving any information against his country:

> You were asking me to give you information in order that you may report on the matter. I am a soldier, … and I have taken an oath. I prefer to abide by my oath. The very fact that you are asking me these questions means that you are interested in it [*sic*] and it is my duty as a soldier not to help you in that interest. All I can say is that the fortunes of war have been against me and I have nothing further to add.[39]

Another pilot, Captain Stefano Castagnoli, was captured in November 1940 after his aircraft had been shot down in south-western Italian Somaliland. Badly injured and the only survivor of his crew, he refused to divulge any operational material concerning his unit or its strength except to say that it was based at Mogadishu. What he did reveal however was that he was tired of the war and hoped that it would end soon whatever the result.[40] This was not an uncommon remark for men serving in the isolated Italian East African empire, despite the fact that Italy had only joined the war in June 1940. Shot down on the same operation as Castagnoli, another captured pilot held a completely opposite view. His interrogator noted that the officer was 'somewhat aggressive and was convinced that the war would end in [Italy's] favour within a short period'. His crewmen were less convinced and showed 'no enthusiasm' for the war. Homesick, they longed to return to Italy.[41]

The gulf in confidence in an Italian victory displayed between officers committed to the Fascist cause and enlisted men who at best were indifferent politically was reiterated by another series of interrogations in Nairobi several months later. 'Whilst the officers interrogated maintained an air of bravado', remarked one intelligence officer, 'it is safe to say that the NCOs were definitely depressed. One of them regarded the war as already having been won by the English.'[42] This theme was regularly commented upon by intelligence officers in Cairo and Malta as well. In one Middle Eastern POW censorship summary, the difference in tone about a forthcoming Italian victory in the mail of officers and enlisted men was noticeable, recorded the chief censor. The NCOs constantly referred to how pleased they were with the food, accommodation and overall treatment while in captivity, especially the provision of free cinemas. Others declared they were getting fat in captivity and contrasted this to their starvation rations before capture! On the other hand, the officers' mail contained the familiar 'brand of Fascist optimism'.[43] Indeed, the whole issue of enemy morale and ways of exploiting it for British propaganda purposes, which will be discussed in greater detail below, was an item which interrogators explored with vigour after the sweeping victories in Abyssinia and North Africa in 1940–1.

Political warfare and propaganda

In April 1940 plans were initiated by the Anglo-French Enemy Propaganda Committee to establish a shadow organisation that would conduct a propaganda offensive against Italy if and when it joined the war on Germany's side. One of the tasks of this joint venture was to create the necessary propaganda machinery and direct it against Italian garrisons in Libya and Abyssinia.[44] Little, if anything, had been accomplished when Italy declared war on 10 June 1940. Major-General Dallas Brooks, a key individual in SO1 who was later appointed Deputy Director-General of the PWE in August 1941, refrained from commenting on the propaganda operations that were being directed against Italy except to say that 'I am unable to find either a policy or an object!'[45]

Nevertheless, over the summer of 1940 and well before the stunning victories in Libya, British intelligence officers in both Britain and the Middle East began formulating plans to conduct a political warfare campaign against the Italians. In late August, Section D of the Special Operations Executive (SOE) made preliminary enquiries about the availability of possible agents for sabotage work overseas amongst the Italian community resident or incarcerated in Britain. While SOE (dubbed by Churchill as the Ministry of Ungentlemanly Warfare)[46] consulted officials at the Foreign Office, MI5 and the Home Office over procedural matters, in December 1940, Lieutenant-Commander George Martelli RN, was sent to the internment facilities located on the Isle of Man to see if any 'thugs' were available for clandestine and propaganda work.[47] Not unexpectedly, his investigation revealed very meagre results. Of those interviewed by Martelli most were found to be anti-Fascist. However, they were not pro-British either and therefore would be 'hopelessly compromised' if deployed in the field to suborn their counterparts to work for Britain against Fascist Italy.[48] The same was true of those Italians who had been interned but were later released or recommended for release by the Loraine Committee, established in September 1940 under the chairmanship of Sir Percy Loraine, a former ambassador to Italy (1939–40). Interrogations disclosed that of those few internees who had volunteered to serve with the British, several had done so simply to escape internment.[49] Dr Hugh Dalton, the forceful Minister for Economic Warfare (and the minister responsible for SOE), was equally disappointed. 'Italy is still a black spot,' he lamented to Churchill. 'Though we [are] combing all possible sources of supply, we have not [so] far been able (with one exception) to find Italians willing to risk going back home as our agents.'[50]

The lack of success with the internees on the Isle of Man forced Martelli to explore other avenues. In January 1941 he made several visits to an Auxiliary Military Pioneer Corps (AMPC) training centre at Ilfracombe, north Devon, which housed several hundred pro-British Italian recruits. The pioneers, according to Martelli, were the 'pick' of the Italians in Britain from the point of view of fitness, political reliability and 'willingness to serve our cause'. Broadly speaking, there were two categories of men. The first group were Anglicised Italians with no interest in politics, most of whom had family or business connections in Britain, and were 'not of the adventurous or idealistic' type. The second group was comprised of political refugees and Jewish émigrés, mostly middle-class intellectuals (students, teachers, lawyers and doctors), who had arrived in Britain from Italy after the enactment of anti-Semitic laws in November 1938. Both groups expressed their willingness to fight, but with few exceptions, remarked Martelli, 'their apparent willingness derived from what they thought was expected of them, rather than from genuine enthusiasm'.[51]

Fifty of just over 100 potential candidates were interviewed at Ilfracombe, but in the end only nine were deemed satisfactory. Even then, Martelli was forced to admit that they were the best of a bad lot. It was found that most of the pioneers could not speak fluent Italian, having been born or bred in Britain. Additionally, many were former café proprietors and cooks who had not been back to Italy for years, and whose accent was poor. More significantly, these men expressed no desire to go on active service, as most were perfectly satisfied with their present employment. 'Anti-Fascists can ... live a secure life and earn comfortable money by working for [the] PWE and [the] B[ritish] B[road-casting] C[orporation]', reported one intelligence officer. The younger intellectuals and Jewish refugees, although the most vocal and possessing the necessary linguistic skills, were not the most serviceable because, as fugitives, they were probably well known to the Italian secret police.[52] Failure to tap the human material closest to hand, which was unsuited for SOE's plans, forced it to look overseas. But the well was equally dry in Canada and Malta.[53] However, it was suggested without any factual foundation that the neutral United States might hold the key to SOE's recruit conundrum, as the 'toughest' type of Italian 'desperado' was 'mostly to be found in America'.[54]

What of SOE's operations in the Middle East? The Military Liaison Officer for SO1 at GHQ, Cairo, Colonel C. J. M. Thornhill (an experienced intelligence officer who had been attached to the British embassy in Petrograd during the First World War), was responsible for the dissemination of subversive propaganda, both overt and covert, in Libya and Italian East Africa. In addition, his department was assigned to convert the 45,000 Italian civilians resident in Egypt from a Fascist into an anti-Fascist community. Finally, perhaps the most important, as well as the most challenging, task of his mandate was to spread anti-Fascist feeling throughout Italy and its empire.[55] Success, however, would depend upon the co-operation and co-ordination between Thornhill's department, local civilian authorities, the British Army, the RAF, the Foreign Office and the BBC.

In August 1940 a detailed memorandum was tabled at GHQ Cairo that set out the measures to be adopted, including the conversion, segregation and organisation of Italian POWs 'into anti-Fascist instruments'. Thornhill admitted that this programme would take time to produce results; but he argued that the potential long-term benefits would far outweigh the 'trouble' involved. 'In the event – not improbable – of Italy ... making a separate peace', he continued, 'it would be very useful to be able to flood her with some thousands of pro-British Italians.' Moreover, it was not enough to have them 'vaguely friendly', for Thornhill insisted that they be carefully trained to 'say what will be most useful to our purpose. We should, in fact, be training a "Fifth Column" of our own.'[56] The basis of a Free Italy movement had been tentatively laid. In October 1940 these embryonic ideas were taken one step further when the Foreign Office initiated discussions on the creation of a Free

Italian committee and embarked upon a search for a potential leader of a Free Italy movement.[57]

The capture of huge numbers of Italians during the first four months of 1941 prompted a great deal of discussion in London and Cairo on the potential propaganda windfall the British had been given and how best to conduct a political warfare campaign amongst Italian POWs; and it was Thornhill's August memorandum that may have been the catalyst in stimulating discussions at a higher level. For instance, one idea that attracted growing attention from high-ranking British military and civilian authorities alike was the raising of a 'Garibaldi' Legion or Free Italian force from amongst the Italian captives. The Foreign Office was aware that from a political point of view the formation of such a force held potential, not least of which was its usefulness for propaganda purposes. More importantly, however, its formation might provide a nucleus round which anti-Fascists in Italy could identify themselves. Indeed, initial intelligence reports from the Middle East indicated that there were some Italian captives who suggested the creation of just such a force.[58] Churchill added his endorsement. He informed the War Cabinet in February 1941 that he saw no reason why the raising of an anti-Mussolini or Free Italian force in Cyrenaica should not be considered.[59]

Dalton was equally keen to pursue this idea. Taking soundings from several of his field officers, he agreed that the best course of action was to segregate 'disgruntled' POWs from their Fascist comrades by removing them to separate camps. He urged that all Italian POWs should be 'combed in order to discover genuine and gallant anti-Fascists' who were prepared to risk their lives in order to free their country. Slovenes, Croats and Piedmontese were, he told Gladwyn Jebb, SOE's Chief Executive Officer, the most likely candidates for work in and against Italy.[60] It was also suggested that Sardinian POWs with separatist leanings might also serve as willing agents. When told that the use of POWs for such clandestine operations was contrary to the Hague and Geneva Conventions, Dalton vented his displeasure. This was the first he had heard of this 'new snaghunter's triumph'. Unwilling to accept this 'formula of frustration' the minister asked Jebb: 'From whom does this fatuous defeatist inhibition emanate?'[61] Convinced that the mass of information from Italian POWs offered 'very great possibilities' for political and military purposes, the impatient Dalton insisted that he see 'without fail and without delay' all future telegrams dealing with the British exploitation of Italian POWs.[62] Citing precedents during the First World War, in which the Germans recruited Irish POWs as help-mates for Roger Casement, and sought agents amongst Flemish-speaking Belgian POWs for anti-Allied work, Dalton thought it 'utterly intolerable that we should be warned off the great host of more than 100,000 Italian prisoners of war, on some thin-lipped and thin-blooded pretext of pseudo-legality, ... I just won't have it!'[63]

The War Office did not share Churchill's, Dalton's or the Foreign Office's optimism. The Director of Military Intelligence, Major-General F. H. N. Davidson, acknowledged that it was true that some captured officers had expressed a willingness to fight against their former Fascist masters, but 'Italian words [were] usually better than their deeds', and it was doubtful if a Free Italian force would have much combatant value. On the other hand, Davidson saw some benefit in using Italian POWs as civilian or military labour. If units composed of technically skilled personnel such as motor drivers and mechanics could be raised they would be of immense value, especially in the Middle East, where there was an acute shortage.[64] Despite War Office reservations, and doubts amongst some of its own officials about the value and loyalty of such combat units, the Foreign Office thought the idea of creating a Free Italian force was still worth pursuing. This was endorsed by the JIC which had become interested in the 'moral education' and instruction of POWs. In February 1941, it pushed for the prioritisation in the development of enemy POWs as sources of propaganda and military intelligence.[65]

General Sir Archibald Wavell, Commander-in-Chief Middle Eastern forces, advised caution. Although in principle not against the idea of raising a Free Italian force, he recognised that in practice there was a number of obstacles that had to be overcome. For instance, it took time for intelligence officers to assess the quality and value of all military and political information gleaned from POW interrogations. Moreover, even if it was possible to raise such a force, Egypt was far from secure. Therefore, when it was suggested by SOE that it would establish a Middle Eastern training centre and recruit potential agents and saboteurs amongst 'friendly' Italian POWs incarcerated in Egypt, Wavell did not support the initiative. Instead, he suggested Eritrea would be a safer base for such operations once it was wrested from the Italians. For Wavell the essential point was the need to choose a leader of sufficient calibre 'to command respect and avoid jealousies'.[66] Concomitant with this, was the proper screening and segregation of potential recruits. Initial indications were that it was going to be a slow and painstaking task. One intelligence officer, Lieutenant-Colonel John de Salis, warned that most Italian POWs interviewed in Egypt at Geneifa Camp No. 3 were quite prepared to say that they were non-Fascists if they thought they would obtain better food or privileged conditions. Unable to 'trust a single one of them', de Salis firmly believed that 'a good many pretend to be Non- or Anti-Fascist in order to find out what we want and so warn the others, who are in collusion with them'.[67] Later that year, SOE came to the same disappointing conclusion about its raw material in Egypt. Complaining that the vast majority of its Italian captives were unsuited for covert work, one war diarist commented that for the most part they were 'perfectly content to remain prisoners, and showed no desire whatever, either for money or for any other reason, to return to their country in an adventurous capacity'.[68]

Senior military authorities in London realised very soon after the North African victories the need to separate Fascists from non-Fascists if British propaganda and political warfare were to have any chance of success amongst their Italian POWs. In late January 1941, the War Office also canvassed the Commander-in-Chief India, General Sir Robert A. Cassels, about his views on the segregation of Italian regulars from the specially recruited Fascist or Blackshirt battalions. This initiative, argued the War Office, offered 'considerable political advantages' for Britain in the conduct of its propaganda war against the Axis. Indeed, if 'de-Fascisation' was to have any chance of success, segregation had to be applied to both officers and other ranks in both categories and made effective as soon as possible after capture. The strategy was twofold. First, it would break the authority and discipline that existed between the Italian officers and their men. Secondly, and more important, the resultant segregation of Fascists from non-Fascists would eliminate the influence of hardline Fascism. This would allow the British to conduct almost unhindered their own political warfare campaign amongst the non- and anti-Fascist POWs.[69] However, this was easier said than done. Continued military successes increased dramatically the tally of Italian POWs, which by March 1941 had mushroomed to 160,000.[70] Wavell demanded that for strategic and political reasons as many as possible be evacuated immediately from Egypt to destinations such as India and Australia. The successful Axis counter-attack launched in April 1941 by the newly arrived German commander, General Erwin Rommel, reinforced Egypt's vulnerability. Such urgency therefore precluded the careful sorting that was vital if a Free Italian force was to be recruited.

If Egypt was deemed infertile for propaganda work, then this raised the question of where within the British empire could a selected team of experts 'conduct an experimental campaign of propaganda' and recruit a Free Italian force amongst the thousands of Italian POWs. Martelli recommended that efforts be concentrated in India, not only because the bulk of the Italian prisoners would eventually be transported there, but also because it was thought by political warfare officers such as he that India possessed the conditions necessary to conduct this sensitive work.[71] The War Office and Foreign Office agreed. Lieutenant-General Sir Claude Auchinleck, Wavell's successor as C-in-C Middle East, was informed that upon review of the situation and owing to the persistence of 'adverse conditions' in Egypt all propaganda aimed at raising a Free Italian force or the enlistment of Italian POWs to fight for the Allied cause would cease immediately.[72] Efforts for such a mission were redirected towards India, helped it seems by Dalton's robust intervention in support of Martelli's initiatives.[73]

The Indian government had indeed been quick to respond to Wavell's desperate appeal in early 1941 to evacuate and accommodate Italian POWs. In January it had agreed to accept 16,000; but the quota was quickly raised to 68,000 in mid-March. Shortages of shipping dictated the rate at which the captives arrived in India, but by the end of May there were 4,867 officers and 26,993 other ranks distributed in six (later five) POW groups or cantonments throughout the subcontinent. Officers, including most of the general staff, were billeted in four camps at Dehra Dun, designated Group No. 4, which was nestled in the spectacular scenery of the Himalayan foothills. At Yol in the Punjab, Group No. 5 was being prepared. Here, four camps were under construction, which were supposed to house half the estimated 24,000 Italian officers assigned for removal to India. Non-commissioned officers and other ranks were incarcerated at Bangalore, Bhopal and Ramgarh, that is, Groups 1–3 respectively; a total capacity of 60,000. POW numbers increased steadily over the summer, and were expected to climb to 84,000 by the autumn, including one camp (probably Yol) that would house at least 9,500 officers. However, by November 1941 shipping constraints had interrupted the steady flow of Italian POW traffic to India; by then the numbers had reached 45,676 officers and men.[74]

Meanwhile, as the Italian POWs were being processed in India, the British government was undertaking a major review of its propaganda machinery and political warfare strategy which had important ramifications for the Indian experiment. A key issue was ministerial jurisdiction. Even before the establishment of SOE in July 1940, fierce battles had already been fought between the Foreign Office and the ministries of Information and Economic Warfare for control of both overt and covert – white and black – propaganda activities. The infighting intensified with the creation of SOE, as ministers jockeyed for the political and operational high ground. Indeed, more energy was probably expended between Dalton and his colleagues at the Ministry of Information and the Foreign Office than was directed against the Axis during the first two years of the war. This unnecessary internecine warfare was thankfully halted during the summer of 1941, when the War Cabinet decided to restructure the political warfare machinery.

In July, the JIC had decided that SOE would be responsible for all propaganda amongst POWs. However, it was decided to create a new agency – the Political Warfare Executive – which would be under the joint ministerial control of the heads of the Foreign Office, Ministry of Information and Ministry of Economic Warfare. Dalton lost his coveted SO1 to the new agency, and the more amenable Brendan Bracken, Duff Cooper's successor as Minister of Information, agreed to relinquish his control of the BBC's European Service to the PWE.[75] The PWE was now solely responsible for waging the propaganda war against the Axis.

As we have seen, the conduct of political warfare in the Middle East had been assigned to Colonel Thornhill, who, after the reorganisation of SOE, was now transferred to the PWE. Before the restructuring in August 1941, and in addition to his Middle Eastern responsibilities, Thornhill had co-ordinated propaganda work amongst the Italian POWs in India from Cairo through the Director of Military Intelligence (DMI), India. This had proved highly unsatisfactory. Wavell, now C-in-C India (and one of the few military commanders who saw the real potential of political warfare),[76] recognised this, believing that it was extremely difficult to conduct propaganda work in India from the Middle East, where POW conditions were totally different. He recommended that SOE (later the PWE) should have direct representation in India, for this 'would ensure [that the] political condition and attitude of [the] prisoners of war [was] being correctly gauged and propaganda suitably applied'.[77] Martelli needed no prompting.

The Indian experiment

As we have seen, discussions had taken place concerning the secondment of Italian nationals to conduct propaganda work amongst their captured countrymen. Martelli wrote in early June 1941 that propaganda work should be 'conducted chiefly by Italian representatives of some recognised patriotic Italian body, in co-operation with our own organisation. We would assist and if necessary, subsidise these representatives, but they should be as independent as possible.' He also advocated that similar steps be taken in East Africa, South Africa and Australia. If the results achieved by the propaganda work in the first stages justified it, then Britain could proceed with the next step of raising a Free Italian force. This force would be put on the same footing as the other Free forces, such as General Charles de Gaulle's Free French, and be provided with uniforms, equipment and pay. The British government, concluded Martelli, having announced its intention to raise this force, was then to make a concerted effort to obtain support of Italians world-wide, especially in the United States.[78]

The idea of using Italo-Americans for political propaganda was first sanctioned as early as mid-February 1941. Unfortunately for SOE and later the PWE, the attempt to recruit democratically-minded Italians in the United States and train them to win the hearts and minds of the Italian POWs incarcerated in India was an utter failure. The details of this farcical episode need not detain us, except to say that right from the beginning, the so-called Mazzini mission was wracked with deep internal divisions, severe personality clashes and contradictory aims. When the first and only group of ten 'toughs' and 'thugs' arrived in India in late September 1941 it was obvious that only one or two were suitable for the sensitive task of political re-education. The mission was quickly scrubbed in December 1941.[79]

The demise of the Mazzini mission, although an embarrassing disaster for the PWE, taught it an invaluable lesson on the limits of using foreign operatives without first providing in-depth training in the subtle arts of subversion. Forced to re-evaluate its propaganda work in India, Thornhill's understaffed team worked hard to overcome this initial calamatitions entry into POW indoctrination. The arrival of Major F. L. Stevens and Major Ian Munro (formerly of the Ministry of Information) at GHQ New Delhi on 20 November 1941 was none too soon. Three days before, the military authorities in India had despatched an urgent telegram demanding policy guidelines on the conduct of political propaganda in their POW camps. Without it, they argued, the reorganisation of the POW administration in India could not be completed, as the propaganda programme had a direct bearing on the restructuring being undertaken.[80] Growing impatient, the DMI India asked what was the basis of British propaganda in the POW camps:

> Is it [the] creation of [an] impression of our strength and invincibility and that it will pay them to support [the] winning side [?] Or that we are essentially liberal and peace-loving and [that] Anglo-Italian interests could be coincident [?] Or that they are in their present position because of misgovernment and misdirection of their nation by [the] Fascist regime [?][81]

Answers were forthcoming. Earlier that month, the PWE's plan of action towards Italian POWs was tabled and approved by a high-ranking ministerial committee consisting of the Foreign Secretary, Anthony Eden, Brendan Bracken, Dalton and the British Chiefs of Staff (COS). Its strategy was based on the overarching principle 'that the treatment of prisoners is a powerful means of influencing Italian morale'.[82] The objects of the policy were twofold. First, it was necessary to exploit the treatment of Italian captives in British hands in order to influence Italian domestic opinion. Secondly, the prisoners themselves had to be imbued with 'friendly sentiments' towards Britain, so that upon their return home at the end of the war they would become pro-British propagandists. This had been a major tenet of the new standing order on British propaganda towards Italy which had been tabled three months earlier during the creation of the PWE. Central to the directive was its uncompromising stance on the use of derogatory or racist language. If the war for Italian hearts and minds was to be won, and Italian POWs were to be encouraged to co-operate with the Allies: 'DO NOT CALL THEM WOPS'.[83] In addition, the POWs might be persuaded, if circumstances presented themselves, to perform a combatant role for the Allies against their former Fascist masters during the remainder of hostilities. Short of this, they could give 'valuable assistance to our war effort by their willing labour as agricultural workers [and] road-makers'.[84]

In order to fulfil these objectives, the PWE's policy depended upon the careful implementation of a six-stage programme. The sympathetic and humane treatment of the prisoners was essential for success, because such treatment implied not only decent living conditions but also a level of understanding towards the prisoners on the part of their captors. 'Italian prisoners who are contented morally as well as materially are usually willing workers and not unresponsive to propaganda. On the other hand, if they are treated with contempt or indifference, they will rapidly turn sour and become useless for our purpose.'[85] A key factor in ensuring that the prisoners remained contented was to prevent boredom. Recreation was the answer, through games, concerts or theatrical performances; or by arranging other occupations during leisure periods, such as workshops in carpentry, carving or basket-weaving. Another highly recommended 'pastime' was education, especially the teaching of basic English.

Equally important was their segregation from 'incurably hostile elements'. The PWE believed that the majority of Italian POWs had no strong political opinions. In other words they were non-Fascist, but were 'often terrorised by the presence of a small number of ardent Fascists, some of whom are police agents, belonging either to the

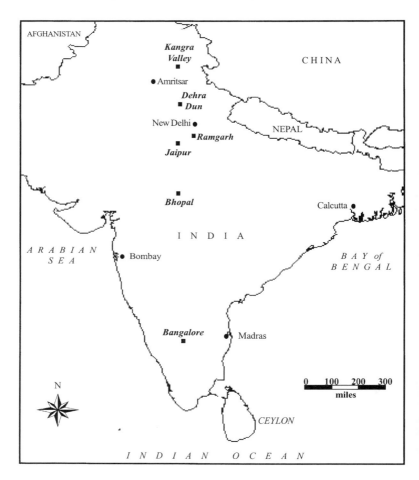

Map 6 Prisoner of War Camps for Italians in India, 1941–7

O.V.R.A. (the Italian secret police) or the Carabinieri'. For this reason it was deemed essential that these small but disruptive elements were removed to a separate camp whenever possible. Under no circumstances were ardent Fascists to occupy positions, such as camp leaders, where they could exercise influence or authority over their fellow inmates. Furthermore, camp intelligence officers were warned to monitor the camp chaplains and doctors, who, by abusing their status as Protected Personnel, might operate unmolested as Fascist agents in the camps.[86]

Only when the above two conditions had been fulfilled would it be possible for the four remaining objectives to have any prospect of success. These included the initiation of propaganda among the prisoners, the publication of a prisoners' newspaper in Italian, the raising of a Free Italian force, and the use of POWs as propaganda material in the war for hearts and minds. It was recognised that the process of 'de-Fascisation' or political re-education would be a gradual one, involving careful planning and forethought. For years the prisoners had been brought up in a Fascist atmosphere in which they had been taught that Britain and the other democracies were their enemies. Therefore, direct attacks on Fascism had to be avoided, because many prisoners would equate these with attacks on Italy itself. The need therefore was to concentrate on attacking the Fascist political ideology and leadership, but not the Italian nation. A more subtle approach was recommended, which concentrated on explaining the disastrous consequences for Italy if she continued the alliance with Nazi Germany:

> We should constantly keep before them the picture of what the German New Order means for Italy and the individual Italian, and thus lead them to realise for themselves the terrible position in which their country has been placed by Mussolini and the men around him, and make them see that these men are serving the German and not the Italian interest.

The ideal aim was not to classify the POWs as Fascists and anti-Fascists, but 'to unite them all spiritually as anti-Germans'.[87]

The best medium for such propaganda was an Italian-language newspaper whose staff should be recruited if possible from among the POWs themselves. At first, the weekly *Il Corriere del Campo* was introduced to the POWs from Cairo, before printing facilities were organised in India. As well as publishing leading articles, this paper not only printed the communiqués of all the belligerents, but also supplied POWs with puzzles, chess problems, English lessons, and, eventually, the serialisation of Rudyard Kipling's *Kim*. In mid-1942, *La Diana*, the Italian edition of a Government of India monthly publication known as *The Bugle*, was also circulated to provide more of a focus on Indian events and issues.[88]

Newspapers were supplemented by radio broadcasts, lectures and open discussions. For example, prisoners were allowed to listen to the BBC, Vatican Radio and Radio *Roma*, so that they could make up their own minds about the 'veracity' of British and Italian propaganda. Guidelines were laid down as to the best approach to use in the implementation of these policies; the central tenet being that the various media, especially the newspapers, should not be seen as propaganda tools. For instance, the newspapers were to confine themselves to 'objective news about the war, ... world events, the situation in Italy and life in the prisoners' camps'. Correspondence and suggestions from the POWs were to be encouraged, and from this would 'emerge currents of opinions, which should help in formulating editorial policy and facilitate its gradual development on lines favourable to our cause, without provoking too violent reactions'.[89] Eventually, it might be possible to recruit a Free Italian force or labour corps. In fact, the first step towards raising a combat force amongst the anti-Fascist POWs would be the establishment of a pioneer corps under British command to work in the rear echelons. Finally, there was no doubt as to the immediate propaganda value provided by the indulgent treatment of these men. Descriptions of camp life, and sound recordings of typical scenes or amusing incidents, supplemented by broadcasts of personal messages from prisoners to their families and sweethearts in Italy, provided first-rate material for the British propaganda campaign to Italy.[90]

The basic outline of these principles was telegraphed to GHQ India two days after Stevens and Munro had arrived in New Delhi.[91] The PWE were confident, on the basis of their experience with Italian captives in the Middle East and the United Kingdom, that their policy directive was sound. However, they clearly recognised that its execution would have to be carried out chiefly by the military authorities, 'who alone can judge what is practicable' in the camps under their charge.[92] Herein lay the source for future conflict between the PWE and the military authorities in India. The PWE mission relied on the goodwill and whole-hearted co-operation of all levels of command of the British military in India, in particular the Director of Military Intelligence (DMI). Without it, the PWE mission was helpless, if not stillborn.

The immediate task that Munro and Stevens had to tackle upon their arrival in India was the establishment of clear lines of communication and responsibility between themselves and the various military agencies involved with POW administration. In this, they were firmly supported by Wavell. At a conference of POW group commanders held at GHQ New Delhi between 2 and 4 December 1941, Wavell circulated a secret directive that stressed that uniformity and centralised control were essential conditions if the ultimate aims of the PWE's policy amongst the Italian POWs was to succeed. Thus, the Chief of the General Staff (CGS), India, would be responsible through the DMI India, for the execution of the political policy. The Adjutant-General, working through the Director of Prisoners of War, India, would ensure that the provisions of the 1929 Geneva Convention were observed, and that the administration of POW affairs was kept as far as possible in accordance with the political policy. This meant that group commanders and their camp commandants would be restricted to the housing, clothing and feeding of POWs. Orders regarding the treatment, discipline and security within the camps would be issued directly from GHQ alone through the group commanders. The co-ordination of both the administrative and political policies was the sole responsibility of the CGS, India.[93]

The overall structure and demarcation of responsibilities seemed clear enough; but the mechanisms by which this policy was to operate were not. Matters arising out of the political aspects of the directive were to be forwarded by the group commanders to the Directorate of Prisoners of War (DPW) at GHQ. To facilitate the co-ordination and execution of both the political and administrative policies, a military intelligence section under the control of the DMI was installed in the DPW. It was this branch of military intelligence that was the all-important linchpin between the military authorities in India and the PWE mission, which was ultimately responsible to the Foreign Office in London. Although Stevens and Munro were attached to the DMI, they were not part of the intelligence section that was attached to the DPW, which meant they had no direct line of communications with the POW authorities in India.[94]

There was a real danger, therefore, that vital intelligence material of a political nature would not necessarily reach these officers, whose primary responsibility was to gauge political opinion in the camps and advise accordingly. In addition, the PWE mission did not have direct communication with London. In theory, the PWE had to process all its correspondence through the General Staff at GHQ. In practice, the DMI saw all reports and messages before their dispatch, and had the right to refer them to the DPW and Adjutant-General for comment.[95] In other words, not only could the military authorities monitor the PWE's communications with London, but they could also defer or delay the implementation of PWE policy. The lack of a direct channel to London, compounded by the exploratory nature of its work, was later to prove a serious bone of contention between PWE personnel in India and their military superiors at GHQ New Delhi. For, as the PWE staff argued, it delayed unnecessarily the implementation of policy objectives and subsequently limited their effectiveness in the camps.

One of the fundamental requirements for the successful operation of the PWE mission in India was the active support of the camp authorities.

Thornhill, writing shortly after Munro's departure for India in October 1941, informed him that the camp commandants would be instructed to offer assistance, but that it was vital for him to meet them individually and

> endeavour to interest them in the work and open their eyes to the importance of the task in which they are asked to co-operate. Few commandants have any knowledge of the political situation in Italy, or of the value of the long-term propaganda policy of converting as many prisoners as possible into friendly emissaries working for understanding and co-operation with England in postwar Europe.[96]

This was sound, practical advice; but the job of proselytisation was fraught with many pitfalls.

Discussions held at the group commanders' conference in early December and subsequent visits to their facilities by Stevens made it abundantly clear that drastic alterations in attitudes, camp conditions and policy were needed. A trip to Group No. 2 at Bairagarh near Bhopal, which comprised eight POW camps and housed just over 15,000 captives, revealed that nothing had been done to 'de-root Fascist activities'. It was 'utterly impossible' to initiate any PWE policy, wrote Stevens, and that unless segregation was carried out 'thoroughly and completely' it would prove an absolute waste of time for the PWE to initiate its political warfare campaign.[97]

Equally worrying for the British was the fact that morale and Fascist discipline had improved markedly among the POWs since their capture and relocation to India. At one POW facility, Fascist membership cards had been fashioned from cigarette cartons, and a nominal roll of all members and their activities within the camp was kept, as well as a record of the movements of Fascists between camps. 'The Fascists have made it known that they are keeping a tally of each prisoner for report back to Rome', reported Stevens. As a result, the POWs were

> consequently more in awe of the secret Fascist cells than of the British authorities. Collective bravado and love of heroics without danger is a contributory factor to this state of mind. Men who in Italy joined with everyone else in feeling bored when *Giovanezza* was sung now join in its choral chanting with the utmost fervour. Fascism has become identified in their minds with patriotism.[98]

The distribution of *La Diana* also met with widespread and organised opposition. One senior Italian officer went so far 'as to buy up all the copies allotted to his wing and have them publicly burnt. Any P.O.W. found reading literature published by us became a marked man, and went in danger of being beaten up.'[99]

Meanwhile, some commandants tolerated Fascism in their camps because it was the Fascists who maintained order and discipline. To ignore or turn a blind eye to these political activities in order to ensure a quiet or cosy billet was self-defeating, argued the PWE. Vigorous action was needed to suppress these manifestations if the Italian POW was to be turned against Fascism. Firm discipline had to be imposed in all camps and any undue dependence upon Fascist POWs for the maintenance of order was to be deprecated.[100] In addition, Munro recommended that the status and powers of intelligence officers and interpreters in the camps be increased. This was supported by the DMI, India, which admitted that the quality of many of its camp commandants and interpreters was poor. The main stumbling-block, however, remained the inability of the military authorities to segregate and sieve the officers and the known Fascists from the remainder. Until segregation had been completed it was deemed unwise by the PWE to enforce political discipline among the Italian POWs.[101]

Why were the military authorities apparently dragging their feet over this matter? Part of the problem was organisational, while another was operational. The sudden influx of Italian prisoners from North Africa during the winters of 1940–1 and 1941–2, coupled with the fact that Egypt was threatened on both occasions by an Axis invasion shortly after each campaign, had made it imperative that as many enemy POWs as possible should be evacuated from the Middle East. Given this state of flux, it was not possible to carry out any but the most rudimentary classification of captives. Once in India, there were the logistical challenges of housing, feeding and guarding the Italian POWs. Delays ensued, in particular the construction of the POW compounds. Men were shunted from place to place while the camps were built and expanded. Prisoners were 'herded into camps', wrote one officer, and, 'provided they did not attempt to escape, they were allowed to organise themselves as they liked' without interference from their captors. By apparent good behaviour and the maintenance of discipline, the Fascists gained the confidence of the camp staffs and took control.[102] The pressures generated by the initial administrative chaos therefore made it extremely difficult for the Indian military authorities to establish a systematic segregation policy. General Cawthorn claimed that 'the delay in the arrival of the Mission and in the issue by the P.W.E. of a definition of policy [had] been an adverse factor'.[103]

The latter point is debatable and, in part, could be interpreted as sour grapes on the part of the DMI. Nevertheless, the PWE agreed that under the circumstances the segregation of hostile elements into separate camps had to be sacrificed to the need to evacuate enemy POWs from operational areas.[104] The entry of the Japanese into the war in December 1941 and their subsequent conquest of Burma in the first four months of 1942 compounded the problem. Intensive troop movements necessitated by the defence of India's eastern frontier had absorbed all available rolling-stock at the very moment orders for the concentration of officers at Yol in the Punjab were about to be enacted; an essential prerequisite of the segregation strategy. Nonetheless, General Brooks stressed in an *aide mémoire* that unless some measure of segregation was undertaken, however dire the operational situation or however overstretched the military authorities were in India, the task of the PWE mission would be rendered impossible. It was imperative, he continued, not to lose sight of the far-reaching political repercussions the creation of a Free Italian force, however insignificant militarily, would have not only in Italy, but also amongst her Axis partners and the neutral countries and, especially, in the United States.[105]

The strength of Fascist opposition in the camps must not to be underestimated. The number of known Fascists, or 'blacks', which included most of the Italian officers, was put at 12,000 by Munro in January 1942. The DMI, India, believed that this was an exaggerated figure and that Munro was overstressing the point,[106] perhaps to give further credence to his continual demands for segregation. However, Munro countered that an orderly camp was not necessarily a 'politically healthy' camp, because the discipline that prevailed was more than likely being imposed by Fascist cells rather than by British administrators.[107] As another PWE officer observed in January 1943, 'From the top to the bottom of the group organisation the attitude was that trouble must be avoided at all costs, [one] which had as its source the indifference of the [DPW] to the possibilities of turning this mass of P.O.W. from a liability into an asset.'[108]

The central factor that lay at the heart of the tensions between the PWE officials and certain powerful elements within the military bureaucracy in India was control. The mission's independent authority must have rankled with some senior officers, who, as a result, were unprepared or unwilling to extend their full co-operation. Similarly, political warfare was no doubt a strange and unfamiliar concept to many Indian Army officers. To them 'the methods of fighting a war began and ended on the battlefield, and they were unable to fit propaganda [and] POW[s] into the larger strategic picture'.[109] It was a learning process for all who dealt with POWs, and there were bound to be misunderstandings, petty jealousies and jurisdictional disputes between departments and individuals during the first stages of implementation.

The confusion and delay that plagued the implementation of the mission's policy during the winter of 1941–2 were eventually overcome. The policy of educating group commanders and their staffs as to the aims and objectives of the PWE's strategy, although painstakingly slow, began to pay dividends. At a second group commanders' conference held in May 1942 problems were identified, recommendations were made and steps were taken to rectify many of the organisational and administrative problems that had led to inefficiencies and misunderstandings in the past. Indeed, the conferences provided an excellent forum to air concerns and settle disagreements. The greatest achievement was recognition of the fact that group intelligence staffs could communicate directly with the PWE mission and the DPW on intelligence matters. The appointment of PWE liaison officers to each POW group was another major improvement, for under the old system this material went first to the DMI, which was supposed to, but did not always, forward it to other departments.[110] Furthermore, the upgrading in status of camp intelligence officers and interpreters was a marked step forward in improving intelligence-gathering and the waging of a political warfare campaign.

Italia Redenta

These were indeed trying times for the beleaguered band of PWE officials in India. Despite scoring some successes, especially the promise of closer co-operation with the military authorities, there were moments when enthusiasm for the mission seemed to be wavering. Confidence among some of the mission's personnel was fragile. Most of the pessimism stemmed from the lack of progress made in segregating the POWs. Moreover, as Colonel Stevens remarked, doubts had arisen concerning the usefulness and scope of the mission because of the unfavourable military developments in Burma. The question arose, would the Government of India continue to support a venture that was experimental in design, bearing in mind that the obstacles to a vigorous segregation of prisoners seemed insurmountable.[111] As far as the Foreign Office was concerned nothing had arisen to make them want to abandon the project. Reassured, the PWE sanctioned funds for the establishment of a 'rallying centre' at Jaipur in Rajasthan, where anti-Fascists could be removed from existing camps 'with a view to exploring the possibility of inducing them to form a Free Italian Force'.[112]

Thornhill, who had arrived in India in February 1942 to become head of the mission, informed his superiors in London that Stevens had compiled a list of 3,000 anti-Fascist Italian POWs. The Jaipur proposal also had the enthusiastic support of the DMI, India:

> All other heads of departments have given [their] approval and [have] promised assistance. I and the senior officers of my Mission consider it to be the only way of putting to a practical test the possibility of success of the task entrusted to us. It is not possible to assess the prospects one way or the other unless and until we have a camp apart such as Jaipur will provide.[113]

The plan was to send the first instalment of 1,000 POWs to a special facility at Jaipur. The balance would remain in their present camps until additional accommodation was built.

Construction began in late August 1942. However, difficulties in finding building materials, further delays in segregation work and the inability of the Quartermaster's branch to supply rations meant that by December the camp, which was still unfinished, had billets for only 400 of the proposed complement of 1,000 'white' (anti-Fascist) POWs. It was not until the end of January 1943 that accommodation for 200 officers and 1,000 other ranks was completed. Despite these annoying hold-ups, Stevens was convinced that, given more resources, the Jaipur facility could be expanded. A further 3,000 'whites' were earmarked for transfer as soon as accommodation became available. Given the right conditions, Stevens assured his superiors in London that up to 10,000 could be relocated to Jaipur in just five months.[114]

At long last a nucleus of POWs who were willing to assist the Allied war effort had been formed. Jaipur would be the base of operations for specially formed Italian POW labour battalions, which would be employed in technical support in India or to provide guides for Allied landing parties in the forthcoming invasions of Sicily and mainland Italy. They would be led by their own officers, and it was proposed that they wore a uniform of British design with *Italia Redenta* (Italy Redeemed) embroidered on the right sleeve. These men would also provide the core of 'something more ambitious', that is, the basis of fighting units for a Free Italian force. 'To take full advantage of the potentialities of this scheme there must be no delay in the provision of special accommodation and improved living conditions for those who wish to declare themselves anti-Fascists' reported the Indian mission to Sir R. H. Bruce Lockhart, Director-General of the PWE, in January 1943. 'We are gaining the confidence of the POW, and to lose it at this juncture will endanger the whole scheme.'[115] However, only the War Cabinet in London could sanction expansion, and time was of the essence.

The idea of the *Italia Redenta* received Eden's fullest support and his approval for the expansion of the Jaipur experiment. There were three advantages in the formation of these anti-Fascist labour battalions. In light of the shortage of manpower they possessed a utilitarian value. In addition, they were useful weapons in the propaganda war and, finally, as pioneer battalions they could be quickly converted into military units and deployed during the forthcoming liberation of Italy. This was an attractive idea, and one which the PWE and Foreign Office had continually supported. There was an additional reason for pushing the PWE's argument forward according to one senior Foreign Office official, Pierson Dixon. The Americans might well raise their own anti-Fascist units in North Africa, and it was therefore advisable for the British to have a body of anti-Fascist Italians under their control so that, for example, if 'they were ever needed in connection with an invasion of Italy, we should not be dependent on the Americans'.[116] Indeed, such military potential could hardly be ignored, as the number of Italian POWs in British hands was approximately 274,000 in February 1943, 68,000 of whom were located in India. The question now posed by Eden to his cabinet colleagues was how desirable was it to extend this scheme to the 98,000 Italian POWs in East Africa and the United Kingdom?[117]

The War Cabinet endorsed Eden's proposal four days later; but refused to extend the labour battalion scheme to the United Kingdom because, argued the Ministry of Agriculture and Fisheries, Italian POWs were already engaged in work of national importance, namely agriculture. Therefore, it did not see the advantage of creating special, anti-Fascist labour battalions in the British Isles. The War Cabinet was also unwilling to sanction the creation of armed anti-Fascist units.[118] As officials grappled with the possibility of expanding the labour battalion scheme, there were indications that Thornhill's men in India were winning the propaganda war in the camps and turning the tide against the hardline Fascists. The yardstick that measured the change in attitude was information gleaned by the censors from POW correspondence. Accustomed to grumble about food, the POWs were finding themselves impressed by the more disturbing home news and the worsening situation within Italy. 'I am alright and the treatment meted out to us … is excellent', wrote Captain Antonio Lombardi. However, when he contemplated what his children ate, which he claimed was not even a third of what he was rationed, 'I feel very sad.'[119] An extract from a letter sent to India from a loved one in Italy revealed the severity of the situation that ordinary citizens faced on a daily basis. 'We suffer famine here. The farmers have enough, but the country is in a plight. The Axis fares badly and the tide of war is turning against us.'[120]

Morale within most of the Italian POW facilities in India was adjudged to be 'precariously balanced'. This prompted Munro to suggest that the propaganda directed from London should now encourage the flow of correspondence with Italians abroad; 'that all broadcasts, open and covert, make as much as possible of Free Italy Movements, and that every emphasis be laid on any scraps of information which indicate bad feeling between Italians and Germans'.[121] The PWE mission was adamant that the opportunities now being presented should not be squandered as they had been in the past. One long-standing complaint lodged by PWE liaison officers was that British propaganda concerning the Italian POW had always been negative. A more positive approach was required. It was not enough, argued Thornhill, 'to rub in that Mussolini has bartered the Italian people to the Germans. The [POWs] want a constructive vision of the future of Italy' after the war. If the Foreign Office failed to confront this issue then the POWs would be looking to Washington or Moscow for solace.[122] This was why it was vital for the Foreign Office to expand the facilities at Jaipur and give those POWs who had openly committed themselves to helping the Allies, an opportunity to contribute to the war effort. Failure to enlarge Jaipur or a delay through lack of funds might jeopardise the entire project. As one field officer noted: 'We have already lost prestige among the P.O.W.[s] on account of our inability to house those Whites who have openly declared themselves for us ... a repetition of this might have serious consequences.'[123]

For the moment it looked as if the PWE mission had finally secured the proper environment and support that it had demanded for such a long time. Unfortunately for Thornhill and his hardworking team, old problems resurfaced, and several new obstacles were introduced which by July 1943 had effectively stymied the mission and led to its recall from India. At the War Office, some officials were still at a loss as to the objects of Thornhill's activities.[124] The real difficulties, however, remained with elements within GHQ, India, especially the Adjutant-General's Branch. PWE officers commented repeatedly that the co-operation given them by GHQ was marred and overshadowed by the Indian military's lack of interest and understanding of political warfare. It was a new idea, and was inclined to be viewed as a 'waste of time'. The Adjutant-General's Branch were singled out as the chief offenders. 'Full co-operation is continually

promised, but our projects are apt to be hindered by administrative difficulties, which, by the use of a little imagination, could be overcome. The
Adjutant-General's Branch do not like doing anything which will disturb
the even tempo of the life of the camp staffs.' The PWE were adamant
that the amount of co-operation their mission had received and was still
receiving from the military authorities in India left much to be desired.[125]

The death-knell came with the Australian request in May 1943 for the
removal of 10,000 anti-Fascist Italian POWs from India for agricultural
work in the dominion.[126] This, argued the PWE, rendered the formation
of the Labour Corps units 'well-nigh impossible'. The entire programme
depended upon the combing out of 'white' and 'grey' (anti-, non- or
slightly Fascist) personnel from the camps. Eden was informed by one
disgruntled official that

> if all converts and likely converts are now to be removed to Australia,
> the retention of our Mission will not … be worth while. Clearly, so
> far as [the] P.W.E. is concerned, nothing can be gained by attempting
> to re-educate prisoners who, as soon as they are reaching a standard
> which would enable us to make use of them for the purposes of polit-
> ical warfare, are removed.[127]

The same official bemoaned the fact that after two trying years the
labour corps scheme, which was now in its opening stages and which
had been 'carried out in the teeth of very considerable difficulties', was
being terminated.[128]

When the news reached Lieutenant-Colonel A. C. Johnston, who had
replaced Thornhill in March 1943 as head of the Indian mission, it came
as a 'complete bombshell'. Shocked and angry, Johnston raised the all-
important point that it was those POWs who had openly declared their
support for the Allied cause who would suffer the bitterest disappointment. They and their families had taken great risks in wholeheartedly
assisting the PWE in the formation of the *Italia Redenta*. Men had been
intimidated and beaten up by 'blacks' in the camps, and there were
several unconfirmed cases where the families of several co-operators had
been made to suffer as well.[129] One senior PWE official in London, Air
Commodore P. R. C. Groves, complained that there were no mechanisms through which these 'whites' could be compensated for the risk
that they and their families had undertaken by volunteering to fight
against their Fascist masters. The Jaipur camp was now a dead end; 'the
prisoners find themselves treated precisely as they were before the transfer with no hope of preferment'.[130]

When Brooks notified the War Office of the decision to recall the mission from India it came as something of a surprise. According to R. Evelyn-Smith, Deputy Director of the War Office's DPW, both Wavell and his successor as C-in-C India, General Sir Claude Auchinleck, had not been consulted. Furthermore, the suggestion that the mission's work had been vitiated by the decision to transfer 10,000 anti-Fascist POWs to Australia was based on a misapprehension. Thus, the premise on which the PWE had decided to withdraw the mission was inaccurate, and moreover, the decision had been taken without reference to the War Office.[131] Similarly, GHQ India vigorously denied that the transfer of Italian POWs to Australia precluded the continuance of the PWE recruitment policy for the *Italia Redenta*. They also stated that they were not transferring any of those already enrolled or earmarked for the labour corps.[132] Besides, the availability of shipping would dictate the flow of prisoners to Australia. The damage, however, had been done.

Throughout July, discussions took place between officials from the PWE, the India Office and the War Office on the future conduct of political warfare in the Italian POW camps in India. It was unanimously agreed that recruitment to the *Italia Redenta* be maintained. The PWE would continue to finance *La Diana* on condition that GHQ India undertook guidance as provided by the PWE's weekly directives. Acknowledging the importance of the radio broadcasts, GHQ India also agreed to take full operational and financial responsibility for them. All wireless apparatus on charge to the PWE was handed over to GHQ India, again on the stipulation that the PWE would waive demands for reimbursement provided that GHQ continued to use its weekly directives for the broadcasts. Finally, English would still be taught in the camps, but on a much reduced scale. With the exception of the clerical staff and those personnel who would be redeployed to GHQ India to assist in the continuation of the propaganda work, all members of the mission were withdrawn to the United Kingdom or the Middle East.[133]

It was ironic that when the decision to withdraw the PWE mission in India was being made the Allies were scoring successive victories against the Axis in the Mediterranean theatre. On 13 May 1943 Axis forces surrendered in Tunisia. Two months later the Allies invaded Sicily, which was conquered on 17 August. Meanwhile, Mussolini had resigned on 25 July. The Allied invasion of mainland Italy was launched on 3 September, and five days later Italy surrendered. Shortly afterwards, on 13 October, Italy declared war on Germany and became an Allied co-belligerent. The sudden and dramatic turn of events during the summer of 1943 seemed to preclude the need for a Free Italy movement.

Did the Italian surrender mean that the PWE's political warfare campaign was unnecessary or wasted? The answer must be an unqualified no, even though there was no apparent need for an armed *Italia Redenta* after July 1943. Admittedly, the Italian surrender in September meant that the importance of propaganda directed to the Italian POWs had diminished.[134] However, it did not mean that the knowledge and expertise gained during this entire process was lost, as some of the techniques and personnel were incorporated into those 're-education' programmes later undertaken amongst the growing number of German POWs. Meanwhile, the return in terms of the numbers of 'white' Italian POWs recruited and actively engaged for political purposes with the Allies was small, although the number of 'co-operators' employed as labourers was indeed significant.[135] However, the dramatic turn of political and military events that took place in 1943 should not be overestimated. While the changed circumstances had a great impact on the PWE's policies, the challenge now was to adapt to these new conditions in order to reap some postwar political dividends however small.

More specifically, what of India and the work that the PWE had initiated amongst the Italian POWs there? Once the mission had been recalled, the idea of transforming the *Italia Redenta* from a pioneer unit to a fighting force was quickly and predictably shelved by the military authorities. They had strongly deprecated the formation and employment of armed POW units in India. Instead, GHQ India welcomed the formation of unarmed labour units, which could be deployed anywhere in India on vital military projects, such as road-building and airfield construction. The preferred option involved the release of the 'white' prisoners and their formation into small units of 250 men each. This, argued GHQ India, was the most effective use of surplus Italian POWs. As 1943 progressed the military authorities in India took a harder line. A severe famine was ravaging India, and threatened the internal security of the country. Stocks of military food supplies were already being diverted for famine relief, and those designated for the POWs had been the subject of 'acid comment' by members of the Legislative Assembly. The War Department of the Government of India welcomed their removal from India altogether.[136] Over the next few months many thousands were in fact relocated to Australia, the Middle East and the United Kingdom. In turn, PWE staff were transferred to the Middle East and the United Kingdom to carry on work amongst the growing number of prisoners in those two theatres.

The failure of the PWE mission to move beyond the exploratory stage of its work was due, in part, to the fact that it had no executive authority over the Italian POWs in India. This was firmly in the hands of the Adjutant-General. As the mission was limited in scope to an advisory capacity, it had neither the executive power nor the resources to implement an effective or large-scale propaganda campaign. Segregation had been piecemeal. Therefore, despite the initial interest and support of Wavell, the effectiveness of the small cadre of PWE officials in India was constrained from the very beginning, because of their dependence on the goodwill and co-operation of the Indian military authorities. As we have seen, this was not always forthcoming. The shortage of trained personnel, in particular Italian-speaking intelligence officers, hampered further the mission's efforts. In the end, the immediate demands and manpower requirements of the military were to triumph over the long-term political aims of the PWE. The Free Italy movement, although an interesting experiment, was not to be.

6
The Watershed Year of 1943: From Enemies to Co-Belligerents

The worsening military position of the Italian Armed forces towards the end of 1942 and rumours that elements in Rome were attempting to negotiate with the Allied powers served to focus attention on what would happen if and when a surrender came. The Casablanca conference of 14–24 January 1943 highlighted the differences in the British and American positions with regard to their Italian enemy. While insisting on unconditional surrender for the Germans and Japanese, the Americans were prepared to countenance the possibility of negotiation with the Italians. Prime Minister Winston Churchill concurred with this view, seeing it as a means to encourage the collapse of the Mussolini regime, but the War Cabinet in London led by the Foreign Secretary, Anthony Eden, and the deputy prime minister, Clement Attlee, were far more sensitive to British public opinion. They argued for the inclusion of Italy in the communiqué demanding unconditional surrender,[1] not least because British forces had borne the brunt of the war against the Italians and because 74,000 of their servicemen were still held as prisoners in Italian camps.[2]

The Anglo-American debate on the political and military policies to be followed towards a liberated Italy continued throughout the spring and summer of 1943. It took place within the wider context of the debate on postwar security, and also within the framework of the increasingly fraught relationship between the Atlantic alliance and its Soviet ally. As David Ellwood makes clear, even as the collapse of Fascism became inevitable a whole series of questions remained unanswered:

> Besides the issue of the form and content of the armistice, and to what extent it signified an end to hostilities or the surrender of the entire country, decisions were required on machinery for its enforcement,

on the nature of the provision of an Allied regime, on the status of Italy's assets as a great power – colonies, armies, fleet – and on the responsibilities which might have to be assumed for the welfare of the Italian people in the event of a total social and political collapse ...[3]

However, although these matters of high politics remained the central agenda for Britain, the US and the Soviet Union, specific plans to deal with Italian POWs were also being formulated while the war continued.

The diverse use of prisoners' manpower

In February 1943, a War Cabinet paper from the Foreign Office pointed out that while prisoners were of value in alleviating manpower shortages, their incorporation into labour battalions might also be used for propaganda purposes and allow for their ultimate conversion to anti-Fascist fighting units.[4] As we have already seen, Middle East Command's use of prisoners as an unofficial labour supply had actually begun in late 1941 when volunteers had been used in messes and other places where armed supervision was impractical. In June 1943, Allied Forces Headquarters (AFHQ) informed its commanders that volunteer Italian prisoners would be organised into 'more or less *ad hoc* Pioneer Companies for battlefield clearance' and soon after that they could be employed as 'cooks, mess waiters and [in] kindred occupations'.[5] Intriguingly enough, units taking prisoners as labour could only do so against a vacancy on their war establishment, although the prisoners were never counted into that war establishment and remained on the strength of the POW camp from which they had come. Such were the shortages that nearly all units took up the offer of additional manpower, and Italian prisoners found themselves working in reinforcement base depots, transportation and storage companies, dock groups, base petrol transport companies, field butcheries, ordnance depots, base medical laundries and workshops, canteen depots and transit camps. The unofficial nature of this use of prisoner labour also had other advantages, as a later report on the subject from the POW camp at Suez made clear:

> Reinforcement of wastages in these units was a simple affair unencumbered by set instructions. Bribes and corruption are of course unknown in the British Army and it would be monstrous to suggest that so many prisoners equalled any commodity. That the gratitude of a commanding officer to a PW Camp Officer for supplying him with several prisoners might sometimes express itself in a bottle of

whisky or something equally scarce is beside the point. And so all units with an enterprising [commanding officer], authorised to hold PW or not, suffered little or nothing from the prevailing and greatly advertised shortage of manpower.[6]

During the Tunisian campaign, both British and US forces continued to make extensive use of their Italian POWs in labour battalions, ostensibly at least within the terms of the Geneva Convention. So large were the numbers of captives as the war in North Africa came to an end that the Supreme Allied Commander, General Dwight D. Eisenhower, estimated that it would take four months to evacuate all of them.[7] Captured Germans could not be used as labour because they had to be so closely guarded and their use was therefore uneconomic in military terms. As a result, they were the first to be shipped across the Atlantic while the more docile Italians were employed in North Africa to plug gaps in the manpower provisions of the Allied armies, making their contribution to the war effort that much more important. For the most part, there were few Italian complaints about the treatment of their servicemen. Marshal Pietro Badoglio's memoirs, perhaps not surprisingly, record only positive comments about British and American treatment of his compatriots,[8] but this lack of concern is largely borne out by the British files on the subject.[9]

While the Italians were beginning to make a practical contribution to the Allied war effort in Britain and East Africa as agricultural labourers and road-builders, and in North Africa as military ancillaries, their use for political purposes was also being considered. For, as mentioned above, the PWE had been instrumental in stressing another aspect of prisoners' usefulness, namely as a tool in the political struggle against Mussolini's Fascist regime and in winning the hearts and minds of the Italian people once the war was over. Italian prisoners in India were already being screened for anti-Fascist leanings, with a view to their incorporation into new political movements sponsored by the British. However, the PWE's attempts to extend the scheme to prisoners in Britain was rejected, mainly at the behest of the Ministry of Agriculture, on the grounds that the 'Italian prisoners [were] already being used for work of national importance'.[10]

Apart from their usefulness as propaganda tools, the prisoners were also seen as bargaining counters. While the possession of some enemy soldiers had always been an important factor in ensuring the reciprocal treatment of prisoners in Axis hands, the Italian prisoners became especially important during 1943. Shortly after the conquest of Tunisia,

Major-General R. A. D. Brooks, Deputy Director-General of the PWE, suggested that it would be 'advantageous' to issue a statement concerning the repatriation of Italian POWs, 'since the morale of the Italian fighting services will be our primary target during this phase' and 'every effort should be made to make the Italian soldier feel that our attitude to him is different from our attitude to the Germans'. The most effective method of achieving this, he argued, would be a declaration promising that the repatriation of Italian prisoners would begin immediately after the expulsion of the last German from Italian soil and after Italy had laid down her arms. 'Should there be any attempt to transfer British prisoners in Italian hands from Italy to Germany, such repatriation would be delayed until the defeat of Germany'.[11] From this, it is clear that some thought was being given in British government circles to the use of prisoners to meet short-term propaganda objectives in the campaign against Italy, and to use them to bargain for the safety and release of British prisoners held in Italy. Additionally, prisoners were intended to play their part in the longer-term objectives of political reconstruction being undertaken by the PWE through the 'recruitment' of Italian officers and men in India. However, these plans remained marginal to the overall Allied strategy towards Italy and were often overridden if they conflicted with more immediate objectives.

The events following the dismissal of Mussolini on 25 July 1943 undoubtedly had the greatest impact on the future treatment of the Italian POWs. Eisenhower was keen to have King Victor Emmanuel III of Italy send an emissary to negotiate quickly for peace. To that end, he was prepared to offer the Italians peace with honour, including the repatriation of Italian prisoners.[12] Four days after Mussolini's downfall, Eisenhower was given permission by his political masters to broadcast directly to the Italian people in order to encourage an early end to hostilities by offering them an honourable capitulation.[13] Among other guarantees, Eisenhower promised that the Allied occupation of Italy would be 'mild and beneficent'. Life would return to normal, and, 'provided all British and [A]llied prisoners now in [Italian] hands were restored safely to us, and not taken away to Germany, the hundreds of thousands of Italian prisoners captured by us in Tunisia and Sicily [would] return to the countless Italian homes who long for them'.[14]

Originally the speech had not specified which Italians would be released if all Allied prisoners were returned and it was at Churchill's behest that this act of generosity was limited to the most recent captures, thereby excluding all the prisoners taken earlier in the war who were now, as he put it, 'parked around the world' and in many cases contributing materially to the Allied war effort.[15] Churchill's priorities were clearly reformulated as the war situation changed. Obtaining the release of all British prisoners in Italian hands was now considered 'of the highest importance' and ranked only just below the essential military aims of controlling all Italian territory, ensuring the surrender of the Italian fleet and Italian forces occupying south-eastern France, the Greek islands and Balkan territories. Nevertheless, he did not seem prepared to commit the Allies to returning all their Italian prisoners to realise these objectives.[16]

This tension between political expediency and military necessity had been most clearly demonstrated after the successful invasion of Sicily on 10 July 1943. The drain on resources caused by the capture of tens of thousands of Italian troops on the island at a time when the Allies were about to try and dislodge a hard core of 65,000 German troops cornered on its north-eastern extremity, led to an alteration in overall Allied policy on POWs. Eisenhower hoped to carry out a plan originally suggested by either the Deputy C-in-C North Africa, General Sir Henry Maitland Wilson, or General Sir H. R. L. G. Alexander, C-in-C 15th Army Group, Sicily. This involved a number of Italian POWs captured in Sicily being released to help with the harvest.[17] On 23 July, the Joint Staff Mission in Washington passed the idea on to the British Chiefs of Staff suggesting approval provided that the Allied Military Government Occupied Territories (AMGOT) were satisfied that the POWs were bona-fide local farmers and labourers and 'not actively pro-Fascist'. In addition, it was considered that the proposal, if handled properly, possessed immense and wide-ranging propaganda value. For instance, its impact would not be confined to Sicily alone for such propaganda 'might have [a] strong psychological effect on Italian troops [on] the mainland who may be called upon to fight near their homes and who do not relish [the] possibility of internment in North African camps'.[18] Moreover, it might further weaken Italian morale in the Balkans.[19]

The British Chiefs of Staff approved the suggestion but did not consult the diplomats at the Foreign Office. Predictably, this annoyed the latter who were sensitive to the fact that any decision ought to be postponed until the position of the Allied POWs had been clarified. In any case, senior Foreign Office officials were doubtful about the scheme's propaganda value. The Deputy Under-Secretary, Sir Orme Sargent, was convinced that any move of this nature would be misunderstood by the British public at a time when the expectation of the return of British POWs in Italian hands had been heightened. The debate rumbled on into August. Harold Macmillan, as resident minister in Algiers, represented Foreign Office fears to Eisenhower, who responded by pointing out that an official statement of the 'true' facts might assuage the British public. If they were told of the military advantages which would accrue from this policy, and were reassured that the Sicilians were only paroled and could be re-imprisoned at any time, this might serve to lessen the anxiety over a 'soft' treatment of a defeated enemy who still had some control over British prisoners.[20] The British Chiefs of Staff were nevertheless anxious that no bargaining would take place that might prejudice an unconditional surrender. Moreover, they were adamant that Sicilians held in POW camps overseas should not be returned to their homes, and that calls on POW labour for work outside Italy should continue to be fully met.[21] Initially, the issue was a storm in a teacup, as early reports from General George S. Patton, commander of the US Seventh Army in Sicily, suggested that there were no Sicilians among the early prisoners taken by US forces; the inference being that Mussolini had doubts about their reliability on home soil and had moved them elsewhere.[22] However, after the conquest of Sicily, Eisenhower paroled thousands of Italian soldiers captured during the campaign to help the Sicilian farmers bring in the harvest. Eventually, in July 1944, the parole scheme in Sicily was cancelled and all Italian POWs on the island were immediately released.[23]

Equally significant was the threat these policies posed to British domestic interests as outlined by Sir John Anderson, Lord President of the Council. Even with Churchill's modifications, Eisenhower's radio broadcast of 29 July had caused further complications to British plans merely by promising that all Italian prisoners taken in Tunisia and Sicily would be returned home provided that no United Nations prisoners or internees were handed over to the Germans. In a memorandum dated 19 August, Anderson pointed out that if Britain had to comply with the promise, 28,000 prisoners taken in these areas and earmarked for use in the United Kingdom as agricultural labour would be lost. In addition, ships would have to be provided to transport the prisoners back to Italy and enormous friction would be created if those captured much later in the war were sent home first while others remained in captivity.[24]

The end of Italian involvement in the war also created a potential threat to the continued use of the 74,900 prisoners already employed in the British economy. Major-General Sir Hastings Ismay, as Deputy Secretary (Military) to the War Cabinet, commented to Sir Alexander Cadogan, Permanent Under-Secretary at the Foreign Office, that he did not think any action was required:

> If the Italians have failed to retain our prisoners in Italy, then our pledge falls to the ground. On the other hand, if we recover all our

prisoners, it will be cheap at the price of some awkwardness over manpower. In any case, there was no timetable in the broadcast. Moreover, we may capture plenty of Italians in Italy, and we are not pledged to return *them*.[25]

Ismay's comments and Cadogan's concurrence were reflected in the War Cabinet discussion of the memorandum on 10 September when it was decided to continue the plan to import Italian prisoners to Britain, albeit with the stipulation that any Sicilians should be screened out if possible.[26] In line with Ismay's rather cynical approach, it was also decided to try to ensure that prisoners brought to Britain were from northern Italy so that there was little or no chance of a demand for their repatriation while the Germans occupied this region. The Cabinet was further reassured by a rumour that the Italians had been unable to prevent 2,500 of their British prisoners being taken by the Germans which would mean that Eisenhower's offer could indeed have been deemed to have lapsed.[27]

If this solution promised to solve the immediate problems faced by the British government, it could not hide the fact that an imminent Italian surrender would require a complete reappraisal of the status to be awarded to incarcerated Italian military personnel. As far as the Foreign Office was concerned, Eden was adamant 'that whatever their status is to be, Italian Prisoners of War as a whole must be regarded as a pool which Allied Governments will continue to draw on in whatever way will best contribute to [the] solution of [the] manpower problem'.[28] Yet Eden, like the rest of his cabinet colleagues, realised that any future negotiations with a defeated Italy would have to include the POWs on the agenda.

The problems of co-belligerency

In the short term, military necessities and political expediency could be dovetailed, but the contrasting treatment handed out to prisoners captured at different times was to become one of the major problems to be reconciled after the Italian surrender on 8 September 1943. The surrender terms agreed between Eisenhower and the Badoglio government did little to clarify the future status of the defeated Italian state or of its government. The negotiations to produce a settlement ending hostilities and acceptable to all parties occupied more than a month. The prime Anglo-American considerations were to ensure the participation of Italy in the war against Nazi Germany while at the same time not making commitments which would offend their Soviet ally or domestic public opinion. For this reason, the Badoglio regime was to be granted the status of a co-belligerent rather than an ally as and when the new government declared war on Germany. This went too far for the Foreign Office which felt that recognition as a co-belligerent should come as a reward for future Italian actions rather than as an inducement to make war on a former ally.[29] Moreover, the British diplomats were afraid of public reaction to any such announcement, fearing that 'the newspapers sooner or later will conclude that military expediency in the Mediterranean and electoral expediency in America (with its 600,000 Italian voters) will have outweighed long-term political considerations'.[30] Nevertheless, co-belligerency did have some advantages. Ellwood argues that it 'signified little beyond compromise and postponement ... [a] postponement in the name of practical flexibility and unprejudiced freedom of action'.[31] Its imprecise nature was a major benefit to those concerned about the Italian POWs because it imposed no obligation on the Allies to hand back their Italian captives, and there was no question of negotiating a peace treaty which would have made repatriation mandatory.

The Allied success in Italy culminating in the surrender of 8 September was to be the catalyst which transformed the politics and economics of using POWs as a labour force. By that time, the British and Americans had control over more than 500,000 Italian prisoners,[32] and decisions had to be made about their future. As might be imagined, there was a whole series of legal complications created by the changed circumstances, not least the fact that Italy was effectively changing sides in the middle of the war. The 1929 Geneva Convention made no provision for such an eventuality and there were conflicting views on how the Italian servicemen captured in the war should be treated.

Italian POW camps in Britain were reported to be full of 'effervescence' after the news of the surrender reached them.[33] Prisoners were beginning to ask questions and London feared that they might become discontented and their willingness to work would be affected. Moreover, could the planned transportation of a further 8,000 Italian prisoners to Britain actually be carried out in the light of the changing political situation?[34] Even before the armistice, Eisenhower had intimated his intention not to remove any more Italians from the Mediterranean theatre to Britain or the United States 'in view of the altering status of Italy', until their position had been established. This caused consternation in London, where the COS noted that this endangered a very valuable supply of labour. General Sir John Dill, British representative on the Combined Chiefs of Staff Committee in Washington, emphasised that the manpower situation in England was 'very acute and obviously reliance had been placed on the continuous flow of prisoners into the United Kingdom'. Admiral William Leahy, an American representative on the Combined Chiefs of Staff Committee, supported by Dill, pointed out the difficulty of shipping Italian prisoners to the United Kingdom in view of the Allied attitude towards the new Italian government. At the same time, he was clear that the decision was based on political rather than military grounds. Eisenhower's stance undoubtedly endangered the proposals under consideration by the War Office to import a full quota of Italian POWs for 1943, and to extend the scheme in 1944. Similarly, Sir Ronald Campbell, British minister in Washington (1941–5), reported to the Foreign Office that the United States would refuse or at least would not approve the shipment of any Italian prisoners to the United Kingdom if they had been originally captured by US forces because of the domestic political implications involved.[35]

The State Department was also antagonistic to the idea of further shipments and a diplomatic clash seemed inevitable until it was pointed out that the United States War Department also wanted to hold onto its quota of prisoners.[36] In this way, a dispute was avoided and the immediate threat to supplies of Italian labour to the British war effort was removed. Certainly, Churchill was adamant that the Italians should continue to be used to provide a labour supply:

> Where are [*sic*] the great mass that we have taken? Over 250,000 were captured by General Wavell alone. It would be rather difficult to move to England, men taken after the armistice who have done their best to help us or have not resisted at all, but we have these larger pools to draw on, and work in the UK is more important than in India or South Africa … I certainly look forward to getting 100,000 more Italians into England for work purposes during 1944.[37]

Although the prime minister saw the difficulty in transferring prisoners from the Italian and North African theatres to Britain once an armistice had been agreed, he remained happy to countenance the shipment of prisoners from the dominions in order to meet the demand for further labour.[38] South Africa was reported to have up to 40,000 prisoners who could be transferred for work in Britain, but, as the planners pointed out, it was not supply but the lack of accommodation in Britain for prisoner labour which would dictate that only a further 11,000 could be brought in during 1943.[39] This continued to be the main stumbling-block into 1944, when Attlee reported to the War Cabinet that the Ministry of Labour thought that a further 250,000 prisoners could be usefully employed in Britain, but that there was only accommodation for 18,000, and then not necessarily where the work existed.[40]

Once the surrender terms had been signed, a debate ensued about the precise status of the prisoners in Allied hands. During October, a whole series of discussions took place to decide on a solution which would meet the legal requirements and practical needs of the Allied powers. Various possible options and designations were discussed by the British and Americans. There was some thought given to employing the prisoners as civilians, but this was ruled out of the question, not only because it involved the *de facto* demobilisation of Italian military personnel but also because it would give the Allies little or no control over their erstwhile prisoners. Enlisting them officially in Allied (British) units was also ruled out, mainly because they would then have had to be treated like any other Allied soldier and this was again considered unacceptable. Finally, there was a plan to enlist them in military units of the Italian government under overall British or US control. This third option emerged as a result of the US view that continuing to treat captured Italians as POWs was incompatible with their country's co-belligerent status. Washington felt that the benefits of keeping these men as prisoners were outweighed by the advantage that they would no longer be protected by the Geneva Convention. This would allow them to be used more flexibly and for a much wider range of tasks.[41] Although the British negotiating team in the United States was effectively won over by the idea, the Foreign Office looked at the legal position more carefully. While the scheme would work in Italy or on Italian ships where Italian officers could enforce Italian jurisdiction, this could not be applied to the 250,000 prisoners held in the British Empire, as neither British nor Italian officers would have the legal right to discipline or sentence their men. While it was accepted that this could be remedied through legislation, it would inevitably take some time.[42] A more immediate problem was that in many areas, including the United Kingdom, there were few Italian officers or suitable linguists to lead such units.[43]

A War Cabinet committee discussed the various proposals on 27 October 1943, and having ruled out all these options returned to the idea of negotiating some form of agreement with the Badoglio government whereby the Italians would remain prisoners but would have their conditions ameliorated and would continue to assist the Allied war effort. In favour of this option was the fact that disciplinary control would be complete and easily ensured throughout the world; it provided a flexible system which could be adapted to all situations, including mainland Italy; it would allow recusants and undesirables to be kept in (or returned to) camps; it would be wholly acceptable to Allied and British public opinion; and finally it would provide an immediate solution. Ultimately, only the PWE dissented, pointing out that it retained the anomaly of a co-belligerent being asked to fight and work for the Allied cause while its soldiers remained POWs. Moreover, the stigma of POW status would be retained which might in turn discourage the Italians from wholehearted support for the Allied cause and it might also be used by German propaganda to dissuade other satellite states from breaking with the Axis.[44] Any agreement on this basis would be regarded by the Italians as 'humiliating and unfair' and would work against the Allies' (and the PWE's) attempts to win over the hearts and minds of the Italian people.[45] Although the committee took note of the PWE's objections, a draft agreement between the Allies and the Badoglio government was prepared. The only remaining obstacles to British plans were to obtain American concurrence and Badoglio's signature. In the event, neither proved easy to obtain.

To some extent, the British desire for a proper legal basis for the treatment of Italian POWs had been circumvented by direct negotiation between Eisenhower and the Italians. In responding to the Anglo-American debate on the future treatment of prisoners, Eisenhower was at pains to point out that any liberation of Italians would both anger and affront the French, who were anxious that their former enemies should not evade the consequences of having gone into the war on the side of the Axis.[46] Moreover, the Supreme Allied Commander also made the point that no further agreement was really necessary as he had already come to an arrangement with Badoglio within the terms of the Geneva Convention. Under Article 83 of the Convention, belligerent powers could modify the terms and conditions of the Convention and remove the need for protecting powers through direct negotiation. In October 1943 Eisenhower had reached an unwritten agreement with Badoglio that employment restrictions under the terms of the Geneva Convention could be disregarded for Italian prisoners in Sicily and North Africa.[47] Volunteers were organised, first into Allied units and then as separate Italian service units as pioneer or transport companies.[48] As incentive and reward, their living and working conditions were also improved. Eisenhower had no doubts as to the efficacy or correctness of this procedure. It was a secure and practicable solution which the Italian government had recognised and agreed.[49] Indeed, one might argue that this was no more than a regularisation of what had been happening in practice since June 1943. The only difference was that it was now being openly and officially sanctioned. Badoglio's memoirs put a rather different gloss on events:

> After the armistice the Allies decided that our men were to remain prisoners. But under co-belligerency the Allies asked if the prisoners could be employed in the rear areas, to which the Head of Government necessarily agreed in principle, while waiting for detailed agreements ... as Italy has always desired to give the greatest possible support to the armed forces of the co-belligerents. On the basis of this general agreement, the British military authorities, declaring that they were working in full agreement with the Italian government, tried to induce the prisoners in many camps to state in writing that they were willing to undertake any work, even if it were forbidden by the Geneva Convention, while still remaining prisoners, although under improved conditions.[50]

Badoglio noted that the Americans had behaved similarly in Morocco and Algiers but were apparently prevented from doing the same in the United States by 'a senior general' who pointed out the irregularity of their actions.[51] Although Badoglio's account of events is anything but reliable, it does serve to show the problem from the Italian side. While wishing to seem in complete concert with the Allied war effort against Germany, the new Italian government could not be seen to trade away the rights of its servicemen being held by its present friends but erstwhile enemies. Some sense of national honour had to be maintained and Badoglio was undoubtedly aware that the Italian public would hold him responsible for the fate of Italian prisoners and would find it hard to understand why they could not be returned home now that circumstances had changed. Senior British officials agreed. Britain's Resident Minister in Algiers, Harold Macmillan, reminded his Whitehall colleagues that however satisfied Badoglio himself might be about the wording and intent of the agreement, he knew full well that his signature on the document would mean 'political suicide'.[52]

An American memoir gives yet another slant to the problem. Captain Harry C. Butcher, Naval aide to Eisenhower, noted in his diary for 28 October 1943 that

> Ike is now puzzling over one of his many complex problems. Badoglio's government is recognised as a co-belligerent. This government asks for the release of prisoners. They have few, if any Allied prisoners to exchange. As co-belligerents they have reason to expect

all their prisoners. Yet the Italians are contributing to the Allied war effort by their labour in England and America. If they are returned to Italy they become an economic burden not only to Italy, but to the Allies, particularly America, who have the job of supplying essential food and clothing. The Badoglio government is showing its good faith by pressing for inclusion of at least one Italian division in line of combat in addition to supplying troops for labour and lines of communication.[53]

All of these postwar commentaries merely serve to highlight the confusion on both sides in the immediate post-surrender period and the continued paradoxical position of personnel originally conscripted into the Italian army. Those recently captured in North Africa were being used for war-related work, others in Britain were employed in agriculture and other approved tasks, still more were in camps in the dominions while many of those captured on the Italian mainland had already been paroled by Eisenhower and allowed to return home to work in liberated areas. If this was not enough, some Italian army units which had not been captured were actually fighting alongside the Allies against the Germans.

In assessing the situation in the autumn of 1943, a number of issues become clear. Unlike his compatriots in the United States, Eisenhower was perfectly happy to allow the status quo to remain and for the Italians to retain their prisoner status and for the anomalies in treatment to persist. At the same time, it was clear that others wanted a more permanent solution. Undoubtedly, the Badoglio government was expecting some further discussions and agreement on the fate of its servicemen in Allied hands. In addition, it was an issue of vital domestic importance to a regime with only a tenuous hold on power and an uncertain future. In Britain also, some further action was expected. Apart from the legal arguments of the Foreign Office, the end of the war with Italy had brought new problems for the War Cabinet to consider and new uncertainties for the Italian prisoners in British hands.

Negotiations towards some form of agreement to be placed before Badoglio's government continued beyond October. In the light of Eisenhower's preference for retaining the Italians as POWs, the US authorities in Washington withdrew their objection to this proposal, but it remained for an agreement to be reached with the Italians. In January 1944, the Allied proposals were rejected by Badoglio. As a matter of national honour,[54] his government could not agree to the terms being proposed. The objections were that Italians who volunteered could be used anywhere in the world, on any type of work but would still remain prisoners. Moreover, there appeared to be no protection afforded to those prisoners who did not volunteer. The Italian conclusion was that, 'any Government who signed [this agreement] would undoubtedly be overthrown by public opinion in liberated Italy and would be utterly discredited in the eyes of all Italians in occupied territory'. Moreover, 'the agreement would not only constitute no incentive to collaboration of prisoners ... but, on the contrary, its very harsh disposition would have a most discouraging effect'.[55]

The Italians for their part proposed a mixed commission to discuss the issue and referred back to discussions between their representative in the United States, General Pietro Gazzera, and certain high-ranking American military figures. This was wholly unacceptable to the British who feared that any further negotiations would bring about extensive delays to the proposals. Major-General E. C. Gepp, Director-General of the Prisoner of War Department at the War Office, was in no doubt that they should rely on the verbal agreement between Eisenhower and Badoglio and put the agreements into force as if they had been signed. Badoglio could then be sent explanations of the terms and any guarantees he might 'reasonably demand'. As Gepp pointed out:

> The Italian Government's intention to co-operate fully in the war effort of the United Nations can best be judged by their readiness to enter into these agreements which are designed to enable Italian prisoners of war to render the greatest assistance to the common cause. The powers which it has been found necessary to take under these agreements have only been sought because they are regarded as essential if the maximum assistance is to be derived from the labour of these members of the Italian Armed Forces. Their treatment under these agreements will be generous and will represent a considerable amelioration of the excellent conditions which they already enjoy.[56]

Negotiations dragged on until April 1944. Italian counter-proposals met with rejection by the Allies, and a US idea that an exchange of notes might suffice could still not get round the intractable problem that if Badoglio were to sign an agreement which sanctioned the continued captivity of the Italians as POWs, his position at home would become untenable. On this, the talks foundered.[57] While Badoglio remained intransigent at an official level, a further exchange of communications between him and Lieutenant-General Sir Noel Mason-MacFarlane, Chief Commissioner of the Allied Control Commission, led Mason-MacFarlane to conclude that the Italian was not going to complain about the Allies changing the terms on which Italian prisoners were held.[58] Certainly, Badoglio felt that he had reached some form of verbal agreement with Mason-MacFarlane on 5 April, even if the latter did not see it in quite the same way.[59]

After these exchanges, the Allies decided that there was no point in reopening the negotiations as neither side was going to give ground. As Churchill informed Cadogan, there was no need to 'maul or weaken' Badoglio:

> We ought not to make too much of this or insist on signatures on the dotted line to legal documents. Gentlemen's agreements and [the] development of good feeling, as it becomes clear to the Italians that we are winning, will be the most convenient line to follow ... There is no need to bring these matters to a head at an awkward time.[60]

Consequently, it was decided that the Allies would continue to rely on the verbal agreement of October 1943 and that Italian prisoners could be used in 'any and all noncombatant employment ... in the war against Germany'.[61] A formal system was devised to cover Italians held outside the Mediterranean theatre where prisoners were offered the chance to become 'co-operators' who would be employed in a much wider range of employment, including war work, in exchange for better conditions and other concessions. Those who chose not to co-operate were returned to camps, while co-operators were given greater freedom and financial rewards for their work.[62]

It is clear that Allied policy towards Italian POWs had to adapt to rapidly changing political and military circumstances during 1943 as the Italian involvement with the Axis war effort ceased and accommodations were reached with the Badoglio regime. Prior to 1943, the Allies (and for the most part this meant the British and dominion armed forces) had treated their Italian prisoners according to the terms of the Geneva Convention. This ensured reciprocal treatment for Allied soldiers in Italian hands and for some limited negotiations between the belligerent powers to improve conditions on both sides. During that time, Italian prisoners were also moved away from Egypt and other African war zones lest they became a threat to the political stability of the area, but their sheer numbers were both a complication and an advantage. Only in 1942 did Middle East Command manage to reduce its prisoner holdings to manageable levels by 'exporting' captives to other parts of the Empire. In the meantime, Britain and the dominions had discovered that the Italians represented a wonderful source of apparently docile labour for non-war work. In addition, the Italian soldiers were seen as having a role in the political warfare being waged against the Fascist regime, and Italian service personnel held in India were screened as potential recruits for Allied-sponsored political movements.

Even before the surrender in September 1943, the Allies had found new uses for their POWs. Rumours of an Italian capitulation were rife from the beginning of the year, and prisoners were increasingly being used as substitutes for civilian labour in Britain and the dominions, and as substitutes for Allied military personnel in the rear echelons in North Africa. In both cases, it seems that the distinction between war and non-war work was on occasion deliberately blurred when it was deemed desirable. Moreover, in all these cases, expediency was the key word, but the military commanders had to tread carefully, as other Allied powers, and British public opinion was considered hostile to the idea of special treatment for the Italians. The prisoners' importance as a political warfare tool also increased, although once the Fascist regime had been overthrown, the prime objective of the Allies was to use them to win over the hearts and minds of the Italian people as part of the process of post-war political reconstruction.

While the increased importance of the prisoners to the Allied war effort in this period cannot be denied, their existence did not protect many of the Allied prisoners in Italian camps from being handed over to the Germans. Moreover, their continued use depended on the nature of the agreements made with the Italian government to bring hostilities to an end. Both the British government and her armed forces had a vested interest in the surrender terms, if only to safeguard what had become a very important source of ancillary labour. While the surrender terms said nothing about POWs, and Eisenhower's offer to return prisoners taken in Tunisia and Sicily lapsed when the Italians were unable to hand over all their prisoners, it was clear that the anomalous position of captured or surrendered Italian service personnel could not be allowed to continue indefinitely.

Although the Americans and to some extent the British Foreign Office wanted to regularise the position, the acceptance of the Italians as co-belligerents meant little or nothing. Attempts to find a more flexible way of using the Italians after their surrender foundered on the legal problems of their status, the need to have some continued means of control and discipline, and the Badoglio government's refusal to put its signature to any document which involved Italians remaining as prisoners of war. Ultimately, the Allies wanted it both ways. They needed the labour force and ideally wanted it to perform any and all tasks associated with the war effort. At the same time, they realised that the interests of discipline and order required that the Italians retained their prisoner status, but this effectively excluded them from much of the work the Allies wanted them to do. Ironically, the misfortune for many Italian POWs was to have been captured too early, and to have become too useful to an Allied war effort which was constantly short of manpower and willing to extend to the limit the boundaries of international treaties in order to make use of all available resources. In the end, although Badoglio was not prepared to sign an agreement which would keep Italians as prisoners of war, the Allies were able to fall back on his verbal agreement with Eisenhower in October 1943 that Italians might be used for all types of work in the Allied cause.

7
Neither Enemies Nor Allies: Italian Prisoners in the United Kingdom After the Armistice

Co-operators and non-co-operators

The Armistice with Italy had been greeted in the corridors of Whitehall, and in Britain as a whole, as the first practical indication that the war in Europe was being won. In its aftermath, as we have seen, the Churchill administration went to great lengths to protect the status of its Italian prisoners in order that they could continue to be used as a labour supply, both in the United Kingdom, and in its Empire and the dominions. Yet even as the diplomats were pulling out all the stops to protect this supposed asset, the first doubts were being cast on the utility of the Italian labour force, as a telling internal memorandum from the Ministry of Agriculture made clear:

> When these prisoners started work the general experience was that they were first class workers. I am sorry to report that they have steadily deteriorated ever since, particularly where the prisoners have been working in small gangs without a proper ganger ... The prisoners have discovered that nothing happens if they don't work very hard.[1]

Nevertheless, their numbers in the United Kingdom continued to increase as more were brought from camps in various parts of Africa, and their geographical and occupational distribution across the country continued to widen. Moreover, in spite of these disparaging comments from central government, the demand for labour showed no signs of abating. The Ministry of Agriculture remained under pressure as its potential domestic labour supply was decimated by conscription. Hence the draft for Italian prisoners was set at 44,000 for 1943.[2] There was no shortage of prisoners to meet the demand, with the camps full to overflowing after the North African campaigns and the invasion of Southern Italy. Indeed, such was the pressure on British military resources that the British and Americans agreed on a division of prisoners under the so-called 50:50 agreement which involved the United States acting as detaining power for some Italians nominally under British control.

However, the problem of bringing prisoners to Britain remained one of accommodation and transport rather than of supply. At the same time, the near monopoly exercised by the Ministry of Agriculture on the uses of prisoner labour was also under threat. Now that conditions on employment were being relaxed, other government departments began to stake claims for what was still very much a scarce resource. A memorandum from the Ministry, couched in very 'possessive' terms, stated:

> We should be the chief sufferers in any such proposal ... [for diversifying the use of prisoner labour] ... So far we have been able to resist the Ministry of Labour interfering with any of our prisoners, though we have lent small numbers to other departments from time to time. I fear, however, that if the matter is raised with Minister... we shall lose control over at least a proportion of our prisoners.[3]

As has been shown, with the Armistice it became difficult for the British government to justify the removal of Italians to the United Kingdom once the invasion of Italy had begun, and more or less impossible in the face of Eisenhower's objections.[4] Nonetheless, projected domestic demand for prisoner labour in 1944 was put at a staggering 250,000 by the Lord President, Clement Attlee, although he also admitted that there was only accommodation for 18,000, and then not necessarily where the work existed.[5] On the supply side, there were also calculation revisions at the end of 1943. There was no question of Italians taken prisoner on Italian soil being taken out of the country, and many were rapidly paroled for agricultural work at home to prevent their becoming a charge on the Allied armies.[6] Thus any future prisoner labour would have to come from those already in captivity in the Empire. A paper to the War Cabinet Chiefs of Staff Committee revealed that there were approximately 73,000 men still available, but that the 40,500 in East and South Africa would be impossible to transport in the short or medium term.[7]

The Armistice and surrender on 8 September 1943 also had major effects on the Italian prisoners already in Britain. Even before the surrender, large numbers of Italians had been used as auxiliary labour in North Africa, but this had been almost entirely under military supervision. After the surrender they were organised into Labour Companies to perform all manner of tasks.[8] Any transfer of such a scheme to the United Kingdom and other parts of the Empire in order to maximise the Italians' use as a labour supply beyond the terms of the Geneva Convention had to be carefully considered. Four possible alternatives were suggested: namely that Italians could be enlisted in the Pioneer Corps; that they could be made subject to the Allied Forces Act (1940); that they could be treated as civilian enemy aliens; or that they could be retained as prisoners but with a view to negotiating their status with the post-surrender Badoglio regime. The idea of civilian status was quickly dismissed as it would leave the authorities with little practical control and few sanctions. In any case, it would involve the demobilisation of Italian troops, their incorporation into civilian life in Britain and the possibility that they could claim settlement or naturalisation rights after the war.[9] Incorporation into the Pioneer Corps or application of the Allied Forces Act (1940) was also rejected. While this had some advantages in taking the Italians outside the terms of the Geneva Convention, these were heavily outweighed by the possibilities of adverse public opinion, opposition from the fighting services, the lack of suitable Italian officers to provide a command structure and a similar lack of Italian linguists from the Allied forces to make good this deficiency.[10]

This meant that any decision about changing the status of Italian prisoners in the United Kingdom, or in any part of the Empire, was dependent on some form of agreement with the Badoglio regime. As has been seen, this was consistently refused, with the result that by the spring of 1944, the British authorities were desperate to maximise the labour potential of the Italian prisoners and had decided to act without a formal agreement.[11] Towards the end of April 1944, the War Office sent out a substantive letter[12] outlining a scheme whereby Italian prisoners would be invited to become volunteer co-operators who would engage in work 'directly connected with the operations of the war'. This was seen as paralleling the existing scheme in North Africa, where Italians had been organised into Labour Battalions with the sanction of the Badoglio regime and had performed such 'valuable work'.[13] The volunteers were to be organised into Labour Battalions of around 250 men commanded by Italian Warrant Officers. It was assumed that in most camps, the vast majority of men would volunteer and the few who did not would then be removed elsewhere. The camp would then be redesignated as a Labour Battalion, but retain its original number. Co-operators were to be issued with chocolate-coloured battledress and with the word 'Italy' as a shoulder tab. The general idea was that conditions for co-operators should be made more appealing than those for non-co-operators, with better conditions and liberties being offered to those who volunteered. Rates of pay were increased to 7 shillings per week for unskilled work and 9 shillings for skilled work. NCOs were paid even more and there were no deductions for sickness, mealtimes or travelling times. Henceforward, only co-operators would be allowed to reside in billets, and camps designated for co-operators would have their perimeter fences dismantled, with the inmates allowed to exercise outside the camps during daylight hours. Guards were also removed from working parties and only the restrictions on fraternisation and limitations on access to public houses and places of entertainment were retained.[14] Any prisoner could volunteer for the scheme but known Fascists and bad characters, those permanently unfit for work and psychotics were to be excluded.[15]

The scheme was implemented as from 1 May 1944 and in theory should have capitalised on the perceived desire of the majority of Italians to assist the Allies, not least in the liberation of their own country from the Germans. However, it was pointed out by the PWE that 'the ungenerous, procrastinating and equivocal policy' towards these men had turned a 'general willingness to co-operate' into 'disillusionment, resentment and hostility' as they received little or no mail from their families at home, and had been kept completely in the dark for more than six months about what Italian co-belligerency might mean for them.[16] Nevertheless, early returns showed that just over 60 per cent of all the Italians in the United Kingdom had volunteered.[17] A high proportion, but nonetheless a disappointment to the War Office. Many camps had split more or less down the middle, necessitating the removal of large numbers of men to render individual camps either completely co-operator or non-co-operator. However, it was also noted that the whole system of ascertaining the Italians' intentions was flawed in many respects. Choices had often been made in public, leaving individuals subject to the opprobrium of their fellows if they volunteered, and the majority was against co-operation. Moreover, it allowed influential individuals such as the medical officers or chaplains to exercise a possibly unhealthy level of power over the men's actions. Another factor was raised by the Commandant, Camp No. 56 (Brockenhurst), who noted: 'A fair proportion of POW[s] decided against co-operation, not because they were unwilling to do so, but for fear of reprisals on their families in the unoccupied [German controlled] portion of Italy, [thus] as more places are freed, so more men will be willing to co-operate.'[18]

This report also highlighted the unsatisfactory way in which those who changed their minds were treated – being left with their non-co-operator comrades but with co-operator privileges until an appropriate reallocation could be effected. It soon became apparent that the organisation of initial or subsequent choices was not the only flaw in the system. By early July, there was an increasing level of complaints from co-operators that the improved conditions they had been offered had not materialised. As one co-operator wrote to his family: 'as a genuine anti-Fascist and a political victim, I have been allowed to take part in the potato and beet campaigns, and in the digging of ditches. So I do the same work as the Fascists ... '[19] They were being asked to work longer hours with no payment for overtime (non-co-operators received cigarettes in lieu), they were excluded from places of entertainment, and while given additional money to spend were restricted by the lack of available NAAFI supplies in canteens. One report noted that co-operators had begun to feel that promises had been made to attract them which the authorities had no intention of fulfilling.[20] There were further difficulties when it was realised that Italians being used by the Americans in Britain had better working conditions and rates of pay.[21] This had first been noted among Italians employed by the two powers in North Africa,[22] and while some of the anomalies on payment and conditions were ironed out, problems remained. For example, while non-co-operators in British hands were still initially subject to the exchange rate agreed under the Geneva Convention of £=72 lira, AMGOT (Allied Military Government of Occupied Territories) was using a rate of £=400 lira.

One further disincentive to co-operator status was noted by the Labour Officer attached to Italian Pioneer Company 668:

> The issue of chocolate battledress is having a very adverse effect on the work of this company, who started in with great keenness, have proved willing and easy to train in stores work, and in general a very satisfactory unit. ... Since the issue of *chocolate* battledress was enforced, the sickness rate has increased considerably, and output has fallen off in some instances by as much as 50%.[23]

It may be that the uniforms were perceived by the prisoners as a deliberate affront to their sense of style and fashion, but more likely was the fact that they had been promised proper khaki uniforms when they had been evacuated from North Africa.[24] However, it seems that this was not an isolated protest as by August 1944 the authorities had issued instructions that the battledress colour would henceforward be 'spruce green', ostensibly to make a contrast with the clothing worn by agricultural workers.[25]

A more pressing need began to assert itself after the initial successes of the Normandy landings in June 1944. From an early stage, it was decided to bring German prisoners to the United Kingdom. Initially, this was because there was no space or accommodation to house them in France and the Cabinet sanctioned a first draft of some 17,200 in July.[26] Later, however, other factors came into play. A report to the Cabinet in September revealed the poor conditions being endured by Germans held in France, the difficulties of feeding them and the dangers from the diphtheria outbreak in the Low Countries.[27] All of this meant that space had to be found for the Germans, and the only remedy was to try and create more secure camp space and guards by persuading more Italians to become co-operators.[28] To that end many of the restrictions were relaxed. Some earnings were made convertible into sterling, local shops, post offices and telephones were placed within bounds and visits to the cinema were made easier. Cycles could now be used for pleasure as well as work in an extended radius of five miles from the billet. Co-operators had only to observe a 10 p.m. curfew and were permitted to talk to members of the public and accept invitations to private houses. Two air-letters to Allied-occupied Italy were also to be allowed.[29] To try and persuade more non-co-operators to change their minds, subversive elements were to be removed from camps, and the remaining men balloted in secret.[30]

As the German prisoners began to arrive in the summer of 1944, so the import of Italians was halted.[31] With increasing numbers opting for co-operator status and the general relaxation of conditions, the Italians became almost an everyday sight in the many parts of the United Kingdom where they were employed. In addition, the range of work they did was greatly expanded. There was some discussion of their employment in factories, or even in mines. This latter idea was taken no further, but prisoners were now often placed in sole charge of lorries or tractors. Some co-operators even found themselves working directly for the RAF and there was discussion as to whether their officers could use the RAF Officers' mess.[32] For as long as the war in Europe continued, there were further concessions made to the Italian prisoners in terms of their security, ability to travel, mode of transport, access to public facilities and contact with the civilian population. Thus by November 1944 they had been permitted to exercise within five miles of their camps, enter shops and cinemas, have part of their remuneration paid in sterling, use bicycles for leisure activities and accept invitations to visit private houses.[33] Some activities did remain out-of-bounds although the authorities often had difficulty in producing precise guidelines to legislate for all eventualities. One example will have to suffice.

The Home Defence (Security) Executive (HD(S)E) had taken the view in July 1944 that in spite of the increased liberty granted to Italian co-operators, they should not be allowed in public houses, 'partly because of the danger of careless talk, and also because of the probable effect on the discipline of the co-operators and the effect on public opinion'.[34] Some months later in December, it was reported that the Doncaster police were considering legal action against an off-licensee who had sold beer to two Italian co-operators. This led to a complaint from the retailer's trade association pointing out that there was nothing in the existing regulations prohibiting such a sale. As it was deemed that the main thrust of the original HD(S)E regulation was to prevent the prisoners obtaining alcohol, a further explanatory circular was issued to off-licences throughout the country, albeit not until 9 March 1945.[35]

As the war ended, the Italian prisoners in Britain had achieved a degree of freedom unthinkable some four years earlier. This had come about as a result of several interrelated factors, all of which contributed to the amelioration of the prisoners' conditions of captivity. Firstly there was the need for maximum flexibility in the use of prisoners at minimum cost. Thus hostels and billeting replaced camp accommodation to bring the labour closer to where it was required. Increased access to public and personal transport served the same purpose. Guards were kept to a minimum and then dispensed with altogether. All of these measures were based on the stereotypical official British perception of the Italians as a docile and malleable labour force, a perception which was largely borne out by the prisoners' behaviour in captivity. After the Armistice and surrender, incentives had to be found for those prepared to co-operate in labour tasks beyond those permitted by the Geneva Convention. Further concessions on living conditions, rates of pay and access to civil society followed. These concessions were reinforced by pressure from the PWE. Its agenda was based on winning over hearts and minds rather than on labour productivity and the interests of the British war economy, but it nonetheless contributed to the climate of increasing acceptance of the Italians as more than just prisoners.

The British attitude to the prisoners was therefore dictated primarily by pragmatism and the need to make best use of the captives in order to further the war effort. However, most of this was done within the terms of the Geneva Convention, and even after the Italian surrender it was clear that every attempt was made to put changes onto an appropriate legal and therefore defensible basis. While it seems clear that the United Kingdom authorities did try to play by the rules as they understood them, the prisoners' perception of their treatment was another matter entirely.

In his study of the Italian prisoners' attitudes towards their captors and captivity in Britain, Lucio Sponza concludes that it was

> very complex, as it was affected by such factors as their individual cultural, political and social background; the prevailing sentiments in the camp; the way men related to each other, and to the more influential personalities amongst them; the unfolding of world events and the way prisoners came to know about them; changing personal circumstances; the type and frequency of the news they received from their kin in Italy; and – last but not least – the duration of their captivity and the expectation of it coming to an end.[36]

Given these many variables, it is impossible to draw many detailed conclusions about how the Italians reacted to their enforced captivity in the British Isles. However, some general trends can be identified. There is no doubt, for example, that the early arrivals did conform to the British authorities' stereotypical picture of them, not least because they had been specially selected to meet that very stereotype. Nonetheless, their passivity, eagerness to work and general lack of political opinion was remarked upon by many who came into contact with them. In the first years, dissent was rare, either at an individual or collective level, and usually involved protests against work which was either considered dangerous, or beyond that permitted by the Geneva Convention.[37] Almost inevitably, as the demand for prisoner labour increased and the screening became less intense, so a greater number of 'less reliable' prisoners found their way to the United Kingdom. Thus when Italy surrendered, the PWE produced an approximate categorisation of the prisoners which suggested that around 35 per cent were loyal to the house of Savoy and were prepared either to fight alongside the Allies or to work in British factories for the war effort; 50 per cent were of apolitical peasant stock; and the remaining 15 per cent were either Fascist, pro-German or malcontents who were against any form of co-operation.[38]

The same detailed memorandum also assessed the prisoners' responses to the rapidly changing war situation in the summer and autumn of 1943. Mussolini's fall was greeted initially with disbelief and dismissed as enemy propaganda. This was followed by a polarisation where the majority were 'secretly pleased' but the minority of ardent Fascists remained 'disappointed, apprehensive and downcast'.[39] This underwent something of a reversal when news of the surrender arrived, with all shades of opinion distressed and disheartened, although this may have been more a reaction to the lack of a compromise peace and the fact that Italy was to remain a battleground, than a feeling of national humiliation engendered by defeat. Polarisation returned with news of Mussolini's escape but the report indicates that those with continuing Fascist loyalties remained very much a minority group. However, this did not prevent some trouble in camps where both sides were well-represented, for example at Camp No. 40 (Tonbridge) where the Fascists tore down a portrait of the Italian King, only for it to be replaced by pro-Badoglio loyalists; or at Camp No. 46 (Petworth) where neither Victor Emmanuel nor Mussolini were mentioned at roll-call, to prevent disturbances.[40] These PWE reports tended to concentrate on the political agendas of the prisoners and their reaction to the Italian military and political situation, but for many of the men held captive in Britain their main concern was the material and physical well-being of their families in the light of changing circumstances.

The introduction of the scheme for Italians to become co-operators in April 1944 was to some extent mishandled by the authorities. Resentment had undoubtedly been building in all camps, and among all shades of opinion, that the surrender in September 1943 had not brought any material changes to the prisoners' status, nor any indication about their future. As a result, declining morale within the camps had become a cause for deep concern amongst PWE officials. Sir Percy Loraine, for one, had 'persistently, but in vain' warned his superiors of the poor psychological effects produced by the enforced retention of their POW status.[41] The co-operator scheme invited prisoners to volunteer their labour for the Allied war effort and receive certain privileges in return. Ostensibly, this could have benefited all parties, but in practice there were many difficulties. In July 1944, a letter from a woman who had been used as an interpreter and hospital visitor to Italian prisoners in Cambridge reported that co-belligerents had seen their initial privileges slowly withdrawn to the point where, only a few months after the scheme had begun, they were 'in a much unhappier situation than when they were prisoners'. Hospital and camp visits were now forbidden, as was reading material in Italian.[42] The apparently draconian attitude of the camp commandant in Cambridge may have had something to do with the 'mutiny' at the Ely camp a few weeks before, and have been locally inspired, but there was clear dissatisfaction with the scheme from co-belligerents in many parts of the country.

The situation was summed up by a PWE report which noted the scheme's damaging effect on its political warfare campaigns. Co-belligerency was thought to be failing because there had been no prior agreement with the Italian government, the authorities had failed to explain the scheme to the prisoners properly, the NCOs and chaplains in the camps who owed their status and appointment to their Fascist zeal had been left in positions of authority, and perhaps most telling of all, the rewards offered to co-operators were insufficient.[43] Two other practical factors were also noted: the continuing penal rate of exchange for prisoners attempting to send money home, and the unsatisfactory postal arrangements between the UK and liberated Italy.[44]

By the end of 1944, postal censorship of Italian prisoners' letters reported a good deal of praise for their treatment. Their British officers came in for praise, as did their employers. One long-established prisoner at Camp No. 63 (Alyth, Perthshire) even went so far as to say that 'I no longer remember that I am an Italian. I have already been two and a half years in Scotland, which seems like my own country.'[45] Another made the telling point that 'we had a very good Christmas – a hundred times better than last year'. Conversely, there were also complaints that they were worked too hard or that working conditions were poor. However, the most vitriolic complaints were reserved for the postal and censorship systems and the Red Cross. Three comments extracted by the censors give a flavour of the prisoners' thoughts on the subject:

> Those brigands at the Censorship do not let the mail through. What fault is it of ours if they have made us prisoner? I would be glad if it were they who never heard news from their families.

> How does the Red Cross fulfil its obligations? … Can the expense of forwarding a few hundredweights of mail be so great? I am sure that it is not the expense but the lack of will and of understanding. They should all be ashamed of themselves.

> These barbarians keep us without mail. I am tired of writing because these wretches only tear up and burn my letters. Then they say the Red Cross looks after prisoners. Let them put a Red Cross on their stomachs in memory of their interest.[46]

For men out of contact with their families for years, this venting of spleen is hardly surprising, especially when it was obvious that their letters would be read by one of their targets. While the humble censors could do little to change matters, they did note that complaints about postal communication were twice as numerous from prisoners with families in German-occupied Italy than from those who communicated with Allied-occupied zones.[47]

While the vast majority of prisoners accepted the inevitability of an Allied victory and expressed themselves well pleased with their treatment, for the minority of self-declared Fascists, the events of 1944 and early 1945 provided a mixed diet. As the prisoners were encouraged to become co-operators, it was the diehard Fascists who were isolated by their refusal to co-operate and ultimately collected together in non-co-operator camps. To some extent, they were able to dismiss bad news as propaganda while welcoming good news such as the Germans' Ardennes offensive. It was also noted by the Foreign Office that this one German advance had also exposed the true feelings of many who had become co-operators: 'when the Germans made their push through the Ardennes at the end of December, the Italian co-operator prisoners in the Midlands immediately became idle and extremely insolent – so much for the genuineness of their anti-Nazi feelings'.[48] Many non-co-operators were also moved to record in letters home their thoughts on Mussolini's broadcast from Milan on 16 December. 'Imagine our joy on hearing our leader's broadcast!' wrote one, while another reflected on his change of mood: 'I am now tranquil because five days ago I heard the voice of the Master. In accents stronger than ever he declared that our beautiful Italy will surely rise again soon. How glad I shall be when you return into his hands.'[49]

At least one group of Fascist prisoners at Camp No. 14 (Doonfoot, Ayrshire) had been unable to hear Mussolini, having previously been deprived of their radio set by their camp commandant, making it impossible for them to hear news from German-occupied Italy. Ostensibly because of this, a mass escape took place on the night of 15–16 December when a total of 94 men used a tunnel under the camp wire and dispersed into the Scottish countryside. While this had clearly been planned in advance, the escapees had little idea of what to do with their freedom. Police and soldiers were mobilised and most of the fugitives were recaptured within a matter of days; some were found trying to scrounge food in the vicinity while others were apprehended on the outskirts of Glasgow.[50] The authorities noted that the camp contained only malcontents who had been removed from labour camps as unfit for employment or difficult to control, particularly by the types of guard available. However, their escape seems to have been little more than a protest. Most expressed themselves 'refreshed' by their experience of freedom and others were just happy to have made some trouble for their captors.[51] Although mass breakouts were rare, the monthly reports of the Imperial Prisoners of War Committee record a steady stream of Italian escapes from camps, hostels and billets. Many of these were really cases of men going absent without leave rather than attempts to escape and leave the country. For example, in January 1945 there were only three individual escapes, and apart from another collective attempt by 39 non co-operators in March 1945, the number of escapees seldom attained double figures in any one month. Besides, observed one senior Home Office official: 'If a prisoner managed to reach the continent in a small boat he would be little better off than in this country.'[52]

Nevertheless, there were several near successes by a small hard-core element determined to escape. For instance, during the night of 10–11 July 1944, four 'special class' Italian prisoners escaped from a POW camp near Haddington in East Lothian. They were discovered missing during the morning roll-call, but were arrested five hours later at the nearby RAF station at East Fortune. The four men, all members of the Royal Italian Air Force, had spent a remarkable three-and-a-half hours skulking around the aerodrome before being discovered. It was revealed during their interrogation that, using a map taken from an old atlas as their guide, they had planned to steal an aircraft and escape to Germany or Italy to continue the fight against the Allies. The problem was that the prisoner pilot, who had been captured in 1942, was not, unsurprisingly, conversant with the control panel and gauges of the Mosquito bomber he had chosen for their flight to freedom. As a result, he could not get the aircraft started and 'was therefore afraid to take off'. When confronted by his comrades as to why they were not going anywhere, he assured them that the plane carried no fuel. On the contrary, upon closer inspection it was discovered that it had 560 gallons in its tanks![53]

While the general perception of the Italians as a docile, if slightly less than efficient, workforce may have been generally true, it would be wrong to assume that problems did not exist. The monthly return for January 1945 recorded a number of strikes: 75 co-operators refused to work without greatcoats, having been issued with capes instead; prisoners at Romsey in Hampshire complained about wages and food in kind; and non-co-operators employed at St Columb in Cornwall struck for higher wages and protested about working in snow and the severe punishments meted out by the guards. In fact, of the 154,000 Italian POWs in the United Kingdom by April 1945 over 40,000 or 37 per cent remained on non-co-operative status despite the new work incentives.[54] Subsequent months saw stoppages when prisoners were forced to walk to work rather than use the train, or where working hours had been lengthened. Strike action seems to have died away as the war against Germany ended, as did other recorded forms of crimes and misdemeanours. Most numerous were charges of fraternisation with (female) civilians, including women from enemy alien families. There were also cases of insubordination, larceny, gross indecency and assault on men, women and children. Occasionally there were charges of unlawful intercourse with

under-age girls, and cases of rape. The last were habitually dealt with by
the civil courts but the others remained under military jurisdiction.[55] The
decline in recorded cases may have been due to the war's end and heightened expectation of early repatriation, but may also have been a function
of the authorities now seeing fraternisation and minor assaults as less
important and unworthy of further action.

By May of 1945, the Italians were still voicing some complaints about
their treatment. A sympathetic PWE reported that the co-operators felt
that they were still not being afforded the respect that their status
demanded. Their uniforms, although green, were not proper military
uniform, and they were not paid the same rates as British soldiers or
civilians for the work they did on behalf of the war economy. Furthermore, their leisure activities continued to be limited by curfews and by
local restrictions imposed by military commands on their movements
and access to cinemas, cafés, barbers' shops, restaurants and dance
halls.[56] These measures continued to cause irritation among the co-
operators, although as we have seen, the number of serious complaints
seems to have fallen off by the spring of 1945.

Even at this stage, there was still some attempt being made by the PWE
to persuade Italians to become co-operators, something that at least
49,000 had steadfastly refused to do. The reasons for this were manifold.
Some were considered far too dangerous to be offered the opportunity to
co-operate. Dyed-in-the-wool Fascists and members of Fascist militia or
political units were always excluded, as were elements from the
Carabinieri. Among those who were eligible, some of the reasons given
for retaining their original prisoner status were that they would otherwise sacrifice their protection under the Geneva Convention,[57] that
there were few real material advantages to becoming a co-operator, and
that it was for the Italian government to instruct them to co-operate.
Discussion of this third point produced an interesting response from
the PWE. While it was thought that a large number of prisoners would
agree to change their status if the Italian government was allowed to
contact its soldiers, the disadvantages probably outweighed the advantages. Propaganda from the Italian government was to be avoided

> because some of this literature would undoubtedly be Communist or
> literature representing extreme Leftist views. Togliatti, a Minister
> who is generally regarded in Italy as Stalin's representative on the
> Italian Government, would certainly wish to send Communist liter-
> ature, and it would be difficult for us to veto this without the fact
> reaching the ears of the Russian Government.[58]

Clearly, in these last days of hostilities, Cold War agendas and wider issues of inter-allied co-operation were beginning to take precedence over more mundane issues surrounding the conduct of the war.

The chief reason given for non-co-operation by the prisoners was the possibility that those with families in German-held areas of Northern Italy would be victimised by the Nazis or the Fascists.[59] Some prisoners were reported to have received letters from family members indicating that this had happened, but it must also have been a very potent weapon in the hands of ardent Fascists inside the camps to stop their comrades defecting. In some respects, this factor had been exacerbated by British policy (and specifically Churchill's injunction) after the surrender to bring in prisoners whose homes were in German-occupied northern Italy and who could have no claim for early repatriation. Only the gradual rolling back of German forces and the liberation of all Italian territory early in 1945 removed this constraint on the prisoners' actions.

With hindsight, the complaints of the Italians in captivity in the United Kingdom did not amount to much, especially when compared with the sufferings endured by their compatriots who had been captured by the Red Army or interned by the Nazis after September 1943 and deported to work for the German war economy. Nevertheless, their grievances were keenly felt and undoubtedly coloured their attitudes to their captors, even if some of their complaints were probably based on misconceptions. The PWE again provides some evidence of this confusion, noting in September 1944 that many prisoners billeted in isolated areas remained unsure as to whether they were co-operators or not. Similarly, much of the animosity towards the authorities on the conversion of earnings into lira and their remission to relatives in Italy was based on out-of-date information and abandoned practices. By this time, the British government had undertaken to provide a more realistic conversion rate of £ = 400 lira rather than the penal £ = 72 lira insisted upon by Mussolini in 1940.[60] Ultimately, however, these grievances were afforded less and less attention as the war in Europe came to an end, and the whole question of morale among the 154,000 Italians then held in the United Kingdom became inextricably linked to the possibilities of repatriation.

The Italian prisoners and the British public

Almost from the moment when Mussolini's Fascist regime came into the war in June 1940, public opinion in Britain had been ambivalent towards the Italians. They were perceived as less threatening than their German Axis partners, but at the same time they were despised, both for their actions in Abyssinia, and for the 'cowardly' way they had joined the war against France. Events in the Middle East early in the war tended to reinforce the idea that the Italian Army was not very strong militarily and their soldiers had little heart for the fight. Thus public perception largely mirrored that of the authorities who were prepared to countenance the import of Italian prisoners to supplement the domestic labour force. Moreover, this view of the Italians was, if anything, reinforced when they began to arrive in the United Kingdom in large numbers. The arrival of a troopship with 10,000 prisoners on board led a *Times* correspondent to comment on the differences between the Italians and their Axis allies:

> As they came ashore from a liner the contrast in the attitude of the two peoples was very noticeable. The Italians ran down the gangway, some smiling, a few silent, but all obviously thankful to be out of the war, and gave no trouble as their escort shepherded them to the train ... Arrogance and surliness were portrayed by the Germans. Nearly all turned their faces away from the camera.[61]

If these official reports made the Italians appear benign and ideally suited to the tasks of prisoner labourers, this was reinforced by the public's first-hand experiences. As early as November 1941, another correspondent to *The Times* wrote to praise prisoners in one particular camp for having offered the value of their week's wages to the poor of the parish.[62] In March 1943, Mass Observation attempted a survey of their reporters' and diarists' views on specific nationalities. While this was no more than a snapshot, the results do provide an interesting insight to public perceptions of the Italians in general and, occasionally, of the prisoners in their midst.[63] The timing of this exercise is important. By March 1943, the war in North Africa was coming to an end, and attention was shifting to the expected assault on Italy itself. At one level, British propaganda at home seems to have been directed towards belittling the Italian war effort and making fun of the Italian armed forces. At the same time, there were attempts to break up the Axis and to dissociate the Italian people, who were portrayed as being war-weary, from their leadership who, it was argued, had misled them. In other words, they were more sinned against than sinners and therefore deserving of some compassion. These differing pictures were mirrored in the responses from Mass Observation reporters and diarists about Italians:

The contempt shown by many of our cartoonists, music-hall jokers and journalists is greatly overdone. The Italian is, to me, a more acceptable member of the European family than many who think themselves their superiors. They are the victims of a swash-buckling regime that has vainly tried to make a blood and iron breed of them. I hope that we shall eventually re-establish our traditional friendship with them – though not with Mussolini.[64]

Or more directly: 'For all the jokes about the Italians, they are not such a bad lot.'[65]

There were some respondents who had not a single good word for the Italians. 'Mediterranean rats' and 'Small fry' were two of the printable replies.[66] Another had a more extensive line in bile: 'a gang of treacherous, screaming pimps with a flair for stabbing in the back. Any nation whose "men" drench themselves in perfume as many Italians do is not worth the concern of decent people.'[67] However, the overwhelming majority were far more charitable than this. While there were some who professed to despise the Italians, many others focused on their non-military character and their having been led astray by Mussolini's leadership:

We have a proprietary feeling towards the Italians. Did we not help form their nation? We cannot believe they are malignant, as the Germans are, or treacherous and cunning, as the Jap(anese). They are fat and rather lazy, they sell us ice cream when we are young, and chianti when we are older. It is monstrous that they should be terrorised into war by that bandit Mussolini.[68]

When it came to direct contact with prisoners, the responses were even more positive. 'Pleasant' and 'friendly' were frequently used as descriptions.[69] Others went into greater detail. 'Affable, easy going [and] content to make the best of their incarceration' was one response; 'Glad to be out of the war', another.[70] A farmer in Worcester who had prisoners working for him noted that they were: 'charming, gay, hardworking and entirely illiterate. "War no good" is one phrase they know well from frequent practice. They are of peasant stock from the South, hate the Germans and believe all news to be propaganda.'[71] Another report of Italians working on the land in the autumn of 1941 noted their enthusiasm and the farmer's opinion that two of them were worth any ten casual labourers he could employ.[72] On the whole, the public response to the prisoners was a positive one. One Mass Observation diarist summed this up: 'Few people, I think, dislike the Italians, even today. Prisoners in this country are shown kindness not demanded by the most liberal interpretation of International Law.'[73]

Certainly there was little animosity shown towards the prisoners. A number of women recorded how good they were with children,[74] and there were plenty or references to them being 'nice' and 'hardworking'. Some young women were able to get closer to the prisoners than the authorities (or their parents) would have liked. Given the numbers of Italians employed in agriculture, it was inevitable that they would find themselves working alongside girls from the Women's Land Army. A former member recalled one such encounter in the autumn of 1943:

> The mob of Italians were not wanted and only three came. We were stacking a hay-rick, three Italians and three girls, and then things started happening. Two in long kisses, and then the other two started larking about throwing hay which smothered the remaining Italian and myself … I thought everything appalling and disgusting, yet how sorry for those fellows I feel, prisoners for nearly three years, a girl on a haystack must be a very tempting proposition with no one around.[75]

Other Land Girls were less well disposed towards their Italian fellow workers:

> The Italians were disgusting, and bone idle. They'd spend all day cutting up one log. We were supposed to be picked up by their lorry every morning to go to the forest where we were working. When we climbed in, their hands would be everywhere and whoever was supposed to be in charge of them did nothing. When we got to the forest you didn't dare go to the lavatory … they'd be lying in wait to grab you. We were only kids. It really wasn't fair. It got so bad we refused to go in the lorry with them. We said we'd rather walk to work.[76]

Apart from their general behaviour, the Italians were also resented because they received better clothing and better working conditions and hours than the women working alongside them, a point made forcibly in February 1945 by the MP for Fyfe East, Henderson Stewart in an article for the *Daily Sketch*.[77]

Resentment also came from other quarters. Stereotypes and prejudices were trotted out, but some of these were undoubtedly deep-rooted or based on negative wartime experiences. For example, one woman employed as a bus conductress during the war whose husband had been captured in Libya by the Italians and remained a prisoner in German hands until 1945 explained her personal bitterness. 'There were so many prisoners of war … going with English girls, getting on English buses, going where they liked. … Your husband was behind wire and there [they were,] running around everywhere.'[78] Other views were derived from the general thrust of British propaganda. Italians were 'lazy', 'childlike', 'easily led' or characterised as ice-cream sellers, but many responses were more considered and demonstrated sympathy for those who had traditionally been regarded as friends.

While this may have been true at a general level, it did not preclude the possibility of friction between the prisoners, who had increasing levels of freedom, and local populations. In April 1943, the MP for Grantham, W. D. Kendall, received a complaint from a constituent about Italian prisoners being seen riding 'almost new' bicycles unescorted when war workers were 'unable to obtain cycles except after very long waiting periods'.[79] While the War Office excused both the lack of escorts and the use of bicycles on the basis of getting the maximum value from the prisoners' labour, a further complaint from the same county came from women land workers who had stopped work because Italians from a nearby stone quarry had been allowed to roam 'almost at will'. They categorically refused to return until the Italians were placed under 'proper' guard.[80] Reactions of this type were quite common by 1943, and there were also complaints about prisoners being conveyed in lorries when ordinary workers had to walk, and their being given preference for severely rationed supplies.[81]

As co-operator Italians were given greater freedom during their leisure time after the spring of 1944, different tensions started to appear. There were complaints in the House of Commons about Italians being 'permitted to overcrowd omnibuses and the cinema at Coleshill',[82] and about their being accommodated at Shaftesbury in Dorset, where the Council protested to every conceivable department in Whitehall 'in the strongest possible terms' that women in the town had already been molested by Italians stationed nearby.[83] In Saffron Walden, the mayor had agreed to ban Italians from Town Hall dances after protests from British and American servicemen. Interestingly, he had earlier refused to impose a colour-bar on negro soldiers after objections from their white American counterparts.[84]

There remained some further problems – for example, when the siting of new camps and hostels collided with the burgeoning number of military airfields being constructed, or when the only available hostels for essential work were too close to other military installations and additional restrictions had to be placed on the prisoners' movements.[85]

These, however, were exceptional and the general trend was for greater freedom. Guard details on prisoners were gradually reduced and further concessions were made for their material and spiritual health. In May 1943, the War Office's DPW suggested that prisoners be allowed to cycle unescorted to church on a Sunday. By March 1944 the HD(S)E raised no objections to the employment of Italian POWs on work which would involve them being away from their quarters during the hours of darkness, provided the necessary escorts were available. This relaxation, however, did not apply to prisoners whose work or camps were in a restricted area.[86]

Virulent protests also emanated from London, where some co-operators were brought in to work for the Ministry of War Transport and to clear bomb damage.[87] Although there were some reservations about this plan, early signs were encouraging. One hundred and fifty men were brought in to work side-by-side with local labour on a standard 65-hour week. Within a month, both Surrey County Council and Croydon Borough Council declared the scheme an 'unqualified success', noting that the best work was obtained if they were kept apart from British labour and put under the supervision of a suitable and understanding foreman.[88] In addition, on 1 August 1944, the *News Chronicle* reported that an Italian had been severely injured while shielding a young boy from a bomb blast. Six other prisoners were also badly injured.[89]

This sympathetic treatment did not last. Men were moved out of tents into vacant housing in Acton, Pinner and Hatch End in order to comply with the terms of the Geneva Convention.[90] In some cases, they were used to renovate the houses, but so great was the local protest, and the concomitant press campaign,[91] that they were rapidly removed to make way for bombed-out families from other parts of London.[92] Elsewhere in the metropolitan area, there was at least one report of a fight between prisoners and civilians on Kew Bridge, but more problems were encountered in the East End which required the attention of the Metropolitan Police Commissioner himself. Bethnal Green had seen a number of 'incidents' between prisoners and the local population, and the police were worried that the 'very rough elements' in that area might provoke more serious breakdowns of public order.[93]

A Home Office circular to survey the behaviour of Italian POWs in all Metropolitan Police divisions in January 1945 revealed very few causes for concern.[94] Superintendents were asked about the prisoners' general behaviour, and any instances of their accosting or insulting women, or being encouraged (by women) to break disciplinary rules. They were also asked to comment on public attitudes towards the prisoners and whether a greater use of Military Police might be advisable. In every division bar one, such an idea was deemed unnecessary and general behaviour was uniformly described as 'good'.[95] Only isolated incidents of indiscipline were recorded, usually when locals engaged in verbal provocation, or in cases of fraternisation. Occasionally this resulted in violence. For example, when a prisoner working at New Cross Gate railway station was reprimanded by a foreman for striking up a friendship with a female carriage-cleaner, the prisoner assaulted the foreman, biting him in the ear and neck, and was imprisoned for two years by a subsequent court-martial.[96] Most cases were more minor in nature, but it was accepted that the prisoners' camps did provide a 'source of attraction to young females' and that 'in the poorer districts some females, particularly young girls, [were] inclined to force their attentions on the Italians'.[97] Thus in some divisions, steps were taken to provide a greater police presence to act as a deterrent. Most police reports, however, indicated little ill-feeling towards the Italians. The Superintendent at Cannon Row station reported that the matter had not even been discussed at Hyde Park Corner, 'a favourite spot for observations by speakers and listeners on current or "thorny" subjects'. There were some objections to their using shops or cinemas, especially when it meant that ordinary citizens were excluded or disadvantaged,[98] and only some degree of envy when they were conveyed to work by specially provided motor bus while other workers had to queue for public transport.[99]

Although there were few serious problems recorded by the authorities, there is no doubt that Italian prisoners were subjected to a good deal of verbal and sometimes physical abuse from local people throughout the war. The first drafts of agriculturalists in 1941 and 1942 apparently neither spoke nor understood much English, and therefore could not understand the precise import of what was said to them, but this level of incomprehension did not last long. In November 1944, the commandant of the 122nd Italian Labour Battalion stationed at Rayners Lane in North London received a long letter from an Italian Major outlining the treatment being meted out to his men. He spoke of an 'incessant' press campaign against his men, and 'cases of insults, provocations and even spitting … as everyday occurrences'. He went on: 'It is not comforting, Dear Commandant, for a soldier who after having worked conscientiously for eight hours, to be spat on. The public has described the co-operator with the most injurious titles, i.e. "WOP", "Lazy Devils", "Third Rate People".'[100] In the same month, Ernest Bevin as Minister of Labour reported to the Cabinet on the peculiar problems of using Italians in London, noting that the accommodation of prisoners in houses which might otherwise have been used to accommodate the bombed-out was the only alternative if the urgent work they were doing was to be completed. Interestingly, Bevin blamed part of the problem on a press campaign stirring up ill-will and asked for the Ministry of Information to try and moderate the line taken by the newspapers.[101]

Even allowing for the possibility of a concerted press campaign against the Italians, the authorities nevertheless had to tread a narrow tightrope between making enough concessions to attract and maintain the morale of Italian prisoners as co-operators while at the same time maintaining sufficient restrictions to satisfy public opinion which, although willing to take a benign view, had a clear view of what was acceptable and what was not. Careful note was taken of public reaction to the increased privileges granted to co-operators.[102] Certainly, public opinion became noticeably less well-disposed towards them. They were often excluded from canteens, including those of the Women's Voluntary Service. There was a widespread view that they should be sent home to liberate their own country, epitomised by the phrase 'why should our boys be killed while Italians are living off the fat of the land'.[103] Elsewhere, there were complaints about their amorous disposition, their insolence, their laziness, their bicycles and the fact that they received Players cigarettes in tins while British soldiers got Park Drive loose.[104]

This highlighted the dilemma of the authorities. Faced with continuing public disapproval of the freedoms granted to the Italians, they nonetheless had to find ways to make co-operator status more attractive to the prisoners. This became even more important as Allied forces sustained heavy losses in the campaign to liberate Northern Italy and was reflected in a War Office memorandum in early November 1944 which commented on the implementation of these more relaxed rules for co-operators:

> Fraternisation with females. This is strongly resented by the public although it is admitted there is often encouragement by irresponsible girls. Co-operators have been seen walking arm in arm with females and this practice must cease. They will not be permitted to make ... unwelcome approaches to women and will refrain from forcing their attentions on anyone.[105]

Interestingly, this did not deal specifically with occasions where the approaches were not unwelcome, but Commandants were also instructed to use their initiative in restricting prisoners' visits to the cinema and public places, and to exclude them from public transport. This was widely reported in the press as the War Office yielded to public pressure by issuing guidelines on the interpretation of these new freedoms.[106]

The other complication as far as the authorities were concerned came from the trade unions' response to the use of prisoners as a labour supply. Government records indicate the care taken to make sure union opinion was canvassed and taken into consideration throughout the war. In the early stages, there was no question of the prisoners being paid, and union concern was mainly directed towards making sure that employers were charged a market rate for their Italian labour force by the state. As the range of employment was extended beyond the agricultural sphere, the authorities continued to tread warily and made clear that prisoners would only be introduced into new trades with the agreement of the (local) workforce and the trade unions.[107] This did not mean that friction was entirely absent. At a meeting of the liaison committee between government and unions at the end of 1944, some disquiet was voiced by the trade union side about a proposal to employ appropriate Italians as skilled labour to maximise their usefulness. This had been raised in a paper at the beginning of the year, but not fully discussed. However, the TUC representatives noted that they had received a number of complaints from the Engineering Joint Trades Movement about the use of Italians to replace British men in that industry called up into the services.[108] For the time being at least, these complaints could not be addressed as the state began to look towards manpower planning beyond the end of the war in Europe.

With hindsight, it is clear that a good deal of time and effort was wasted on schemes for Italian prisoners that never came to fruition. For example, whatever plans PWE may have had for the political re-education of Italians on British soil, these were invariably subordinated to the needs of the Ministry of Agriculture, and later other government departments. While the battle for hearts and minds was considered important in some government circles, most saw its main purpose as providing a docile labour force in the short term. Only the PWE and the British administration in liberated Italy had visions of a bigger picture which involved influencing postwar political reconstruction in the aftermath of the Mussolini regime.

It is also remarkable that, just as the tortuous negotiations to create a status for the Italian prisoners which would allow their continued and increased use as a flexible labour supply were being resolved in the late spring of 1944, military and political imperatives effectively brought increased use of Italians in Britain to an end. Although co-belligerency and the creation of co-operators provided the legal framework for the continued employment of Italians already in the United Kingdom, further imports of labour were ended to make way for the increasing numbers of Germans being captured after 6 June 1944. Thus the number of

Italian prisoners reached a peak of 158,029, and although their fate continued to be bound up with the course of the war in Europe, by the late summer of 1944 the defeat of Nazi Germany was becoming more and more likely, and with it the possibility of a return home. Finally, while the British public's perception of the Italians in their midst remained conditioned by a wealth of different factors, there is no doubt that they were widely, if sometimes grudgingly, accepted and undoubtedly left an indelible and enduring impression on many people who encountered them during their sojourn in the British Isles.

8
Freedom, Farming and Frustration: Italians in Africa and Australia, 1943–5

One of the key problems for the British and their Commonwealth partners throughout the war was the maintenance of good morale amongst the Italian POW population. Without it, their use as an all-important stopgap in the domestic labour market would have been negligible. However, as we have seen, the surrender of Italy in September 1943 actually threatened to unravel the entire policy at a time when the restrictions on the use of Italian POW labour were being eased and more captives were being earmarked for work outside the camps. Using censored extracts from outgoing POW mail, Middle Eastern intelligence summaries noted the confusion which existed within the POW ranks throughout Africa brought about by Italy's collapse. A large but unspecified number of POWs conceived the idea that as soon as the Armistice had been signed that they would be released. One soldier declared that his chief cause of concern was that 'he and his comrades [were] prisoners not of the Allies but of fellow Italians'. In East Africa there continued to be a 'strange mixture of sentiments' on the question of co-belligerency. Some were nonchalant about their future while others were adamant that they would never volunteer to co-operate with the Allies as long as they remained POWs. Others expressed utter contempt for the Germans, while yet more stated they would never fight for the Allies, especially Russia, whatever happened.[1]

Running in tandem with the fluid nature of POW morale was the equally problematic issue of the relationship between the civil population and the increasing number of POWs on outside employment. If POWs grew more resentful of their POW status now that Italy was a co-belligerent, became more truculent and began to withdraw their labour in protest, what would be the consequences for the POW authorities responsible for maintaining discipline both within and outside the camps? Moreover, what consequences would this have for those who still wanted to work for the Allies, but were increasingly exposed to hostile elements within the civilian population who refused to accept the need for POWs to be granted what they saw as unlimited freedom outside the barbed wire? In the end, the value of their work far outweighed these concerns over internal security. Nevertheless, there are noticeable differences in the way in which each of the detaining powers handled these delicate issues between 1943 and 1945.

Economic benefit: political threat

One of the problems which contributed to the increased tension between prisoners, especially in South Africa, was the delay in the implementation of a segregation policy. Regular and detailed censorship reports from the Middle East throughout 1941 had alerted Pretoria of the need to monitor the situation, in particular the swings in POW morale. However, the immediate concern that year had been the urgent removal of as many POWs from the Middle East as possible and the establishment of a suitable camp system to accommodate a rapidly expanding prisoner population. Therefore, attempts by the military authorities in South Africa, as elsewhere, to separate the 'sheep from the goats' had made very little progress by late 1942.[2]

Eventually, segregation plans were drafted and resources mobilised for what became an important wartime activity. However, the tardiness with which the segregation policy was initiated in South Africa, combined with the internal threat from elements of the Afrikaner right, not only increased the tension between elements within the POW community, but also added an extra dimension to internal security if and when these prisoners were to be paroled to work outside the camps. One of the key security dangers came from protected personnel such as medical officers and chaplains. In early 1942, Auchinleck, as C-in-C Middle East, had raised 'strong objections' with the War Office over the issue of captured Italian officers being allowed to take long strolls without an escort while on parole. He was particularly concerned with those regulations regarding chaplains. Under the Geneva Convention chaplains were granted parole and allowed to attend mass without an escort within a three-mile radius of the camp. With over 50,000 Italian inhabitants in Egypt and unsettled political conditions in nearby Palestine, however, escorts were deemed essential because of the 'known political tendencies of Italian padres'. The primacy of security, especially in such a valuable strategic location, was paramount, whatever the legal privileges granted under international law.[3]

This lesson did not go unheeded in Pretoria. In October 1941, Union Defence Force (UDF) authorities were experiencing difficulties in controlling effectively the movement of POW chaplains and medical officers who insisted on claiming their full rights, to the freedom of movement under the Convention. Pretoria had refused to concede these rights, arguing that Zonderwater was located in a sensitive military area. After consultation with London, it was decided that only the medical officers would receive their entitled parole and that it would be restricted to a one-mile radius from the camp with an unarmed escort. The wisdom to exclude the camp chaplains from this concession became evident in December 1941 when the Chief Censor in Cape Town recorded that: 'Altars continue to form the rallying points for pseudo-religious enthusiasm which too lightly veils the patriotic and Fascist current underlying it, and shows that some Chaplains whilst caring spiritually for their flock are not averse to injecting some Fascist dope along with the heavenly manna.'[4]

In September 1942, the Adjutant-General's (AG) branch informed the Defence Department that the Camp Commandant at Zonderwater had from time to time been specially instructed to deal with Fascist elements in his camp. The censorship of POW mail had been a crucial weapon in the scrutinisation of potential troublemakers. As a result, several thousand had already been segregated and moved to separate blocks, which the authorities hoped would stop the active spread of Fascist propaganda amongst the remaining inmates at Zonderwater. In other words, 'birds of a feather were best [kept] together in a camp of their own', thus preventing the contamination of the rest of the population. But Colonel R. D. Pilkington-Jordan had to admit that the difficulty his colleagues faced when confronting Fascism amongst the POWs was that by far the large majority of them *were* Fascists. 'The most that can be done is to deal with the active elements amongst them and to suppress such positive mischief as they may be able to create.'[5]

Unquestionably, despite the efforts of Allied intelligence officers, Fascist cells carried out their activities, in some cases even expanding them. Reports from Cairo in May 1942 indicated that Zonderwater in particular was a centre of well-organised Fascist activities which, it was alleged, the South African authorities did very little to check. Interviews with prisoners and reports from POW stool pigeons indicated that a clear chain of command existed where orders were issued by Fascist medical officers in the camp hospital and enthusiastically carried out by NCOs. Cell activities included the blacklisting of anti-Fascists and the sanctioning of disciplinary action against recalcitrant individuals. Beatings were a common occurrence, and although rumours of murder could not be confirmed, POWs were of the opinion that had they taken place the camp authorities would have been none the wiser, 'as they never seemed to know whether the correct number of POWs was in the camp at any given time'. These, and other allegations which included charges of collusion amongst camp staff – some of whom were accused of being Nazi sympathisers – were immediately contested by Pretoria.[6] Slowly but surely, South African authorities began to master the hard lessons their counterparts in Britain and the rest of the Empire had had to learn about controlling Fascist activity within the camps. Throughout 1942, rules and regulations were tightened and a series of countermeasures were implemented including a more rigorous segregation policy. Eventually, progress was made, but Fascist activities at Zonderwater never entirely disappeared. One British military liaison officer, Captain C. Wilson, reported as late as March 1944 that propaganda campaigns within and between camps continued to be orchestrated by unrepentant Fascists against their non-Fascist comrades. For instance, prisoners were intimidated with the threat of a 'Special War Tribunal' which they were told they would have to face on their return to Italy.[7]

It is worth remembering, however, the comment made by one Foreign Office official that 'the best propaganda among prisoners is good food, comfortable quarters and facilities for recreation' – hence the emphasis by the Imperial Prisoners of War Committee (IPOWC) to encourage camp commandants throughout the empire to develop robust programmes of organised sport, arts and crafts and amateur dramatics within the POW compounds. Not only were these activities the best antidotes to boredom, but also, and more significantly, the simple things in life could do more in winning the battle for hearts and minds than any officially sponsored re-education policy.[8] Nonetheless, some military authorities questioned the quantity of rations that POWs were consuming. In May 1941, one official noted during his tour of Italian POW camps in India that the POWs were putting on 'considerable weight' owing to the 'unnecessarily large ration' being issued.[9] And there were, at times, striking differences between the quality and quantity of food provided in camps in the United Kingdom as opposed to those in Egypt, Kenya and South Africa. The prisoners themselves were keenly aware of the differences in the conditions and standard of living, not only between individual camps but also between the host countries and colonies. A Pietermaritzburg inmate, Eugenio Bizzarro, wrote to a friend and fellow prisoner incarcerated at POW Camp No. 359 at Burguret in Kenya, of the treatment he was receiving in Natal. Lodged in comfortable tents complete with electric light, Bizzarro gleefully told his friend that in the morning they had coffee with real milk. Food was plentiful, especially the fruit and vegetables, which were fresh. There was discipline, but Bizzarro praised the organisation of the camp as perfect:

> Luxury kitchens run with coal ranges, water the whole 24 hours of the day. Payment in cash … In the canteen … you can buy all God's good things. Clothing: civilian felt hat, colour blue; black civilian overcoat, lined; personal linen and jerseys of the most special kinds, fully fitted razor, 'Autostrop'. Altogether a Paradise. At noon everybody in a comfortable mess served by guards. Everything in greatest abundance from food to clothing … No more [Kikuyu] but South Africans who are treating us quite differently from what it used to be in Kenya. In short, dear Forte, this is the life in South Africa, climate very good, camp very spacious.[10]

Another contented POW in the same camp summed up his treatment quite succinctly: 'I eat well and have got fat.'[11]

Such glowing reports of conditions in South Africa created problems for POW administrators in Kenya. In March 1944, the GOC East Africa protested that POWs transferred from East Africa to South Africa found the conditions in South Africa much more congenial. As a result, POWs in East Africa were becoming increasingly non-co-operative in the hope that they would be transferred to South Africa. This, in turn, threatened to undermine the co-operator programme and reduce the pool of POW labour in East Africa. In order to stabilise the situation, they advised London to suspend the transfer of able-bodied Italian POWs to South Africa.[12]

The War Office was also increasingly concerned with the pampered lifestyle many Italian POWs seemingly enjoyed in South Africa. The most flagrant breaches of discipline stemmed from those who had been paroled to work for employers, mainly farmers, outside the camp system. They were treated far too leniently by employers, recorded one officer, and as a whole enjoyed 'almost unrestricted freedom', in spite of the explicit instructions contained in the employment agreement which every civilian employer had to sign.[13] There were problems of supervision, which in some cases exposed POWs to politically minded Afrikaner employers who, sympathetic to the *Ossewabrandwag*, the

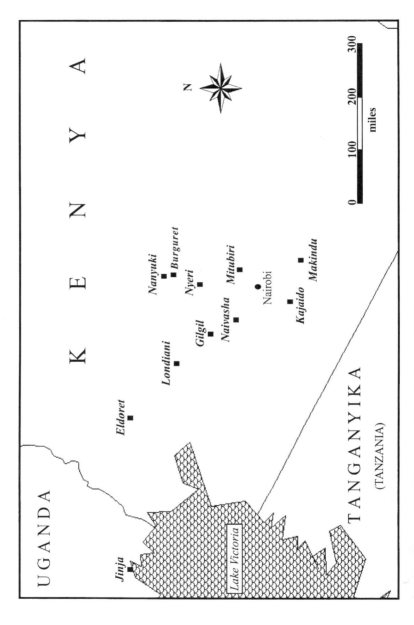

Map 7 Prisoner of War Camps for Italians in Kenya, 1941–7

pro-Nazi paramilitary Afrikaner organisation, deliberately encouraged anti-British, anti-war sentiments.

For example, in January 1943 the *Cape Argus* was disgusted by the actions taken by some anti-British farmers in the Paarl and Stellenbosch regions. It accused them of 'lavishly entertaining the Italian prisoners, who are permitted to roam at large at all hours and display sickening arrogance'.[14] One correspondent, who had been on holiday in another wine-growing area, reported that upon his arrival a local farmer brought five POWs to the local hotel and entertained them in the bar. Several nights later, several POWs were in the audience at the local cinema. What really angered the reporter was that one evening he witnessed three unescorted prisoners taking the 'belles of the village out for a stroll to the woods'.[15] The Native Commissioner at Taung in the Vaal-Hartz region of the Cape claimed that enemy captives were mixing freely with members of the *Ossewabrandwag*. Not only were they entertaining them, but also in one case one of the prisoners had become engaged to a settler's daughter! Such flagrant hobnobbing with the POWs had to stop, demanded the Native Commissioner. Moreover, as many of the 'loyalist' settlers were on active service, the wives of these settlers were anxious about these unsupervised prisoners who had the open sympathy of their anti-government neighbours. The local magistrate warned the Secretary of Native Affairs that the latitude given to these prisoners had reached dangerous levels. In fact, one 'loyalist' farmer had already accidentally killed one prisoner in the district. Tired of the constant trespassing and pillaging of his crops, J. D. S. Behr chased several prisoners off his property. While in pursuit, the gun discharged, hitting one of the prisoners in the back, killing him. Behr was cleared of culpable homicide.[16]

The conduct of Italian POWs in the Paarl and Stellenbosch regions continued to worry Prime Minister Smuts's loyal United Party supporters. A constituent claimed that one farmer in the region, whose brother had been interned at the outbreak of the war whilst endeavouring to leave South Africa to join the German Air Force, was himself 100 per cent Nazi and had 12 Italian POWs billeted to him. Charges were levied that farmers with pro-Nazi or anti-government leanings were deliberately giving the POWs tremendous latitude. Alcohol was being purchased for them in direct contravention of the parole agreements, while many Italians, dressed in civilian clothes, were seen fraternising with local girls and women. To add insult to injury:

There is a very strong feeling in Stellenbosch by loyal United Party members against the anti-English sympathies amongst the students at the Stellenbosch University, which are openly expressed by street parades of students wearing the swastika armband, who also commit acts insulting to Britain and the Royal family. This is made more blatant when it is considered that the Government pays pound for pound for the upkeep of Stellenbosch University. On several occasions indignation at the latitude allowed to Italian prisoners of war was expressed to us by residents of Stellenbosch and Paarl who have sons serving in the fighting forces.[17]

The National Council of Coloured Welfare Organisations lodged similar complaints. The secretary, C. Ziervogel, reported that a large number of Italian POWs were let loose to move about freely in Stellenbosch in early March 1943. As a result, a number of Cape Coloureds were assaulted and molested, particularly women. Ziervogel warned the authorities that resentment was running high in the Cape Coloured community and demanded that the government take measures to 'stop any uncalled feeling arising'. Blaine was also told by his officials that such incidents, which had also occurred in Paarl and Wellington, could lead to serious trouble and might even hamper the government's war effort if something was not done to assuage local feeling in both the European and non-European communities. 'One hears of frequent complaints of this sort', minuted Blaine, but he did not offer any concrete suggestions as to how to improve a potentially volatile situation.[18]

Such flagrant displays of ill-discipline by POWs on outside employment, and in some cases with the full knowledge, if not encouragement, of their employers, many of whom were alleged anti-government supporters, prompted the Commissioner of the South African Police, G. R. C. Baston, to remark that this 'is becoming much too serious for my liking and I urge that immediate steps be taken to remedy the position. Enemy flags at concerts, secret meetings with schoolgirls, love letters etc., seem difficult to believe but here is the evidence.'[19] Indeed, there was, and plenty of it. For instance, in March 1943, one UDF Captain on the staff of a POW work camp reported that rumours were running rife throughout the camp that at the 'Cullinan Hotel one was unable to get a seat in the Dining Room [because] it was taken up by Italian officers with women'.[20] The Magistrate in Rustenburg, a hotbed of anti-government sentiment and strong *Ossewabrandwag* connections, bitterly complained that known anti-government farmers who had already been convicted of cattle theft and who had had earlier requests for POW labour turned down, had now been considered fit to billet POW labour. Not only did the magistrate complain of poor communications between the AG's department and his office, but also that these decisions were undertaken without consultation with his office and the local South African Police (SAP) detachment. In the end, it was the fact that it was his office that would have to take the full brunt of public criticism that the magistrate was clearly uncomfortable with.[21]

Colonel R. C. Wilson, who was an imperial officer and not South African-born, responded to this growing litany of ill-discipline in an intriguing manner. In his opinion, his fundamental role as Deputy AG(POW) was to ensure that the basic conditions as regards feeding and housing the men were observed by the farmers who had contracted the POWs on outside employment. Obviously, with thousands of POWs scattered across the country his office could do no more than attend to specific complaints of ill-treatment against farmers or of specific cases of misconduct by POWs that were brought to his attention. 'The matter of the general treatment of POWs by the community as a whole must be left to the good sense of public opinion', he exclaimed. 'Unfortunately … [throughout the Union] there seem to be two schools of public opinion, neither of which is conspicuous for its sense. One takes the vague pleasure in treating POWs extravagantly while the other is making vague complaints against the first.' Wilson commented that in his capacity as purveyor of POWs he was not interested if people were Nazi sympathisers or had strong feelings about POWs whatever they were. Both groups were entitled to POWs and there was little he could do to control the manner in which they were treated.[22]

Brigadier Blaine and the Chief Control Officer, Colonel Sir Theo Truter, were alarmed at this attitude. In the small village of Reitz in the Orange Free State, a member of the NRB recalled how POWs were taken into cafés, given lavish attention and spoken to by the locals who were very derogatory about UDF soldiers. Indeed, Wilson admitted that it was now 'customary' for many South African civilians to encourage POWs into their homes, to associate freely with them and to allow them to meet their womenfolk on equal terms, which generated much public dissatisfaction. 'Colonel Wilson as a recent arrival in the Union is perhaps not acquainted with our numerous and very difficult internal problems', minuted Blaine, who suggested that Truter have a quiet word with him on South Africa's domestic political situation. If Blaine was expecting help in this matter from Smuts, as Minister of Defence, his faith was misplaced. Blaine lamented that: 'The Minister says it can't be helped if POW[s] are hired to Nazi or anti-War sympathisers if they do "treat POW[s] like Lords" – it's their trouble.'[23]

In June 1943, existing regulations under the War Measures Act were tightened up; and in no small part due to pressure from the SAP and Smuts' United Party faithful who were concerned about how these incidents were undermining wartime morale and public opinion. Under the new regulations, prisoners would only be allowed to leave the working premises when in possession of a special pass signed by the employer. The pass would include the prisoners' destination, the purpose of their visit and its duration. While out on the pass, prisoners were forbidden to fraternise with the public, travel on public vehicles other than local buses, or visit any place of public entertainment such as bars, cafés or dance halls. Nor were they allowed to enter any private residences except with special written permission of the employer or the officer in charge of the work detail.[24]

Herein lay the crux of the issue of employing POWs outside the camp network: how best to balance the needs of maintaining proper security, while at the same time maximising the labour potential of these prisoners in an increasingly demanding war economy where labour was at a premium. In other words, the pressures to bolster production, especially of foodstuffs, forced the Union government to expand the outside employment schemes even if that meant risking public criticism over the conduct of the POWs when they came in contact with less loyal elements within white rural South Africa. By using a combination of tighter restrictions on the movement and social interaction POWs had with South Africans while paroled to farmers outside the camp system, combined with stiffer vetting procedures of prospective employers and heavier penalties if these employers failed to adhere to their obligations, Pretoria hoped that the number of embarrassing incidents involving POWs and South African citizens would be curtailed.

Meanwhile, pressure mounted as farmers complained that the shortage of labour was now critical in many regions. In February 1943 Smuts was asked in the House of Assembly to make the restrictions on the employment of POWs by private individuals more 'elastic' so that deserving farmers throughout the country could avail themselves of this labour. Of note, was that despite having one of the largest POW populations in the empire, Pretoria had not yet fully exploited this resource. It was revealed that only 2,730 Italian captives were employed on government works projects in contrast with 2,209 by private farmers and 152 by other unnamed agencies. This, out of total inmate population of just under 50,000.[25]

The number of POWs employed on outside contracts rose sharply after May 1943. The fundamental problem was the growing shortage of indigenous labour. Since 1942 maize producers had experienced some of the most acute labour shortages throughout the agricultural sector. This was compounded in 1942 by an unusually small maize harvest.

Severe food shortages loomed if the 1943 harvest was not taken off soon; a situation which had reached critical as untimely autumn rains and the general shortage of indigenous farm labour threatened to aggravate an already worsening situation. Following intense lobbying by these producers and with the full support of the Minister of Agriculture, Smuts created – on grounds of 'national importance' – five temporary harvesting camps in the Orange Free State. Each camp would accommodate 300 POWs and between 50 and 60 administrative staff. A total of 1,500 POWs would be placed under canvas near Kroonstad, Hennenman, Wesselsbron, Bothaville and Groenebloem. A similar scheme was established for wheat and mealie producers in the 1943–4 season, but instead of establishing reaping camps, batches of POWs would be despatched to regional camps to augment the POW labour supply.[26]

Expansion continued apace throughout the latter part of 1943 and early 1944. In October 1943 approval was granted to open a POW camp for 400 POWs at Standerton to assist farmers in the Eastern Transvaal and Orange Free State. By late February the two largest outside employment camps at Worcester in the Western Cape, and Kroonstad in the Orange Free State, held 4,221 and 4,529 prisoners respectively. Another camp located just outside Pietermaritzburg in Natal contained 3,506 Italian captives. In April 1944 another facility holding 500 POWs was established at Warmbath in the Northern Transvaal. Here, the Waterburg District Farmers' Union had successfully appealed to Prime Minister Smuts arguing that the extra labour was urgently needed. They admitted that despite their efforts to minimise the serious effects of the region's labour shortage, thousands of bags of groundnuts had already been lost. Other crops, such as beans and maize, were also threatened. The only way to stop this unnecessary waste of the country's food supplies was the immediate establishment of the Warmbath camp.

The government approved the construction of this camp, despite warnings from public health officials. Some of the new work camps in the Transvaal and Orange Free State were near areas where outbreaks of plague and/or proven rodent infestation had occurred in the previous few years. If the necessary precautions were not adhered to, argued the public health officials, the crowded conditions at these sites provided perfect breeding grounds for bubonic or septicaemic plague that could give rise to pneumonic plague. Although these concerns were duly noted, the risk was deemed negligible. By the end of 1944, 18,000 Italian POWs were working on outside contracts employed in weeding, planting and harvesting; almost a five-fold increase from May 1943.[27] Moreover, Pretoria remained confident that it could maintain this quota for outside contracts for the duration of the war, despite the request from London to transport 22,000 additional POWs to Britain from the Union in 1944. The POW census of February 1945 demonstrated that Union officials in fact had succeeded. Out of a total POW population of 39,136 still resident in the Union, approximately 22,700 co-operators were recorded working out of Zonderwater and ten other satellite camps throughout the country.[28]

The expansion of the outside employment scheme was a notable success. In May 1943, when the parole regulations were tightened up, farmers in the Western Cape reported that in 90 per cent of cases both farmers and POWs were satisfied with their working arrangements. As a result, demand for this labour in the Western Cape continued to grow. Moreover, now that the SAP had undertaken to keep an eye on the welfare and behaviour of the POWs on outside employment 'the immediate result of their action has been a gratifying reduction in the number of complaints by members of the public'.[29] Previous restrictions on the employment of POW labour were also eased. For instance, POWs were forbidden employment within 30 miles of the sea for fear of attempts to communicate with Axis submarines offshore. In March 1943, this regulation was amended to 15 miles provided the prisoners did not have a view of the sea. The exclusion of POWs from specific magisterial districts such as Cape Town, Simonstown, Wynberg, Bellville, Somerset West, Hopefield, Port Elizabeth, East London and Durban was however maintained. Nonetheless, after further protests from fruit growers in the Cape, Pretoria was forced to make more concessions. In districts where a complete ban was not in force, POWs were now allowed within five miles of the coast.[30]

The South African military authorities were also forced to make concessions in two other hitherto sensitive policy areas. In September 1943, and after the Italian surrender, the CGS drew attention to the need for the employment of POWs in military messes in place of unattested indigenous personnel in order to relieve the shortage of this type of labour in the agricultural sector. Until now, this practice had been strictly forbidden. What had changed? According to General van Ryneveld: 'Natives were being employed privately in messes at rates of pay far beyond what they normally received, and this continued to have an adverse effect on the supply of native labour available in rural areas.' Particular attention was drawn to the Barberton and Piet Retief areas near the Swaziland border in the Eastern Transvaal where the CGS instructed the AG to 'popularise the idea, and draw the attention of units to the advantages that would accrue from the employment of

POW[s] in the direction indicated'.[31] Individual requests from influential private citizens, however, such as Rear Admiral J. H. Kay Clegg, the former Commodore of Convoys East Indies, or C. J. Burchell, the Canadian High Commissioner in South Africa, for the use of Italian POWs as batmen, chefs or butlers were given short shrift.[32]

The policy of employing Italian POWs in or near large native reserves such as the Ciskei or Transkei in the Eastern Cape had, until May 1943, been resisted vigorously by the Department of Native Affairs. The danger was that Fascist POWs might stir up racial confrontation between the white farmers and their African neighbours, especially in areas like the Eastern Cape where tensions between European farmers and Africans over land tenure and grazing rights were never far from the surface. Such dry tinder needed only the smallest of sparks for it to ignite. Therefore, Pretoria was determined to avoid providing the fuel for any kind of indigenous uprising. Smuts's administration had enough problems maintaining a watchful eye on dissident Afrikaners. The last thing his government needed was the added threat from an unsettled indigenous population – the much feared *swart gevaar* or 'black peril'. Nevertheless, farmers' organisations in the Eastern Cape were able to score some small successes. If limited numbers of POWs were not provided, and quickly, their crops would rot where they stood. As a result, departmental objections were withdrawn in several instances, such as the Mount Currie district and Cedarville section of the Matatiele district in the Transkei.[33]

Not surprisingly, the expansion of the outside employment programme was not without its risks. Complaints ranged from the trivial to the tragic. In July 1943, the Minister of Railways and Harbours, F. G. Sturrock, complained to General van Ryneveld that Italian POWs in Upington in the Northern Cape were being housed in modern up-to-date accommodation. Why could they not be housed in tents like UDF soldiers? As more prisoners obtained limited freedom by working on outside contracts, and as the South African government had to respond like their British counterparts with extra inducements to keep their 'co-operators' content, the supervision by some private employers began to falter. The SAP received complaints that Italian POWs were regularly found driving motor vehicles on public highways. Although strictly forbidden, Commissioner Baston admitted, despite some tough talk, that there was very little his officers could do other than fine offenders and revoke those licences which had been granted in error by local magistrates.[34] Prisoners were also accused of trespassing on nearby farms in the vicinity of the Cookhouse POW work camp, near Grahamstown in the Eastern Cape, where they 'roamed at will' destroying wild game.[35] In the Worcester region, prisoners were accused of indecent or obscene behaviour. In the Transvaal at Vereeniging similar charges were levelled against ten POWs who were evicted by Military Police from a football match as they were in direct contravention of their parole. Whilst being removed one POW 'gesticulated wildly and spoke volubly in Italian which, fortunately for him, was not understood'.[36] The South African Air Force did not escape criticism either. Now allowed to employ Italian POWs as cooks, waiters and batmen either on an individual basis or in the officers' mess, supervisory slackness had reached new heights when it was reported that some of these POW cooks and waiters had been seen drinking and fraternising in the bars of Pretoria![37]

Unscrupulous employers who abused their contract privileges were another source of trouble which aroused sporadic protests from organised labour and ex-servicemen's groups. The Building Workers Industrial Union, the Amalgamated Society of Woodworkers and the Amalgamated Bricklayers Trade Union of South Africa lodged a series of complaints with the AG's office complaining that many farmers were not using their POWs for agricultural labour, but were instead employing them as tradesmen building barns, out-buildings and chicken runs. Several Chambers of Commerce also complained that their members' businesses were suffering because of the illegal employment of the POWs. As many of these POWs had been employed as artisans in the farm machinery, automotive or building trades prior to the war, South African farmers were able to circumvent local tradesmen, to the detriment of these businesses.[38] In March 1944 Smuts received a strongly worded cable from the Springbok Legion protesting about attempts to introduce Italian POWs as skilled labour into the engineering industry. They reminded the prime minister that: 'These jobs belong to South Africans.'[39]

The temptation to employ cheaper POW labour continued after the war had ended. In October 1945, it was brought to the attention of Major-General G. E. Brink, Director-General of Demobilisation, that POWs were still being employed to the exclusion of returning African, Cape Coloured and European veterans. Brink's department subsequently investigated these charges. By June 1946 it was abundantly clear that the first priority was the reabsorption of all Union volunteers into civilian occupations. As a result, despite pleas from the agricultural sector to maintain POW labour to bring in the 1946 harvest, the Department of Demobilisation could not recommend the continued retention of Italian POWs in the Union for very much longer.[40] In part, the need to reintegrate returning veterans into the South African economy provided some impetus for the acceleration of the repatriation process.

POWs were victims as well. Organised theft by non-European guards was one complaint often lodged by POWs, especially those who were in transit or on work details outside the camp. In 1944 South African censors in Cape Town recorded a letter from Vincenzo Bosco, an inmate at the Pietermaritzburg camp, one of the three largest POW work camps in the Union. He complained bitterly to his wife that roll-call was simply an excuse for the guards to plunder and commit armed robbery. He alleged that during one such roll call 'a command of armed Zulus surround[ed] us whilst about 400 soldiers or rather South African brigands … search[ed] our tents'. The greed of these South African 'wolves' knew no bounds. Obvious valuables such as money, watches and jewellery were taken as well as cigarettes, matches, family correspondence and photographs. According to Bosco, the 'rapacious claws' of these bandits and looters had snatched everything the POWs had managed to save during the preceding three years of captivity. And it was stolen from them 'in such an undignified manner that it would raise a blush of shame on the black snouts of the uncivilised and primitive Zulus, who with arms in their hands guard us'. But one has to be careful with such remarks. For as the military intelligence officer reported, there was still a 'steady flow of abusive' correspondence from the Pietermaritzburg camp which was evidence of a determined and organised Fascist propaganda campaign.[41]

Conflict between Fascists and anti-Fascists continued despite Pretoria's determination to isolate diehard Fascists within the camps. In February 1944 five anti-Fascist POWs were attacked by Fascist elements within the Pietermaritzburg camp. In March, a serious assault was committed by several Italian POWs at Worcester who attempted to murder one of their junior officers; but investigations revealed there were no obvious political motives involved.[42]

As in other parts of the British Empire, increasing tensions between POWs and their civilian hosts marred the post-surrender atmosphere of September 1943. Perhaps one of the more bizarre stories occurred in Durban in 1943. When Italy joined the Allies as a co-belligerent, the submarine *Ammiraglio Cagni* which had been operating with German U-boats in South African waters since November 1942, surrendered. The commander and a few officers and crew lived on the vessel under guard of the Royal Marines. This meant that the interned vessel and the crew living on it were the responsibility of the Royal Navy. The remaining officers and crew were relocated to Kings Park Camp and were a UDF responsibility. Instructions were issued by the GOC Coastal Area that the crew were to be treated as 'privileged internees', which meant that they were allowed out of camp under UDF supervision. On their second night an incident took place on a tram when several civilians reinforced by UDF soldiers took exception to Italian POWs using local transport. The *Natal Daily News* reported that as co-belligerents these men should have been treated with respect. Had not many Italians risked their own lives to help South African POWs escape from Italy? 'It would be churlish indeed not to be grateful to them' or to have reciprocated one's appreciation to them in some way. However, popular feeling could not change overnight, for had not these same men been torpedoing Allied shipping of the East Coast just several weeks earlier? To add insult to injury, the submarine commander had been taken to a local nightclub and then to the racetrack by his escort![43] This highly embarrassing incident raised the hackles of the British High Commission who had criticised the South African POW authorities earlier that year for serious lapses of judgement and breaches of security.

Feelings throughout some parts of the country continued to run high as many South Africans, both European and non-European, objected to the increasing liberties being given Italian POWs. In January 1944, a POW was set upon in Pretoria by a civilian wielding a bicycle chain.[44] Unprovoked attacks by civilians against POWs were rare, but not uncommon. Trespassing continued to be a common complaint, particularly in the rural areas. At Schoemansville on the shores of the picturesque Hartebeestpoort dam, north of Pretoria, a series of complaints were lodged by the Meerhof Chronic Sick Home for European Children. Italian POWs were seen on the property at all hours, reported the hospice's secretary, and had already led to one 'unfortunate' case of fraternisation between a patient and a POW.[45] Popular nightspots, cinemas, cafés, tearooms and restaurants continued to pose potential flashpoints where civilians and POWs competed for space. In February 1945 an altercation between POWs from the nearby Boschpoort work camp and patrons of the local spa in Warmbath threatened to escalate into a full-blown fight as the veranda had become 'overrun' with POWs. The POWs were told to clear off while the civilians were told to either go inside or go home. Subsequently, the mineral baths were made out of bounds to the prisoners. Another example of high spirits occurred at the local cinema near Zonderwater in October 1945. UDF soldiers stormed out when Italian medical officers sat down in the front block of the cinema which had been reserved for serving UDF officers. The cinema operator was afterwards placed under close arrest and the men who walked out were sharply rebuked for their actions, although one soldier denied that their protest was made with any mutinous intent.[46]

Lax supervision by employers or poor communications with the POWs as to their obligations while on parole were two of the fundamental factors responsible for incidents between POWs and South Africans. A scanty knowledge of English, let alone of Afrikaans or some of the indigenous tongues, was another problem. All the regulations in the world could not prevent determined individuals from inviting these men into their homes. Perhaps the most contentious issue that caused the most consternation amongst Union authorities was the fraternisation between the prisoners and women, in particular relationships between POWs and local women. The Weza forest incident of 1941–2 is a case in point, where 'lustful' Italian POWs persistently trespassed into the nearby reserve looking for sexual favours from African women. And as has been noted above, Cape Coloured women were equally vulnerable to molestation by 'marauding' groups of unsupervised POWs in Stellenbosch and Paarl. It was not always one-way traffic however. In August 1944, five women, three Cape Coloured and two African, were convicted in Kimberley for entering a nearby POW camp for illicit purposes. Their punishment was a £3 fine or 30 days' hard labour.[47]

Regular appeals to senior government officials were made by concerned citizens that South African women and children must be protected from these men. For example, when a POW assaulted a seven-year-old girl from Pretoria North while in the employ of her father, Commandant Prinsloo at Zonderwater was keen to prosecute. In nearby Hatfield, a POW in the employ of a landlord had come over unsupervised to fix a broken window, and had kissed the wife of a serving sergeant against her will in her own home. 'My wife and other women in that neighbourhood feel very unsafe whilst these prisoners are [around]', reported the women's husband, Sergeant J. D'Arcy-Searle.[48] Such crimes could only be prosecuted with the supporting evidence, but the files contain no indication of what legal measures, if any, were taken in these cases. Touting for sexual favours seems more commonplace, but recorded cases of rape and sexual abuse by POWs in South Africa, as in other parts of the empire, seem the exception rather than the rule. Nevertheless, POW officials became alarmed at the sexual promiscuity of their charges when it was revealed that there was a slight increase in reported cases of venereal disease amongst inmates in the Zonderwater camp between September 1944 and August 1945 (a similarly worrying trend noted in Kenya at the same time).[49]

Legitimate affairs of the heart were more numerous and more difficult to police. Although strictly forbidden, as early as April 1942 the AG had already received enquiries from South African women and Italian POWs on outside employment concerning marriage. Censored mail from POWs also revealed the extent of some of these liaisons. 'Just imagine I am engaged to an English girl already', wrote Giuseppe Pisano from Kroonstad camp to a friend in Sardinia. '[S]he gives me everything, cigarettes and a bit of everything one can think of, I need nothing, you can guess everything that I wish to explain.' The AG took a firm line that such marriages should be proscribed during the course of the war. Furthermore, there was no means of assuring the validity of these marriages. The issue was raised of whether the government should promulgate a measure prohibiting marriages of this kind, but subsequent discussions revealed that there were serious doubts whether such a war measure would be valid, let alone enforceable. The government line was that all such marriages had to be 'discouraged in every possible way'. Besides, argued Colonel Wilson of the AG's department, these women 'are often uneducated and ignorant girls with no knowledge of the conditions of life to which they may be subjecting themselves after the repatriation of their POW husbands'.[50] Little comfort to the indeterminate handful of women who bore children from these liaisons; women whose love for these men was genuine.

Putting the human cost aside, what did the final balance sheet reveal for South Africa in keeping these men in captivity in the Union between 1941 and 1947? In March 1945 the bill was put at £7,273,165 of which the South African government contributed £1,143,114.[51] By September 1946 the revised total stood at £8.5 million. The figures revealed that since 1941 the total cost of holding both German and Italian POWs in South Africa had been just less than £40 per prisoner per year. Of this, £6.3 million had been allocated to maintenance allowances that were covered by a capitation grant, which by October 1945 had been calculated at 2 shillings per diem per prisoner.[52] Unfortunately, there are no separate figures which would indicate the exact amount spent on just the Italians prisoners. But it is obvious that the lion's share of the money was allocated to their maintenance and upkeep. As far as their financial contribution to war production is concerned, these statistics either do not exist or have not yet been unearthed. Nevertheless, their contribution to South Africa's war economy was, as we shall see in the case of Australia, significant.

Prisoners for profit: Australia 1943–5

The acceleration of the POW work programme in Australia in 1943 was, as in South Africa, the result of pressing labour shortages in agriculture and on the railways. Once the magnitude of the manpower shortage was exposed, the Commonwealth government responded in December 1942 by establishing an inter-departmental committee to explore new approaches to the problem. In April 1943, the committee tabled two recommendations. First, it reported that private citizens should be allowed to employ selected prisoners in groups no larger than three per farm or in rural industries without guards. At the same time, it recommended that more Italian POWs be brought into the country 'subject to the standard safeguards about health, hygiene, security and rates of pay'.[53]

The inter-departmental committee's recommendations made interesting reading. Prisoners designated for employment without guards would be contracted to private employers in primary industry. They would be carefully screened, having good records and being passed as medically fit for manual labour. Approved work areas would be within a 25-mile radius of the Army-administered POW Control Centre. Each employment area was allocated a minimum of 200 prisoners to be located in areas without a substantial enemy alien population. Restrictions of movement while in the employ of the farmer, who also had to undergo security clearance, were imposed on the prisoners to prevent their congregation with other prisoners or undue fraternisation with local people. The Army provided clothing, pay, medical and other services on behalf of the prisoners and had the right to withdraw or replace any POWs at its discretion. Local security measures involved the co-operation and co-ordination of the security services, the War Agricultural Committees and police, which was organised through the Army POW Control Officer, attached to each Control Centre. Ultimately, it was this officer who exercised administrative and disciplinary authority over all the prisoners in his area. Hours of work and rates of pay were to be arranged between the employer and the Department of Labour and National Service. Where no pay award existed employers were subject to pay a minimum of £1 per week plus keep per prisoner.[54]

Interestingly enough, the government's medical officers raised no serious objections to this scheme. Acknowledging that 20 per cent of the POW employees were capable of infecting members of the employers' families and other citizens with amoebic dysentery, the Director-General of Health, Dr J. H. Cumpston, believed that the risk was not, 'under the generally arid conditions of Australian country life', very great despite their distribution into the countryside. This contention was reinforced by the knowledge that to date there had been no transmission of any tropical disease into the wider community because of the rigid precautions undertaken prior to and immediately upon the prisoners' arrival in Australia. Admittedly, there was no sure-fire guarantee that the existing precautions would prevent the eventual transmission of diseases such as malaria or enteric fever into the wider community. Nonetheless, provided unscreened prisoners were not allowed to work in non-government irrigation areas, and those firm medical practices were continued, the risk to the Australian public was deemed inconsequential. Cumpston realised, however, that unless the medical arguments were overwhelmingly adverse to the initiation of this scheme, the new employment provisions would be determined 'largely on considerations of national necessity', rather than issues of national health.[55] In early April the Australian War Cabinet approved the inter-departmental committee's recommendations.

In May 1943 the Commonwealth government approved the importation from India of 10,000 Italian POWs of whom 5,000 were desired immediately. The Australian High Commissioner in London, S. M. Bruce, was asked to confirm that the transfer could be arranged on the same conditions which already applied to those presently held in Australia under the agency principle. Canberra did not envisage the construction of new camps, as it was confident that the extra POWs would be held in existing staging facilities before being drafted out for employment; although they intimated that a few work hostels might have to be built. Of note was that Canberra requested that the Indian military authorities eliminate Fascist elements and select those best suited for agricultural work.[56] The War Office agreed to the transfer but refused to pay for any increased expenditure, such as the construction of new hostels.[57]

As with the first transfer in 1941, the availability of shipping once more governed the pace of the second transfer to Australia. The shipment of these men was further complicated by complaints lodged by the PWE mission in India who rightly feared that because of the demand for anti-Fascist POWs, it was their charges at Jaipur which were being targeted for trans-shipment to Australia. Such a demand would mean the death-knell to their experiments in political warfare and re-education, as the number requested by Canberra matched that in PWE custody. Resistance from the PWE forced Whitehall to look to POW sources held in the Middle East, Kenya and South Africa which might be used to fill the quota. This proved difficult. Shipping from these destinations was also in short supply, which was compounded by the fact that these regions were also accelerating their own POW work programmes because of the chronic shortages of labour which existed in these territories. Competition for Italian POW labour also came from an unexpected corner – New Zealand. In October 1943, attracted by the labour potential of Axis POWs, the New Zealand government explored possible sources in India, the United Kingdom and the United States. Its efforts, however, remained stillborn largely due to the worldwide shortage of shipping. By October 1943, despite Canberra's determined efforts, only 1,500 of the 10,000 Italian POWs had arrived in Australia from India.[58]

During the initial War Cabinet discussions in April 1943, the Minister for the Army, Frank Forde, argued that the contemplated increase in POW numbers posed no serious threat to domestic security. 'Our subsequent experience with Italian P[O]W[s] shows that, if the Fascist agitator type are excluded, [the rest remain] docile and, if firmly but humanely handled, [are] reasonably good workers. Physical security problems with lower rank Italian prisoners of war have not been serious. Only a few escapes, due mainly to bravado or boredom have occurred. All escapees have been recaptured.' Whilst accepting that large numbers of additional prisoners posed problems in providing sufficient garrison personnel, Forde considered that the transfer of these POWs from the sub-continent deserved serious consideration because of the obvious benefits it afforded in partially relieving the existing manpower shortage.[59]

However, despite Canberra's emphasis on proper screening and the recruitment of the 'best available types' of prisoner, the fundamental question remained: did these types exist and in sufficient numbers? The Australians thought so, for they resurrected the idea of accepting up to 50,000 lower-rank prisoners first made in 1941. In subsequent inter-departmental discussions held between the Treasury, Supply and Shipping, Labour and National Service, Commerce, the Interior, the Directorate of Prisoners of War and Internees (DPW&I) and the Directors-General of Health, Security and Manpower, the now familiar stereotype of the Italian was continually trotted out. Lieutenant-Colonel J. McCahon, Director of the DPW&I, commented that the general experiences of the Australian Military Force (AMF) had been that if the 'small percentage of ardent Fascists, agitators, and lazy types' were excluded, the remainder of the Italian prisoners would work quite satisfactorily 'when handled firmly but with humanity and understanding'. As many of the POWs were of peasant stock, they made good, hard-working agricultural labourers for hard-pressed Australian farmers.[60]

Confident that most Italian POWs had abandoned their Fascist faith, and combined with the growing manpower crisis, the Australians continued to press the British and Indian authorities to expedite swiftly the screening and trans-shipment of these additional POWs. Events in

Europe, however, intervened to stall Australian efforts to acquire more POW labour. The invasion of Sicily, the fall of Mussolini in July 1943 and the surrender of Italy in September put a temporary brake on the shipment of these POWs, as the Allies not only focused on the larger strategic and diplomatic issues, but redeployed existing POW labour in the Middle East to meet these Mediterranean contingencies. This included the possible redeployment of POWs from India to meet labour shortfalls in North Africa. Further complications arose during the wrangling over Italian co-belligerency and what this meant for the future status of Italian POWs, frustrating Australia's carefully laid expansion of its POW employment schemes. It was not until February 1944, when the Allies finally resolved not to release those Italians already in custody and to maintain the POW status amongst those captured before the Italian surrender, that the remainder of the 10,000 from India were finally transferred to Australia.[61] At last, by May 1944 10,117 Italians had finally arrived from India; a figure which was predicted to increase by a further 5,000. Meanwhile, Canberra had been examining the importation and use of 7,500 German POWs if the appropriate number of Italians could not be found. This project was eventually rejected. In ability, the German POWs were adjudged to be superior to their Italian counterparts, but as their morale had not yet been broken senior officials argued that it was at present unwise and unsafe to employ these men without sufficient guards in the back blocks of Australia.[62]

In June 1943 the extension of the camp network was initially undertaken in the 'safe' states of Victoria and South Australia, but New South Wales was quickly added to the list because of the large number of Italian POWs held there. At first, approval was given to establish five POW Control Centres in New South Wales and three in Victoria, two of which included Hamilton and Colac in the Western Districts. The first instalment of 1,000 POWs would be drawn from the POW Groups at Hay (500) and Cowra (200) in New South Wales, and from the Murchison Group in Victoria (300). Selected prisoners would work within a 25-mile radius of each POW Control Centre. To secure an economy of administration, after three months it was expected that each area would possess a minimum of 200 POWs. Since the ultimate objective was the reduction of garrison personnel employed in outside compounds, it was vital to formulate a proper set of guidelines. Throughout June, a series of comprehensive regulations were drawn up. They included clearly delineated chains of command between the parent and outreach camps; the selection of experienced, trustworthy POW Control Officers; a detailed set of recommendations for the allotment of prisoners, rates of pay and their conditions of employment; procedures for the selection of employers, as well as the terms and conditions employers had to observe while employing POW labour; and finally, the all-important notes for employers on how to handle and discipline their Italian charges while in their custody.[63]

Despite the earlier fears and prejudices concerning the suitability of the POWs for work on private farms, their employment without guards proved an instant success. During the first month of the scheme, the *Hamilton Spectator* reported that Italian POW labour was working well in the district, and that the men were contented and anxious to please their new employers. This was substantiated in the initial reports submitted by senior land inspectors and National Service Officers (NSOs) to D. Cameron, the Deputy Director-General of Manpower in Victoria. The 25 POWs already working in the Hamilton district had created a very favourable impression. 'By their unfailing courtesy, industry and willingness, they have won the admiration of those to whom they have been allotted', commented P. J. O'Connor, the NSO in Hamilton. 'The Prisoners of War themselves are quite happy with the conditions under which they are working.' Cameron himself was glowing in his praise for the enthusiasm, respect and eagerness with which the POWs engaged in all aspects of their work. Although acknowledging the necessity of proceeding carefully with the scheme in the first instance, the practical experience gained so far in Colac and Hamilton had demonstrated conclusively to him that it 'should be pushed ahead with vigour and confidence'. W. Findlay, the senior land inspector in Hamilton, noted that the 'news of the success of the scheme is certainly getting well known and the local bush telegraph is apparently very busy.'[64] Similar success was recorded in Colac (where 15 POWs had been billeted out to local farmers), which prompted Cameron to urge his superiors in Canberra not only to remove the severe publicity restrictions originally imposed, but also to adopt a more liberal attitude in the placement of these men in the vital interests of wartime production.[65]

Demand for prisoner labour was so high, however, that Australian authorities never filled the steady stream of requests from graziers, wheat, dairy, fruit and vegetable growers for this extra labour. It was estimated that by the end of 1943 between 15,000 and 20,000 POWs could have been absorbed effortlessly into the domestic labour market.[66] In May 1944, 56 POW Control Centres had been opened with over 6,500 POWs employed through them. By November 1944 there were 13,000 Italian POWs established in 96 POW Control Centres labouring in rural communities in all states throughout the Commonwealth. The largest proportion of captives had been allocated to individual farmers; the remaining balance being employed unguarded on primary production at special POW hostels, or working under guard in POW camps across the country. Still eager to extend the project and bring in several thousand more prisoners, according to the Department of the Army, the scheme had 'reached the stage where it may be considered an important factor in maintaining national production'.[67]

In fact, POW and civilian internee labour had become indispensable to the Australian war effort to the extent that throughout 1944–5 Canberra was willing to relax and even forgo a number of its medical and security practices in order to get more prisoners into private rural employment. For instance, in October 1943 the DPW&I requested that the medical regulations be modified so that the period of quarantine upon arrival in the POW camp be reduced to a minimum in order to facilitate their quick release for outside work. In May 1944 the Advisory War Council recommended to the Australian War Cabinet that despite the risk from a public health point of view, the distribution of POWs in specific agricultural practices previously restricted, like private irrigation projects, be overturned 'in view of the stringent manpower position'. Arguing that the indiscriminate distribution of POWs in agricultural areas was not a safe procedure in the absence of a preliminary medical examination or a period of quarantine, the Director-General of Health acknowledged that in view of 'national necessities' it was decided to accept whatever medical risk was involved.[68] The Commonwealth health authorities warned, however, that state health authorities would lodge strong protests about the government's deliberate acceptance of the risks to public health; and urged that a clear understanding be made as to any action which was needed if an epidemic disease was traced to a POW. Furthermore, they repeated their concern about the indiscriminate employment of POWs in the dairy industry, of which 2,290 screened POWs were already working; and about the employment of POWs infected with malaria in regions where malaria-transmitting mosquitoes existed. It was evident, however, that the need to increase essential foodstuff production, especially dairying in the irrigable districts, whatever the remaining medical concerns, would receive priority. In September 1944 the original embargo on the employment of Italian POWs on private irrigation schemes was repealed.[69]

Manpower priorities also put pressure on Canberra to employ Fascist POWs. Of the 10,000 earmarked for shipment to Australia from India between October 1943 and April 1944, only 3,000 were deemed politically acceptable. This left 7,000 alleged Fascists that were hitherto unemployable outside the camps. As the scheme of employing Italian POWs on farms was proving highly successful, and as the potential demand was far outstripping the labour available, the practice of regarding *all* Italians arriving in Australia as a pool of labour available for allocation to rural industry by the Director-General of Manpower under Army administration was to be continued.[70] That meant even employing the POW 'dregs' whatever their political views.

Prior experience had shown that extreme Fascists were unco-operative but, according to the DPW&I, many others who had professed to support Fascism were quite satisfactory workers. Provided constant vigilance was maintained in weeding out the troublesome and hardcore political activists, the Australian authorities were confident that more Italian captives could be employed on outside work. Indeed, the best results could be obtained by placing the men on farms almost immediately. The advantage was that it would prevent them from establishing any organised influence among them, 'and without ready contact with their confederates, any Fascist tendencies they might have would…fade away'.[71] A further bonus was that they would be segregated completely from non-Fascists, as they would be placed together on farms with only members of the same political inclination. To employ them in the hostels was ruled out completely as this would allow large numbers of Fascist prisoners to congregate for long periods of time, and thus, Fascist ideals would be maintained and the leadership would reassert its authority, endangering those non-Fascists who would be targeted for intimidation. This, in turn, would undermine POW morale and put at risk the whole rural employment scheme. Firm treatment, proper discipline and the removal of truculent elements back to the permanent camps allowed the POW authorities to employ even some of the more hard-line elements. 'It was found', recorded the DPW&I, 'that as soon as some were advised of early movement to farms, the others were only too glad to volunteer for work.'[72]

Just as the last instalment from India disembarked in Australia in May 1944, requests were made in June for a further 7,000 Italian prisoners. Labour requirements in South-East Asia Command meant that it would retain all its employable POWs other than its outstanding transfer commitments. Middle Eastern and Northwest African commands were themselves short of labour. Efforts to effect transfers from East and South Africa fell on equally stony ground as the United Kingdom had priority on any surplus labour held in these two territories. If Australia wanted more Italian labour it would have to take those hard-line Fascists whom the Indian authorities did not want and could not employ.[73]

But the decision to take these ne'er-do-wells was not, as Gianfranco Cresciani claims, one which the Australian authorities 'meekly' acquiesced in. GHQ India reported in July 1944 that it believed that many of those classified as Fascist were not confirmed Fascists because they had been prevented from volunteering through intimidation from their seniors. If these agitators could be weeded out, in Delhi's opinion, the 3,000 so classified were willing to work on the land. Besides, the Australians were becoming desperate for this labour. Bolstered by recent public opinion surveys which revealed that the much feared antagonism by the Australian public towards the employment of POWs had proved groundless, domestic circumstances looked favourable. This was reflected in the ease with which Italians had been placed and were welcomed into the Commonwealth's farming community. What Cresciani fails to realise is that the Australians were supremely confident that even the known and 'arrant' Fascists could be usefully employed behind the barbed wire on camp fatigues. At a meeting of senior camp officers at the end of June 1944, those attending were unanimous that another transfer from India, even if most of these men could not be employed on parole schemes, would release at least 1,500 Italians to the POW Control Centres; men who were at present behind the wire in the permanent camps.[74]

If any one thing was going to stop the employment of Italian POW labour it was the contemplated adjustment in the weekly rate from £1 to £2 plus keep per prisoner which private employers currently paid the government. It was economics, not political ideology, which seriously threatened to dislocate and retard the scheme; for a substantial alteration in pay rates would make it prohibitive for the smaller producer, especially the dairy farmer, to compete. There were some, like E. J. Holloway, the Minister for Labour and National Service, who thought an upward revision of the scale should be introduced. But the consensus in cabinet was that such a progressive scale would endanger the success of the scheme. Weekly POW rates were for the time being kept at £1 plus keep. As the rewards of importation once again far outweighed the risks, the Australian War Cabinet eagerly approved the acquisition of the hard-line Fascists from India. Confident that these men could be controlled, two batches totalling 3,067 prisoners were sent to Australia from the subcontinent in December 1944 and February 1945.[75]

The ambitious expansion of the POW labour scheme paid enormous dividends throughout the remainder of the war and beyond. In October 1943, when the issue of co-belligerency threatened to undermine Australia's POW scheme, Canberra informed London that the employment of Italian prisoners without guards appeared to be the 'most economical and effective method of using their labour' and was likely to absorb all those who could be made available.[76] South Australia illustrates the utility of POW labour in the private sector. By the end of April 1944, 489 employers had been approved to use 525 POWs for labour on their farms. In fact that month alone had seen a substantial increase: 125 employers being allocated 167 POWs. One year later, the number of approved employers in the state had more than tripled to 1,578 (this included 215 terminations and cancellations) with a POW allocation which peaked at 2,055 in February, but fell inexplicably to 1,454 by the end of April 1945.[77]

Even more revealing is the profitability of the entire scheme. In April 1945, the Department of the Army informed the Treasury that as of 31 December 1944 the POW and internment camps in Australia had made an accumulated profit of £144,135. The largest profits generated by POWs were at Murchison (£57,671) and Cowra (£23,067), with the civilian internment camp at Loveday, South Australia, registering a profit of £32,028.[78] Not only had fears been dispelled that the costs of camp maintenance and security would be exorbitantly high, but it was also lamented that if some projects had been better managed and the seasonal conditions in 1944 had been better, even more of a profit could have been made. In fact, the final balance sheet makes for remarkable reading.

Between December 1943 and March 1945 the total amount raised by the Department of the Army in the form of charges billed against employers and employing authorities for work performed by POWs was a staggering £918,062. This represented a total of 4,926,705 man/days worked by POWs on behalf of employers. Moreover, the credits accumulated on behalf of the British government helped offset the capital costs it had incurred under the agency agreements in the construction and maintenance of the permanent camps. As of 30 June 1945 the total cost for the construction of the six camp complexes at Myrtleford, Murchison and Tatura in Victoria, Cowra and Hay in New South Wales and Loveday in South Australia was estimated at £993,000; of which a residual value of £139,900 was realised.[79] Compare the difference of the remaining capital costs incurred (£853,100) with the gross total of revenue generated in the audit period listed above and we see strong indicators of a well-managed, commercially orientated administration which more than offset its operating costs.

Maintaining morale in the outback

The establishment of the outside employment programme coincided with the final collapse of Italy between May and September 1943. Prior to the placement of the first drafts on outside duties, camp intelligence reports at Murchison in Victoria revealed that boredom was becoming problematic for some prisoners. One POW wrote to a family friend in Salerno that despite the good treatment by the Australians there was little to combat the 'intense monotony and the depressing inactivity which reigns in this camp situated [as it was] in an uncultivated and uninhabited district'.[80] Several weeks later a vast improvement in morale was noted when the POWs at Murchison were informed that the farm employment scheme was to be initiated in the Western Districts. Camp officials recorded a 'remarkable uplift in morale'. Not only did the prospect of working outside the wire immediately improve the low state of prisoner morale, but it was also noted that the announcement had provided an effective antidote to the news of the Allied capture of Pantellaria and Lampedusa islands; operations which were part of the Allied preparations for the invasion of Sicily. One POW, when asked why he was so cheery, replied: 'Soon I go farm and pulla the cow teat'![81] Leask also commented that similarly enthusiastic reports were being received from *all* the Italian POW compounds throughout the Commonwealth. At Hay, prisoners were endeavouring to create a good impression with their captors in the hope of selection for farm work. The question on all the POWs' lips was, 'How soon we go out on farm?'[82]

Nothing was as astonishing as the reaction of the first 100 Italian POWs transferred from Hay to Cowra prior to their allocation to the rural employment scheme. Never had these men been so willing, recorded the camp intelligence officer. 'Nothing was a trouble; they fell over themselves to oblige the camp authorities. Final departure was an orgy of tearful embraces, and kissing was the order of the day.' The camp padre gave a 'sound' address 'telling his men to conduct themselves always as soldiers', and emphasised that the continuation of the scheme depended on their good conduct. 'One slip and they would return behind the wire for good.' Finally, he reminded his flock how privileged they were, and 'was forceful in [his] advice as to their contacts with womenfolk who, he said, must be treated with the greatest respect'.[83] Therefore, the prospect of living and working outside the barbed wire was proving a welcome tonic to flagging morale.

The fall of Mussolini in July 1943 provided another insight into the Italian psyche. The reaction of the majority of Italian POWs to this war news at Cowra was stunned disbelief. It was significant, remarked the camp intelligence officer, 'that pictures of Mussolini have disappeared from huts, and the crude drawings of the late *Duce* are now appearing in latrines accompanied by chalked terms of coarse abuse'.[84] Evidently, the news had barely 'disturbed the apparent calm' of the POWs at Hay and

Yanco. One interpretation was that many captives had already resigned themselves to Italy's impending collapse. Moreover, many more may have been preoccupied with their new-found freedom obtained by participating in the rural employment scheme. As a result, Canberra was informed that the POWs were now obeying orders without the customary protests which had once been commonplace. For diehard Fascists the news was met with a sense of bewilderment or tersely dismissed as Allied propaganda. At Murchison the same mixture of wide-ranging emotions was recorded. Interestingly, the older captives seemed rather relieved, expressed hope that Italy would soon be out of the war, discussed their repatriation and eagerly awaited a speedy return to their peacetime occupations.[85]

Italy's capitulation in September 1943 was met by the same mixture of relief, stupefaction, depression and truculence. At Myrtleford, censored mail revealed the overwhelming feeling of thankfulness that the war was over for Italy, combined with a pervasive melancholy. There were a few POW officers who continued to dismiss these reports as blatant propaganda, but it was noticeable amongst the letters written by the younger officers that their minds now turned to settling down in Australia. One remark passed at Yanco to a member of the AMF was: 'Come on; give a hand; we are all cobbers now!'[86]

For the remainder of 1943 and most of 1944, morale within the Italian POW compounds remained high. The expansion of the rural employment scheme continued to attract more POW volunteers, including officers, who were anxious to escape the confines of their barbed-wire enclosures. Prisoners at Yanco, for example, grew impatient, as many wanted to 'change from gang farm work to a touch of individual effort and private life'. Some even vented their displeasure at not being included in these outside employment schemes.[87] One of the biggest complaints lodged by POWs was the lack of or sporadic delivery of mail, which did have adverse effects on morale. In Western Australia at the Marrinup camp, intelligence reports indicated that the recent arrival of a large consignment of mail from southern Italy and Sicily via India had a pronounced and beneficial effect on the spirits of the POWs at the camp and the surrounding rural areas.[88] War news also had an effect on morale. In October 1944, intelligence officers at Marrinup reported that the morale of Italian POWs engaged in rural work schemes was generally high; but doubts were raised at the POW Control Centres as to whether the standard would be maintained if the POWs were disappointed in their belief that as the war in Europe was nearing an end, their return to Italy was imminent.[89]

The need to monitor the ebb and flow of POW morale was useful in identifying potential trouble. As in Africa and the United Kingdom, camp authorities were presented with a deepening resentment among an increasing number of Italian POWs at their continued incarceration when the granting of co-belligerency to Italy seemed to indicate to them that the war, and hence their captivity, was now over. Confused by the inability of the Allies to come to a written agreement with the Badoglio regime, compounded by the incessant haggling between Britain and the United States over the future status of the Italian POWs well into 1944, many POWs, who had willingly co-operated with the Australian authorities, became recalcitrant. Some POWs refused to undertake certain tasks. Others organised their comrades and embarked upon work-to-rule or go-slow campaigns. Downing tools or sabotage were other forms of protest increasingly used by disgruntled captives. Fed up, some tried to escape; while others withdrew into themselves, became sullen and even suicidal.

Many of these protests had nothing to do with political ideology. More often than not, they were demonstrations by frustrated men who were bored and homesick. This is not to say that organised Fascist cells had been eliminated. After the shock of Italy's surrender had worn off there was a resurgence of Fascist activity, especially at Cowra and Myrtleford. Conflicts between Fascists and Royalists within the camps continued, as did the vendettas between feuding Calabrian, Umbrian, Sicilian and Neapolitan gangs within some of the compounds. So too did punishment beatings. The more diehard elements still used the Fascist calendar, continued to induct new arrivals from other camps and insisted on their members using the Fascist salute. Indeed, part of this resurgence was assisted by the arrival of new drafts of captives from India, in particular those who arrived in late 1944–early 1945, and who were known to be staunch Fascists.[90] The realisation that there was always going to be a small core of intransigent Fascists was balanced by the Australian military's determination to identify, weed out and punish wrongdoers before a situation got out of hand. In this task, the ever-vigilant camp authorities were largely successful.

Australia, like the rest of the Empire, found it difficult to prevent fraternisation between POWs and women. In 1943, when the Australian War Cabinet was formulating its rural employment scheme, it attempted to learn from South African experiences. Leask noted that one of the 'unpleasant' features in the use of Italian POWs on road work and agriculture had been the 'frequent' report of amorous relations between the prisoners and women from all racial backgrounds. He realised that part of the problem lay squarely with the POW authorities themselves. Poor discipline by the escort troops and lax supervision by their officers were to blame, in part, for these unfortunate liaisons. The prisoners, however, were not the only ones to make advances. '[W]omen of loose character make full use of their opportunities and, in some cases, anti-government sympathies on the part of the farmers and their families are responsible for this undesirable state of affairs.'[91] The simple message here was that Australia would learn from South Africa's experiences.

Obviously, contact between POWs and Australian women was unavoidable, especially after 1943 when hundreds of Italians were being billeted out to private residences and farms throughout the Commonwealth. Many POWs were eager to strike up innocent friendships with the wives and daughters of their employers. It was one way of combating the loneliness and isolation of captivity. For those who had families in Italy these friendships provided a useful coping strategy as they were one way of trying to salvage a bit of normality. For instance, one junior officer wrote home that on one of his parole walks he had encountered a young 'lonely' female child of 3–4-years-old. She lived in a nice one-storey house surrounded by trees, he recalled, and it was evident that he had encountered her on more than one occasion. 'Yesterday she graciously accepted my candies.' An innocent enough remark at one level, but the censors were alarmed and advised careful monitoring of this prisoner in case this charitable act was in fact motivated by a more sinister intent.[92]

Isolated acts of indecent assault on under-age girls were indeed reported. In Western Australia, one Italian POW in the employ of a farmer near Kulin in the Albany district was alleged to have indecently assaulted three little girls. He was tried in a civil court, the military authorities providing him with a defence attorney.[93] Common assault against women was another problem. In most cases, charges were filed when POWs attempted to kiss or molest these women against their will. In all cases the POWs were immediately returned to the permanent camps and placed in detention awaiting a military tribunal. If found guilty, the accused were sentenced to 28 days and more than likely never allowed on outside employment again.[94]

Charges of rape, although rare, were also made against several POWs. In July 1944 a farmer's wife from the Mudgee area of New South Wales made a complaint that a POW in their employ had made sexual overtures toward her. Highly embarrassed by the episode, she requested his immediate transfer, which was sanctioned. Further investigations by her husband revealed that the POW had in fact been boasting about his sexual exploits with her. The husband now wished him charged with attempted rape. He alleged that although his wife had managed to beat off her attacker, the POW implored her not to tell her husband and promised to never come near her again. She told him that if he dared come near her again she would tell her husband, and agreed not to say anything. The following day the POW reportedly made another unsuccessful attempt. The lack of corroborative evidence and the delay by the women in reporting the incidents meant that a conviction of rape was near impossible to prove. Instead, the POW was charged with common assault and given 28 days.[95]

Cases of serious sexual assault were the exception rather than the rule. It was legitimate affairs of the heart that were more commonplace. In the Orange district of New South Wales one POW had been making a persistent nuisance of himself with a female cherry-picker. Having, it was alleged, enticed her to his hut, he kissed her. When the employer came on the scene he saw the POW and the girl standing in the room. The POW had lipstick on his face. The next day, the employer witnessed the POW standing in the orchard at the foot of a tree from which the girl was picking cherries. A fracas ensued when the POW refused to leave the orchard. However, the intelligence officer revealed that the girl's statement left no doubt that the POW's 'attentions were not as unwelcome' as one might have at first imagined. The POW was charged with assault and fraternising with the public.[96] In several other cases, it was the farmers' wives who had made the first romantic overtures. There was another case where a POW who had been transferred to another farm deliberately sought to fall out with his new employers so that he would be transferred back to his previous employer where he had been fraternising with several females on nearby properties.[97]

At times, prostitution was a problem. At Cowra, the local racecourse had been turned into a market garden, the labour force being provided by POWs. The racecourse was on the other side of the river, so it was necessary for the POWs to travel each day through town and cross the bridge to get to work. The men were transported on slow-moving wagons. As they proceeded through the streets they were closely followed by dozens of children and some women to whom the POWs threw sweets purchased from the POW canteen. Two of the women, 'alleged prostitutes known as "Two Ton Tony" and "Dirty Dora" constantly meet the wagons', reported the camp intelligence officer. On a number of occasions they were also seen walking behind the returning wagons as they crossed over the bridge back into town at the end of the day! These and other complaints prompted a visit to the POW camp by the police vice squad. Investigations revealed that a 'considerable number of undesirable women' had been detained for medical examination.[98] It is unknown whether these women were charged with solicitation, or if the POWs themselves were also punished.

POWs in the Empire: balancing advantages and risks

At one level, the incarceration of Italian POWs in Africa and Australia was quite similar. Almost immediately both dominions understood the labour potential of these prisoners. It was clear by 1943, as the pressures of their respective wartime economies mounted, how indispensable the POWs had become, particularly in agriculture. Evidence also suggested that many more POWs would co-operate with the Allies if paroled to work in the countryside. There was a price however. Their labour could only be maximised if security and quarantine regulations were relaxed. Similarly, this raised the potential for increased conflict between the prisoners and the civilian population as thousands more captives were contracted out to private individuals after mid-1943. Nonetheless, if it meant that agricultural production levels could be maintained, that valuable foodstuffs would be prevented from rotting in the fields or a vital railway link could remain open, it was a price worth paying whatever the inconvenience a few malcontents or molesters might cause to public order and decency.

To some extent, the cultural stereotype of the Italian POW, which pervaded most of the Allied wartime commentary on this issue, came into play. Government and military officials on both sides of the Indian Ocean firmly believed that most Italians were not ideologically driven, unlike their German or Japanese allies. The relative ease with which Italy had been knocked out of the war had confirmed this belief. The descriptions of Italian captives as 'docile', 'malleable', 'child-like' and 'happy to be out of the war' were commonplace. To be sure, the attitude of and response by many Italian POWs during captivity also reinforced the stereotype. However, as Gianfranco Cresciani has noted, this is a dangerously over-simplistic and highly inaccurate picture.[99] The story of Italian captivity in Kenya, South Africa and Australia was written on a much richer tapestry, threaded with a multitude of individual experiences and emotions.

Nevertheless, there were fundamental differences in administration and circumstance between Australia and her African partners. Compared with Pretoria or Nairobi, Canberra had developed a much more effective and efficient POW administration, but it also had better resources.

In addition, the shortage of shipping between the Middle East, India and Australia had proved a blessing in disguise, as the numbers and flow of prisoners were somewhat regulated, allowing the military authorities to prepare for their guests well in advance of their arrival. Moreover, the crucial factor in this comparison was that the number of Italian captives sent to Australia was only one-third of the number incarcerated in either Kenya or South Africa. The African administrations never had the luxury of time to plan, and it was evident that their POW administrations were under-manned, under-resourced and under pressure right from the beginning. As prisoners flooded in, and faced with such an enormous task, it is no wonder that there were a number of important POW issues to resolve in Kenya and Pretoria in 1941–2. What is remarkable is how well these agencies coped under such trying conditions. More significantly, Australia unlike South Africa did not have to face a serious threat to its internal security from elements within its own citizenry. The menace posed by the *Ossewabrandwag* and other right-wing factions within Afrikanerdom did not exist in Australia; nor did the added complication of a majority non-European population living in a segregationist society fashioned and policed by a white minority government.

9
The Long Road Home

Prisoner exchanges in wartime

Arrangements for the reciprocal repatriation of Italian and British-held prisoners of war within the terms of Article 68 of the 1929 Geneva Convention had been in place since the summer of 1941. As early as December 1940, the British government had requested such an arrangement through their protecting power to facilitate the exchange of sick, wounded and 'protected' personnel. A basic draft agreement was drawn up with little difficulty. However, the machinery needed to effect exchanges was cumbersome in the extreme. On the British side, it involved two inter-departmental repatriation committees that included representatives from the armed forces, civilian ministries, the dominions, and later even the United States. In addition, there was the need to negotiate through the protecting powers and to arrange guarantees through the neutral states where the exchanges were to take place, and to enlist the help of neutral observers such as the International Committee of the Red Cross to monitor the actions of all sides.[1]

Unlike the planned exchanges with the Germans, which encountered enormous difficulties due to Berlin continually making additional threats and demands, and the perceived need to organise parallel repatriations of British and United States servicemen, relations with the Italian government were far more straightforward, if not always smooth. A British suggestion to exchange around 500 sick and wounded Italians for a smaller number of British prisoners in September 1941 had been agreed on 12 January 1942. This led to a formal exchange in the Turkish port of Smyrna on 8 April the same year when hospital ships brought 344 wounded Italians and 575 'protected personnel'[2] to be exchanged for 59 wounded and 69 'protected personnel' from British Imperial forces.

These included men from Australia, New Zealand and South Africa as well as from the British Isles.[3] At this stage, the exchanged Italians had come exclusively from prisoners held in the Middle East theatre, but the success of this first exchange encouraged a further British approach in August 1942 which encompassed Italian prisoners held throughout the Empire and the dominions. Removing sick and wounded prisoners would undoubtedly reduce the burden on the detaining powers, but there was also a domestic political motive involved. The British authorities believed that there were many British prisoners in Italian hands that had been deemed eligible by Mixed Medical Commissions who had not been included in the first exchange. Thus it was considered politically expedient to make every effort to have all British servicemen qualifying under Article 68 repatriated at the earliest opportunity.

This led to a much more extensive exchange which lasted for more than six weeks from 19 April to 3 June 1943 as ships were used to ferry Italians collected in Alexandria from various parts of the Empire to Smyrna. At the same time, British prisoners were brought from Italy to Smyrna to make the return voyage. In addition, other Italians were brought from the United Kingdom to Lisbon to form a third element in the exchange process. In total, some 9,114 Italians and 1,916 British Imperial servicemen were allowed home.[4] London requested a third exchange through Lisbon, involving 500 Italians and 170 British soldiers, two days before the fall of the Mussolini regime. The proposed date was 13 September, but the fall of Italy some five days earlier meant that the British soldiers were caught in the chaos as the Germans flooded Northern Italy with troops, while the hospital ship carrying the Italians had already sailed from the United Kingdom. Rather than send them back, the British authorities contrived to land the Italians in Algiers from where they were ultimately conveyed back to Southern (liberated) Italy during 1944. The British soldiers were destined to remain in German hands for a much longer period.[5]

One final and more unusual exchange took place during 1942. The neutral government of Saudi Arabia had interned a large number of Italian naval personnel whom they were keen to remove from their country. The British, seeing a useful opportunity to recover 'valuable reinforcements for the Royal Navy in exchange for an Italian party of naval officers and men of doubtful worth', welcomed the idea of their being used as exchange material for men held by the Italians. Through the intercession of the Turkish government, the exchange took place between ships moored at the port of Mersin, involving 788 Italians, 25 German civilians and an equivalent number of Royal Navy and merchant mariners.[6] According to Foreign Office figures, in excess of 11,300 Italian sick and wounded servicemen and protected personnel were returned to a belligerent Italy between April 1942 and September 1943.

For nearly all the Italians in British hands after September 1943, there was to be no change in their status or conditions. Certainly, there was to be no early return home. The only exceptions were, as had been the case during hostilities, those that were sick or wounded. Thus, for example, 4 officers and 120 men were sent back to Italy from Britain in January 1945.[7] One minor anomaly in this policy arose when the authorities in India pointed out that they had some 40 Italians who were wounded or disabled in the First World War, and therefore technically not eligible for repatriation as their injuries had not been sustained in the current conflict! The War Office expressed itself at a loss to understand how these men could have become prisoners-of-war in the first place, but wanted the matter settled and decreed that the date of the injury was not to be deemed relevant to their consideration for repatriation.[8]

British policy on repatriation

Although the wholesale repatriation of Italians held in Britain and the Empire had been debated since the surrender in 1943, it was not seriously considered until the beginning of 1945, when the end of hostilities against Germany and the liberation of Northern Italy was in sight. The Foreign Office remained concerned that every effort was made to ensure that, for political reasons, Italian hearts and minds were not turned against their Allied 'liberators'. However, the return of prisoners from abroad, and the status of those being used as labour battalions inside Italy was becoming an increasingly important domestic issue. In February, the British Embassy in Rome reported an article quoting Count Sforza who reflected on the perceived injustice of the prisoners' continued incarceration and how this reflected on both the Italian government and the Allies.[9] Pressure also came from the Italian Representative in London, Count Carandini,[10] who wanted the British government to reclassify the prisoners and make some statement about repatriation. This, it was felt, would remove the stigma attached to prisoner status and encourage the men to work harder, knowing that they were really contributing to the Allied war effort. The Foreign Office were keen to go some way to helping the Italian government, pressing the matter with the War Office as one 'in which we really can do so at no cost to ourselves'.[11] A memorandum from one Foreign Office Counsellor, F. R. Hoyer Millar, at the end of April pointed out the weak moral case for doing nothing on account of the Italian contribution to the war effort and the potential for protest among prisoners. Certainly, he saw nothing unreasonable in Carandini's request as it would make 'no practical difference but would satisfy the Italian government'.[12] At this stage, the War Office was not prepared to move on the issue, again stressing the problems of controlling the Italians if they were relieved of prisoner status. The DPW were adamant that, 'until it is known when and to what extent their labour can be replaced by demobilised British personnel or by German prisoners of war we cannot give any kind of undertaking on their repatriation'.[13] However, it was also pointed out that many of Carandini's other demands, in relation to remittances and mail, were already being met.[14]

While it was clear that the Foreign Office was keen to do something to assuage Italian opinion, even *it* was sceptical about some of the claims being made. For example, it was felt that the removal of POW status might make the Italians 'much less disposed to work' rather than encourage them to redouble their efforts. In this matter, coercion was felt to be more efficacious than kindness. The idea of having the Italians reconstituted as a military force under the Allied Forces Act was also resisted, not least because of the plans put forward by General Gazzera to bring this about. These involved the establishment of a headquarters in Britain, staffed by a plethora of generals and equipped with numbers of motor cars. This was felt to be unnecessary in the extreme. Some low-ranking officers were essential, but 'all our experience with the Allies in this country is that the fewer high-ranking officers there are, the more smoothly matters proceed'.[15]

For the time being, the position was not to change and on 18 May 1945, the Cabinet agreed that no repatriations should take place without further discussion.[16] However, as had been the case with the prisoner question in 1943, their American allies forced the British government's hand. On 28 May, Field Marshal Alexander informed the War Office that the Americans had agreed with the Italian government to begin the repatriation of the 33,000 Italian co-operators held in the United States at the rate of 10,000 per month, beginning in July. If the non-co-operators were to follow, it would mean that all American-held Italians would be sent home within nine months. It would be inequitable and politically disastrous if the Americans were to repatriate their non-co-operators before co-operators in British hands were sent home.[17] This American initiative prompted a rapid British reappraisal of their policy. Aside from the imperative created by the actions of their ally, the Foreign Office was keen to exploit the potential political advantages. Announcement of a repatriation policy would help 'moderate elements in the Italian Government

and in Italy at large who look to us for support'. Somewhat more cyni-
cally, it was argued that 'the credit which would accrue to us for such a
decision would be quite out of proportion to the limited scale of repatriation which could, in fact, be achieved'.[18] Although these two political
considerations may have been paramount, it was also recognised that
the gesture would be more or less costless given that German replacements were available. Once hostilities had ceased, German prisoners had
been held pending their use as substitutes for Italians, but this meant a
double commitment to guarding, feeding, accommodating and clothing
prisoners for as long as the Italians were retained.[19]

Finally, it seemed that both the War and Foreign Offices were in agreement that British international, military and domestic interests would
best be served by expediting, or at least signalling, the beginning of a
repatriation policy for the Italians. However, as was already recognised,
there would be some substantial logistical difficulties in returning the
prisoners to their homeland. The Army Council thought there would
be few problems finding shipping to move men from India and the
Middle East, but transport from East and South Africa, and from the
United Kingdom would be more constrained. Their initial suggestion
was that 500 men could be sent home each day by air, beginning in July,
and that Italian cruisers being used for transport from the Mediterranean
could be used to take Italian prisoners home on their outward voyages.
Even the financial difficulties had been sorted out. For a United Kingdom
desperately short of funds, the idea that the Italians could take home
the monies accrued to them while in captivity was unthinkable and
steps were taken to substitute a 'chit' as evidence of the debt.[20] No indication was given as to how these chits might be redeemed but presumably these were to be honoured by the British authorities in Italy and
paid in appropriate amounts of lire.

Whatever the advantages of this course of action may have been, the
disadvantages were exposed when the matter was finally debated
in Cabinet again on 15 June. The Italian co-operators employed individually or in small groups on farms were essential for the coming harvest
and could not be replaced by Germans (who would need to be guarded
and could not be lodged outside camps). Similarly, those employed in
the building or food-processing industries could not be spared in the
immediate future either. The only alternative was to allow the non-
co-operators to be sent home first, something that would be unfair, but
more importantly 'give rise to trouble with the co-operators'. It was clear
that domestic considerations were now paramount. Certainly Churchill
was in no hurry to see the Italians go, seeing it as 'unnecessary ... to

hasten to make any concessions to meet the views of the Italian government'.[21] His view and those of Ministries of Labour and Agriculture prevailed. There were to be no repatriations before the late autumn.

It was left to the Imperial Prisoners of War Committee to sort out the problems caused by this ruling. The American decision to begin repatriation was a major complication, but even some prisoners in British hands and held in Italy had already been released. Those over fifty who had been in captivity for more than two years and all those over sixty had been handed over to the Italian military authorities, and some others had also been released on compassionate grounds.[22] However, the committee remained keen that a common policy should govern the repatriation of Italian prisoners in British hands in whatever country they were held, and that co-operators should be released before non-co-operators.

The Cabinet decision did nothing to alter the pressures building elsewhere. At the very moment that ministers were discussing the issue, the Foreign Office had received yet another plea for action from the Italian government via Count Carandini. Its representatives continued to press for a statement at least, which would prevent Britain being adversely compared with the United States on this issue or ultimately credited only with 'an unwilling conformity'. There was no advantage to keeping the Italians as they were perceived neither as docile nor as hardworking as the Germans, and 'however much we "educate" them or call them by another name, we shall not gain their affection by keeping them here now that the war is over'.[23] The War Office was also far from happy. Without a positive decision on when the repatriations of Italians were to begin, the Germans being held to replace them remained in limbo and were regarded as a drain on the resources of 21st Army Group.[24] Moreover, it would eventually be necessary to arrange the 'disposal' of the 300,000–400,000 German troops still in Norway, thus increasing the pressure still further. More galling still was the fact that transport was currently available to repatriate anything up to 4,000 prisoners a month, but this would not be the case by the end of the year.[25]

When the topic was raised with Churchill again, he responded in characteristically belligerent fashion:

I hate 'gestures' which nearly always take the form of giving things away at our expense. These Italian prisoners of war probably shot down a lot of our men and afterwards begged for their lives, and have been handsomely maintained ever since. I daresay we should be forced into a peace with the US, but this will not happen immediately ... Have the Russians released all their prisoners, or did they kill them all and have none. Anyhow, I cannot see the urgency.[26]

This merely served to convince Cadogan and one of his Assistant Under-Secretaries, Oliver Harvey, that raising the issue with the Prime Minister again would be useless.[27] Nonetheless, the debate continued on into July, with the Ministry of Agriculture anxious to hang onto their 30,000 Italian farm labourers until the potatoes (November) and sugar beet (December) had been harvested. The Ministry of Labour was likewise keen to retain prisoners for reconstruction work. Their representatives suggested that prisoners might be persuaded to volunteer to stay in exchange for incentives, but this argument drew more or less the same objections raised when first discussed during the previous year.[28] In early July Carandini raised the stakes by making a public statement to the effect that 150,000 Italian prisoners would be sent home when shipping permitted. As was observed in a Cabinet meeting of 10 July, he had neither the authority nor the grounds for saying this. Moreover, 'the statement was likely to arouse false hopes among Italian prisoners of war in this country, and was also disturbing to farmers who were relying on Italian labour for [the] year's harvest'. This did not stop one Italian newspaper from denouncing British duplicity: 'Let me tell you Mr. Attlee the war has been over quite a bit. In Italy too we await the harvest … Haven't the English ladies and gentlemen got hands of their own to collect up their potatoes and beetroot?'[29] Clearly, this was an attempt to force the government's hand, and to some extent it succeeded.

The issue was again discussed in Cabinet on 15 July when the Minister of Agriculture once again stressed his need to keep the 30,000 prisoners, albeit on a wage-earning basis. This was reinforced by the Secretary of State for India, Leo Amery, whose officials were also anxious to retain the skilled and unskilled prisoners being used for ship repairs, airfield construction and as drivers in motor transport companies. Moreover, they were eager to obtain more of the same from East Africa and the Middle East. Far from being repatriated, some of these men were likely to be moved further from home than they had been in wartime captivity. The ministers agreed the desirability of these measures,[30] but this left everyone unsure as to whether the Cabinet had intended that this new provision should modify the decision reached in June, and gave no indication on how the practical problems associated with this step could be solved.

A further inter-departmental meeting debated the meaning of the Cabinet decision some four days later. Ministry of Agriculture representatives suggested that if repatriation was to take place, the prisoners might be paid civilian rates for the job as an incentive for them to volunteer to stay. However, the Ministry of Labour thought this would still be unacceptable to the trade unions; the Foreign Ministry insisted that rates could not go above those paid to the lowest rank in the British Army (and co-operator rates had already nearly reached that level); and the War Office maintained that if the Italians were paid at civilian rates they could no longer be retained as prisoners of war.[31] There were no easy solutions, although the meeting did suggest that the billeting of Germans (as opposed to keeping them in camps) should begin so that they could provide ready replacements for Italians when the latter were sent home.[32] However, even this was complicated by the fact that any Germans brought across from continental Europe would affect the transport for British troops coming home on leave.[33]

In May 1945, there were 153,779 Italian prisoners held in the United Kingdom: 78,763 in camps, 54,214 in hostels and 20,802 in billets.[34] Their sense of frustration at continued incarceration undoubtedly increased as the war ended but their circumstances remained unchanged. Collective acts of protest had tended to be a feature of the winter when working conditions worsened, but there were also complaints about other restrictions, such as those applied to public transport. As the warmer months of 1945 arrived, so the levels of protest and other forms of disobedience and crime decreased. There were fewer absconders or attempted escapes and even charges of fraternisation lessened over the summer.[35] For their part, many of the petty restrictions imposed on the Italians were considered essential by the British authorities. They had to be paid less than British soldiers and civilians – not least because the latter had to house and feed themselves, things that the Italians had had provided for them. The question of access to public transport, cinemas and dance halls was also fraught with pitfalls. It was considered essential to keep the Italians away from the civil population as much as possible outside working hours. The cinemas and dance halls were so crowded that it was considered indefensible to allow access to the Italians, not least because it would 'inevitably lead to trouble with the locals over girls'.[36] There were also problems over the payment of prisoners. Italian other ranks were paid largely in tokens to prevent them making ostentatiously large purchases that might inflame local opinion. Officers, although paid entirely in sterling, also had to have their purchasing restricted. If this was not bad enough, the fact that none of the prisoners were liable for income tax (then levied at ten shillings in the pound) meant that they were potentially much better off in money terms than their British counterparts.[37]

However, as the war with Japan ended and no firm statements on repatriation emerged, so the mood worsened. As there had been little political re-education of prisoners, most of them were described as disappointed and discontented with Britain.[38] Worse still, although co-operators had been promised that they would be the first to be sent home, the reality was that British and Italian manpower needs took precedence, with some non-co-operators being sent home early at the request of the Badoglio government and all co-operators being kept back. By the late summer of 1945, a relatively innocuous broadcast from the BBC about Italians ceasing to be prisoners when the peace treaty was signed was greeted with despondency by many Italians who had been led to believe, both by letters from home and by Carandini in London, that they would be home before Christmas.[39]

This was to remain the position until early autumn. The end of the war against Japan had fundamentally altered the military, strategic and logistical calculations of the British government, but no further decisions were taken and there was little debate. Moreover, the wartime national government under Churchill had been replaced by a Labour administration under Clement Attlee. The new Foreign Secretary, Ernest Bevin, was kept apprised of the situation. His colleague George Isaacs, the Minister of Labour, reported a conversation with Baron Malfatti, the Italian Labour Attaché, who had once again raised the whole question of prisoners.[40] At the same time, Carandini had had a further meeting with Cadogan, during which he warned of a general strike being planned by the Italian prisoners to coincide with the meeting of the Council of Foreign Ministers. While the Foreign Office professed itself unhappy at this form of blackmail, Cadogan was clearly sympathetic. 'I think the prisoners here have had rather a raw deal and that Count Carandini, who has been doing his best for them, is now being put in a more and more difficult position.'[41]

Bevin took up the question of the Italians on 10 September and submitted a paper to Cabinet. To all intents and purposes, the situation was now becoming positively embarrassing. The decision of the United States to repatriate had been problematic for British interests, but with the end of the war, the Soviet Union and even the French were now committed to sending home Italians who had been their prisoners. Bevin clearly wanted to move Britain into line, if only to prevent British reticence being used by her detractors inside Italy.[42] He submitted a draft communication for the Italian government announcing in principle the repatriation of Italians from the United Kingdom that was agreed in Cabinet on 18 September.[43] Progress had undoubtedly been made, even if it remained only on paper. However, the ministers' decision had done nothing to alter the prospects of Italians held elsewhere in the Empire or in the dominions. Moreover, Bevin's paper had raised a supplementary issue that was to cause some problems in the future. Baron Malfatti had let it be known that there was a good deal of industrial unrest in Italy, that the Italian Communist Party had grown in size to around one million members and that anything up to two million people were in possession of firearms. At the same time, 'there was practically no police ... [and] ... all the elements of considerable danger in the situation'.[44] In this instance at least, the Italian pleas did have some effect. The Foreign Office was keen to do all it could to help the Italian government and professed itself 'anxious' to send home any available *Carabinieri* 'to improve the standard of the Italian police'.[45] The problem arose because the *Carabinieri* concerned had been largely non-co-operators and could not legitimately be sent home before their co-operator colleagues unless they were deemed a special case. Certainly, this appears to be what the Foreign Office wanted. However ideologically or practically wedded to Fascism these men might have been in the past, this was now to be forgotten in the face of their practical value in keeping order, and thereby bolstering a liberal democratic regime in Italy which was sympathetic to western (British) interests. In this instance, as in many others, the politics of the Cold War were already more important than purging key elements of the Fascist system. In the event, the Defence Committee, in line with Foreign Office plans, agreed that the 1,280 *Carabinieri* held in the United Kingdom and 729 others held in the Middle East should not be sent home in advance of others, but be included in early repatriation parties.[46] As insurance, it was suggested that it be made public that the repatriation of the *Carabinieri* had taken place at the express request of the Italian government.[47]

Planning the timetable

Once the decision had been taken in principle, it became a question of time and the practical difficulties of arranging the replacement and repatriation of the Italians. The basic principles were set out by the Imperial Prisoners of War Committee. First of all, it was considered essential that there should be a common policy throughout the Empire, but with repatriations beginning in the United Kingdom because it had the largest holdings of prisoners. In principle, co-operators were to be sent home before non-co-operators, and age and length of captivity should determine the order of repatriation within these categories. As a special measure, priority was to be given to members of the Cuneo and Regina divisions who had escaped from the Dodecanese and fought against the Germans, and who were currently being held in the Middle East.[48] There was an element of guilt here as assurances had been given to the Badoglio government that these men would not be treated as prisoners, but it had proved impossible to deliver on these assurances.[49]

In agreeing that Italians prisoners should be repatriated as soon as was practical, the Cabinet not only left problems of how this could be expedited, but also created a series of potential difficulties in sectors of the domestic economy where the prisoners' contribution was still deemed essential. Apart from the overriding need to collect the harvest, including the potatoes and sugar beet, Italians were also employed in the sugar beet refineries and could not easily be replaced. Uninterrupted production was essential. The Ministry of Works wanted to keep its Italian building labourers for 'as long as possible', and the Ministry of Fuel and Power was adamant that the 700 employed in gas undertakings were essential for the continuity of supply. If they were repatriated without replacement before March 1946 then a breakdown would be inevitable. There was no obvious local labour supply to replace any of these workers, and all the Germans currently in the country were already allocated to employment. However, there were also instances where replacement Germans were not wanted as an alternative, as with the 15,000 Italians at work on the railways. In spite of these reservations, the departments agreed that repatriation would commence in December, subject to suitable replacement labour being found and transport being available.[50]

The problem of manpower losses through repatriation was to be solved by Camp Liaison Officers and User Departments either reallocating their labour force – that is, making their operations more efficient – or by accepting the loss. Only in exceptional cases would essential workers be replaced by other Italians. In this way, sugar beet processing and gas production could be safeguarded through the coming winter.[51] Even at this late stage, the government's opinion of the Italians as a labour force was ambivalent. While the utilities, railways and food processors seemed anxious to retain their services, there were also countervailing forces with reports of strikes and of farmers unhappy with the amount of work done by prisoners. This ambivalence was summed up by Hoyer Millar of the Foreign Office:

> Everyone with whom I have spoken recently who has had anything to do with prisoners of war – farmers in this country and landlords in Scotland, etc. – have unanimously condemned the Italians and said they were a lazy lot of good-for-nothings who expected to be fussed over and treated like pets and went on strike for extra food or extra privileges on every possible occasion! These remarks may be exaggerated and admittedly a certain proportion of the highly skilled Italian agricultural workers have done good work and have made themselves popular with the farmers. On balance I think, however,

that opinion is definitely unfavourable to the Italians and everyone will be glad to see the last of them.[52]

Certainly, the various government departments involved did not wish to see the Italians allowed to remain to compete on the open labour market as it would only enrage the trade unions. It was also argued that, unlike Belgium and France, Britain had no tradition of employing foreign labour on any scale, or incorporating foreigners into the labour market. However, Isaacs had noted unofficially to Bevin that employers benefited from using prisoners, as they did not have to pay National Insurance contributions.[53] While this would not change if the Italians were merely replaced with German prisoners, there was some reticence in a number of quarters about using the far more disliked Germans than the amenable Italians, and a fear that there would be trouble if Germans were put to work alongside British civilians, or allowed the sort of freedom which had been afforded to the Italians.

The decision to begin repatriation finally came on 6 November 1945 after a further paper to Cabinet from Bevin which asked for 3,000–4,000 repatriations at an early date, as even a trickle was better than nothing at all.[54] Tom Williams, the new Minister of Agriculture, was persuaded to agree to an initial draft of 3,000 at the beginning of December, with a further 2,000 to be ready by the middle of the month. The War Office was instructed to assemble the first draft at Kempton Park by 3 December, and the second draft on 9 or 12 December. In the interim, nothing was to be published lest there were last-minute problems in carrying out the plan. Indeed, even in mid-December, Bevin was still uncertain about the availability and regularity of the shipping needed to carry out the programme.[55] Disappointing the prisoners was to be avoided at all costs, especially as morale was said to be improving. A report covering the month of October painted an optimistic picture:

> Repatriation is still the main topic of interest. Since the announcement that this will begin in the not-too-distant future, morale has risen considerably. The knowledge that about 2,000 are to be sent home undoubtedly has helped to lessen the strong anti-British feeling which had arisen. As the majority of prisoners have voted for co-operation they have been able to mix to a certain extent with the civil population. This has helped to bring about a gradual awakening towards political and world events.[56]

This view was not entirely shared by Carandini, who continued to press the Foreign Office for some type of limited military mission to carry out political re-education among men prior to their return home.[57] This had been discussed for some time before, but the British authorities felt that this was essentially the province of the Italian Representative and his staff.[58]

Once the repatriations from Britain began, the pace was intense. An initial draft of 6,639 officers and men sent home in December 1945[59] was followed by monthly totals which never fell below 10,000 and reached a peak in May 1946, when 82 officers and 32,267 men were repatriated. By the end of July, the last transport had departed, leaving only 1,391 men who had been released from POW status and then taken on as contract labour by the Ministry of Agriculture and Fisheries, and ten men who had been likewise discharged and employed by Carandini in London.[60] A small number of escapees also remained unaccounted for, but few efforts were apparently made to track them down. Even the small number of contract labourers seems to have generated a good deal of inter-ministerial correspondence. The Ministry of Agriculture, keen to hang onto any type of labour force, still had to convince the Home Office that the men were no threat, and the trade unions that the contracts amounted only to a deferred repatriation with no long-term consequences.[61] While the trade unions appeared satisfied, Home Office policy actually conspired to undermine attempts to keep some Italians in Britain. It was reported by the Foreign Office that there had been some requests from prisoners to be allowed to stay permanently in the country. However, the Home Office upheld the principle that they would all be sent back eventually and that permission to stay would only be granted in the most exceptional cases.[62] Thus the Home Office even refused to allow such 'civilianised' Italians who had subsequently married British women to stay permanently. This changed only in April 1947 when these few labourers were given permission to remain and given the same conditions as other aliens – including the right to bring their families from Italy. At the same time, they forfeited their rights to repatriation as prisoners of war,[63] and remained restricted to employment in agriculture unless given permission by the Ministry of Labour.[64] Although only a small number of former prisoners actually stayed in the United Kingdom, a few others returned in later years. However, it was their letters to family at home in Italy which undoubtedly had an effect in stimulating what became a much larger civilian immigration to Britain under the European Volunteer Worker schemes of the postwar years.

The pace or repatriation from Britain was inevitably governed by the availability of transportation, but was also driven by the necessity of finding placements for the huge numbers of German prisoners still being held by British forces. In the space of eight months, 143,854 Italian officers and men had been sent home. However, the pace of events elsewhere was governed by other considerations. In the case of those held in India, Noel Charles in the Rome Embassy had to defuse a protest by concerned wives at the end of November.[65] This was followed in March 1946 by further protests when it became clear that non-co-operators from the United Kingdom as well as generals and known Fascists were arriving back in Italy before co-operators from India.[66] This pressure was reinforced by the Political Intelligence Department, which noted the poor morale and dissatisfaction among the Italians in Italy and expressed worries about the prisoners returning to Italy with 'any prejudicial anti-British bias'.[67]

In spite of this, the Cabinet had decided that demobilisation and repatriation of British Imperial troops and civilians should take precedence over other demands and that no shipping should be specifically designated for the movement of enemy POWs. As a result the Ministry of Transport used whatever spare capacity became available. This favoured certain routes above others. For example, almost empty troopships sailing to India to collect British forces returning from the Far East facilitated the evacuation of Italians from the United Kingdom. In spite of the traffic from India, these same ships were also used to convey prisoners on troopdecks when only the cabins were required for British personnel. East and South Africa were less well served by the system, but even here a flow of returnees had been possible. However, it was Australia which remained the 'blackspot' as no troopships were being sent to the Antipodes. This had prompted a plea from the Australians who, having removed their Italian prisoners from farms early in 1946 in the expectation of a rapid repatriation programme, found that they were now forced to maintain the men in camps where the 'deterioration in [their] mental and moral outlook' would continue to grow.[68] As the Foreign Office was keen to point out, 'the Australians are obviously fed up with being told there is no shipping to repatriate these people' and saw this as useful ammunition against the Ministry of Transport.[69] Thus it was not until October of 1946, some months after all the Italians had been sent home from the United Kingdom, that the first major repatriations from Australia began. In spite of these difficulties, the Ministry of Transport hoped to complete the 'whole task' (of repatriating prisoners) by the end of the year.[70] More or less true to their word, all 1,004 officers and 18,631 men had been shipped out of Australia by the following January.[71]

The military authorities in East Africa raised the issue of repatriation as early as 30 May 1945, having assumed that this would begin soon after the war in Europe was ended. The main concern was that the prisoners were spread over such a huge area that they could not be gathered together for travel back to Italy if shipping was made available at short notice.[72] The situation in East Africa was complicated by the fact that many of the prisoners there had been raised from the Italian colonial territories. There was no question that they should be allowed to return there, but initial repatriations had taken place to Italy on a voluntary basis. This would not solve the entire problem, as a Foreign Office memorandum made clear:

> We must soon decide what is to be done with the residue of prisoners who do not wish to be repatriated to Italy or who are not accepted by the Colonies, the Dominions or other countries as permanent settlers. I cannot see that we have any alternative to repatriating them whether or not they want to go to Italy and whether or not the Italian government is prepared to settle them. This point has become a hard core to such prisoners – probably ex-active Fascists and other undesirable people – and someone will have to be compelled to take them. It seems to me preferable that this should be Italy rather than our own Colonial territories.[73]

By October, 20,985 still remained in East Africa[74] but sailings had been arranged, and presumably a degree of coercion was brought to bear on the prisoners unwilling to leave. However it was achieved, the last major shipment of prisoners was sent in December 1946 and nineteen further stragglers were embarked in February 1947.[75]

In South Africa, local conditions also played a part in the repatriation process. At the end of hostilities, the Union still held about 38,000 prisoners of whom some 15,000 were in active employment. Originally, the Union government had pressed for the non-co-operators and known Fascists to be sent home first as they represented a greater liability to the authorities. However, this policy was reconsidered in the summer of 1945, ostensibly to meet the possibility of complaints from co-operators. Thus it was asked that the latter 'be given the first chance of returning home'.[76] While the complaints may have been real enough, the change of heart was also motivated by two other factors that had a direct impact on the fundamentals of white rule in the Union. Firstly, there was the question of finding employment for returning non-white soldiers, where the removal of the Italians would create new opportunities in agriculture. Secondly, 'it would be most embarrassing for the Union authorities, for political reasons and because of the Italian prisoners' tendency to fraternise with natives and coloured people, if the Italians were to be given some sort of civilian status while they remain in the Union'.[77] More obscure was the fate of ten Italians who had been held in Jamaica. Because there was no shipping to take them home direct, they were brought to the United Kingdom and then taken overland with a police escort all the way to Milan 'to ensure [their safe] arrival'.[78] By the end of February 1947, the process of repatriation was all but complete, with the last sailings from South Africa, Australia and East Africa. The Imperial Prisoners of War Committee was reasonably certain that it had accounted for all the Italian captives held in the British Empire. The overwhelming majority had been sent back to Italy, a few had been accepted as migrants, and the remainder comprised those who had escaped and succeeded in evading the authorities. Even then, the totals were not large, with only 7 escapees in India, around 100 in South Africa, 140 in East Africa, 109 in Australia and two in Bermuda. As with the escapees in the United Kingdom, it appears – with the exception of Australia – that no great efforts were made to find these men.[79]

The fruits of fraternisation

The return of the Italians to their homeland was not always the end of the story. Even before repatriation had begun, Carandini had drawn the attention of authorities in Britain to 'quite a number of children' born to prisoners during their captivity. He wanted the men to be able to recognise their children before they were sent home,[80] but at this stage, the government chose not to respond. However, the problem did not disappear. Once repatriations began, the Foreign Office received requests, either directly or via a solicitor, from women who had become involved with prisoners during their stay.[81] For the most part, they had been made promises of marriage and many were expecting or nursing illegitimate children. The War Office had been particularly clear on the issue. Prisoners had been forbidden to 'establish relations of an amorous or sexual nature' with women in the United Kingdom. It was therefore impossible to 'allow a prisoner to marry a woman in this country, even where a child has been born, as this would be tantamount to condoning a very serious breach of existing regulations and would have a grave effect on the discipline among prisoners'. Liaisons of this nature were, of themselves, punishable by close imprisonment and loss of privileges.[82] Some prisoners had undoubtedly fallen foul of this regulation but the majority of cases concerned men who had subsequently been repatriated.

In general terms, there were three categories of cases. The first concerned women with illegitimate children, who having been promised marriage, were subsequently unable to contact their 'betrothed'. In these circumstances, the officials felt that the mother had 'had it' and the only course was to consider trying to obtain some alimony. However, even this was considered impractical. British consuls were often employed to track down recalcitrant fathers. One such enquiry to the consul in Milan produced a denial of paternity, but also a few crumbs of comfort for the wronged woman. 'It may be of some slight consolation to the mother to know that G. appeared here rather shabbily dressed, has been without work for some time, according to his statements, and does not appear to us to be a type able to give a home or care to a British born girl.'[83] In these circumstances, former prisoners found it relatively easy to avoid responsibility by claiming that the woman in question had been involved in other relationships.[84] There were instances of women who seemed determined to go to Italy and confront their paramours, but here the diplomats' self-interest was clear. They did everything possible to dissuade would-be travellers on the grounds that they would undoubtedly 'land in trouble for lack of funds' and the officials would then have 'another repatriation case on [their] hands'.[85] There was a suggestion that a policy could be formulated based on what was done in cases where British servicemen had allegedly fathered children in Northwest Europe, but this was rapidly shelved.[86] Clearly, the Foreign Office had no desire to enquire too closely into these most intimate of inter-allied relations.

These cases of desertion were only one aspect of the problem. For every Italian who tried to evade his responsibilities, there were others who were anxious to legitimise their relationships. Some wanted their fiancées to join them in Italy. This was perfectly possible provided the woman obtained a passport and Italian visa. For the Foreign Office, this had at least one advantage as, on marriage, the woman would become an Italian citizen and 'cease to concern us'.[87] However, worried parents would sometimes contact the authorities to check on the prospective son-in-law, his home and the wealth and respectability of his family before allowing their daughters to venture abroad.[88] To some extent, the Foreign Office shared the reservations of these parents, realising that conditions in many parts of Italy were far from ideal.

The third category concerned former prisoners who wished to come back to redeem their promises and then settle in Britain. This was certainly the preferred option of Foreign Office officials but was opposed by the Home Office who had received some thirty to forty requests. Some 70 per cent of such applicants intended to work on their prospective father-in-law's land, indicating that they had reasonable assurances of employment, and, subject to further checks as to their good character, the Foreign Office hoped that their Home Office colleagues might be persuaded to reconsider their policy 'and human felicity thereby perceptibly increased'.[89] In the final analysis, the restrictive Home Office attitude was overridden by the small numbers involved and the insatiable demand for labour in the United Kingdom which gave rise to huge schemes for the import of workers from Europe and the Caribbean in the later 1940s. Apart from the relatively small numbers of Italian prisoners who managed to stay in Britain without being repatriated, others chose to return to settle permanently, or influenced family members to do so. Similar patterns occurred in other parts of the Empire such as Australia and South Africa where former prisoners also chose to settle and augment existing Italian communities.[90] In the South African case, there is an interesting postscript that may be mirrored elsewhere. Some men, having lived for more than fifty years and taken citizenship in their adoptive country, have nonetheless chosen to be buried with their wartime comrades in the military cemetery at the former Zonderwater Camp, as recent gravestones there testify.

Although provision had been made in all theatres for the screening of Italian prisoners, and especially the officers, for those suspected of war crimes, this was never really carried out. Surviving files suggest only the most cursory examinations were carried out, and then only to isolate individuals who might have committed crimes against British nationals or interests. Indeed, it has been suggested that the British government policy went further, and deliberately did everything to prevent Italians from being handed over to the Ethiopian or Yugoslav authorities. The British government backing of the Badoglio government made it especially difficult to indict men who had been the Marshal's subordinates during the war without undermining the political settlement. It seems that maintaining the status quo and preventing Italy from falling into the hands of the communists were already more important features of British *realpolitik* than the identification and prosecution of war criminals. As a result, whatever crimes they may have committed in the colonial wars or in the Balkans before falling into British hands, the Italian commanders were never called to account.

Conclusion

In surveying the British captivity of Italian servicemen during the Second World War, it is clear that the diversity of experience catalogued in the preceding chapters was conditioned by the interaction of military, political, economic and cultural factors. Thus the initial treatment of Italian captives in North and East Africa was based primarily on the assumptions that the 1929 Geneva Convention should be upheld, but qualified by the imperatives of military security at a time when the front line was fluid and the stability of the Egyptian base could not be guaranteed. At the same time, racial assumptions also came into play. The difficulties of dealing with huge numbers of Italian captives was to some extent ameliorated by the almost immediate disarming and demobilisation of non-European conscripts and militias, who, it was assumed, were of little military value, uncommitted to Fascism and who could be relied upon to return home and cause no further trouble.

Plans for the dispersal of captured Italians throughout the Empire continued initially to be based on military imperatives, but these were soon overtaken by other considerations, most notably the economic value which these prisoners might have as a source of labour. Nowhere is this convergence of interest more apparent than in the transfer of prisoners from the Middle East (and later South Africa) to the United Kingdom. Domestic labour shortages and the need to remove prisoners from North Africa led the Churchill cabinet to approve the transfer of specially selected men to the United Kingdom. Faced with severe restrictions on the billeting and the use of these men, the government rapidly altered its stance on the treatment of prisoners in the mother country. Having been so keen to remove all Axis prisoners from the UK in the aftermath of the fifth-column scare in May 1940, the import of Italians represented an almost complete volte-face.

Even before the first Italian drafts arrived in the UK, the potential problems of guarding and finding acceptable accommodation for these men within the existing regulations and obligations to the Geneva Convention while at the same time maximising their potential as a source of labour were neatly avoided by the authorities, simply through the expedient of altering the regulations in force. This official change of heart over attitudes towards the Italian enemy was undoubtedly conditioned by underlying cultural assumptions about the Italian people as a whole. Thus it was widely assumed in government circles – albeit with little empirical evidence – that the Italians were uncommitted to Fascism, unlikely to cause much trouble if brought to the UK, and possessed the natural attributes to make good 'road menders, mechanics and market gardeners'. These assumptions, while undoubtedly grounded in the need for expediency, also betray a level of cultural stereotyping amongst the ruling elite in Britain which is clearly evident in the official records, and mirrored in the attitudes of the public at large. These same attitudes were also apparent in both the dominions and colonial empire where, with the exception of India, the same loosening of controls was very much in evidence from late 1941 onwards.

Although this loosening of control was evident in nearly every corner of the Empire, the prisoners' experience of captivity was primarily conditioned by the geographic and climatic conditions in the territory to which they were sent. Most officers were incarcerated in camps in India unless they were considered of sufficient importance to be further interrogated by the military authorities in the Middle East or United Kingdom. The only other exceptions were the small numbers of protected personnel of doctors, orderlies and chaplains who accompanied the NCOs and other ranks. The vagaries of warfare, the chaos of surrender and capture and the often-arbitrary division of captives helps to explain why men from the same unit could have very differing experiences of captivity. Many were engaged, at least initially, in farm, forestry and reclamation work, albeit in environments which varied from the cold and damp of Scotland and northern England, through the temperate valleys of the Western Cape in South Africa to the extremes of climate in the Australian outback. Others found themselves employed on road and runway construction, quarrying and even mining in different parts of the Empire, while small numbers could even be found in West Africa making artificial limbs for returning British colonial troops.

By the summer of 1943, there were some 500,000 Italians in British captivity, spread over five continents and in innumerable camps, hostels, and billets. They all continued to be treated more or less in accordance with the terms of the Geneva Convention, although there were various attempts by the British civil or military authorities to circumvent or ignore certain 'inconvenient' clauses, such as the precise meaning of what constituted 'war work' or the stipulation that prisoners should not be subjected to public ridicule. In many cases, the captives undoubtedly colluded with the bending of rules when it suited them, but they could be equally vehement with their protests when it did not. However, it was the fall of the Fascist regime and the surrender by Badoglio's government on 8 September 1943 which was the watershed in the subsequent treatment of the Italians in British hands. The uncertain status of the new regime, and indeed of Italy itself, in the continuing war against Nazi Germany created enormous complications for the new Italian government, the captor and detaining powers (which by now included the United States and the Free French), and the prisoners themselves.

For the British War Cabinet, the priority as the war with Italy came to an end was to hang on to the prisoners who were now playing such an important role in the labour force, both at home and in the Empire. The war for the hearts and minds in the POW camps, and in liberated Italy was entirely subordinated to this end, despite the protests of Foreign Secretary, Anthony Eden, the PWE and the British officials in Italy itself. More of a complication for the mandarins in Whitehall was the attitude and policy adopted by Eisenhower in relation to Italians captured in Sicily. His cavalier attitude to their parole and demobilisation set alarm bells ringing in London, bells that became ever louder as the US State Department began to consider the repatriation of Italians in their hands. This threat was only overcome when it became clear that the US War Department was also eager to retain prisoners for labour and other purposes.

A more general problem arose in relation to the precise status to be afforded Italy and her POWs in Allied hands after the formal surrender. The debate between London, Washington and the Badoglio regime on this issue dragged on well into 1944, but it is notable how large a role the POW issue played in the final designation of Italy as a co-belligerent rather than as an associated Allied power. The new regime under Marshal Badoglio faced a different set of imperatives. Eager to be seen as co-operating with the Allied war effort (perhaps in part to mask its leader's previous career as a central figure in the Fascist war effort), domestic political considerations dictated that the Italians could not countenance, at least openly, agreeing to the continued incarceration of their countrymen in Allied hands. This inability to reach a settlement was only resolved by British recourse to some semantic sleight of hand that allowed a previous, but apparently limited, verbal agreement to apply to all Italians in captivity. This nevertheless allowed Badoglio to maintain the fiction at home that he was doing everything in his power to bring about immediate repatriation.

For the prisoners it was a period of many uncertainties. News of the fall of Fascism and surrender was greeted with a range of emotions, from relief, jubilation and the hope and expectation of an early repatriation, to outright disbelief and condemnation of the reports as another example of Allied duplicity and black propaganda. In the event, all were to be disappointed. Co-operation with the Allies did not lead to early release, as Churchill remained adamant that the prisoners had a role to play in the defeat not only of Hitler's Third Reich but also of the Japanese Empire. Conversely, the sceptics and dyed-in-the-wool Fascists who refused to have any truck with such collusion and who continued to believe in Mussolini's ultimate victory were equally disillusioned by their continued captivity and the lack of positive news about the Axis war effort. Whether co-operator or non-co-operator, the reality for nearly all the prisoners was that they remained in captivity until long after the war in Europe was over. This was essentially determined by the economic needs of Britain and her imperial partners, and perhaps epitomised by the deliberate delaying of repatriation from many parts of the Empire until after the 1946 harvests had been gathered in.

This survey does allow for some conclusions to be reached. While it has often been assumed that the terms of the Geneva Convention were the major factor in protecting the interests of prisoners-of-war, the detailed negotiations between 1940 and 1945 suggest that this was only partially true, and that reciprocity was also important. Thus the British government was keen to abide by the rules for as long as the Fascist regime possessed a substantial number of British and Commonwealth servicemen, but became somewhat less wedded to the principles underlying the Convention once the Italian state had no further bargaining power. While the discipline of the Convention was never severely breached, the redesignation of prisoners as co-operators and their state as co-belligerent was to some extent a precursor for events and policies adopted towards a defeated Germany at the end of hostilities in 1945.

It could be argued that the 'diaspora' of so many Italian prisoners spread throughout the British Empire provided the first contacts between civilians and 'the enemy' in the Second World War. For the authorities, the possible friction that their presence might have caused had to be offset against their usefulness as a source of labour, and in the event, there seems to have been little trouble between prisoners and civilian populations in any part of the Empire where they were utilised. To that extent, the Italians seem to have lived up to the stereotypical expectations of the British War Cabinet and its civil servants. Disputes over rates of pay, access to resources and places of entertainment were largely resolved without undue dispute with the local populations.

In the final analysis, the sheer numbers of Italians taken prisoner in the years 1940–3 make any generalisations over their capture, captivity and ultimate repatriation impossible. In effect, this is a history made up of 500,000 individual stories. Some clearly have experiences in common, but even these collectivities were to some extent mediated by the individuals' perception of captivity and adjustment to life in enemy hands. While many prisoners have provided accounts of their experiences, they fail to provide a clear picture and perhaps inevitably range between those which have a positive view of their captivity and those who saw it in a purely negative light – as wasted years away from their homes and families.

The final irony is perhaps that, in spite of their numbers, their story remained untold and ignored in the years after 1945. The political and economic reconstruction of Italy as a 'western' democracy and European partner in the NATO alliance meant that the Fascist past and the war against the west were conveniently forgotten. Only their comrades lost or taken prisoner fighting on the Eastern Front fitted the image that the postwar Italian state wished to portray to the outside world during the Cold War. This case of selective national memory may have served the interests of postwar Italy extremely well, but nevertheless served to marginalise the experiences of so many of its wartime servicemen.

Appendix

Table 1 Directorate of Prisoners of War. Return of Enemy Prisoners of War detained in United Kingdom and Dominions as of 15 September 1943

Italians	Officers	Other ranks	Total
Great Britain	364	76,491	76,855
Middle East	2,723	56,732	59,455
Persia & Iraq Command	5	1,196	1,201
East Africa	4,938	53,174	58,112
West Africa	1	577	578
India	11,029	55,703	66,732
Australia	473	4,119	4,592
Canada	–	60	60
South Africa	202	48,118	48,320
Jamaica	–	31	31
Caribbean	6	24	30
Total	19,741	296,215	315,966

Notes:
1. The classifications for officers and other ranks include Army, Navy, Air Force, Merchant Seamen and Merchant Navy.
2. Not included in the Italian figures were 10,586 native troops, 10,570 of whom were in the Middle East.

Source: FO 898/323.

Table 2 Demands for Prisoner of War Labour After Cessation of Hostilities with Germany

Ministry	Numbers of POWs
Ministry of Works	300,000
Ministry of Agriculture	
Dept. of Agric. (Scotland)	250,000
Ministry of War Transport	27,000
Ministry of Supply	20,000
Ministry of Food	5,000
Ministry of Fuel and Power	1,400
Air Ministry (Service Units)	11,000
(Maintenance)	2,600
Admiralty	1,000
Army (Service Units)	108,000
Total Requirement	730,000

Source: CAB 66/65, War Cabinet memorandum entitled 'Employment of German Prisoners of War Outside Germany after the Cessation of Hostilities in Europe', 10 May 1945, annex A.

Table 3 Statement of Prisoners of War Held by British Commonwealth and USA

The British Commonwealth now hold 295,000 Germans and 380,000 Italians. The USA hold 604,000 Germans and 120,000 Italians. The detailed distribution is as follows:

(a) British Commonwealth

Region	British Captives		US Captives	
	Germans	Italians	Germans	Italians
United Kingdom	102,000	154,000	54,500	–
Middle East	36,000	66,000	–	–
Persia and Iraq	–	2,000	–	–
East Africa	–	37,000	–	–
West Africa	–	1,000	–	–
India	–	33,000	–	–
Australia	1,500	16,000	–	–
Canada	34,000	–	–	–
South Africa	–	39,000	–	–
Jamaica	500	–	–	–
N.W. Africa & Italy	13,500	28,000	–	–
Gibraltar	–	600	–	–
N.W. Europe	53,000	–	–	–
TOTAL	240,500	376,600	54,500	–

Total British Commonwealth holding: 671,600
Source: CAB 66/61, WP(45)89, 'Disposal of Prisoners of War Captured in North-West Europe', 10 February 1945, annex B.

(b) United States

Region	British Captives		US Captives	
	Germans	Italians	Germans	Italians
USA	130,000	45,000	170,000	5,000
N.W. Africa & Italy	–	–	–	64,000
N.W. Europe	–	–	304,000	6,000
Total	130,000	45,000	474,000	75,000

Total United States holdings: 724,000
Source: CAB 66/61, WP(45)89, 'Disposal of Prisoners of War Captured in North-West Europe', 10 February 1945, annex B.

Notes and References

Introduction

1. MacGregor Knox, *Hitler's Italian Allies* (Cambridge: Cambridge University Press, 2000), pp. 5–21, and 'The Fascist Regime, Its Foreign Policy and Its Wars: An "Anti-Anti-Fascist" Orthodoxy?', in Patrick Finney (ed.), *The Origins of the Second World War* (London: Arnold, 1997), pp. 148–68.
2. Brian R. Sullivan, 'The Italian Soldier in Combat, June 1940–September 1943: Myths, Realities and Explanations', in Paul Addison and Angus Calder (eds), *Time to Kill: The Soldier's Experience of War 1939–1945* (London: Pimlico, 1997), p. 190. The Italian troops consisted of 47,000 regular army, 27,000 Fascist militiamen and 17,000 military policemen. Also see Knox, *Hitler's*, pp. 78–80.
3. Sullivan, 'The Italian Soldier', p. 188 notes that the scale of the Italian defeat and the number of prisoners was in large part due to the infantry's lack of motorised transport to effect an organised retreat. However, the reasons behind Italy's military failure were much more systemic. See Knox, *Hitler's*, chs 2–3, and for economic factors see Vera Zamagni, 'Italy: How to Lose the War and Win the Peace', in Mark Harrison (ed.), *The Economics of World War II* (Cambridge: Cambridge University Press, 1998), pp. 177–223.
4. M. R. D. Foot, 'Prisoners-of-War', in I. C. B. Dear (ed.), *The Oxford Companion to the Second World War* (Oxford: Oxford University Press, 1995), p. 914.
5. Australian War Memorial (AWM), AWM 54, item 84/370/28, 1st Australian Corps weekly intelligence review, 13 Jan. 1941, compiled by Lieutenant-Colonel J. D. Rogers. In 1942 Rogers was appointed Director of Australian Military Intelligence. For personal insights of several Australian field commanders, see AWM, Lieutenant-General Sir S. G. Savige Papers, 3 DRL 2529, item 017, folder 1, war diary (1941), pp. 113–14; Lieutenant-General Sir F. H. Berryman, PR 84/370, item [1], war diary, 5 Jan. 1941 (Bardia). Berryman was GSO1, 6th Australian Division and the mastermind behind the division's first campaign in Libya. Savige was the commander of 17th Brigade, 6th Division during the Libyan campaign.
6. Quotation cited in MacGregor Knox, *Mussolini Unleashed 1939–1941* (Cambridge: Cambridge University Press, 1986), p. 256.
7. CO 968/45/1, Wavell to WO, 7 Jan. 1941. Unless otherwise indicated all references referred to are from the Public Record Office, London.
8. Bob Moore, 'Axis Prisoners in Britain during the Second World War: A Comparative Survey', in Bob Moore and Kent Fedorowich (eds), *Prisoners of War and their Captors in World War II* (Oxford: Berg, 1996), p. 27.
9. Louis E. Keefer, *Italian Prisoners of War in America 1942–1946: Captives or Allies?* (Westport, CT: Praeger, 1992), p. 28.
10. A. J. Barker, *Behind Barbed Wire* (London: Purnell, 1974), p. 43; Ben Shephard, *A War of Nerves. Soldiers and Psychiatrists 1914–1994* (London: Jonathan Cape, 2000), pp. 313–23.

11. Bob Moore, 'Unruly Allies: British Problems with the French Treatment of Axis Prisoners of War, 1943–1945', *War in History*, 7, 2 (2000), 180–98, see p. 184. In 1944, 120 Italian POWs were sent to West Africa from Kenya to make artificial limbs for wounded African soldiers from the Gold Coast and Nigeria. With the cessation of hostilities in Europe and the Italian government's demand that they be repatriated immediately, the colonial governments in each territory were able to contract 11 men (5 in Nigeria and 6 in the Gold Coast) to continue on with this work. In 1944 the Governor of Sierra Leone, H. C. Stevenson, reported to the Colonial Secretary, Oliver Stanley, that a party of five Italian POWs were employed by the Department of Agriculture on rice cultivation and irrigation schemes. CO 968/67/5, minute by A. H. Poynton, Principal, CO, 4 Oct. 1943; CO 968/117/2, Stevenson to Stanley, 10 Aug. 1944; CO 967/162, Sir Henry Monck-Mason Moore, Governor of Kenya, to Sir George Gater, Permanent Under-Secretary of State, CO, 26 May 1944; CO 980/18, FO to Rome, 13 July 1945 and despatches from the Gold Coast and Nigerian administrations to the CO, 6 and 26 Oct. 1945 respectively. The decision to send Italian POWs to the port of Fao in Iraq in 1943–4, although never carried through, was contemplated because of the ill-temper of the British dredging crews who were finding the extreme heat, boredom and high humidity of the Persian Gulf soul-destroying. The FO thought the idea a sound one, but officials at the Ministry of War Transport saw the employment of these prisoners as 'a very doubtful expedient'. MT 9/3872, minute by unknown MWT official, 26 Nov. 1943; Alan Reid, Port and Transit Control, to W. H. Kimpster, MWT representative at Basra, 27 Nov. 1943; Reid to J. Chaplin, FO, 19 and 20 Jan. 1944, and Chaplin's reply dropping FO support for the idea, 1 Feb. 1944.

12. See, for example, Luigi Pignatelli, *Il Secondo Regno: I prigionieri italiani nell'ultimo conflitto* (Milano: Longanesi, 1969); P. Enrico Gallo, *Ricordi di Guerra e Prigionia* (Marano di Napoli: Società dei Missionari D'Africa, 1955).

13. A complete list of the primary sources consulted can be found in the bibliography.

14. James J. Sadkovich, 'North Africa and the Mediterranean Theater, 1939–1945', in Loyd E. Lee (ed.), *World War II in Europe, Africa and the Americas, with General Sources: A Handbook of Literature and Research* (Westport, CT: Greenwood, 1997), pp. 139–56, especially pp. 142–3.

15. Sullivan, 'The Italian Soldier', pp. 177–87. For the debate on Italian military effectiveness and proficiency of the Italian Army, see MacGregor Knox, 'The Italian Armed Forces 1940–43', in A. R. Millet and W. Murray, *Military Effectiveness*, vol. 3, *The Second World War* (Boston: Allen & Unwin, 1988), pp. 136–79; Domenico Petracarro, 'The Italian Army in Africa 1940–1943: An Attempt at Historical Perspective', *War and Society*, 9, 2 (1991), 103–27; James J. Sadkovich, 'Understanding Defeat: Reappraising Italy's Role in World War II', *Journal of Contemporary History*, 24, 1 (1989), 27–61; Lucio Ceva, 'The North African Campaign 1940–43: A Reconsideration', in John Gooch (ed.), *Decisive Campaigns of the Second World War* (London: Frank Cass, 1990), pp. 84–104.

16. Barker, *Behind Barbed Wire*, but see also Richard Garrett, *P. O. W.* (Newton Abbott: David & Charles, 1981), and Pat Reid and Maurice Michael, *Prisoner of War: The Inside Story of the POW from the Ancient World to Colditz and After* (London: Hamlyn, 1984).

17. Gerald Davis, 'Prisoners of War in Twentieth Century Economies', *Journal of Contemporary History*, 12, 4 (1977), 623–34; S. Paul MacKenzie, 'The Treatment of Prisoners of War in World War II', *Journal of Modern History*, 66, 3 (1994), 487–520, and 'Prisoners of War and Civilian Internees: The European and Mediterranean Theatres', in Loyd E. Lee (ed.), *World War II in Europe, Africa and the Americas*, pp. 302–12.

18. J. A. Ball, 'Italian Prisoners of War in South Africa 1941–1947', *Military History Journal*, 1, 1 (1967), 21–3; Gianfranco Cresciani, 'Captivity in Australia: The Case of the Italian Prisoners of War, 1940–1947', *Studi Emigrazione*, NO. 26 (1989), 195–220; Bob Moore, 'Turning Liabilities into Assets: British Government Policy towards German and Italian Prisoners of War during the Second World War', *Journal of Contemporary History*, 32, 1 (1997), 117–36, and 'Axis Prisoners in Britain', pp. 19–46; Kay Saunders, 'Down on the Farm: Italian POWs in Australia, 1941–1947', *Journal of Australian Studies*, no. 46 (1995), 173–85; Lucio Sponza, 'Italian Prisoners of War in Great Britain, 1943–6', in Moore and Fedorowich (eds), *Prisoners of War*, pp. 205–26; Alan Fitzgerald, *The Italian Farming Soldiers. Prisoners of War in Australia 1941–1947* (Melbourne: Melbourne University Press, 1981).

19. Keefer, *Italian Prisoners*; George C. Lewis and John Mewha, *History of Prisoner of War Utilization by the United States Army 1776–1945* (Washington: Government Printer, 1955). See also, Louis E. Keefer, 'From Captive to Ally: Italian Prisoners of War in Virginia, 1943–1945', *Virginia Cavalcade* (Spring 1990).

20. Giorgio Rochat, 'Die italienischen Militärinternierten im zweiten Weltkrieg', *Quellen un Forschungen aus italienischen Archiven und Bibliotheken* (Tübingen: Max Niemeyer Verlag, 1987), pp. 336–420; Lutz Klinkhammer, 'Leben im Lager. Die italienischen Kriegsgefangenen und Deportierten im zweiten Weltkrieg. Ein Literaturbericht', ibid, pp. 489–520; Nicola Della Santa (ed.), *I militari italiani internati dai tedeschi dopo l'8 settembre 1943* (Firenze: Giunti, 1986); Giorgio Rochat 'Bibliografia sull'internamento dei militari italiani in Germania (1943–1945)', in Della Santa (ed.), *I militari italiani internati*, pp. 197–210; Gerhard Schreiber, 'Die italienischen Militärinternierten – Politische, humane und rassenideologische Geschichtspunkte einer besonderen Kriegsgefangenschaft', in Günther Bischof and Rüdiger Overmans (eds), *Kriegsgefangenschaft in Zweiten Weltkrieg: Eine vergleichende Perspektive* (Ternitz: Höller, 1999), pp. 393–406, especially p. 396.

21. Anon, 'I prigionieri Italiani nel mondo', *Revista Militare* (1987), 114–23, see pp. 117 and 123. This gives the total number of returnees as 10,030. Carlo Felici, 'I prigionieri nella seconda guerra mondiale', *Revista Militare*, 1 (1988), 132–8, see p. 135.

22. Giorgio Rochat, 'I prigionieri di guerra, un problema rimosso', *Italia Contemporanea*, 171 (1988), 7–14, see p. 8.

23. Romain H. Rainero (ed.), *I prigionieri militari italiani durante la seconda guerra mondiale: Aspetti e problemi storici* (Milan: Marzorati, 1985), p. 1. For early examples of memoirs of captivity by the western allies, see also, Felice Benuzzi, *Fuga sul Kenia* (Milano: L'Eroica, 1947); Alfio Berretta, *Prigionieri di Churchill* (Milano: Edizioni Europee, 1951); Alfonso del Guercio, *Campo 25* (Roma: L'Arnia, 1951); Donatello Gabrielli, *I prigionieri di Saida* (Pisa: Industrie Grafische V. Lischi, 1947); Roberto Mieville, *Fascist's Criminal Camp*

(Roma: Edizioni Corso, 1947); Camillo Milesi Ferretti, *Ventimila rupi di taglia* (Roma: Danesi, 1948); Cappuccino Pio, *Convento e galera* (Siena: La Poligrafia, 1949); Elios Toschi, *In fuga oltre l'Himalaja* (Milano: Edizioni Europee, 1954).

24. Gallo, *Guerra e Prigionia*, p. 8.
25. Pignatelli, *Il Secondo Regno*.
26. Flavio Giovanni Conti, *I prigionieri di guerra italiani 1940–1945* (Bologna: Il Mulino, 1986).
27. Rainero (ed.), *I prigionieri militari*, on Italian prisoners in western Allied hands, see pp. 19–34, 79–104, 139–82, 249–54.
28. Jean Louis Miège, 'I prigionieri di guerra italiani in Africa del Nord', and Alberto Rovighi, 'Obiettivi, metodi e risultati dell'azione politica condotta dalla Gran Bretagna nei riguardi dei prigionieri di guerra italiani', in Rainero (ed.), *I prigionieri militari*, pp. 171–82 and 249–54.

1   British Planning and Policy for Prisoners of War, 1939–41

1. Sir Victor Warrender, Financial Secretary to WO, in answer to a question from George Strauss MP, *Hansard*, House of Commons, fifth series (1939–40) vol. 358, col. 824, 8 Mar. 1940; Moore, 'Axis Prisoners', p. 19.
2. Louis de Jong, *Het Koninkrijk der Nederlanden in de tweede Wereldoorlog*, vol. 3 (The Hague: Staatsuitgeverij, 1970), p. 402; E. H. Brongers, 'De Meidagen van 1940: De afvoer van Duitse krijgsgevangenen naar Engeland', *Terugblik '40–'45*, 36, 12 (1998), pp. 342–8.
3. The files of the HD(S)E can be found in three government record groups: PREM 3, CAB 93 and CAB 114. The former remain largely closed but minutes and discussions on POWs from CAB 114 were released at the end of 1998.
4. Moore, 'Liabilities into Assets', p. 120. For Australian internment policies, see the excellent study by Margaret Bevege, *Behind Barbed Wire. Internment in Australia during World War II* (St Lucia, QLD: University of Queensland Press, 1993). There are no comprehensive studies on the internment of enemy aliens of European origin in Canada or South Africa during the second World War. However, useful insights can be found in Ninette Kelley and Michael Trebilcock, *The Making of the Mosaic. A History of Canadian Immigration Policy* (Toronto: University of Toronto Press, 1998), pp. 250–310; Franca Iacovetta, Roberto Perin and Angelo Principe (eds), *Enemies Within: Italian and Other Internees in Cananda and Abroad* (Toronto: University of Toronto Press, 2000). Also see the personal narrative of one interned Italian civilian, in Mario Duliani, *The City Without Women*. trans. by Antonio Mazza (Oakville, ON: Mosaic Press, 1994). Buried in Home Office files is an intriguing report by one of its officials, Alexander Paterson, which dealt with Canadian policy on the UK internees transported to Canada in 1940. See HO 45/23515, 'Report on Civilian Internees sent from the United Kingdom to Canada during the Unusually Fine Summer of 1940', July 1941. For South African policies, see H. J. Martin and Neil Orpen, *South African Forces. World War II*, vol. 7, *South Africa at War* (Cape Town: Purnell, 1979).
5. FO 916/2580, marginal notes by Harold Farquhar and Sir H. W. Malkins, Legal Adviser, FO, 17–18 June 1940; Sir George Warner, head of PWD, to

C. W. Dixon, Assistant Under-Secretary of State, DO, 20 June 1940; Moore, 'Axis Prisoners of War', pp. 24–5.

6. FO 916/2580, memo by D. J. M. D. Scott, Assistant Under-Secretary of State, FO, 15 June 1940.

7. Peter and Leni Gillman, *Collar the Lot! How Britain Interned and Expelled its Wartime Refugees* (London: Quartet Books, 1980), pp. 192–201.

8. H. Wolff, *Die deutschen Kriegsgefangenen in britischer Hand: Ein Überblick* (Munich: Gieseking Verlag, 1974), pp. 3–4, 126–31.

9. Liddell Hart Centre for Military Archives, King's College London, Major-General Sir Ronald F. Adam Papers, Adjutant-General to the Forces (1941–5), typescript narrative, chap. 9 for Gepp description. There was a series of senior Foreign Office personnel in charge of the PWD, sometimes with overlapping periods of appointment, as follows: Sir F. M. Shepherd (27 Oct. 1939–1 May 1940); Sir George Warner (17 Feb. 1940–24 Mar. 1941); W. St. C. H. Roberts (24 Mar. 1941–July 1945); J. W. O. Davidson (Jan. 1944–May 1946); Sir Harold E. Satow (6 Feb. 1940–31 Aug. 1944 *passim*). Sir Harold Satow and M. J. Sée, *The Work of the Prisoners of War Department during the Second World War* (London: Foreign Office, 1950) p. 175.

10. Satow and Sée, *Prisoners of War Department*, p. 5. This notes that some lessons from the First World War had not been learned. For example, properly constituted organisations were not created at the outbreak of war, in spite of their importance in the previous conflict. Similarly, there were no agreements of competence, and rivalries and conflicts between the FO and WO continued throughout the war.

11. Originally entitled the Inter-Governmental Committee on Prisoners of War, the IPOWC continued to meet regularly until well after the cessation of hostilities. Satow and Sée, *Prisoners of War Department*, pp. 169–70.

12. FO 916/161, FO to Italian Government, 5 July 1940, and Italian reply, 10 Dec. 1940.

13. Ibid, Admiralty to FO, 29 Jan. 1941.

14. Satow and Sée, *Prisoners of War Department*, p. 75.

15. FO 916/271, 'Report on Special Agreements with Germany and Italy on Geneva Convention and Sick and Wounded Convention' (draft), initialled by Satow, 16 Dec. 1942.

16. FO 916/86, Roberts, PWD, to Sir Alexander Maxwell, Permanent Under-Secretary of State, HO, 1 Aug. 1941.

17. ADM 116/11640, statistical information, enemy naval POWs, nd.

18. FO 916/86, memo on responsibility for interned enemy merchant seamen, Apr.–May 1941.

19. Ibid; Australian Archives (AA), CRS A7711/1, item 1, 'History of the Directorate of Prisoners of War and Internees, 1939–1951', pp. 105–6. The custom in South Africa was to place all enemy merchant seamen in the civil internment camps, a practice which by Jan. 1942 the Union government and its 112 Italian merchant seamen seemed completely satisfied with throughout the remainder of the war. The men did receive, however, all the benefits entitled to a POW under the 1929 Geneva Convention. SADDA, Box 3065, DC 1472/1, chap. 4, IPOWC, sub-committee A, Paper PWCA/P(42)9, 30 Jan. 1942; Secretary for Interior to C. H. Blaine, Secretary for Defence, 29 Apr. 1942. Canada never took Italian combatants and instead opted for

Italian internees from the UK and captured merchant seamen. However, with the transfer of status of these seamen from civilian internees to POWs in 1942 the Canadian government had to adopt new policies. By Oct. 1942 there were approximately 3,000 enemy merchant mariners held in a number of camps located throughout Eastern Canada. According to PWE statistics there were 60 Italian merchant seamen POWs in Canada as of Sept. 1943. All had been transferred from the UK. By Feb. 1944 this figure had increased to 88, twenty-eight of which had been captured by Canadian naval forces. National Archives of Canada (NAC), RG 24, reel C-5389, f. HQS 7236-43-1, memo by Major D. J. Donahoe, Works Programme-Internment and Refugee Operations, 2 Oct. 1942; draft memo for Cabinet War Committee, 'Acceptance of further prisoners of war by Canada', 19 Sept. 1944; FO 898/323, return of Italian POWs detained by British empire as of 15 Sept. 1943; WO 32/11123, Canadian High Commission, London, to Lieutenant-Colonel R. E. A. Elwes, WO, 26 Sept. 1944; RG 24, reel C-5369, f. HQS 7236-0-10, circular D239, Deputy Minister (Army) to N. A. Robertson, Under-Secretary of State for External Affairs, Feb. 1944; 'Draft on Italian POWs held in Canada as a consequence of World War II', Feb. 1947.

20. Winston S. Churchill, *The Second World War*, vol. 2, *Their Finest Hour* (London: Cassell, 1971), p. 542.
21. Hugh Gibson (ed.), *The Ciano Diaries 1939–1943*, unabridged (New York: Howard Fertig, 1973), p. 323, entries for 10 and 11 Dec. 1940.
22. India Office Library and Records, Linlithgow Papers, MSS Eur. F125/10, Amery to Linlithgow, 17 Feb. 1941.
23. CAB 106/537, Nares to Brigadier H. Latham, Office of the War Cabinet, Historical Section, 17 Dec. 1943. Similar astonishment was expressed by Major-General Sir Hastings L. Ismay, Deputy Secretary (Military), War Cabinet to his close friend Air Chief Marshal Sir Robert Brooke-Popham, the newly appointed C-in-C Far East, when he stated that British successes had been beyond 'our wildest dreams'. LHCMA, King's College London, Brooke Popham Papers, V/1/6, Ismay to Brooke-Popham, 9 Feb. 1941.
24. CAB 106/380, 'Report on Operations in Libya from September 1940 to April 1941', written by O'Connor while a POW in Italy, n.d.; Rear-Admiral Algernon Willis, Chief of Staff to Admiral Sir Andrew B. Cunningham, C-in-C Mediterranean Fleet, wrote O'Connor: 'I'm afraid you've got a nasty problem with all these prisoners. We are sending ships along as fast as we can but it'll take some time to relieve you of 35,000. The 13th Corps certainly deals in large numbers.' LHCMA, Lieutenant-General Sir Richard O'Connor Papers, 4/2/27, Willis to O'Connor, 6 Jan. 1941.
25. I. S. O. Playfair, *The Mediterranean and the Middle East*, vol. 2, *'The Germans Come to the Help of their Ally (1941)'* (London: HMSO, 1956), p. 224; CO 968/45/1, Wavell to WO, 7 Jan. 1941.
26. CO 968/45/1, Wavell to WO, 7 Jan. 1941; Gavin Long, *To Benghazi* (Canberra: AWM, 1952), pp. 238–9.
27. CO 968/45/1, Wavell to WO, 7 Jan. 1941; WO 169/53, war diary of HQ Western Desert Force, 11 and 12 Dec. 1940; LHCMA, O'Connor Papers, 4/2/19, O'Connor to Brigadier A. R. Selby, commander of Matruh Fortress, 14 Dec. 1940.

28. Ministry of Information, *Destruction of an Army: The First Campaigns in Libya: September 1940–February 1941* (London: Ministry of Information, 1941), pp. 53–5.

29. CAB 123/136, WP(41)114, memo by Captain David Margesson, Secretary of State for War, 29 May 1941.

30. For insightful analysis of the Abyssinian campaign including POW tallies, see CAB 106/469, despatch by Wavell, 'Operations in East Africa, November 1940 to July 1941', 21 May 1942; 'Report on Operations from 1 November 1940 to 5 April 1941', by Lieutenant-General Sir Alan Cunningham, 22 July 1941; CAB 106/404, 'The Rise and Fall of the Italian African Empire', 21 Jan. 1943; CAB 106/401, 'Notes on Operations in East Africa, 11 February to 3 July 1941' (July 1941); CAB 106/390, report by a Major Graham of East African Command on the battles of Keren, Asmara, Massawa and Amba Alaji, 12 July 1941. Useful accounts of the campaign can be found in A. J. Barker, *Eritrea 1941* (London: Faber & Faber, 1966); Michael Glover, *An Improvised War: The Ethiopian Campaign 1940–1941* (London: Leo Cooper, 1987); I. S. O. Playfair, *The Mediterranean and the Middle East*, vol. 1, *The Early Successes against Italy* (London: HMSO, 1954), pp. 391–450, and vol. 2, pp. 303–25; Neil Orpen, *South African Forces. World War II*, vol. 1, *East African and Abysinnian Campaigns* (Cape Town: Purnell, 1968); B. Prasad (ed.), *Official History of the Indian Armed Forces in the Second World War 1939–1945. East African Campaign 1940–41* (Agra: Orient Longmans, 1963).

31. CAB 103/143, memo by J. A. I. Agar-Hamilton, Union War Histories Section, Pretoria, showing Italian strength in East Africa, 11 July 1950. Brigadier Latham wrote to General Sir William Platt, former C-in-C East African Command, that the Cabinet Historical Section had never been able to discover what happened to the official Italian records in East Africa. 'Rumour has it that they were buried. If so I should think that ants had finished them off.' Ibid, Latham to Platt, 12 July 1950. For the volume and speed with which Middle Eastern Command embarked their captives overseas, see assorted war diaries for camps in Egypt: WO 169/6759, Camp No. 304, Helwan (near Cairo), July 1941–Oct. 1942; WO 169/2547, Camp No. 308, Alexandria, Apr.–Dec. 1941; WO 169/2548, Camp No. 309, Qassasin (Suez Canal North Sub-area), Feb.–Dec. 1941; WO 169/2549, Camp No. 310, entries for May 1941.

32. PREM 3/363/1, cypher telegrams sent to and from W. C. Huggard, Acting British High Commissioner in South Africa, 11 and 22 Jan. 1941; CO 968/45/1, Governor of Ceylon, Sir A. Caldecott, to CO, 22 Jan. 1941.

33. CO 968/45/1, Wavell to WO, 8 Apr. 1941; FO 898/323, POW accommodation table, 2 Oct. 1943; CO 968/45/1, Huggard to DO, 29 Apr. 1941; WO to Wavell and reply, 28 May and 1 June 1941; Auchinleck to WO, 10 July 1941.

34. PREM 3/363/1, 'Italian POW location in Middle East, East Africa and Sudan as on 15 April 1941'; CO 967/160, Cunningham to Moore, 10 Apr. 1941; Moore to his predecessor as governor, Air Chief Marshal Sir H. R. Brooke-Popham, C-in-C Far East, 20 May 1941.

35. CO 968/45/1, WO to Wavell, 10 Jan. 1941; WO 193/352, unauthored note for Vice-Chief of the Imperial General Staff, Lieutenant-General Sir Robert Haining, Feb. 1941, on the establishment of 18 POW labour companies or 9,000 captives for battlefield salvage work. It was noted that Turkish prisoners had been used as labour in the rear-echelons during the First World War.

36. WO 32/9904, Wavell to WO, 6 Jan. 1941.
37. CO 968/45/1, minute by J. A. Calder, Assistant Secretary, CO, 11 Jan. 1941.
38. Rainero, 'I prigionieri italiani in Africa', pp. 154–5.
39. PREM 3/363/1, Churchill to Ismay, War Cabinet, 26 Dec. 1940; Lieutenant-Colonel L. C. Hollis, Senior Assistant Secretary (Military), War Cabinet, to Churchill, 31 Dec. 1940.
40. Heather Parkin, 'British Policy Towards Italian Prisoners of War in Great Britain from 1940–1945', unpublished undergraduate dissertation, Bristol Polytechnic (1989), p. 9; FO 916/161, part 1, Warner to Sir James P. Grigg, Permanent Under Secretary of State for War, 2 Jan. 1941; US embassy, London, to Warner, 16 Jan. 1941; ibid, part 2, PWD to DPW, 24 Nov. 1941; FO to US embassy, London, Nov. 1941; John Rylands Library, University of Manchester, General Sir Claude J. E. Auchinleck Papers, fols. 510 and 519, Lieutenant-General Arthur Smith, Chief of Staff, to Auchinleck, 3 and 5 Dec. 1941 concerning parading of captured soldiers through the streets of Cairo.
41. Rainero, 'I prigionieri italiani in Africa', pp. 154–5; Conti, *I prigionieri*, p. 32.
42. Rainero, 'I prigionieri italiani in Africa', pp. 156–7.

2   The Essential Labour Supply: The Import of Italian POWs to the United Kingdom

1. PREM 3/364/2, 'Employment of Italian Prisoners of War (Other Ranks)', table, n.d. (probably Jan. 1944).
2. Conti, *I prigionieri*, pp. 289, 435–6. Precise statistics are difficult to compile. Conti uses figures from the Italian state records which are impossible to reconcile, except in broad outline, with those kept by the British. CAB 66/61, WP(45)89, annex B, 'Disposal of Prisoners of War captured in North West Europe', 10 Feb. 1945, gives a figure of 154,000. The IPOWC report for May 1945, sections 13 and 15, in WO 32/9890 gives a more precise figure of 153,779. (By this stage, all movement of Italians to Britain had been halted) See Appendix Table 3(a).
3. MAF 47/54, WO to W. C. Tame, Principal, Man Power Division, MAF, 19 June 1941; Moore, 'Liabilities into Assets', pp. 124–5.
4. Conti, *I prigionieri*, p. 446; Sponza, 'Italian Prisoners', p. 208.
5. MAF 47/54, G. W. Lambert, Assistant Under-Secretary of State, WO, to Sir Reginald Dorman-Smith, Minister of Agriculture (1939–40), 4 Nov. 1939.
6. WO 32/9902, WO to Forestry Commission, 29 Nov. 1939.
7. CAB 118/65, PX(40)68, interim report by Manpower Requirements Committee, 8 Nov. 1940; MAF 47/54, Robert Hudson, Minister of Agriculture (1940–45), to Captain David Margesson, Secretary of State for War, 8 Jan. 1941.
8. Martin Middlebrook, *Convoy* (New York: Quill/William Morrow, 1976), p. 8.
9. CAB 67/9, WP(G)(41)6, memo by Hudson, 'Italian Prisoners of War and Land Reclamation Work', 13 Jan. 1941.
10. MAF 47/54, draft memo from Hudson to War Cabinet, n.d.; CAB 114/25, 'Italian Prisoners of War for Land Reclamation Work', note by Secretary, HD(S)E/42, 17 Jan. 1941.
11. CAB 67/9, WP(G)(41)6, memo by Hudson, 'Italian Prisoners of War for Land Reclamation Work', 13 Jan. 1941; CAB 65/17, WM7(41)8, 16 Jan. 1941. For

an insight into the structure and activities of this organisation, see F. H. Hinsley and C. A. G. Simkins, *British Intelligence in the Second World War*, vol. 4, *Security and Counter-Intelligence* (London: HMSO, 1990), chs 3–4.

12. CAB 114/25, itemised minute by Swinton to A. M. Wall, HD(S)E, 19 Jan. 1941; MAF 47/54, memo by H. J. Johns, Assistant Secretary, Man Power Division, MAF, on meeting of POW Employment Committee and decisions of HD(S)E, 21 Jan. 1941. These discussions also revealed that the War Office had intended to bring 7,000 Italian prisoners to the UK to help with Quartermastering and other work. See CAB 114/25, HD(S)E, itemised minute by W. Armstrong, 17 Jan. 1941. Some of the HD(S)E material pertaining to Scottish agricultural labour services can also be found in the National Archives of Scotland, Edinburgh, AF 59/3/4.

13. MAF 47/54, R. E. Stanley, Secretary of Agricultural Wages Board, MAF, to Johns, 5 Feb. 1941; memo on meeting with National Farmers' Union and other unions, 5 Feb. 1941.

14. Ibid, minutes of a meeting on the employment of Italian POWs in UK held at Hobart House, 12 Feb. 1941.

15. WO 199/405, Captain R. Fullerton, notes on a meeting on the employment of Italian POWs in the UK at Hobart House, 12 Feb. 1941; minutes of above meeting contained in MAF 47/54.

16. PREM 3/363/1, Sir Desmond Morton, personal assistant to the prime minister, to Churchill, 24 Feb. 1941; CAB 114/25, Hunter to R. S. Wells, Acting Secretary, HD(S)E, 27 Jan. 1941.

17. FO 371/29920/R 23, Wavell to WO, 23 Dec. 1940 and 13 Jan. 1941.

18. PREM 3/363/1, Churchill to Bridges, personal minute M243/1, 28 Feb. 1941.

19. Ibid, Churchill to Bridges, personal minute M595/1, 29 May 1941; CAB 123/136, memo to War Cabinet from Bridges, 29 May 1941.

20. PREM 4/57/3, Morrison to Churchill, 8 May and 3 July 1941. The supply of labour improved after an agreement between the United Kingdom and the Irish Free State, but workers only arrived in large numbers after lodging allowances were paid to offset low wages in the construction and agricultural sectors. This in turn led to widespread resentment from the rest of the labour force. Also see Tracey Connolly, 'Irish Workers in Britain during World War II', in Brian Girvin and Geoffrey Roberts (eds), *Ireland and the Second World War. Politics, Society and Remembrance* (Dublin: Four Courts Press, 2000), pp. 121–32; CAB 102/398, unpublished official history entitled, 'Irish Labour in Britain 1939–1945', by Professor J. V. Judges (which can also be found in LAB 76/25).

21. PREM 4/57/3, Morrison to Churchill, 8 May and 3 July 1941. Between Jan. and Apr. 1942 the Northern Irish cabinet discussed ways it could obtain power to deny citizens from the Free State the right of entry into the province to safeguard work for its unemployed citizens. Security was another consideration in these wartime measures designed to stem the 'infiltration' of Eire workers into the province. See Public Record Office of Northern Ireland (PRONI), CAB 4/496/5-5A, memo by Minister of Labour, John F. Gordon, 15 Jan. 1942; CAB 4/503/6, Cabinet conclusion 6, 24 Mar. 1942; CAB 4/504/3, memo by Gordon, 31 Mar. 1942; CAB 4/507/6, Cabinet conclusion 1, 28 Apr. 1942. For a fuller picture of wartime Northern Ireland, see Brian Barton, 'Northern Ireland: The Impact of War, 1939–45', in Girvin and

Roberts (eds), *Ireland and the Second World War*, pp. 47–75. Also see the unpublished official history by J. W. Blake in CAB 102/521, 'Northern Ireland in the Second World War'.

22. H. M. D. Parker, *Manpower: A Study of War-time Policy and Administration* (London: HMSO, 1957), pp. 334–9. This ignores the use of British and colonial labour from overseas, but the numbers involved in these schemes were very small. Parker, *Manpower*, pp. 342–3.

23. CAB 123/136, WP(41)120, proposal to bring 25,000 Italian prisoners to UK, 4 June 1941.

24. CAB 65/18, WM57(41)8, 5 June 1941; ADM 116/4443, Admiralty discussions on WP(41)120 concluded that the risk of sending transports full of POWs unescorted throughout their entire passage to the UK did not breach the rules of the Geneva Convention; CAB 65/18, WM63(41)8, 26 June 1941. A draft of the report to Cabinet was shown to Swinton but he made no comments on it. CAB 114/25, minute by W. Armstrong, HD(S)E, 31 May 1941.

25. MAF 47/54, minutes of a meeting on the employment of Italian POWs, 30 June 1941. Anderson's proposal to bring 25,000 Italian POWs to the UK included the use of an undisclosed number to replace Irish labour in the Orkneys. However, the HD(S)E did not think it a practical proposition as yet to allow Italian POWs to be employed for agricultural purposes in Scotland. NAS, AF 59/3/4, Bridges to A. J. Aglen, Scottish Office, 4 June 1941. Also see W. S. Hewison, *This Great Harbour – Scapa Flow* (Kirkwall: The Orkney Press, 1990), p. 308; J. MacDonald, *Churchill's Prisoners. The Italians in Orkney 1942–1944* (Kirkwall: The Orkney Press, 1987), pp. 1–44; Seona Robertson and Les Wilson, *Scotland's War* (Edinburgh: Mainstream Publishing, 1995), pp. 115–22.

26. WO 165/59, IPOWC, summary no. 2, July 1941. This was made public in a response by Hudson to a parliamentary question in the House of Commons. See *Hansard*, House of Commons, fifth series (1940–41), vol. 373, col. 2090, 7 Aug. 1941.

27. MAF 47/54, memo on report from Hunter, 11 Apr. 1941.

28. MAF 47/54, report by A. Carr Williams to Labour Supply Branch, MAF, 12 Aug. 1941; CAB 114/25, HD(S)E, extracts from itemised minutes 28 and 30, 24 Sept. and 22 Oct. 1941, which noted the decisions of HD(S)E(41)48, 24 Sept. 1941 and HD(S)E(41)51, SE(IPW)1, 22 Oct. 1941 meetings which raised no objections to these plans.

29. CAB 114/25, HD(S)E, SE/132, 'Italian Prisoners of War for Agriculture', note by MAF, 8 Nov. 1941; HD(S)E(41)53, 12 Nov. 1941; HD(S)E, minute by Armstrong, 12 Nov. 1941.

30. Ibid, SE/135, 'Italian Prisoners of War for Agriculture', note by Gepp, 25 Nov. 1941.

31. Ibid, HD(S)E, itemised minute 40, 25 Nov. 1941.

32. Ibid, HD(S)E, itemised minutes 41–53, 26 Nov. to 24 Dec. 1941.

33. Ibid, SE(IPW)1, conference on Italian POWs for agriculture, 24 Oct. 1941. This conference, which included representatives from the HD(S)E, DPW, GHQ Home Forces, the Ministry of Agriculture, Postal and Telegraph Censorship and the Security Services, became the ad hoc consultative body for matters pertaining to the administration of Italian prisoners in Britain.

34. *The Times*, 5 Jan. 1942; *Daily Express*, 9–10 Jan. 1942. See also cartoon caption in the *Daily Express*, 19 Jan. 1942: 'I des'say it's different on the Isle of Capri, but in Shepton Mallet we don't have no siesta hour'.

35. CAB 114/25, Johns to Sir Herbert Creedy, Secret Intelligence Centre, 19 Jan. 1942.

36. This had been first suggested in Oct. 1941 by Hudson to Margesson on 28 Oct. 1941. See MAF 47/54; MEPO 2/6871, Home Office circular to Chief Constables, 20 Feb. 1942; CAB 123/136, WO progress report on the transfer of POW from the Middle East to the United Kingdom for labour purposes, 29 Apr. 1942.

37. WO 32/9890, IPOWC minutes, summary no. 11, Apr. 1942.

38. CAB 114/25, HD(S)E, itemised minute 39, 19 Nov. 1941. See also the debate about the siting of a hostel at Leighton Buzzard, itemised minutes 77 and 78, 17 Feb. 1942.

39. CAB 123/136, draft memo to Lord President's committee on employment of POWs, n.d.

40. Ibid; NAS, AF 59/3/4, Anderson to Hudson, 28 May 1942. When he designated the 600 Italian POWs for urgent work at Scapa Flow, he argued that it was essential to make full use of the long daylight of the summer months. At its peak in 1943 Hewison notes that there were 1,200 Italian POWs on Orkney. *Scapa Flow*, p. 308.

41. CAB 123/136, W. S. Morrison, Postmaster-General, to Sir John Anderson, 1 July 1941; Captain Charles Waterhouse, Parliamentary Secretary, Board of Trade, to Anderson, 6 Oct. 1941.

42. Ibid, meeting on Italian POWs, 5 Dec. 1941. The FO expressed concerns about potential complaints to the protecting powers and advised delay until work on camps was completed and shipping could be assured. However the non-arrival of promised drafts of prisoners actually served to exacerbate the situation for the Ministry of Works which was unable to complete the camps on schedule.

43. Ibid, WO to Lord President's Office, 21 Feb. 1942.

44. MAF 47/54, Johns to H. Biggs, Principal, Treasury, 5 Mar. 1942. Johns described the prisoners as 'almost our last hope of obtaining sufficient labour' needed for the extensive drainage and reclamation work.

45. Ibid, minutes of meeting on employment of Italian POWs, 13 Nov. 1941; memo, MAF to Lord President, n.d.; CAB 123/136, Hudson to Lord President, 4 Nov. 1941; memo to Lord President, 7 Nov. 1941; MAF 47/54, memo by J. A. Sutherland-Harris, Principal Private Secretary to Minister, MAF, 15 Jan. 1942, report of 22 Feb. 1942. Nor did the watchfulness of the Ministry of Agriculture diminish. They were quick to notice that 215 Italians had been diverted from timber production to the iron works at Corby and Kettering. CAB 118/65, MAF to Anderson, 28 Apr. 1942.

46. FO 916/170, Auchinleck to WO, 26 Aug. 1941.

47. Ibid, WO to Auchinleck, 28 Aug. 1941.

48. Ibid, Auckinleck to WO, 9 Sept. 1941.

49. Ibid, WO to Auchinleck, 13 Sept. 1941.

50. Ibid, WO to Lieutenant-General Sir Pierre van Ryneveld, CGS South Africa, 29 Aug. 1941.

51. CO 968/45/1, WO to Auchinleck, 8 Aug. 1941; FO 916/170, WO to van Ryneveld, 23 Sept. 1941; CO 968/45/2, WO to van Ryneveld, 29 Oct. 1941.

52. WO 165/62, minutes of meeting on 'Security: Employment of Italian Prisoners of War in the United Kingdom', 9 Dec. 1941; CAB 123/136, WO progress report on the transfer of POWs from the Middle East to the United Kingdom for labour purposes, 29 Apr. 1942.

53. CAB 123/136, WO progress report, 29 Apr. 1942.

54. MAF 47/54, Hudson to Margesson, 28 Oct. 1941; meeting on employment of Italian POWs, 13 Nov. 1941; SADDA, Box 3074, DC 1472/22, South African High Commissioner, London, to D. D. Forsyth, Secretary for External Affairs, Pretoria, 3 Nov. 1941. The WO had made it very clear to the British Military Mission in South Africa that Britain's acute labour shortage should receive priority. When told by the Mission that South African interests were to be given priority it looked as if an embarrassing deadlock would ensue as each party laid claim to this precious pool of labour. Smuts, however, intervened, telling his subordinates that he had decided to comply with the British request.

55. Each camp was intended to serve a number of counties, as follows: No. 25 Farncombe Down, Lambourn (Wiltshire, Berkshire, Hampshire); No. 26 Doddington, Ely (Cambridgeshire, Isle of Ely, Huntingdonshire, Norfolk, Soke of Peterborough, West Suffolk); No. 27 Ledbury, Hereford (Hereford, Gloucester, Worcester); No. 28 Knighthorpe, Loughborough (Leicester, Derbyshire, Nottinghamshire, Rutland); No. 29 Royston Heath Camp, Royston (Bedfordshire, Cambridgeshire, Hertfordshire, Essex); No. 87 Byfield Camp, Rugby (Leicester, Northants, Warwickshire). MAF 47/54, Paper MPB 750/644, by MAF, Labour Supply Branch, to County War Agricultural Executive Committees in England and Wales on employment of POWs, 25 July 1941. For as near a complete list of camps and hostels located throughout the UK, see WO 199/404–409 and HO 215/201. Also see Anthony J. Hellen, 'Temporary Settlements and Transient Populations. The Legacy of Britain's Prisoner of War Camps: 1940–1948', *Erdkunde*, Band 53 (1999), 191–219.

56. MAF 47/54, Paper MPB 750/644, 25 July 1941.

57. WO 32/9890, IPOWC minutes, summary no. 11, Apr. 1942.

58. MAF 47/54, J. M. Ross, Assistant Secretary, HO, to Johns, 11 Mar. 1942.

59. *The Times*, 12 and 13 May 1942.

60. Ibid, 26 Aug. and 29 Sept. 1942.

61. *Daily Express*, 9 Jan. 1942.

62. Ibid, 10 Jan. 1942, 'Italians Pampered on Farms', comment by Mr J. Turner, NFU Council.

63. CAB 114/25, HD(S)E, itemised minute 103, 9 Apr. 1942, and digest of letter and reports from hostels, Johns to Wells, 9 Apr. 1942.

64. Ibid, HD(S)E, itemised minute 116, July 1942, note from Sir Herbert Creedy regarding complaints about Italians with shotguns; NAS, HH 55/59, PWD/45/10/45, complaint about Italian POW touting a shotgun in Special Branch Report by W. A. Black, Chief Constable, Dumfries County Police Force, 1 July 1944; CAB 114/26, Ministry of Information, Home intelligence weekly report, no. 146, 22 July 1943.

65. WO 165/62, war diary, intelligence summary for 21 Sept. 1942, dated 25 Sept. 1942.

66. ADM 1/14864, minutes of an inter-departmental meeting, 'Italian Prisoners of War: 1943 Programme', 2 Dec. 1943.

67. MAF 47/54, memo by Ministry of Works and Planning, 14 Jan. 1943. This was made up of 28,820 originally requested by Civil Departments plus a further 5,550 requested by the Ministry of Agriculture and 2,000 by its Scottish counterpart, plus 7,978 required by the WO as compensation for guards.

68. WO 165/59, IPOWC, sub-committee A, report for Oct. 1942, 10 Nov. 1942; ADM 1/14864, Lord Leathers, Minister of War Transport, to A. V. Alexander, Secretary of State for the Admiralty, 17 Dec. 1942. For the tragic sinking of the *Laconia* by Captain Hartenstein in U-156 see his eerie account of the attack run and saving of some of its passengers, in SADDA, Union War Histories (UWH), Box 220, N12, U-boat war diary, 7 July–16 Nov. 1942. Another ship, the HMT *Nova Scotia* was sunk several months later off the east coast by U-177. Its cargo were Italian civilian internees being trans-shipped from East Africa to Southern Rhodesia. Ibid, Box 221, N16, U-boat war diary, 28 Nov. 1942. Accounts of both sinkings appear in Martin and Orpen, *South Africa at War*, vol. 7, pp. 198, 208–9. British submarines, despite excellent intelligence detailing the cargo and sailing times, also sank Italian cargo ships which were carrying Allied POWs. Between 9 June and 20 Nov. 1942 at least five such ships were sunk in the Mediterranean by British submarines or motor torpedo boats. Casualties were high in several instances. ADM 223/46, NID summary, 20 Nov. 1942.

69. ADM 1/14864, '1943 Programme', 2 Dec. 1943.

70. Ibid; WO 165/59, IPOWC, sub-committee A, report for Oct. 1942, 10 Nov. 1942. See assorted minutes in ADM 1/14864 for intriguing discussions on limitations on carrying POWs in ships.

71. ADM 1/14864, '1943 Programme', 2 Dec. 1943.

72. PREM 4/54/1, WP(42)539, memo on manpower by Lord President, 20 Nov. 1942.

73. MAF 47/54, meeting of DPW, 19 June 1942; HD(S)E, SE/258, 21 May 1943.

74. FO 916/308, ICRC report by R. A. Haccius, 30 Aug. 1942 on Camp No. 34, Mortimer's Cross, near Leominister, Herefordshire.

75. Ibid, ICRC report by M. H. de Pourtalès, 18 Aug. 1942 on Camp No. 2, Glen Mill, Oldham.

76. *News Chronicle*, 8 July 1942.

77. CAB 114/25, Special Branch security work summary, 16–31 July 1942, attached to Wells to Johns, 15 Aug. 1942.

78. *News Chronicle*, 30 Apr. 1942, reported the conviction of an employee of the Surrey War Agricultural Committee for giving (or selling) bread to prisoners. *Hansard*, House of Commons, fifth series (1941–42), vol. 379, col. 1391, 7 May 1942; CAB 114/25, F. Wells, Superintendent of Police, Ely, to Chief Constable, 22 Apr. 1942; Ross to Johns, 11 May 1942.

79. CAB 114/25, HD(S)E, LOC(41)138(2), 25 Aug. 1942.

80. FO 371/29947/R 8297, Middle East POW location table as of 29 Aug. 1941, dated 4 Sept. 1941.

81. FO 916/308, ICRC report by Haccius, 30 Aug. 1942 on Camp No. 34.

82. WO 32/9911, IPOWC, Paper PWCA/P(41)8, 1 Dec. 1941, 'Treatment of Protected Personnel', section B9 (a)–(f) noted the limited parole for walks once a week offered to protected personnel officers (unescorted) and NCOs

(escorted), and the provision for chaplains to travel up to three miles unescorted to attend mass.

83. HO 45/21875/700460/60, Police Constable A. J. Ayling to W. Oliver, Chief Constable, Guildford, 24 Oct. 1942; WO 32/9911, Ross, HO, to Colonel K. M. Noel, WO, 30 Oct. 1942.
84. *The Times*, 18 Sept. 1943.
85. FO 916/308, ICRC report by Haccius, 19 Nov. 1941 on No. 4 General Hospital (Italian POWs).
86. Ibid.
87. Ibid, ICRC report by de Pourtalès, 18 Aug. 1942 on Camp No. 2, Glen Mill, Oldham.
88. Ibid.
89. WO 32/9890, IPOWC minutes, summary no. 8, Jan. 1942.
90. Ibid, summary no. 19, Dec. 1942.
91. Ibid, sub-committee A, 18th mtg, minute 5B, 3 Mar. 1943.
92. CAB 66/34, WP(43)73, memo by Anthony Eden, Foreign Secretary, 18 Feb. 1943; FO 898/323, PWE internal memos, 2 and 8 Apr. 1943.

3 Italian POWs in Africa, 1940–3

1. CAB 106/401, 'Notes on Operations in East Africa'; CO 968/45/1, Advance Force Nairobi to War Office, 2 June 1941; Wavell to WO, 16 June 1941.
2. CO 822/111/12, Wavell to WO, 16 June and 1 July 1941; WO 222/1493, diary notes of Sudan medical services during Abyssinian campaign, Oct.–Dec. 1941.
3. WO 32/9903, minute by Major J. R. Adams, WO, 29 Jan. 1941; CO 822/111/12, minute by D. G. Watherston, CO, 15 Jan. 1941; minute by Colonel S. J. Cole, head of Colonial Office POW and Civilian Internee Department (1942–46), 7 Nov. 1942. There may have been as many as 80,000 British POWs in Italian hands, nearly 50,000 of whom escaped after the Italian surrender in September 1943. See Roger Absalom, *A Strange Alliance: Aspects of Escape and Survival in Italy 1943–45* (Florence: Leo S. Olschki, 1991), and 'Hiding History: The Allies, the Resistance and the Others in Occupied Italy 1943–45', *Historical Journal*, 38, 1 (1995), 111–31.
4. SADDA, POW 2, CE 8/4/2, summary no. 12, 29 Aug. 1941.
5. Ibid, summary no. 16, 26 Sept. 1941.
6. Ibid, summaries no. 7 and no. 22, 25 July and 8 Nov. 1941.
7. CO 822/111/21, draft note by Lloyd, Jan. 1941; Moore to CO, 26 Jan. 1941; minute by unknown CO official, 6 Jan. 1941; Moore to Sir Arthur Dawe, Assistant Under-Secretary of State for the Colonies, 30 Dec. 1942.
8. Ibid, Colonel Sir Edward A. Ruggles-Brise MP, chairman of the House of Commons Agricultural Committee, to Lord Lloyd, 30 Dec. 1940; CAB 103/178, *Supplement to The London Gazette*, 17 July 1946, p. 3712.
9. PREM 3/363/1, cipher from Huggard, 22 Jan. 1941.
10. WO 32/9903, minute by unidentified WO official, 5 June 1941; CO 822/111/12, GOC-in-C East Africa to WO, 8 Feb. 1941.
11. IWM, MS 84/36/1, Colonel J. H. S. Martin Papers, account written in March 1944. For the unit history, see W. V. Brelsford (ed.), *The Story of the Northern Rhodesia Regiment* (Lusaka: Government Printer, 1954).

12. CO 822/111/12, Adams to Rolleston, 21 Feb. 1941.
13. Ibid, Moore to CO, 26 Jan. 1941; Rolleston to Adams, 24 Feb. 1941.
14. CO 980/17, Captain Fraser to J. F. Fraser, Halifax, Nova Scotia, 19 March 1942 examined by East African censor, 17 Apr. 1942.
15. For the policy discussions on the Great North Road project, see CO 537/1524 and CO 822/111/21, East African Governors' Conference, 21–22 May 1941; CO 968/45/2, 'Prisoners of War Location Statement, Middle East as at 19/9/41', 26 Sept. 1941. This does not include the 43,364 Italian and colonial POWs which was still in the forward areas of East Africa Command, a large number of whom was to be despatched to Kenya. See CO 822/111/12, Moore to Dawe, 30 Dec. 1942. It was not all hard work for the Italian captives, as Louise White argues in her article, 'Prostitution, Identity, and Class Consciousness in Nairobi during World War II', *Signs*, 11 (1986), 255–73. She states that for reasons which are still unclear African prostitutes in the Nairobi region charged the Italian POWs less for sexual favours than they did African troops! We would like to thank Professor Keith Jeffery of the University of Ulster (Jordanstown) for this timely reference.
16. CO 967/160, Moore to Major-General A. R. Godwin-Austen, Force HQ Nairobi, 2 Sept. 1941; Moore to Dawe, 18 Nov. 1941.
17. CO 967/55, Moore to A. C. C. Parkinson, Permanent Under-Secretary of State for the Colonies and Dominions Affairs, 28 Sept. 1941. For a more detailed analysis of Kenya's colonial economy during the Second World War, see John Lonsdale, 'The Depression and the Second World War in the Transformation of Kenya', in David Killingray and Richard Rathbone (eds), *Africa and the Second World War* (London: Macmillan, 1986), pp. 97–142.
18. WO 169/14417, 'Weekly strength statement of Prisoners of War in Base Camps in Kenya as at 26 December 1942 for East Africa Command', 6 Jan. 1943; South African National Archives, Prime Minister J. C. Smuts Papers, A1, vol. 259, fol. 11, Lord Harlech, British High Commissioner to South Africa, to Smuts, 23 Feb. 1943; WO 169/14417, East African Command HQ memo, 1 March 1943.
19. CO 822/111/12, minutes by Calder, 4 Jan. 1941 and Watherston, 28 June and 26 May 1941.
20. WO 169/14417, minutes of a conference on the security of POWs employed in East Africa Command, 2 Feb. 1943; CO 822/111/12, Moore to Dawe, 20 March 1943.
21. CO 822/111/12, memo on the employment of POWs, 17 March 1943.
22. Ibid, Moore to Dawe, 20 March 1943.
23. CO 980/17, secret report by Brett on the POW situation in Kenya, May 1942.
24. *The Times*, 22 Feb. 1943; Felice Benuzzi, *No Picnic on Mount Kenya*, 3rd edn (Wellingborough, Northants: Patrick Stephens, 1989). In 1994 an offbeat television film was produced based very loosely on the above book. Called The Ascent, it starred Ben Cross, Rachel Ward, John De Veillers and Vincent Spano.
25. WO 32/11123, annex showing employment of Italian POWs overseas and in the United Kingdom, n.d.
26. SADDA, CGS(War), Box 186/40/9, vol. 1, memos by Colonel later Brigadier F. H. Theron on the organisation and establishment of the South African Internment Battalion and its incorporation into the 1st Reserve Brigade, 12 Apr. and 29 July 1940.

27. DO 119/1132, internment policy in South Africa (German civilians), 1940. Italian civilians were interned throughout British East Africa with camps in Kenya, Uganda, Tanganyika and Southern Rhodesia. FO 916/375, memo on internment camps for Italian civilians in East Africa, 31 May 1942.
28. DO 119/1133, Viscount Caldecote, Secretary of State for the Dominions, to Huggard, 14 June 1940, and Huggard's reply, 16 June 1940; Smuts to UK High Commission, 22 June 1940.
29. SADDA, Box 3066, DC 1472/4/1, chap. 1, Theron to Major-General Len Beyers, Adjutant-General (AG), 7 March 1941.
30. *Cape Argus*, 28 Jan. 1941; SADDA, CGS(War), Box 186/40/9, vol. 1, South African Defence Chiefs to Cairo, 27 Feb. 1941; Secretary for Defence (DC), Box 3066, DC 1472/4/1, chap. 2, Cairo to South African Defence Chiefs, 25 March 1941.
31. *Cape Argus*, 9 Apr. 1941.
32. *Cape Times*, 10 Apr. 1941; *Rand Daily Mail*, 11 Apr. 1941.
33. SADDA, CGS, Box 93, Fortnightly Intelligence Summary (civil and military), no. 7, 12 May 1941.
34. SADDA, Box 3065, DC 1472/1, chap. 3, Attlee to UK High Commission, 24 Apr. 1941; C. H. Blaine, Secretary for Defence, to Brigadier J. Mitchell-Baker, South African Quartermaster-General, 26 Apr. 1941; Cairo to South African Defence Chiefs, 27 Apr. 1941.
35. SADDA, Box 3066, DC 1472/4/1, chap. 1, minutes of first meeting of Hoogenhout committee, 27 Jan. 1941; Dickson to Hansen, 27 Jan. 1941; *Cape Argus*, 28 Jan. 1941.
36. South African National Archives, Pretoria (SANA), Records of the Ministry of the Interior (BNS), BNS 1/1/1, file 23/3, Secretary for South West Africa to Secretary to the Prime Minister, Cape Town, 7 Apr. 1941; Records of the Department of Native Administration and Development (BAO), BAO 614/400, part 1, Trollope to Howard Rogers, Secretary for Native Affairs, 18 Feb 1941.
37. SADDA, Box 3066, DC 1472/4/1, chap. 1, circular from Lieutenant-General Sir Pierre van Ryneveld, Chief of the General Staff, 14 Feb. 1941; Beyers to CGS, 26 Feb. 1941; SANA, Box 3066, DC 1472/4/1, Blaine to Smuts, 9 Apr. 1941.
38. SANA, Box 3066, DC 1472/4/1, minute by Blaine, 16 Apr. 1941.
39. SANA, BAO 614/400, part 1, minute by Rogers, 18 Feb. 1941.
40. SADDA, CGS(War), Box 186/40/9, vol. 2, minute by CGS to Quartermaster-General and AG, 27 Feb. 1941; SANA, Director-General of Supply (DGS), DGS 119, file DWS 950, P. V. Pocock, Director of 'Q' Production, to Dr H. J. van der Bijl, Director-General of War Supplies, 30 Jan. 1941; I. H. Olivier, Assistant Director of 'Q' Production, to van der Bijl, 10 May 1941.
41. SANA, DGS 119, file DWS 950, Viljoen to Blaine, 23 Apr. 1941. In January 1944 oat meal was substituted for mealie meal because the POWs had found it unpalatable, which had resulted in considerable waste. SADDA, Box 3072, DC 1472/15, chap. 5, QMG to Blaine, 18 Jan. 1944.
42. SANA, DGS 119, file DWS 950, Viljoen to Blaine, 19 Feb. 1941 and Blaine's reply, 12 March 1941.
43. SADDA, Box 3065, DC 1472/1, chap. 3, UK High Commission, Pretoria, to Smuts, 11 July 1941. Coincidentally, the figure of 100,000 Italian POWs

matched the recruitment figure of Non-Europeans which had been set for the end of 1942. WO 32/10204, liaison letter, Van Ryneveld to WO, 25 Sept. 1942.

44. Ibid, Diogo to the Department of External Affairs, 17 July 1941.
45. Ibid, Assistant Director of Medical Services, Zonderwater, to Brigadier E. N. Thornton, Director-General of Medical Services, 18 July 1941.
46. Ibid, CGS(War), Box 186/40/10, vol. 1, extracts from weekly staff conferences no. 18 and no. 23, 10 Sept. and 22 Oct. 1941.
47. Ibid, weekly staff conference no. 24, 29 Oct. 1941.
48. Ibid, report by Beyers, 29 May 1942.
49. Ibid.
50. Ibid, Box 3072, DC 1472/15, chap. 3, South African High Commission, London, to D. D. Forsyth, Secretary for External Affairs, 13 and 27 Apr. 1942.
51. Ibid, R. D. Pilkington-Jordan, AG's office, to Defence Department, 28 Apr. 1942.
52. Ibid, CGS(War), Box 186/40/10 vol. 1, report by Beyers, 29 May 1942; Pilkington-Jordan to Forsyth, 5 June 1942.
53. Ibid, Box 3065, DC 1472/1, chap. 3, Edmonds to Minister of Agriculture and Forestry, 17 Sept. 1941.
54. SANA, BAO 614/400, part 1, resolution passed to Blaine by D. L. Smit, Secretary for Native Affairs Department, 15 March 1941; Blaine's reply, 19 March 1941.
55. DO 35/996/PW19/6/35, Harlech to Viscount Cranborne, Secretary of State for the Dominions, 4 Sept. 1941.
56. SADDA, CGS(War), Box 187/40/11, vol. 1, Colonel Campbell Ross to Colonel Pilkington-Jordan, 11 Sept. 1941; Beyers to CGS, 27 Oct. 1941; extract from Staff Conference no. 29, 10 Dec. 1941.
57. SANA, FOR E 1902, memo by E. Grobler, Director of Forestry, to Secretary for Agriculture and Forestry, 23 Dec. 1941; Dr I. J. Craib, Assistant Director of Forestry, to Grobler, 16 Feb. 1942.
58. Ibid, BAO 614/400, part 2, Acting Secretary for Native Affairs to Grobler, 1 July 1942; P. Berry, Native Commissioner, Harding, to C. P. Alport, Chief Native Commissioner, Pietermaritzburg, 2 July 1942.
59. Ibid, Meston to SAP Commissioner, 8 July 1942.
60. SANA, SAP 101, SAP 1/75/43/1, Officer Commanding Troops, Barberton, to Field Security Officer, Ermelo, 16 Feb. 1943; FOR, E 1902, Colonel R. C. Wilson, AG branch, to Secretary for Agriculture and Forestry, 26 Feb. 1943; SADDA, CGS(War), Box 187/40/11, vol. 1, Colonel Campbell Ross, CGS, to AG, 15 Mar. 1943.
61. SADDA, Box 3070, DC 1472/12, chs 2–3, detailed breakdown of labour detachments in the Union, June 1942 to Jan. 1943; DGD 412/29, memo by Van Ryneveld to Smuts, 27 July 1945; DGD 412/14, memo on employment of Italian POWs, 8 Aug. 1944.
62. DO 35/996/PW19/6/35, Harlech to Cranborne, 12 Nov. 1941.
63. DO 119/1133, Smuts to Huggard, 22 June 1940; DO 35/1008/7, WG 429/51, C. R. Price, Deputy High Commissioner, Pretoria, to Cranborne, 26 May 1941; DO 35/588/3, G 91/422, Harlech to Cranborne, 13 Jan. 1942; Martin and Orpen, *South African Forces*, vol. 7, pp. 97–107 and 168–9; CO 968/45/1, WO to Auchinleck, 24 July 1941; Christoph Marx, 'The Ossewabrandwag as

a Mass Movement, 1939–41', *Journal of Southern African Studies*, 20, 2 (1994), 195–219. For a recent analysis of Afrikaner–Nazi links during the 1930s and the Second World War see Albrecht Hagemann, 'Very Special Relations: The "Third Reich" and the Union of South Africa, 1933–39', *South African Historical Journal*, no. 27 (1992), 127–47; Christoph Marx, '"Dear Listeners in South Africa": German Propaganda Broadcasts to South Africa, 1940–1941', Ibid, 195–219; and Werner Schellack, 'The Afrikaners Nazi Links Revisted', Ibid, 173–85. Excellent insights into the South African government's internal monitoring operations of the *Ossewabrandwag* and other right-wing Afrikaner organisations can be found in the papers of Dr E. G. Malherbe, the Director of Military Intelligence and Army Education (1941–8) and Principal of the University of Natal (1945–65). Killie Campell Africana Library, University of Natal, Malherbe Papers, KCM 56975 (89), file 444/7, 'Subversive Activities in the Union' (Jan.–June 1941), by Captain Janie A. Malherbe (wife), 4 June 1941.

64. Louis Grundlingh, 'The Recruitment of South African Blacks for Participation in the Second World War', in Killingray and Rathbone (eds), *Africa and the Second World War*, p. 181, and 'Prejudices, Promises and Poverty: The Experiences of Discharged and Demobilised Black South African Soldiers after the Second World War', *South African Historical Journal*, no. 26 (1992), 116–35.

65. CO 967/161, Harlech to Moore, 30 Dec. 1941; Van Ryneveld also reiterated this point to his British counterpart, Lieutenant-General (later Field Marshal) Sir Alan Brooke in his liaison letters throughout 1942. See WO 32/10204, Van Ryneveld to CIGS, 25 Sept. and 21 Dec. 1942.

66. CO 967/161, Harlech to Moore, 30 Dec. 1941. Harlech's deputy made the same incisive point six months earlier in a brilliant memo to London. See DO 35/1008/7, WG 429/51, Price to Cranborne, 26 May 1941.

67. SADDA, Box 3072, DC 1472/15, chap. 3, AG to Blaine, 4 Apr. 1942.

68. Ibid, CGS(War), Box 186/40/9, vol. 2, secret circular by AG on organisation and establishment of new Active Citizen Force, 25 June 1942; WO 32/10204, Van Ryneveld to Brooke, 25 Sept. 1942; SADDA, CGS(War), Box 186/40/9, Van Ryneveld to AG, 26 June 1942.

69. In early June 1940, 4,000 Nigerian troops en route to East Africa were temporarily housed in an empty grain shed near the main maize terminal at Congella, Natal. Why such a large force had been allowed to land is unclear considering the sensitive nature of South Africa's colour bar. It certainly unnerved the Defence Department, for shortly afterwards verbal instructions were issued by the CGS to the Officer-Commanding Cape Command. 'You should resist requests to land native troops or sailors, no matter whether serving under the British or an allied flag. If requests of this nature are put up by you to the Minister, he would either have to refuse and rigidly enforce the colour bar, possibly to the annoyance of an ally, or he would have to agree, which might result in public feeling being stirred up in the country.' Future applications to land in the Cape would have to be refused 'diplomatically but firmly'. Wartime logistical pressures eventually overrode domestic racial and political circumstances, however uncomfortable for Pretoria. Now that Durban had become a crucial marshalling point for troops and war material moving from Europe and West Africa to East Africa, Egypt and

India, a transit camp for non-Europeans at Durban was completed in October 1940. Men were confined to camp and it was decreed that there would be no shore leave. The only exception to these regulations was that troops would be allowed outside on organised route marches. Furthermore, the weaponry possessed by African troops who arrived in the Union would be impounded on disembarkation and reissued only on re-embarkation. SADDA, CGS(War), Box 283/58/6, verbal instructions by CGS to OC Cape Command, 15 June 1940; Natal Command to CGS, 24 Aug. 1940; QMG to CGS, 2 Oct. 1940; QMG to South African Defence Chiefs and AG, 27 Dec. 1940.

70. Ibid, Box 186/40/9, vol. 1, Middle East Command to South African Defence Chiefs, 5 July 1941.
71. Ibid, vol. 2, Blaine to Natal Command, 16 May 1941.
72. WO 32/9362, Simpson to Lieutenant-Colonel D. MacLeod, WO, 22 May 1941.
73. Ibid, DO to Huggard, 7 May 1941; UK Military Mission, Pretoria, to WO, 12 May 1941; WO to UK Military Mission, Pretoria, 26 May 1941. Ultimately, unpleasant incidents arising out of the colour bar did occur, primarily in Durban. The most common incidents involved Indian service personnel being refused entry to European bars, hotels, service canteens, restaurants and night-clubs. For these incidents and the discussions between the British, Indian and South African governments, see SADDA, CGS(War), Box 283/58/4, vol. 1, Wavell to Smuts, 8 Oct. 1941; Sir Shafaat Ahmad Khan, Indian High Commissioner to South Africa, to Smuts, 28 Sept. 1942; DO 121/107, Harlech to Attlee, 28 Apr. 1943. When Madagascar was occupied by the Allies in May 1942 the Union government in no uncertain terms refused on racial and political grounds to receive the 1,200 Vichy POWs, the majority of which were Senegalese and Annamese. ADM 199/1284, minute by C. H. M. Waldock, Admiralty, 21 May 1942.
74. SADDA, Box 3072, DC 1472/15, chap. 5, report by Magistrate F. F. Terblanche of Victoria West, to Blaine, 4 Feb. 1943. Prisoner's statement taken by Sergeant J. H. Fourie, 4 Feb. 1943; SANA, Cape Archives, KAB, 1/VCW, vol. 21, f. 9/7/16, Terblanche to Blaine, 5 Feb. 1943.
75. SADDA, Box 3068, DC 1472/10/4, successful escape of Mario Valanzano. Captured in March 1941, this prisoner escaped from Zonderwater on 25 Jan. 1942 and was reported to be in neutral Portuguese East Africa in August 1942.
76. SADDA, POW 2, CE 4/20, censorship report, 3 Nov. 1941.
77. SADDA, AG(POW), Box 87/76/6, case file on death of Celestino Faraone, Feb. 1943.
78. Ibid, Box 95, PW/299, confidential minute, 25 March 1943.
79. Ibid, report on riot in 4th CC(V) Battalion, POW Camp Zonderwater, 31 Dec. 1942–1 Jan. 1943.
80. FO 916/661, Major H. J. Phillimore to F. J. du Toit, South African High Commission, London, 6 Jan. 1943.
81. SADDA, AG(POW), Box 95, PW/299, report on riot in 4th CC(V) Battalion, POW Camp Zonderwater, 31 Dec. 1942–1 Jan. 1943.
82. Ibid.
83. Ibid, Smuts to Diethelm, 4 Jan. 1943.

84. SADDA, CGS(War), Box 186/40/16, extract from CGS conference no. 66, 6 Jan. 1943, which contains synopses of reports by Brett and Pilkington-Jordan, 4 and 7 Dec. 1942.

85. Ibid, Smuts to van Ryneveld, 5 Jan. 1943.

86. Ibid, AG to CGS, 13 Jan. 1943; Wilson to Harlech, 26 Feb. 1942; Van Ryneveld to Beyers, 19 Jan. 1943.

87. Ibid, Box 3065, DC 1472/1, chap. 4, progress report no. 1 by Wilson, 24 Feb. 1943; minute by unknown official, 4 Mar. 1943.

88. Ibid, Box 3072, DC 1472/15, chap. 4, progress report no. 2 by Wilson, 17 March 1943; FO 916/661, Satow to a Major James, WO, 26 Aug. 1943, enclosing ICRC reports on the Dec. 1942 and Feb. 1943 visits to Zonderwater.

89. Ibid, AG(3)154, Box 87, X/880, OC Troops, Premier Mine, to GOC Inland Area, 14 June 1943; report of battalion commanders for the 1st, 2nd and 6th Cape Corps, 22 June 1943; AG(POW), Box 95, PW/299, report by Prinsloo, 19 June 1943; Hammond's report on disturbances by 2nd Cape Corps battalion, 13–14 June 1943, dated 24 June 1943; AG(3)154, Box 87, X/899, unnamed colonel in the Non-European Army Services to Beyers, 28 June 1943.

4 'Farming Down Under': Italian POWs in Australia, 1941–3

1. AA, CRS A7711/1, item 1, 'History of the Directorate of Prisoners of War and Internees, 1939–1951', p. 106.

2. Kay Saunders, 'Down on the Farm: Italian POWs in Australia 1941–47', *Journal of Australian Studies*, no. 46 (1995), 28. Australian internment policy during the Second World War is examined by Margaret Bevege, *Behind Barbed Wire*; Kay Saunders, *War on the Homefront. State Intervention in Queensland 1938–1948* (St. Lucia, Qld: University of Queensland Press, 1993), pp. 33–58.

3. Alan Fitzgerald, *The Italian Farming Soldiers. Prisoners of War in Australia 1941–1947* (Melbourne: Melbourne University Press, 1981); Bill Bunbury, *Rabbits and Spaghetti. Captives and Comrades: Australians, Italians and the War, 1939–1945* (Fremantle: Fremantle Arts Centre Press, 1995).

4. Central to this thesis is Gianfranco Cresciani, *Fascism, Anti-Fascism and Italians in Australia 1922–1945* (Canberra: Australian National University Press, 1980), pp. 171–95, themes of which were expanded on in his 'Captivity in Australia', 195–220.

5. Bevege, *Behind Barbed Wire*, appendix A, pp. 238–43; Ilma Martinuzzi O'Brien, 'The Internment of Australian Born and Naturalised British Subjects of Italian Origin', in Richard Bosworth and Romano Ugolini (eds), *War, Internment and Mass Migration: The Italo-Australian Experience 1940–1990* (Roma: Gruppo Editoriale Internazionale, 1992), pp. 91–2; AA (Melbourne), MP 729/6, item 63/402/41, minute paper on internment camps, 21 Mar. 1941.

6. AA, CRS A7711/1, item 1, 'History of the Directorate', pp. 105–6.

7. Cresciani, *Fascism*, pp. 173–4.

8. AA, CRS A433, item 45/2/6098, DO to Prime Minister's Department via UK High Commission, 19 Mar. 1941; CRS A1308, item 712/1/54, War Cabinet Agendum no. 122/1941, 2 Apr. 1941; AA (Melbourne), MP 729/6, item 63/402/41, War Cabinet minute 927, 2 Apr. 1941.

9. AA, CRS A433, item 45/2/6098, DO to Prime Minister's Department via UK High Commission, 24 Apr. 1941; CRS A1308, item 712/1/54, supplement no. 1 to War Cabinet Agendum no. 122/1941, 30 Apr. 1941.

10. Saunders, 'Down on the Farm', 20.

11. AA, CRS A1308, item 712/1/54, War Cabinet minute 1007, 30 Apr. 1941. Mark Johnston, *Fighting the Enemy. Australian Soldiers and their Adversaries in World War II* (Cambridge: Cambridge University Press, 2000), pp. 1–57.

12. Ibid; CRS A816/1, item 54/301/229, Harry F. Walker to A. W. Fadden, Acting Prime Minister, 21 May 1941; CRS A649/4, item 172/600/19, minute 906, 'Prisoner of War and Internment Camps – Utilisation of Labour', Agendum no. 52/1942, supplement no. 6, Apr. 1942; CRS A816/1, item 54/301/229, Acting Chief of the Naval Staff to Secretary of Defence Committee, 12 May 1941.

13. AA, CRS A1308, item 712/1/54, supplement no. 2 to War Cabinet Agendum no. 122/1941, 9 July 1941.

14. Ibid, War Cabinet minute 1197, 11 July 1941; S. J. Butlin and C. B. Schedvin, *War Economy 1942–1945* (Canberra: AWM, 1977), p. 27.

15. AA, CRS SP109/3/1, item 342/11, unnamed newspaper, probably the *Sydney Morning Herald*, 27 May 1941.

16. Ibid.

17. AA (Melbourne), MP 729/6, item 63/402/39, minute papers, Department of the Army, 'Transfer of POWs from Middle East to Australia', May 1941; AA, CRS A1308, item 712/1/54, supplement no. 3 to War Cabinet Agendum 122/1941, 18 July 1941; War Cabinet minute 1263, 23 July 1941.

18. Fitzgerald, *Farming Soldiers*, pp. 171–2 and 7; AA (Melbourne), MP 729/6, item 63/401/387, minute papers and instructions regarding shipping manifests for 4th and 5th shipments, Oct. 1941.

19. AA (Melbourne), MP 729/6, item 63/401/330, vocations of 817 Italian officers and men from second POW shipment, 15 August 1941.

20. Australian War Memorial (AWM), PR 88/178, Captain John L. Hehir papers, briefing paper entitled 'The Wop', 27 June 1941. O'Brien, 'The Internment of Australian Born', pp. 95–6 confirms occupational backgrounds of the internees.

21. AA (Melbourne), MP 508/1, item 255/714/205, Morel's ICRC report, 14 Aug. 1941.

22. Ibid, item 255/726/101, McIntosh to Director-General of Medical Services, Australian Headquarters, Melbourne, 18 Oct. 1941.

23. Ibid, item 255/726/102, summary of steps taken to control dysentery at Hay, 18 Oct. 1941; item 255/726/87, contains extensive instructions discussed in August 1941 to prevent the transmission of dysentery.

24. AA (Melbourne), MP 508/1, item 155/721/281, minute paper, 'Prisoners of War – Employment', 29 Nov. 1941; Ibid, item 255/721/328, War Office memo on employment of POWs and rates of pay, November 1941; Ibid, item 255/721/215, minute paper by C. R. Laffan, secretary of the Military Board, 12 Nov. 1941.

25. AA, CRS A649/4, item 172/600/19, Chief Inspector, Inspector General of Administration, Department of the Treasury, 18 Apr. 1942; E. Harding for Secretary, Department of the Army, to G. P. N. Watt, Assistant-Secretary, Department of the Treasury (Defence Division), 7 May 1942.

26. AA (Melbourne), MP 508/1, item 255/721/499, minutes and briefing papers on employment of POWs and surplus production at Hay, February to August 1942; item 255/721/519, memo provided on the inter-departmental conference on employment of POWs and internees by Lieutenant-Colonel J. McCahon, Director of Prisoners of War, 7 July 1942; AWM 54, item 780/3/2, part 2, report on visit to no. 3 POW Labour Detachment by Military Intelligence supervisor for POW and internment camps, Lieutenant-Colonel J. U. Leask, 4 Mar. 1943; MP 508/1, item 255/721/520, General Manager, Queensland Cotton Board, to Major R. D. Tyers, Quartermaster-General, New South Wales, 7 Aug. 1942.

27. AA, CRS A649/4, item 172/600/19, Chief Inspector, Inspector General of Administration, Department of the Treasury, 18 Apr. 1942.

28. Johnston, *Fighting the Enemy*, pp. 9–25.

29. Bevege, *Behind Barbed Wire*, pp. 1–27.

30. Ibid, p. 10.

31. AA, CRS A472/1, item W3408, National Security (POW) regulations; CRS A7711/1, item 1, 'History of the Directorate', pp. 112–24.

32. AA (Melbourne), MP 508/1, item 255/711/178, minute paper and annexes of POW and internment camp administration conference, 25–27 Nov. 1941, signed by McCahon, 3 Dec. 1941.

33. David Horner, *Blamey. The Commander-in-Chief* (Sydney: Allen and Unwin, 1998), pp. 310–15; Alan Powell, *War by Stealth. Australians and the Allied Intelligence Bureau 1942–1945* (Melbourne: Melbourne University Press, 1996).

34. Bevege, *Behind Barbed Wire*, pp. 10–13; Horner, *Blamey*, p. 311.

35. Horner, *Blamey*, p. 312.

36. AWM 54, item 780/3/2, Roberts to Lieutenant-Colonel J. U. Leask, Military Intelligence Supervisor, POW and Internment Camps, 18 Oct. 1942.

37. Ibid, Leask to Rogers, 16 Oct. 1942.

38. Ibid.

39. Ibid, visit by Leask to Myrtleford Camp (29–31 Oct. 1942), 14 Nov. 1942.

40. Ibid, visit by Leask to Cowra Camp (7–13 Dec. 1942), 23 Dec. 1942.

41. Ibid, visit by Leask to Hay Camp (17–23 Dec. 1942), 31 Dec. 1942.

42. Ibid.

43. Ibid, visit by Leask to Myrtleford Camp (27–29 Apr. 1943), 8 May 1943.

44. Ibid, extract from weekly intelligence summary, Myrtleford (25 Mar. 1943), 19 Apr. 1943.

45. Ibid.

46. Ibid.

47. Ibid, extract from weekly intelligence summary, Hay (28 Mar. 1943), 19 Apr. 1943.

48. Ibid, notes from camp intelligence reports no. 2, Cowra (23 Feb. 1943), 11 Mar. 1943; extract from weekly intelligence summary, Cowra (7 Mar. 1943), 20 Mar. 1943. For insights into the conflict between Fascists and Royalists, see Fitzgerald, *Italian Farming Soldiers*, pp. 55–72.

49. AWM 54, item 780/3/2, minute by Leask to DDMI, 21 Jan. 1943; notes from camp intelligence report no. 1, 5 Feb. 1943. Subsequent tours of Cowra and Hay conducted by Leask in May–June 1943 confirmed the steady progress made by intelligence officers in improving their operations. Ibid, reports on

visits by Leask to Cowra (11–14 May 1943) and Hay (3–9 June 1943), 28 May and 24 June 1943.

5   Intelligence, Propaganda and Political Warfare

1. F. H. Hinsley, *British Intelligence in the Second World War*, vol. 2 (London: HMSO, 1981), p. 33; Australian War Memorial, AWM 54, item 423/4/24, précis of interview between Harrison and New Zealand intelligence chiefs on POW interrogations sent to Army HQ, New Zealand Military Forces, Wellington, 22 June 1942.
2. Kent Fedorowich, 'Propaganda and Political Warfare: The Foreign Office, Italian POWs and the Free Italy Movement, 1940–3', in Moore and Fedorowich (eds), pp. 119–47; and Fedorowich, 'Axis Prisoners of War as Sources for British Military Intelligence, 1939–42', *Intelligence and National Security*, 14, 2 (1999), 156–78; Allison Gilmore, *You Can't Fight Tanks With Bayonets. Psychological Warfare against the Japanese Army in the Southwest Pacific* (Lincoln, NE: University of Nebraska Press, 1998); Brad W. Gladman, 'Air Power and Intelligence in the Western Desert Campaign, 1940–43', *Intelligence and National Security*, 13, 4 (1998), 144–62; Richard N. Armstrong, 'Hunting Tongues', *Journal of Soviet Military Studies*, 2, 4 (1989), 579–95; Kevin Jones, 'From the Horse's Mouth: Luftwaffe POWs as Sources for Air Ministry Intelligence During the Battle of Britain', *Intelligence and National Security*, 15, 4 (2000), 60–80.
3. For policies directed against the German prisoners, see Henry Faulk, *Group Captives: The Re-education of German Prisoners of War* (London: Chatto & Windus, 1977); M. B. Sullivan, *Thresholds of Peace: Four Hundred Thousand German Prisoners and the People of Britain 1944–48* (London: Hamish Hamilton, 1979); C. Fitzgibbon, *Denazification* (London: Michael Joseph, 1969); A. Hearnden, *The British in Germany: Educational Reconstruction after 1945* (London: Hamish Hamilton, 1984); Kurt Jürgensen, 'British Occupation Policy after 1945 and the Problem of "Re-educating Germany"', *History*, 68 (1983), 225–44; Arthur L. Smith, Jr, *The War for the German Mind: Re-educating Hitler's Soldiers* (Oxford: Berg, 1996).
4. Anthony Clayton, *Forearmed. A History of the Intelligence Corps* (London: Brassey's, 1993), pp. 23, 29–30, 38, 49–50; Major J. E. Hahn, *The Intelligence Service within the Canadian Corps 1914–1918* (Toronto: Macmillan Company of Canada, 1930), pp. 39–55; Christopher Andrew, *Her Majesty's Secret Service* (New York: Viking, 1986), pp. 165 and 170–2.
5. In the case of German submariners, the British cabinet in early 1915 debated whether there should be different treatment for these men – in part a response to the horrors this new technology was inflicting and demands by the British public for immediate action to counter this weaponry. Punishments included either segregation from other naval POWs and/or long periods of confinement. The idea of separate treatment was overturned and the policy of isolation discontinued in favour of observing the provisions of the 1907 Hague Conventions. CAB 37/127/40, hand-written minute, 27 Apr. 1915 and CAB 37/129/9, 5 June 1915.

6. AIR 40/1177, report by Group Captain S. D. Felkin entitled, 'Intelligence through Interrogation', 31 Dec. 1945; M. R. D. Foot and J. M. Langley, *MI9. The British Secret Service that Fostered Escape and Evasion, 1939–1945 and its American Counterpart* (London: Bodley Head, 1979); WO 208/4970, 'The Story of MI19' (c. 1945–6).

7. The Conservative MP and arch-imperialist L. S. Amery briefly served as an intelligence staff officer with the 4th Army Corps in Belgium during the First World War. In his autobiography he describes his own technique which, according to him, proved highly successful when extracting information from German rank-and-filers. German officers, he admitted, were a tougher nut to crack and generally revealed very little, unlike their subordinates. L. S. Amery, *My Political Life*, vol. 2 (London: Hutchinson, 1953), pp. 38–40, cited in Clayton, *Forearmed*, p. 23. Also see John Barnes and David Nicholson (eds), *The Leo Amery Diaries*, vol. 1, *1896–1929* (London: Hutchinson, 1980), p. 110.

8. AIR 40/1177, 'Intelligence through Interrogation'; WO 208/4970, 'Story of MI19'.

9. Foot and Langley, *Escape and Evasion*, p. 31; WO 208/4970, 'Story of MI19'. Also see Peter Wilkinson and Joan Bright Astley, *Gubbins and SOE*, reprint (London: Leo Cooper, 1997) for aspects of these pre-war bodies.

10. AIR 40/1177, 'Intelligence through Interrogation'; ADM 1/10579, reports by Admiralty on handling of enemy captives, 19 May and 9 June 1939, and minutes by Rear Admiral J. H. Godfrey, Director of Naval Intelligence (1939–42), 18 and 21 July 1939; Hinsley, *British Intelligence*, vol. 1, pp. 282–3.

11. AIR 40/1177, 'Intelligence through Interrogation'; WO 208/4970, 'Story of MI19'; WO 165/39, MI9 HQ war diary, 30 Apr. and 12 July 1940; Sullivan, *Thresholds of Peace*, p. 49; A. P. Scotland, *The London Cage* (London: Evans, 1957). After the war Colonel Scotland provided invaluable assistance to Canadian war crimes prosecutors who had the task of trying the infamous Brigadeführer Kurt Meyer, commanding officer of the 12th SS Panzer Division (Hitler Jugend), which committed grizzly atrocities against units of the 3rd Canadian Infantry Division during the first days of the D-Day landings. For these war crimes, see Howard Margolian, *Conduct Unbecoming: The Story of the Murder of Canadian Prisoners of War in Normandy* (Toronto: University of Toronto Press, 1998). Scotland's assistance to Canadian investigators is discussed by Patrick Brode, *Casual Slaughters and Accidental Judgements. Canadian War Crimes Prosecutions, 1944–1948* (Toronto: University of Toronto Press, 1997), p. 23. After the war PWIS(Home) became the British War Crimes Investigation Unit. A small cache of Scotland's papers are in WO 208/4294.

12. DEFE 1/21, organisational memo by Edwin S. Herbert, Director, Postal and Telegraph Censorship Department, 6 March 1942; DEFE 1/333, *History of the Postal and Telegraph Censorship Department 1938–1946*, vol. 1, p. 435.

13. DEFE 1/21, memo by Herbert, 6 March 1942.

14. DEFE 1/334, *History of the Postal and Telegraph Censorship Department 1938–1946*, vol. 2, *Appendices*, no. 27, pp. 862–3; DEFE 1/374, memo by Lieutenant-Colonel Aylmer Vallance, 19 Nov. 1941; WO 208/32, report on General Staff Intelligence, East African Force, 3 Sept. 1939–1 Aug. 1941, value of censorsed POW mail to regional intelligence gathering. For POW

censorship regulations and procedures in the Middle East, see NANZ, AD 1, item 336/3/15, July 1942.

15. Foot and Langley, *Escape and Evasion*; also see WO 208/4970, 'Story of MI19'. Also see Ian Dear, *Escape and Evasion. Prisoner of War Breakouts and the Routes to Safety in World War Two* (London: Cassell, 1997).

16. WO 208/4970, 'Story of MI19'.

17. Ibid; AIR 2/4591, Campbell to Deputy Under-Secretary, Intelligence, 26 Feb. 1945; R. V. Jones, *Most Secret War* (London: Hamish Hamilton, 1978), p. 61. Known as 'Oberst King', a further insight into Felkin's personality and interviewing technique is provided by Sullivan, *Thresholds of Peace*, pp. 53–7.

18. AIR 2/4591, 'History of ADI(K)', 24 March 1944. For the organisational breakdown of British Air Intelligence see AIR 22/76, Air Ministry weekly intelligence summary no. 152, appendix A, 30 July 1942. My thanks to Lorne Breitenloehner for this reference. An example of the flow of *Luftwaffe* documents and intelligence therefrom see AIR 2/4591, 'The Handling of German Air Force Documents', 27 Jan. 1945.

19. WO 208/4970, 'Story of MI19', p. 3.

20. See Gladman, 'Air Power and Intelligence', pp. 149–51 for material gleaned from German POWs prior to the Battle of El Alamein.

21. CAB 4/29, CID paper 1548-B, 3 Feb. 1939; CAB 2/8, part 1, CID mtg. 356(6), 11 May 1939; CAB 4/30, CID paper 1556-B, 27 June 1939.

22. WO 165/39, MI9 war diary, 31 July 1940; WO 208/3248, memo by Macmillan, 20 July 1945. Additional facilities were established in Khartoum and Palestine in 1941 to assist with operations directed against the Italians in Abyssinia and the Vichy French in Syria. Malta possessed another important CSDIC unit, while the Red Fort in Delhi acted as headquarters of CSDIC (India). In September 1942 allied intelligence operations were reorganised in the Far East and co-ordinated by the Australians from CSDIC (Australia) based at Brisbane in Queensland. A preliminary investigation was carried out for the establishment of a CSDIC in New Zealand, the implementation of which had the full support of the New Zealand War Cabinet. However, in October 1942, the project was deemed unnecessary as it stretched already limited resources as well as replicating work conducted in Australia. After the Normandy invasion of June 1944 a CSDIC (Western European Area) was established to handle the tens of thousands of German captives. Australian Archives (Canberra), CRS A3269/1, item 011, General Headquarters, Far Eastern Command, Military Intelligence Section, General Staff, *Operations of the Allied Translator and Interpreter Section GHQ, SWPA*, vol. 5, *Intelligence Series*; NANZ, EA 1, item 89/4/17, New Zealand Chiefs of Staff memo no. 140, 1 July 1942 and schedule 8, 104th mtg. of NZ COS, 19 Oct. 1942; CAB 176/4, JIC/1351/44, 'Proposed creation of CSDIC (WEA)', 8 Oct. 1944; CAB 176/6, JIC/567/45 and JIC/834/45, 29 Apr. and 20 June 1945.

23. Fedorowich, 'Propaganda and Political Warfare', pp. 119–47. Required reading is Charles Cruickshank, *The Fourth Arm. Psychological Warfare 1938–45* (London: Davis-Poynter, 1977); Clayton D. Laurie, *The Propaganda Warriors: America's Crusade against Nazi Germany* (Lawrence, KS: University of Kansas Press, 1996).

24. When Algiers fell to the Allies in mid-November 1942, a second CSDIC was established in North Africa under the unified command of Commander

G. G. D. Rodd, RN, who was already in charge of the Cairo centre. Redesignated CSDIC(MED), this expanded agency negotiated the incorporation of the Italian Intelligence Service (SIM) into Allied CSDIC operations when Italy surrendered in September 1943. For a brief outline of these negotiations and the establishment of CSDIC (Central Mediterranean Force) in which SIM was later attached when Italy was given status as a co-belligerent, see WO 208/3249, appendix 6, history of CSDIC (Italian Army Intelligence). AWM 54, item 423/4/24, memo by then Major D. McMillan, Royal Corps of Signals, on CSDIC mobile units, MEF, 25 March 1942.

25. Hinsley, *British Intelligence*, vol. 1, p. 205; WO 208/3248, memo by Macmillan, 20 July 1945.

26. Ibid.

27. WO 208/4970, 'Story of MI19', appendix E, 'The "M" Room', appendix B(1), 'Survey of CSDIC(UK)', and appendix C, analysis of POWs and reports issued; CAB 176/5, JIC/183/45, annexed report by JIC chairman, 11 Feb. 1945; HW 14/8, memo on 'List of Summaries, Reports, etc Received in Hut 3', 28 Nov. 1940. My thanks to Martin Thomas for this last reference.

28. WO 208/4970, 'Story of MI19', appendix E, 'The "M" Room' and appendix K, 'The Army Interrogation Section (Operational)', p. 4. Also see Oliver Hoare (ed.), *Camp 020: MI5 and the Nazi Spies. The Official History of MI5's Wartime Interrogation Centre* (London: PRO, 2000), pp. 119–22 and 129–31.

29. Ibid; Sullivan, *Thresholds of Peace*, p. 52; HS 6/903, minute by Captain A. W. Waterfield, 26 July 1942, on shortage of camp interpreters.

30. AIR 40/1177, report by Felkin, 'Intelligence through Interrogation'; WO 208/4970, 'Story of MI19'; AWM 54, item 423/4/24, notes on the Harrison interview, June 1942. In June 1941, a German seaman who had served as an engineer on one of the *Bismarck's* supply ships, was interrogated in the London cage. A former Social Democrat who had been imprisoned as an agitator by the Nazis, the 30-year-old was deemed by his interrogators as being of 'direct' value to the Allied cause. 'At the end of my interview', recalled the British officer, 'he said something which suggested he would be anxious to do any work against the Nazis that could be found.' FO 898/320, report by a C. O'Neill of an interview with German POWs on 25 June 1941. No material has yet come to light to suggest that POWs were actively recruited by British intelligence for covert operations behind enemy lines. However, the United States Office of Strategic Services did recruit and deploy agents from German POWs held in Italy during 1944–5. See Clayton D. Laurie, 'The "Sauerkrauts": German Prisoners of War as OSS Agents, 1944–1945', *Prologue*, 26 (1994), 49–60; William Casey, *The Secret War Against Hitler* (London: Simon & Schuster, 1989).

31. AIR 40/1177, report by Felkin, 'Intelligence through Interrogation'.

32. AWM 54, item 423/4/24, notes on Harrison interview, June 1942; WO 208/3248, memo by Macmillan, 20 July 1945; WO 208/4970, 'Story of MI19'.

33. For a thorough examination of the use of 'X' material in the Mediterranean and Middle Eastern theatres, see WO 208/2348, appendix 1; WO 208/3256, appendix 1, and AIR 40/1177, 'The Study of the Work of ADI(K) during the War of 1939–1945'; WO 208/4970, 'Story of MI19'.

34. SADDA, CGS(War), Box 186/40/8, vol. 1, Nairobi interrogation report by Lieutenants I. A. Maisels and H. C. Nicholas, 12 Feb. 1941.

35. AIR 40/1862, interrogation report by Lieutenant-Commander M. Dymott RN, of survivors of the Italian submarine *Rubino*, 1 July 1940; AIR 40/1867, preliminary interrogation report by Lieutenant-Commander F. Younghusband RN (Staff Officer (Intelligence) Malta), of survivors of Italian magnetic minesweeper *Rosina*, 30 Dec. 1942; Ibid, report by the Field Security Officer, Gibraltar, on interrogation of two downed Italian aviators about their radio and navigation equipment, 28 July 1941; SO(I), Malta to SO(I), Mediterranean, 27 Nov. 1942 on Italian harbour defences revealed by captured Italian merchant seamen; WO 208/4189-92, CSDIC(UK) SR reports, I/SRN 1–I/SRN 1313 contains extracts from miked transcripts taken in the London cage during the interrogation of captured Italian submariners, divers and motor torpedo crews who participated in these raids. Also see James J. Sadkovich, *The Italian Navy in World War II* (Westport CT: Greenwood Press, 1994), *passim*.
36. WO 169/2874, Intelligence HQ war diary, East Africa Force, 21 Jan. 1941. Also see WO 169/19, notes on armed forces in IEA, summary no. 138 and appendix B of same, 5 Oct. 1940. In WO briefing paper on the capture of Gondar prepared for the War Cabinet it was revealed that as the Allied advance progressed it became increasingly evident that Italian morale had deteriorated in part due to a severe shortage of supplies. The report also noted that desertions were frequent and that there were rumours of mutinies amongst the native troops. WO 208/4384, 'The Capture of Gondar', 1 Dec. 1941. For personal accounts of several key operations in Abyssinia see IWM, Misc 952, MSS by Major-General James G. Elliott: 'An Account of the Battle of Keren, Eritrea, in March 1941'; IWM, 83/21/1, Major-General T. H. Birkbeck, 26th East African Brigade, on Gondar operations.
37. Dawn M. Miller, '"Raising the Tribes": British Policy in Italian East Africa, 1938–41', *Journal of Strategic Studies*, 22, 1 (1999), 96–123; David Shirreff, *Barefoot and Bandoliers* (London: The Radcliffe Press, 1995). Also see Rhodes House Library, Sir H. R. Brooke-Popham Papers, MSS Afr. s1120, III/9/1, Sir H. R. Brooke-Popham, Governor of Kenya, to General Sir W. Edmund Ironside, Chief of the Imperial General Staff, 7 Oct. 1939.
38. AIR 40/1867, interrogation report of Metallo, 27 July 1941; interrogation report of wireless operator Constantino Atzei, 28 July 1941.
39. AIR 40/1862, interrogation of Molinelli by SO(I) Malta, 23 June 1941.
40. SADDA, CGS(War), Box 186/40/8, vol. 1, interrogation report by Captain T. S. Harrison, Air HQ, East Africa, Nov. 1940.
41. Ibid, interrogation report by Maisels, Nov. 1940.
42. Ibid, interrogation report by Maisels and Nicholas, 12 Feb. 1941.
43. SADDA, POW 2, file 2390, weekly Middle Eastern POW summary of outgoing mail, 12 June 1941; ibid, CE8/4/2, summary no. 4 (25 June–1 July 1941). Similar bravado and confidnce in a Fascist victory was noted by CSDIC(UK) concerning Italian naval officers captured in the Mediterranean during 1940. WO 208/4189, SR reports, I/SRN 1–I/SRN 400 (1940).
44. FO 898/161, secret memo, 14 Apr. 1940.
45. Ibid, secret and personal, Brooks to R. J. H. Shaw, Department EH, 11 June 1940.
46. Hugh Dalton, *The Fateful Years* (London: Muller, 1957), p. 366.
47. HS 6/885, minute by Section D, 28 Aug. 1940; Sir Frank Nelson, operational head of SOE (codenamed CD), to AD, 9 Dec. 1940.

48. Ibid, Nelson to AD, 9 Dec. 1940.
49. HS 6/884, JA to D/JG (Martelli's code number), 17 June 1941. Later on in the war, Martelli became a member of the Psychological Warfare Section of Allied Forces HQ in North Africa. FO 371/37274/R 1382, minute by Lockhart, 18 Feb. 1943. For the Loraine Committee's activities see John Curry, *The Security Service 1908–1945. The Official History* (London: HMSO, 1999), p. 166; Lucio Sponza, 'The British Government and the Internment of Italians', in David Cesarani and Tony Kushner (eds), *The Internment of Aliens in Twentieth Century Britain* (London: Frank Cass, 1993), pp. 125–46; and Terri Colpi, 'The Impact of the Second World War on the British Italian Community', Ibid, pp. 167–87.
50. British Library of Political and Economic Sceince, London School of Economics, Dr Hugh Dalton Papers, 7/3, Dalton to Churchill, 24 Sept. 1941. For an insight into the failures of British propaganda and clandestine operations in Italy, see the indispensable William Mackenzie, *The Secret History of SOE: The Special Operations Executive 1940–1945* (London: St Ermin's Press, 2000), pp. 537–57, especially pp. 538–9. Dalton was referring to the Italian agent Fortunato Picchi who was trained as a guide and interpreter for covert airborne operations. He was dropped into southern Italy in February 1941, captured and executed. For details of Operation 'Colossus', see CAB 79/9, COS(41)52nd and 56th mtgs, minutes 1 and 16 respectively. News of his tragic failure stymied further recruitment amongst those Italians interned in the UK. HS 6/888, 'Attempts at Recruiting Volunteers for Italy', no author, 17 Oct. 1941; HS 7/265, extracts from SOE war diaires (Italy), p. 21.
51. HS 6/885, Martelli report on recruiting of Italian internees, 9 Jan. 1941.
52. Ibid, memo on recruiting Italians in the UK, 27 Jan. 1941; J to D/CD(O), 30 Jan. 1943; HS 6/888, 'Attempts at Recruiting Volunteers for Italy', 17 Oct. 1941.
53. FO 371/29936/R 2804, minutes by W. L. C. Knight, 25 and 28 Mar. 1941 on possibility of raising an Italian Legion in Canada; HS 6/882-3, contains SOE's efforts to recruit Italians in Canada; HS 7/265, SOE war diary – extracts (Italy), 30 Jan. 1941; HS 6/885, Nelson to Jebb, 15 Oct. 1941.
54. HS 6/885, Martelli to Nelson, 19 Dec. 1940.
55. HS 3/146, Dalton to Oliver Lyttleton, Minister of State, 9 July 1941; FO 898/110, 'Memorandum on Anti-Fascist Propaganda in the Middle East', by Thornhill and Miss Freya Stark, Assistant Information Officer, Ministry of Information, Aden, 15 Aug. 1940. See Andrew, *Her Majesty's Secret Service*, pp. 204–6, 217, for Thornhill's Russian duties during the First World War.
56. FO 898/110, memo by Thornhill and Stark, 15 Aug. 1940. For a fascinating insight into the murky world of subterfuge, propaganda and personal rivalries in the Cairo office of SOE, see CAB 102/610, unpublished official history of the PWE written by David Garnett, pp. 53–64.
57. FO 898/161 possesses fleeting references to these initial discussions and FO 371/29936 contains a great deal of material concerning the suitability of Carlos Petrone as a potential leader of the Free Italy movement. In July 1941 Petrone was forced off the executive of the Free Italy committee and severed all connection with it. AA, CRS A981/1, ITA 9, Alfred Stirling, External Affairs Officer, London (1937–45), to Lieutenant-Colonel W. R. Hodgson, Secretary, Department of External Affairs (1935–45), 8 Oct. 1941.
58. FO 371/29920/R 23, Wavell to WO, 30 Jan. 1941; minute by Sir Pierson Dixon, 4 Feb. 1941.

59. CAB 66/15, WP(41)51, minute by Churchill, 11 Feb. 1941.
60. HS 6/903, secret minutes 'I' and 'II', Dalton to Jebb, both dated 23 Jan. 1941; HS 3/189, Dalton to Clement Attlee, Lord Privy Seal, 24 Feb. 1941. In his memoirs, Dalton freely admits that when Churchill gave him the additional powers to conduct subversion, sabotage and psychological warfare, 'I was extremist here … eager to go [to] all lengths'. Dalton, *The Fateful Years*, p. 326. For early discussions on the segregation of Slovenes and Croats from the Italian POW population and their training as agents for work in Italy or as a nucleus for a Free Yugoslav movement, see FO 371/29947/R 1263, P. Nicolls, FO, to Sir H. Page Croft, Under-Secretary of State for War, 26 Feb. 1941; R 1337, WO to Wavell, 23 March 1941; R 5569, Wavell to WO, 8 May 1941 and WO reply, 19 May 1941; HS 7/265, SOE war diary, p. 5
61. HS 7/265, SOE war diary, p. 9d; HS 6/903, Dalton's secret minute 'I'.
62. HS 6/903, secret minute 'VIII', Dalton to Jebb, 29 Jan. 1941.
63. Ibid, secret minute 'I'. Angry that his directives were being blocked by some meddling minion, the target of Dalton's ire was Major A. R. Rawlinson, who was in charge of a revived sub-branch of military intelligence, MI1(a), and later transferred to MI9. Its responsibilities included the interrogation of enemy POWs and promoting escape and evasion for Allied personnel behind enemy lines. HS 6/903, secret minute 'IV', Dalton to Jebb, 27 Jan. 1941. For Rawlinson's career as an intelligence officer, see Foot and Langley, *Escape and Evasion*, pp. 31–2, 35–6.
64. FO 371/29935/R 1376, Davidson to Nicholls, Feb. 1941.
65. CAB 65/11, WM19(41)12, 20 Feb. 1941; CAB 66/15, WP(41)51, 'The Formation of a Free Italian Movement in the Italian Colonies', 6 Mar. 1941; FO 371/29936/R 3055, minute by Sir Miles Lampson, British Ambassador, Cairo, 3 Apr. 1941; LHCMA, King's College, London, Major-General F. H. N. Davidson, war diaries, entries for 20 Dec. 1940 and 7 Feb. 1941; CAB 81/98, JIC(40)325, 18 Oct. 1940; CAB 81/87, JIC(40)63, minute 1, 25 Oct. 1940; CAB 81/88, JIC(40)71, minutes 1 and 2, 3 Dec. 1940, and JIC(40)73, minute 1, 24 Dec. 1940.
66. CAB 66/15, WP(41)51, 6 Mar. 1941; WO 193/352, Wavell to WO, 21 Mar. 1941.
67. FO 371/29947/R 5913, report by de Salis on Geneifa POW Camp No. 3, Apr. 1941.
68. HS 7/58, SOE War History: J Section, extract from letter, 15 Oct. 1941.
69. CO 968/45/1, WO to C-in-C India, 23 Jan. 1941.
70. WO 165/59, 'Summary', 6 May 1941.
71. FO 898/111, draft letter to Sir Orme Sargent, 30 June 1941; FO 371/29947/R 5913, minute by Martelli, 7 June 1941.
72. FO 371/29936/R 5642, WO to Auchinleck, 16 July 1941 and FO to Lampson, 26 July 1941.
73. Ben Pimlott (ed.), *The Second World War Diary of Hugh Dalton 1940–45* (London: Jonathan Cape, 1986), p. 244.
74. CO 968/45/1, Wavell to WO, 7 Jan. 1941 and C-in-C India to WO, 14 Mar. 1941; WO 193/344, Middle East POW location table as of 31 May 1941, n.d. (probably June 1941); FO 898/110, C-in-C India to WO, 30 July 1941; WO 193/352, C-in-C India to WO, 14 June and 23 July 1941; CO 968/45/2, return of enemy POWs as on 1 Nov. 1941; WO 222/1360, medical quarterly report on POW camps in India, Dec. 1941. Ramgarh was eventually closed in August

1942 and its POWs redistributed. See FO 939/370, Thornhill to Sir R. H. Bruce Lockhart, Director-General of PWE, mission report for August 1942, 2 Sept. 1942. Useful tables are produced from Italian archival sources by Conti, *I prigionieri*, pp. 452–3. However, they largely deal with the 1943–5 period. Also see Carlo Felici, 'I prigionieri nella seconda guerra mondiale', *Revista Militare*, 1 (1988), 132–8, and Romain H. Rainero, 'I prigionieri italiani in mani alleate', in Romain H. Rainero and Renato Sicurezza (eds), *L'italia nella 2ª guerra mondiale: aspetti e problemi (1944–1994)* (Milano: Marzorati editore, 1995), pp. 383–401. In the India Office Archive and Library there is a two-volume alphabetical list of Italian POWs held in India. The lists contain surname, Christian name, rank, serial number, corps and camp location. Some names have notations as to movements of POWs around India or overseas, plus date of repatriation. IOL, L/MIL/5/1069-70, POW lists, compiled on 24 Mar. 1942 and revised Aug. 1942.

75. Cruickshank, *Fourth Arm*, pp. 28–43; Michael Balfour, *Propaganda in War 1939–45: Organisation, Policies and Publics in Britain and Germany* (London: Routledge & Kegan Paul, 1979), pp. 93–102; FO 898/286, contains PWE directives on the reorganisation of the SOE and the establishment of the PWE.

76. Cruickshank, *Fourth Arm*, p. 57.

77. FO 898/110, Wavell to WO, 30 July 1941; HS 3/195, Dalton to Jebb, 13 Aug. 1941; HS 3/189, Dalton to Wavell, 5 Jan. 1941; Rex Leeper, head of SO1, to Dalton, 5 Dec. 1940.

78. FO 371/29947/R 6065, minute by Martelli, 7 June 1941.

79. Kent Fedorowich, 'Toughs and Thugs: The Mazzini Society, Political Warfare and Italian POWs in India, 1941–43', unpublished paper given at the Eleventh Annual Conference of the British International History Group, University College Worcester, 9–11 Sept. 1999. A brief mention of the mission is mentioned in Mackenzie, *SOE*, pp. 538–9, and in CAB 102/610, pp. 121–5.

80. FO 898/110, telegram from DMI India to PWE, 17 Nov. 1941.

81. Ibid.

82. WO 163/583, IPOWC, sub-committee A, Paper PWCA/P(42)15, 25 Feb. 1942, appendix A, PWE memo entitled, 'Policy towards Italian Prisoners of War', 14 Nov. 1941.

83. INF 1/920, propaganda directive, 15 Aug. 1941.

84. WO 163/583, IPOWC, sub-committee A, Paper PWCA/P(42)15, 25 Feb. 1942, appendix A, PWE memo entitled, 'Policy towards Italian Prisoners of War', 14 Nov. 1941.

85. Ibid.

86. Ibid; FO 898/111, Stevens to Munro, 27 Nov. 1941.

87. WO 163/583, appendix A, 14 Nov. 1941. The concentration on the Italian leadership as opposed to the Italian people is emphasised by a former POW, Alberto Rovighi, in his piece entitled, 'Obiettivi, metodi e resultati dell'azione politica condotta dalla Gran Bretagna nei riguardi dei prigionieri di guerra italiani', in Romain H. Rainero (ed.), *I prigionieri militari italiani durante la seconda guerra mondiale: aspetti e problemi storici* (Milano: Marzorati editore 1984), pp. 249–54.

88. FO 898/112, Thornhill to Lockhart, mission report for July 1942, 6 Aug. 1942; FO 939/402, Thornhill to Lockhart, 28 Nov. 1942; FO 939/370, 'Scheme for the Employment of Italian P. O. W.', 1 Feb. 1943.

89. WO 163/583, appendix A, 14 Nov. 1941. For the development of white propaganda and the importance of the BBC's remaining 'objective' in its news coverage and programming see Cruickshank, *Fourth Arm*, pp. 69–86, and Balfour, *Propaganda in War*, pp. 80–91.

90. Ibid.

91. FO 898/111, WO to C-in-C India, 22 Nov. 1941.

92. FO 898/321, secret memo on treatment of Italian POWs in UK, 9 Oct. 1941; WO 163/583, PWE directive, 14 Nov. 1941.

93. FO 898/110, secret policy directive concerning Italian POWs in India, 1 Dec. 1941.

94. Ibid, circular from GHQ, 2 Dec. 1941.

95. Ibid, memo by DMI, India, 3 Mar. 1942.

96. Ibid, Thornhill to Munro, 27 Oct. 1941.

97. FO 898/112, PWE report by Munro as to progress up to 19 Jan. 1942; Stevens to Munro, 8 Jan. 1942.

98. Ibid, PWE report by Munro as to progress up to 19 Jan. 1942.

99. Ibid, 'Report of the Work of the P. W. E. Mission in India', by Lieutenant A. Trower, submitted to Lockhart, Jan. 1943.

100. Ibid.; FO 898/110, Adjutant-General, India, to Headquarters, POW camps, India, 24 Apr. 1942.

101. FO 898/112, PWE report by Munro as to progress up to 19 Jan. 1942.

102. Ibid, Trower report, Jan. 1943.

103. Ibid, Cawthorn to DMI, London, 21 Jan. 1942.

104. FO 898/111, Brooks to Rawlinson, 10 Feb. 1942.

105. Ibid, Brooks *aide mémoire*, 15 Apr. 1942; Brooks to Rawlinson, 10 Feb. 1942.

106. FO 898/112, Cawthorn to DMI, London, 21 Jan. 1942.

107. Ibid, written report no. 2 by Munro despatched to Brooks, 19 Jan. 1942.

108. Ibid, Trower report, Jan. 1943.

109. Ibid.

110. FO 898/110, notes supplied to Thornhill by Munro for group commanders' conference, 11 May 1942; FO 898/112, Thornhill to Lockhart, mission report for August 1942, 21 Sept. 1942.

111. FO 898/111, Stevens to Air Commodore P. R. C. Groves, PWE, 21 Apr. 1942.

112. Ibid, David Stephens to Groves, 4 Mar. 1942; Brooks to Lockhart, 22 Apr. 1942.

113. Ibid, Thornhill to Brooks despatched to WO via C-in-C India, 8 May 1942.

114. FO 898/112, Thornhill to Lockhart, mission report for August 1942, 2 Sept. 1942; WO 208/841, E. L. Philip to Dixon, 17 Nov. 1942; FO 939/402, Thornhill to Lockhart, 28 Nov. 1942 and Thornhill summary of reports on PWE mission India, 6 Jan. 1943.

115. FO 898/112, report by Trower submitted to Lockhart, Jan. 1943; FO 939/402, 'Summary of reports on PWE mission India', 6 Jan. 1943.

116. FO 371/37274/R 1057/G22, minute by Dixon, 9 Feb. 1943.

117. CAB 66/34, WP(43)73, memo by Eden, 18 Feb. 1943.

118. FO 939/370, PWE briefs, 2 and 28 Apr. 1943; FO 939/404, WO to C-in-C India, 6 Feb. 1943.

119. FO 898/112, propaganda notes for London compiled by Thornhill, 25 Feb. 1943; FO 939/403, extract from a letter sent to PWE mission, 27 Apr. 1943.

120. FO 939/403, extract from a censored letter, 10 Dec. 1942.

121. FO 898/112, Munro note to Thornhill, Feb. 1943.
122. Ibid, extracts from PWE Indian mission propaganda notes, 6 Oct. 1942; FO 939/402, summary of reports on PWE mission India, 6 Jan. 1943.
123. FO 939/363, Trower to Thornhill, 19 Jan. 1943.
124. WO 208/841, WO to D. F. Howard, southern department, FO, 1 Dec. 1942.
125. FO 939/363, PWE mission progress report, 28 Apr. 1943; Groves to Brooks, 22 May 1943.
126. FO 371/37274/R 5404, ministerial meeting of PWE, 10 June 1943; AA, CRS A373, item 6221, War Cabinet Agendum submitted by F. M. Forde, Minister for the Army, outlining employment of POWs in Australia, Sept. 1944.
127. FO 939/370, minute to Eden, 3 June 1943.
128. Ibid.
129. FO 939/398, Johnston to Brooks, 7 July 1943.
130. FO 939/363, Groves to Brooks, 21 June 1943.
131. FO 939/398, Evelyn-Smith to Brooks, 7 July 1943 and Brooks to Lockhart, 29 June 1943; FO 939/370, Wavell to Eden, 28 June 1943.
132. FO 371/37274/ R 5404, C-in-C India to WO, 12 July 1943.
133. FO 939/398, minutes of meeting to discuss questions relating to the recall of POW mission to India, 16 July 1943; minutes of meeting between PWE, India Office and War Office, 22 July 1943; WO to GHQ India, 24 July 1943.
134. Ibid, Brooks to Bracken, 18 Oct. 1943.
135. At the end of the war the Americans had enlisted 31,000 co-operators into Italian Service Units, 1,000 of whom were shipped overseas to serve as support troops behind American forces fighting in Europe. The British scored an even more marked success. In early 1944, in anticipation of serious labour shortfalls in part created by the extensive preparations required for the forthcoming Normandy invasion, the War Office transported 30,000 co-operators to England from the Middle East, East Africa and India. Moreover, Italian POWs were used extensively in North Africa and Sicily and on the Italian mainland. In Sicily in January 1944 there were 2,051 unskilled and 768 skilled Italian POWs employed in pioneer units on the island. In North Africa, the numbers were much higher. Divided into the categories of unskilled, skilled and POWs used within the war establishment of British units, there were 25,798, 5,289 and 4,793 respectively. In April 1944 two pioneer units with a complement of 283 men each and commanded by British officers were transferred to Italy. By the end of June 1945, 5,179 Italian co-operators were retained in North Africa, while 21,702 were employed in the Central Mediterranean Force on a variety of non-combatant duties. According to Foreign Office statistics there were 114,400 co-operators out of a total of 154,728 Italian POWs in the United Kingdom in April 1945. Lewis and Mewha, *Prisoner of War Utilization*, pp. 93–100 and 175–205; Keefer, *Italian Prisoners*, pp. 73–101; CAB 106/453, 'Employment of Co-operators in the Italian Campaign', n.d. , fos. 69–70; FO 898/324, memo, 24 Apr. 1945.
136. FO 939/370, minute for Brooks, 3 June 1943; WO 193/352, minute for Director of Military Operations, 12 Feb. 1943; WO 203/4714, C-in-C Ceylon to SEAC, 29 Nov. 1943; 25th mtg. of Supreme Allied Command, 3 Dec. 1943; WO 203/3756, employment of Italian POW officers, Dec. 1944–May 1945; PREM 3/364/2, War Department, Government of India, to Secretary of State for India, 16 Nov. 1943, circulated to the War Cabinet.

6 The Watershed Year of 1943: From Enemies to Co-Belligerents

1. David W. Ellwood, *Italy 1942–1945* (Leicester: University of Leicester Press, 1985), pp. 22–3. Also see Elena Agarossi, *A Nation Collapses. The Italian Surrender of September 1943*, trans. by Harvey Fergusson II (Cambridge: Cambridge University Press, 2000).

2. FO 954/13, Lord Avon Papers, Churchill to President Roosevelt, 28 July 1943. There may have been as many as 80,000 British POWs in Italian hands, nearly 50,000 of whom 'left' their camps after the Italian surrender. See Roger Absalom, *A Strange Alliance* (Firenze: Leo S. Olschki Editoire, 1991), and 'Hiding History', *Historical Journal*, 38, 1 (1995), 111–31.

3. Ellwood, *Italy*, pp. 25–6. Also see Moshe Gat, 'The Soviet Factor in British Policy Towards Italy, 1943–1945', *The Historian*, 50, 4 (1988), 535–57.

4. CAB 66/34, WP(43)73, memo by Eden, 18 Feb. 1943.

5. WO 169/2549, War diary, Suez POW Camp No. 310, 8 May 1941; CAB 106/452, memo entitled, 'Italian Co-operators and GHQ 2nd Echelon in the Mediterranean Theatres', July 1943.

6. Ibid.

7. Harry C. Butcher, *Three Years with Eisenhower: The Personal Diary of Captain Harry C. Butcher* (London: W. Heinemann, 1946), p. 257. Entry for 12 May 1943.

8. Pietro Badoglio, *Italy in the Second World War: Memories and Documents*, 2nd edn (Westport CT: Greenwood Press, 1976), p. 196.

9. The International Committee of the Red Cross also had little to say about the treatment of Italian prisoners in British or American hands. See International Committee of the Red Cross, *Report of the International Committee of the Red Cross on its activities during the Second World War (September 1, 1939–June 30, 1947)* vol. 1 *General Activities* (Geneva: ICRC, 1948).

10. FO 898/323, internal memo of PWE, 2 Apr. 1943.

11. FO 371/37260B/R 3823, minute by Brooks, 21 Apr. 1943.

12. Butcher, *Three Years*, p. 315. Entry for 27 July 1943.

13. Ellwood, *Italy*, pp. 27–8.

14. Mario Toscano, *Designs in Diplomacy. Pages from European Diplomatic History in the Twentieth Century* (Baltimore, MD: The Johns Hopkins Press, 1970), p. 397.

15. FO 954/13, Churchill to Roosevelt, 28 July 1943; FO 371/37263A/R 6936, Orme Sargent to Eden, 28 July 1943; Winston S. Churchill, *The Second World War*, vol. 5, *Closing the Ring* (London: Cassell, 1952), pp. 55–6; Keefer, *Italian Prisoners of War*.

16. FO 954/13, FO to Washington, 26 July 1943 reporting Churchill to Roosevelt, 26 July 1943.

17. Butcher, *Three Years*, pp. 312–13. General Wilson had apparently suggested the idea based on the German success with a similar policy in Greece. However, evidence suggests that the idea may have originated with General Alexander. See FO 954/13, Resident Minister, Algiers to FO, 29 July 1943.

18. FO 371/37263A/R 3514, Air Ministry to Washington citing COS(W)726, 23 July 1943; Sargent to Eden, 28 July 1943.

19. Ibid.

20. FO 371/37265/R 7687, Harold Macmillan to FO, 17 Aug. 1943.

21. FO 371/37265/R 3514, Air Ministry to Washington, 23 July 1943; Sargent to Eden, 28 July 1943.
22. Butcher, *Three Years*, pp. 312–13.
23. Lewis and Mewha, *Prisoner of War Utilization*, p. 178; WO 214/63A, Earl Alexander of Tunis Papers, secret cyphers from AFHQ to British commanders, Sicily, 10 July 1944 and 10 Aug. 1944.
24. CAB 66/40, WP(43)392, memo by the Lord President, 10 Sept. 1943.
25. FO 371/37265/R 7687, Ismay to Cadogan, 23 Aug. 1943. Authors' emphasis.
26. The reason for their exclusion was presumably to assist the PWE in its campaign to win hearts and minds in Italy by arranging repatriations to Sicily. FO 898/325, Major C. A. H. Harrison, Acting Regional Director, PWE Italian Region, to Director of Plans, 13 July 1943.
27. CAB 66/40, WP(43)392, memo by Lord President on Italian POW, 17 Sept. 1943.
28. CAB 122/670, Eden to Sir Ronald I. Campbell, British minister in Washington, 26 Sept. 1943.
29. FO 371/37271/R 10098, FO memo on co-belligerency, 4 Oct. 1943.
30. Ibid, W. Ridsdale, head of FO News Department, to P. Dixon, Eden's principal private secretary, 1 Oct. 1943.
31. Ellwood, *Italy*, p. 47.
32. C. R. S. Harris, *Allied Military Administration of Italy, 1943–1945* (London: HMSO, 1957), p. 151; FO 898/325, Resident Minister in Algiers to FO, 5 Feb. 1944, quotes the Italian government figure of around 27,000 officers and 420,000 NCOs and men. A table in PREM 3/364/2 gives a total of 556,780 prisoners but this may have included a large number of Italian colonial troops.
33. FO 371/37274/R 8720, FO to Eisenhower (draft), 9 Sept. 1943.
34. CAB 65/35, WM127(43)4 and WM128(43)1, 13 and 16 Sept. 1943; CAB 79/64, COS(43), 225mtg (O)5, 24 Sept. 1943.
35. CAB 122/670, WO to British Army Staff, Washington, 7 Sept. 1943; copy of COS(43)120, 24 Aug. 1943; Campbell to FO, 2 Oct. 1943.
36. ADM 116/5182, AFHQ Algiers to WO, 7 Oct. 1943.
37. PREM 3/364/2, Churchill to Lord President, 16 Sept. 1943.
38. Ibid, Churchill to Eden, 29 Sept. 1943; Churchill to FO, 13 Oct. 1943. It was also the case that this would get round the problem of trying to remove the Italians captured in North-West Africa who had been designated as United States captives. See, Lewis and Mewha, *Prisoner of War Utilization*, p. 90.
39. PREM 3/364/2, W. L. Gorell Barnes, Privy Council Office, to Gepp, 14 Oct. 1943.
40. CAB 66/45, WP(44)36, memo by Attlee, 18 Jan. 1944.
41. PREM 3/364/2, Campbell to FO, 19 Oct. 1943.
42. CAB 78/16, FO to Washington (draft) n.d. ; ADM 116/5182, FO to Washington, 4 Nov. 1943. Lewis and Mewha, *Prisoner of War Utilization*, pp. 180–1.
43. CAB 78/16, Colonel Deneys Reitz, South African Minister of Native Affairs and member of the South African War Committee, to Viscount Cranborne, Secretary of State for Dominions Affairs, 22 Oct. 1943.
44. Ibid, WP(GEN)21(43)1 and 2 submitted to COS on the status of Italian POWs and a draft agreement with Italian government on same, 26 Oct. 1943; FO 1011/218, Loraine to Lockhart, 30 Aug. 1943.

45. FO 898/323, PWE memo entitled, 'Future Status of Italian Prisoners of War', 18 Oct. 1943.

46. CAB 122/670, Viscount Halifax to FO, 6 Nov. 1943; paraphrased report of message from Eisenhower, 30 Oct. 1943.

47. Ibid, Combined Chiefs of Staff memo entitled, 'Treatment of Italian Prisoners of War under the Italian Government's Co-belligerent Status', 20 Dec. 1943. For the International Red Cross perspective on the POW issue, see André Durand, *From Sarajevo to Hiroshima: History of the International Committee of the Red Cross* (Geneva, 1984), and ICRC, *Report of the International Committee*.

48. For the development and extent of this use of Italian labour by the British Army, see CAB 106/452, 'Italian Co-operators and GHQ 2nd Echelon in the Mediterranean Theatres'.

49. CAB 122/670, Halifax to FO, 6 Nov. 1943; paraphrased report of message from Eisenhower, 30 Oct. 1943.

50. Badoglio, *Italy*, pp. 198–9.

51. The American view was that the only restrictions on the use of Italian prisoners in the United States were those created by security considerations. See Lewis and Mewha, *Prisoner of War Utilization*, pp. 99–100.

52. NAC, RG 24, reel C-5369, f. HQS 7236-0-10, Cranborne to Canadian Prime Minister, W. L. Mackenzie King (who was also Secretary of State for External Affairs), 17 Feb. 1944.

53. Butcher, *Three Years*, p. 373.

54. ADM 116/5182, AFHQ Algiers to AGWAR, 29 Jan. 1944, noted Badoglio's refusal to sign the agreement and his preference for resignation.

55. FO 898/323, Macmillan to FO, 6 Feb. 1944.

56. Ibid, Gepp to Palairet, 9 Feb. 1944 (draft). For the semi-official history published by the FO on POW policy, see Satow and Sée, *Prisoners of War*.

57. CAB 122/671, Combined Chiefs of Staff, Washington, to General Wilson, Algiers, 13 Mar. 1944; Eden to Halifax, 21 Mar. 1944.

58. Ibid, General Wilson to Combined Chiefs of Staff, 7 Apr. 1944.

59. Ibid, Badoglio to General Mason-MacFarlane, 6 Apr. 1944.

60. PREM 3/364/2, Churchill to Cadogan, 9 Apr. 1944; CAB 122/671, Halifax to FO, 13 Apr. 1944.

61. Ibid.

62. WO 32/11123, WO note, 9 May 1944; Harris, *Administration of Italy*, pp. 152–3; ADM 116/5182, FO to Washington Embassy, 8 Apr. 1944.

7   Neither Enemies Nor Allies: Italian Prisoners in the United Kingdom After the Armistice

1. MAF 47/54, memo by W. S. Mansfield, MAF, 13 Jan. 1942. See also CAB 114/26, parliamentary reply by Robert Hudson, Minister of Agriculture, to question by W. F. Jackson MP, *Hansard*, House of Commons, fifth series (1942–3), vol. 386, col. 1599, 16 Feb. 1943.

2. MAF 47/54, memo, 'Italian Prisoners of War: 1943 Programme – 2 Dec. 1942', 30 Nov. 1942; memo by Ministry of Works and Planning, 14 Jan. 1943.

3. Ibid, internal memo by W. C. Tame, Man Power Division, MAF, 21 Dec. 1943.

4. CAB 122/670, COS(43)719(O), joint note by WO and Ministry of War Transport, 'Move of Italian Prisoners of War to the United Kingdom', 18 Nov. 1943. Eisenhower had broadcast that the Italians taken prisoner in Tunisia or Sicily would be returned home if all Allied prisoners were handed over. As many had fallen into German hands, this offer was deemed to have lapsed, but Eisenhower remained unwilling to sanction their removal out of the Tunisian or Sicilian theatres of operation. PREM 3/364/2, Attlee to Churchill, 19 Aug. 1943, which included annex to 'Employment of Italian Prisoners in the United Kingdom', WP(43)392.

5. MAF 47/54, internal memo by Tame, 21 Dec. 1943; CAB 66/45, WP(44)36, memo by Attlee, 18 Jan. 1944; PREM 3/364/2, 'Employment of Italian Prisoners of War' cites WP(44)36 but gives total accommodation of +23,000.

6. ADM 116/5182, CCS to AGWAR, 22 June 1944, notes the paroling of around 65,000 men by the British and Americans in Sicily – most of them Sicilians.

7. CAB 122/670, COS(43)319, note by Lieutenant-General Ronald M. Weeks, Deputy Chief of the Imperial General Staff, 'Move of Italian Prisoners of War to the United Kingdom', 29 Dec. 1943.

8. ADM 1/17394, WO memo, 'Employment of Italian Prisoners of War as Co-operators', 23 Apr. 1944.

9. CAB 78/16, War Cabinet Paper, GEN21(43)2, 'Status of Italian Prisoners of War', 26 Oct. 1943.

10. Ibid.; Colonel Deneys Reitz, Minister of Native Affairs and member of the South African War Committee, to Sir James Grigg, Secretary of State for War, 22 Oct. 1943.

11. FO 898/323, Gepp to Sir Michael Palairet, PWD, 9 Feb. 1944.

12. ADM 1/17394, WO to GOC-in-Cs, Home Commands, 23 Apr. 1944.

13. Ibid. The Italian agreement to this previous arrangement was appended to the WO letter, although the Badoglio regime had consistently refused to sanction the use of prisoners outside North Africa in this way.

14. WO 32/10737, MAF memo to County War Agricultural Executive Committees in England and Wales, 29 Apr. 1944.

15. ADM 1/17394, WO to GOC-in-Cs, Home Commands, 23 Apr. 1944.

16. FO 898/325, PWE memo on the proposal to employ Italian POWs on work prohibited by the Geneva Convention, 14 Apr. 1944.

17. WO 32/10737, WO to Home Command HQs, 13 May 1944. The actual figures were co-operators 56,166, non-co-operators 37,091. Ibid, WO to Gardner, 30 May 1944. By Apr. 1945, of the 154,728 Italian POWs in the UK, the PWE claimed that 114,400 were co-operators and 40,328 were non-co-operators. FO 898/324, memo, 24 Apr. 1945.

18. WO 32/10737, C-in-C HQ Southern Command to WO, 11 June 1944.

19. FO 371/49859/ZM 696, 'Postal and Telegraph Censorship – Italian Prisoners of War in Great Britain', report on letters read, Dec. 1944 to 15 Jan. 1945, p. 3 cites E/PW/IT/6308/44.

20. WO 32/10737, C-in-C Western Command to WO, 4 July 1944. Hair oil, toilet accessories and even beer to meet the additional allowances for co-operators was reported in very short supply. Ibid, C-in-C Northern Command to WO, 13 July 1944.

21. Ibid, C-in-C Southern Command to WO, 21 July 1944. Pay differentials also existed between Italians employed by the British. Those employed by the

Admiralty on ammunition loading worked longer hours at inferior rates of pay than their counterparts engaged on agricultural work. ADM 1/17394, W. H. Gardner, DPW to N. J. Abercrombie, Assistant Secretary, Labour Branch, Admiralty, 15 July 1944.

22. ADM 116/5182, FO to British embassy, Washington, 16 Dec. 1943.
23. WO 32/10737, report from Lieutenant-Colonel P. D. Hewat, no. 2 Transportation Stores Depot, Royal Engineers, 13 May 1944.
24. Ibid.
25. Roderic de Normann, *For Führer and Fatherland: SS Murder and Mayhem in Wartime Britain* (Stroud: Sutton, 1996), p. 46, cites Wiltshire Record Office, F5/530/3, Home Office letter, 23 Aug. 1944.
26. PREM 3/364/13, WP(44)421, memo by Ernest Bevin, Minister of Labour and National Service, 31 July 1944.
27. Moore, 'Turning Liabilities into Assets', pp. 133–5, and 'Unruly Allies', pp. 180–98.
28. BT 168/84, WO to C-in-Cs Home Commands, 9 Aug. 1944.
29. Ibid
30. Ibid; WO 32/10737, minutes of a meeting of POW Commandants held at HQ Western Command, 14 Aug. 1944.
31. CAB 65/44, WM160(44)5, 30 Nov. 1944.
32. *News Chronicle*, 29 May 1944; CAB 114/29, itemised HD(S)E minutes 74–5, 29 May 1944.
33. WO 32/9911, DPW administrative instruction, amendment no. 16, parole for protected personnel, 28 Oct. 1943; CAB 114/29, statement by Sir James Grigg, *Hansard*, House of Commons, fifth series (1943–44), vol. 404, cols 1816–17, 14 Nov. 1944. There was one instance in Scotland when a farmer in Aryshire, who had two POWs billeted on his farm, was unable to convey them to their camp as his car had broken down. He loaned them two bicycles so they could make the twelve-mile journey back to camp. NAS, HH 55/58, PWD/45/10/40, Special Branch Report, Chief Constable, Kilmarnock, 31 Jan. 1944.
34. WO 32/10737, HD(S)E, LOC(44)257(1(e)), 27 Dec. 1944.
35. Ibid, LOC(45)269(1(c)), 20 Mar. 1945.
36. Sponza, 'Prisoners of War', p. 206.
37. Ibid, p. 209, notes the strike in December 1942 at Camp No. 155 (Penrith) where more than one hundred men refused to work underground in a lead mine, and an ICRC report on a camp in Essex early in 1943 where 24 prisoners were in detention for refusing to carry out certain work.
38. Ibid, p. 211, cites memo by N. H. Andreoni entitled, 'Political reactions in Italian POW Camps resulting from the downfall of the Fascist regime', 2 Oct. 1943 in FO 939/357. This can also be found in FO 898/323.
39. FO 898/323, Andreoni memo, 2 Oct. 1943.
40. Ibid.
41. WO 32/10737, see for example, Sergeant-Major Raffaele Scalers to Camp Commandant, 12 Feb. 1944; FO 898/324, Wing Commander R. W. Hay, PWE Italian POW section, to Lieutenant-Colonel H. L. Chandler, WO, 2 Oct. 1943; FO 898/325, Loraine to General Dallas Brooks, 24 May 1944.
42. FO 939/356, Cesarina Hudson to FO, 27 July 1944.
43. Ibid, Regional Director, PWE Italy, to Director-General PWE, 29 Aug. 1944.

44. Ibid. The exchange rate of £ = 72 lira had been insisted upon by Mussolini in the initial Anglo-Italian negotiations on the workings of the Geneva Convention, ostensibly as a matter of national pride. Certainly it helped Italian officers in captivity who were handsomely rewarded at these rates, but conversely penalised transfers from sterling into lira, a fact compounded by rampant inflation in Italy. Satow and Sée, *Prisoners of War Department*, pp. 29–30.

45. FO 371/49859/ZM 696, 'Postal and Telegraph Censorship', report on letters read, p. 1 (Privates Mammi and Masini), Dec. 1944 to 15 Jan. 1945.

46. Ibid, p. 2, cites E/PW/IT/133/45, E/PW/IT/8297/44, E/PW/IT/55/45.

47. Ibid, p. 3. The figures for complaints were 44% of mail censored to German-occupied Italy and 22% of mail to Allied-occupied Italy.

48. FO 916/1279, memo by Cavendish Bentinck to Western Department, FO, and PWD, 5 Mar. 1945.

49. FO 371/49859/ZM 696, 'Postal and Telegraph Censorship', report on letters read, p. 4 (Privates Beltrami and Martucci).

50. HO 45/21875/700460/79, HD(S)E, LOC(44)256(1(a)), 19 Dec. 1944; *The Times*, 18–21 Dec. 1944.

51. FO 371/49859/ZM 696, 'Postal and Telegraph Censorship', report on letters read, p. 4; HO 45/21875/700460/79, HD(S)E, LOC(44)256(1(a)), 19 Dec. 1944; *The Times*, 18 Dec. 1944. Charles Whiting (without citing any sources) argues that the British authorities saw this escape as part of the pattern of unrest in POW camps in the United Kingdom linked to the Germans' Ardennes offensive in the winter of 1944. See his *The March on London* (London: Leo Cooper, 1992) p. 95. See also *Daily Express*, 18 Dec. 1944.

52. WO 32/9890, IPOWC, monthly reports, Jan.-Mar. 1945; HO 45/21875/700460/79, minute by J. M. Ross, 28 Dec. 1944.

53. NAS, HH 55/59, PWD/45/10/46, Special Branch Report by Chief Constable of East Lothian Constabulary, July 1944. On 30 July a group of 30 'extreme Fascist types' escaped from a camp in Argyll. They possessed ample supplies of food, blankets and civilian clothes. The escape was not discovered until two surrendered to local police 'and, owing to the country into which they escaped, consisting of miles of bracken and scrub', they were not all recaptured until 6 Aug. Several were found 38 miles from camp! HH 55/59, PWD/45/10/47, Scottish Home Department, monthly report, Aug. 1944.

54. WO 32/9890, IPOWC, monthly reports, Jan. 1945; FO 898/324, PWE memo, 24 Apr. 1945.

55. PREM 3/363/7, S. Redman, personal private secretary to Sir James Grigg, to T. L. Rowan, private secretary to prime minister, 16 Apr. 1943, commented that as of Apr. only 10 cases of common or indecent assault had been committed by Italian POWs in the UK so far. All the cases had been tried by a military court, and sentences up to nine months' detention had been imposed. Also see WO 32/9890, IPOWC, monthly reports, Jan.–Mar. 1945; HO 45/21963/886179/2-3, minutes by G. J. Mathew, HO, 16 Aug. 1944, and illegible signature, 13 Apr. 1945; NAS, HH 55/57, PWD/45/10/37, memo by Sergeant W. W. Wait, Berwickshire Constabulary to the Chief Constable, 31 Oct. 1943; Ibid, PWD/45/10/39, Scottish Home Department, Special Branch Report, Dec. 1943; HH 55/58, PWD/45/10/43, Special Branch Reports by W. A. Black, Chief Constable, Dumfries County Police Force, 30 Dec. 1943

and 29 Apr. 1944; Ibid, PWD/45/10/40, Special Branch Reports, Perthshire and Kinross Constabulary, Jan. 1944; Ibid, PWD/45/10/42, Special Branch Report by David W. Brown, Chief Constable, Roxburghshire Constabulary, Jedburgh, 31 Mar. 1944. All the Scottish cases deal with fraternisation and many deal with school-age girls between the ages of 12 and 14.

56. FO 939/353, PWE memo on the political re-education of Italian prisoners, 1 May 1945; NAS, HH 55/57, PWD/45/10/37, David Baldie, Chief Constable, Kirkcaldy Burgh Police, to Secretary, Scottish Home Department, 28 Oct. 1943; HH 55/58, PWD/45/10/41, Special Branch Report by Robert Mitchell, Chief Constable, Kincardineshire, 28 Feb. 1944; Ibid, Special Branch Report by Black, 28 Feb. 1944; WO 32/10737, WO memo to HQs Home Commands and HQ London District, 2 Nov. 1944.

57. FO 898/324, memo on the re-education of Italian POWs in England, 30 Sept. 1944.

58. FO 939/353, notes for meeting between Air Commodore P. R. C. Groves, PWE, Oliver Harvey, Assistant Under-Secretary of State, FO, and Major-General W. H. A. Bishop, PID, 24 Apr. 1945.

59. FO 916/1279, WO to A. J. Gardner, FO, 23 Mar. 1945.

60. FO 898/324, memo on the re-education of Italian POWs in England, 30 Sept. 1944.

61. *The Times*, 28 July 1943.

62. *The Times*, 21 Nov. 1941, cited in Sponza, 'Italian Prisoners', p. 208.

63. The material from Mass Observation does need to be treated with caution. It was collected via a directive which asked for general feelings about a whole range of nationalities, and at a time when the Italians were considered by many to be more than half-way to complete defeat. As this exercise was not repeated, it is impossible to say if the views expressed here were consistently held or were to change as the war progressed.

64. Tom Harrisson, Mass Observation Archive, University of Sussex, (hereafter MO), DR3164, Mar. 1943.

65. MO, DR2685, Mar. 1943.

66. MO, DR2719 and DR2142, Mar. 1943.

67. MO, DR (unnumbered), Mar. 1943.

68. MO, DR3194 Mar. 1943.

69. See, for example, MO, DR2845, DR2362 and DR3184, Mar. 1943.

70. MO, DR3356, and DR2957 Mar. 1943.

71. MO, DR1093, Mar. 1943.

72. Sponza, 'Italian Prisoners', pp. 206–7, cites FO 916/172, notes by Colonel Harold Stevens on visit to Italian POW Camp, Royston, 23 Sept. 1941.

73. MO, DR3194, Mar. 1943.

74. MO, DR1578 and DR3380, Mar. 1943. See also Sponza, 'Italian Prisoners', p. 208.

75. IWM, 87/5/1, Mrs D. M. Wood made the point of how industrious she found POW labourers, while others attached to the Women's Land Army or Women's Timber Corps make fleeting but unspecified references to contact they had when working with Italian POW labour. See IWM, 88/1/1, Mrs E. M. Hughes; 88/43/1, Mrs M. Waterhouse; 87/21/1, Mrs E. G. Yerbury. Jenny Hartley (ed.), *Hearts Undefeated. Women's Writing of the Second World War* (London: Virago, 1996), pp. 208–9.

76. Nicola Tyrer, *They Fought in the Fields. The Women's Land Army: The Story of a Forgotten Victory* (London: Mandarin, 1997), p. 181. Also see IWM 88/1/1, Mrs E. R. Hazell on problems of working with Italian POWs. For an example of a Land Army girl being grabbed and the POW getting his just desserts, see Donald Brown, *Somerset v Hitler* (Newbury, Berks: Countryside Books, 1999), p. 145.

77. Tyrer, *They Fought in the Fields*, p. 182, cites the *Daily Sketch*, 15 Feb. 1945.

78. Imperial War Museum, Sound Archive 12861/2 (Edie Ford), p. 6.

79. *The Times*, 9 Apr. 1943. See also *Daily Express*, 20 Apr. 1943 and *Daily Sketch*, 19 Apr. 1943.

80. *The Times*, 26 July 1943.

81. CAB 114/26, Ministry of Information, Home Intelligence weekly report, no. 150, 19 Aug. 1943.

82. *The Times*, 25 Oct. 1944; question by Sir J. Mellor MP to Grigg, *Hansard*, House of Commons, fifth series (1943–44), vol. 404, col. 14, 24 Oct. 1944.

83. *The Times*, 8 Feb. 1945.

84. Ibid, 14 Sept. 1944.

85. CAB 114/26, Lieutenant-Colonel R. Evelyn Smith, Deputy Director of DPW, to H. Armstrong, Secretary, HD(S)E, 4 Dec. 1942 and Armstrong's note, 'Italian Prisoners of War in Agriculture', SE/228, 4 Dec. 1942.

86. Ibid, DPW memo entitled, 'Italian Prisoners of War: Use of Bicycles to attend Church unescorted on Sundays', SE/258, 21 May 1943; HD(S)E, LOC(43)88(5), 26 May 1943; NAS, AF 59/3/4, minute by A. W. Sharman, Department of Agriculture for Scotland, 6 Apr. 1944.

87. CAB 114/31, extracts of HD(S)E minutes, LOC(44)233, 4 July 1944, report by Ross of HO on difficulties of clearing bomb damage and offer of 1,000 Italians from Ministry of Works.

88. Ibid, HD(S)E memo, LOC(44)32, 19 Aug. 1944.

89. *News Chronicle*, 1 Aug. 1944.

90. CAB 114/31, parliamentary reply by E. G. Hicks, Parliamentary Secretary, Ministry of Works, to questions by Captain H. C. Longhurst MP and Sir R. Blair MP, *Hansard*, House of Commons, fifth series (1943–44), vol. 403, cols 955–6, 4 Oct. 1944.

91. *Sunday Pictorial*, 1 Oct. 1944; *Daily Express*, 2 Oct. 1944; *Daily Herald*, 2 Oct. 1944.

92. *The Times*, 5 and 10 Oct. 1944; MEPO 2/6871, Superintendent 'X' Division, Harrow Road, to Chief Constable, 6 Jan. 1945.

93. MEPO 2/6871, H. C. Loyd, HQ London District, to Sir Harold Scott, Commissioner of Police for the Metropolis, 6 May 1945.

94. Ibid, Home Office circular 324/44, signed by M. H. Whitelegge, Assistant Secretary, HO, to Chief Constables, 28 Dec. 1944.

95. Ibid, Superintendents to Chief Constable, 6 Jan. 1945. The exception was 'X' Division.

96. Ibid, Superintendent 'M' Division, Southwark, to Chief Constable, 6 Jan. 1945.

97. Ibid, Superintendent 'K' Division, East Ham, to Chief Constable, 5 Jan. 1945; Superintendent 'Z' Division, Croydon, to Chief Constable, 6 Jan. 1945; Superintendent C2 Branch to Chief Constable, 2 Jan. 1945. A number of comments were made specifically about schoolgirls loitering near camps, but

this was usually dealt with by informing the relevant school. In January 1946, the *Daily Herald* reported the sentencing by a military court in Aldershot of a 31-year-old Italian POW to 9 months for kissing a 15-year-old girl against her will. *Daily Herald*, 31 Jan. 1946.

98. MEPO 2/6871, Superintendent 'A' Division, Cannon Row to Chief Constable, Jan. 1945; agenda of meeting on security of Italian Co-operators, 8 Mar. 1945, item 9(a).

99. Ibid, Superintendent 'S' Division, Golders Green, to Chief Constable, 6 Jan. 1945.

100. WO 32/10737, Major G. Rescazzi to Commandant 122nd Italian Labour Battalion, Rayners Lane Camp, 28 Nov. 1944. The use of the term 'WOP' in official correspondence was similarly targeted by the Foreign Office. 'While the exercise of humour in official business may tend to leaven monotony it is thought that this particular specimen of gratuitous tactlessness is one which will tend to render the task of obtaining co-operation all the more difficult. It is perhaps not realised that a number of Italians, more particularly officers and chaplains on whom we have in the past relied and shall in future have to rely to some extent, have a knowledge of English sufficient to enable them to detect and take note of this form of humour. ... May I strongly urge, therefore, that these reference letters be changed forthwith.' FO 898/324, unsigned FO draft, 11 Jan. 1944.

101. PREM 3/363/13, WP(44)686, memo by Bevin, 24 Nov. 1944; CAB 65/44, WM160(44)5, 30 Nov. 1944. Interestingly, intervention had been rejected eighteen months earlier as likely to be distorted and used by the enemy for propaganda purposes. CAB 114/26, HD(S)E, LOC(43)175(7), 11 May 1943.

102. WO 32/10737, WO memo to HQs Home Commands and HQ London District, 2 Nov. 1944.

103. CAB 114/29, Ministry of Information, Home Intelligence weekly report, no. 208, 28 Sept. 1944.

104. Ibid. Also see no. 207, 21 Sept. 1944; no. 209, 5 Oct. 1944; and no. 210, 12 Oct. 1944.

105. WO 32/10737, WO to all HQs Home Commands, 2 Nov. 1944.

106. *Daily Express*, 24 Nov. 1944; *News Chronicle*, 25 Nov. 1944; *Daily Mail*, 25 Nov. 1944; *Daily Telegraph*, 25 Nov. 1944.

107. BT 168/84, committee for the allocation of POWs, 19th mtg, 6 Nov. 1944.

108. WO 32/11131, Ministry of Labour and National Service, Joint Consultative Committee, 49th mtg, minute 7, 12 Dec. 1944; CAB 114/29, Ministry of Information, Home Intelligence weekly report, no. 217, 30 Nov. 1944.

8 Freedom, Farming and Frustration: Italians in Africa and Australia, 1943–5

1. SADDA, POW 1, CE 8/4/6, Middle Eastern intelligence summary no. 101 (1–14 Dec. 1943), 18 Dec. 1943.

2. CO 968/45/1, WO to C-in-C India, 23 Jan. 1941; CO 822/111/12, minute by Watherston, 3 Sept. 1942.

3. WO 32/9911, Auchinleck to WO, 17 Jan. and 13 Apr. 1942. One of the fears raised by officials in MI9 in 1941 was the possibility that protected

personnel would collect information when out on parole and be able to pass it back to Germany or Italy, as it was these men who were liable for early repatriation. Ibid, minute by Lieutenant-Colonel N. R. Crockatt, 30 Sept. 1941.

4. SADDA, Box 3065, DC 1472/1, chap. 3, Secretary for External Affairs to South African High Commission in London, 15 Oct. 1941 and reply 12 Nov. 1941; POW2, f. 2390, POW summary no. 5 (1–30 Nov. 1941), 15 Dec. 1941.

5. Ibid, Box 3072, DC 1472/15, chap. 4, PWIS (Home) officer to MI19(a), WO, 28 May 1942; Pilkington-Jordan to Blaine, 4 Sept. 1942.

6. Ibid. Some prisoners made allegations against Zonderwater's Senior Medical Officer, Lieutenant-Colonel L. Blumberg, charging that he was a Nazi sympathiser. The South African authorities, which immediately dismissed them as ridiculous and the mischievous work of Fascist agitators, vigorously contested these allegations. There is no doubt that Blumberg was a dedicated officer who did more than anyone to maintain the proper standards of hygiene under difficult circumstances during those early days at Zonderwater. SADDA, Box 3072, DC 1472/15, chap. 4, Pilkington-Jordan to Blaine, 4 Sept. 1942.

7. WO 32/9905, POW censorship summary by Wilson, 15 Mar. 1944, pp. 3–4.

8. FO 371/29947/R 5913/G, FO minute, June 1941; SADDA, Box 3072, DC 1472/15, chap. 4, Pilkington-Jordan to Blaine, 15 July 1942. In Sept. 1944 the 'Savoia' Theatrical Company, Block 1, Zonderwater, performed *Cyrano de Bergerac*. Invitations were sent to senior camp officers and officials in Pretoria including the Prime Minister Smuts and Dr E. G. Malherbe. Killie Campbell Library, Malherbe Papers, KCM 56996 (170), file 179/6 A, misc. theatrical productions. The South African National Museum of Military History in Johannesburg also possesses a number of programmes from plays and concerts performed at Zonderwater by the POWs.

9. CO 968/45/1, C-in-C India to WO, 11 May 1941.

10. WO 32/9905, censorship summary by Wilson, 15 Mar. 1944.

11. Ibid.

12. WO 307/2, GOC East Africa to WO, 24 Mar. 1944.

13. WO 32/9905, Major A. Hermelin, Moorby Camp, Revesby, Lincolnshire, to the DPW, 26 Apr. 1944.

14. *Cape Argus*, 9 Jan. 1943. The Superintendent of the Orange River Settlement near Upington made similar complaints to J. J. du Plessis, Secretary of Lands, six months earlier. SANA, LDE , vol. 1878, file 35580, 10 Aug. 1942.

15. *Cape Argus*, 14 Jan. 1943.

16. SANA, BAO 614/400, Magistrate for Taungs to Secretary for Native Affairs, 1 Mar. 1943 which includes the Behr judgement, 23 Feb. 1943. Several other examples of POWs being billeted to members of the *Ossewabrandwag* can be found in SAP 101, SAP 1/75/43/1, case file, Lindley district, May 1943; Ibid, case file, Vryburg district, Jan.–Feb. 1943.

17. SADDA, Box 3077, DC 1472/29, Blaine to AG, 25 Mar. 1943, submitting a statement received from H. G. Lawrence, Minister of the Interior and Public Health on conduct of Italian POWs in Stellenbosch and Paarl areas.

18. Ibid, Ziervogel to Blaine, 15 Mar. 1943; Defence Department clerk to Blaine, 15 Mar. 1943, and minute by Blaine, 16 Mar. 1943.

19. Ibid, Baston to Chief Control Officer, 11 Mar. 1943.
20. Ibid, AG(3)154, Box 87, X/895, report by Captain E. S. Hyland of Modena Work Camp, no. 47, 31 Mar. 1943.
21. Ibid, Box 3077, DC 1472/29, H. Barrett, Magistrate, Rustenburg, to Chief Control Officer, 5 Mar. 1943.
22. Ibid, Wilson to Blaine, 1 Apr. 1943.
23. Ibid, Wilson to Blaine, 6 Apr. 1943 and minutes by Blaine, 16 and 22 Apr. 1943.
24. SADDA, Box 3074, DC 1472/20, chap. 1, annexure to War Measure NO. 49 of 1942, regulation 6, sent by Smuts to the South African Governor-General Sir Patrick Duncan for endorsement, 22 June 1943.
25. SADDA, Box 3065, DC 1472/1, chap. 4, question by H. C. de Wet to Smuts, 9 Feb. 1943; Box 3084, DC 1472/57, AG War Records to Blaine giving POW census figures, 8 June 1948.
26. Ibid, Box 3068, DC 1472/10/6, QMG to Authorities Committee, 4 June 1943; QMG to Blaine, 10 June 1943; Viljoen to Secretary for Finance, 7 June 1943 outlining agreement between departmental representatives for maize project, 24 May 1943; Colonel C. R. Wyche, DAG(POW) to Camp Commandants at Zonderwater, Kroonstad and Standerton, on wheat scheme, 22 Nov. 1943; KAB, 1/IWE, vol. 4/1/8, file 9/7/16, contains Special Press Service bulletins no. 268 and no. 271 by the Ministry of Agriculture and Forestry on the use of Italian POWs for harvesting wheat and weeding maize, Aug. 1943.
27. SADDA, Box 3077, DC 1472/30, chap. 1, weekly POW strength returns for period 5 Mar. 1943 to 25 Feb. 1944; CGS(War) Box 187/40/10, vol. 2, AG to Blaine, 5 Oct. 1943; Box 187/40/11, vol. 1, Honorary Secretary, Waterburg District Farmers' Union, to Smuts, 14 Apr. 1944; Box 3068, DC 1472/10/6, Secretary for Public Health to Blaine, 8 June 1943; Box 188/40/16, Progress Report no. 3, 17 May 1943.
28. Ibid, CGS(War) Box 187/40/11, vol. 1, extract from CGS conference no. 113, 2 Aug. 1944; AG(POW) Box 1, file 1B, folio 2590, number and location of co-operators, 28 Feb. 1945.
29. KAB, 1/BKW, vol. 7/3, file 9/7/16, part 1, application for Italian POWs by P. H. van Wyk, 18 Oct. 1943 and approval by Kroonstad Camp Commandant through Magistrate at Barkly West, 26 Oct. 1943; 1/MTO, vol. 8/1/7, file 9/7/16, processing of POWs for local farmers in the Molteno district, 1944; SADDA, CGS(War) Box 188/40/16, Progress Report no. 3, 17 May 1943.
30. SADDA, CGS(War) Box 188/40/11, vol. 1, Colonel Campbell Ross, Staff Officer, CGS, to Van Ryneveld, 31 Mar. 1943.
31. Ibid, Box 187/40/11, extract from CGS Staff Conference no. 45, 15 July 1942, and no. 92, 15 Sept. 1943.
32. SADDA, Box 3067, DC 1472/10/1, chap. 4, Clegg to H. Lawrence, Minister of the Interior, 11 Aug. 1942; Box 187/40/11, vol. 1, Burchell to Forsyth, 29 Aug. 1944.
33. SANA, BAO 614/400, part 1, Secretary for Native Affairs to AG, 16 Sept. 1942, refusal by Department of Native Affairs of request from Magistrate in Umtata for use of POW labour in territory; Ibid, 13 May 1943, withdrawal of Department's objection; Ibid, part 2, AG to Secretary for Native Affairs, 7 Nov. 1944; Magistrate for Matatiele to Chief Magistrate Umtata, 3 Jan. 1945.

34. SADDA, CGS(War) Box 186/40/10, vol. 2, Sturrock to van Ryneveld, 28 July 1943; SANA, SAP 101, SAP 1/124/43, Baston to Secretary for Labour, 15 Sept. 1943.
35. SANA, SAP 101, SAP 1/75/43/1, Deputy Commissioner, SAP, Grahamstown, to District Commandant, 7 Jan. 1944; AG to Baston, 17 Jan. 1944.
36. SADDA, Box 3074, DC 1472/20, chap. 2, questions in House of Assembly, 24 Mar. 1944; AG(POW), Box 55, file 23, vol. 6, Lieutenant Du Plooy, Field Security Officer, to Officer Commanding 22 Air School Vereeniging, 1 Oct. 1944.
37. WO 32/9905, Hermelin to DPW, 26 Apr. 1944. For British procedures on the hiring of Italian POWs as waiters, cooks and batmen, see WO 32/10735, minutes by Gepp, 21 and 29 Oct. 1942; AIR 2/5834, administrative instruction on the employment of Italian co-operator POWs on RAF stations in the UK, 1944. One of the first examples of employing Italian POWs as waiters and batmen occurred in the Middle East, when a Group Captain from an RAF base approached the authorities of a nearby POW camp to discuss the possibility of utilising these men for domestic service. WO 169/2549, war diary, Camp No. 310 (Suez), 8 May 1941.
38. SANA, ARB vol. 718, file 1183/15, contains correspondence from a variety of Building Trades, Chambers of Commerce and allied professions in 1944–5 which were investigated by the AG; SADDA, AG(POW), Box 1, file 1B, folio 2151, question in House of Assembly, 29 Feb. 1944.
39. SADDA, CGS(War) Box 187/40/11, vol. 1, Springbok Legion to Smuts, 7 Mar. 1944.
40. SANA, DGD 412/29, minute for Colonel P. R. Viviers, Demobilisation Department, 22 Oct. 1945; DGD 412/14, Brink to AG, 1 Aug. 1944; Brink to Mrs A. J. Theron of Fraserburg, Cape Province, 7 June 1946.
41. WO 32/9905, censorship summary for Feb. 1944 by Captain C. Wilson, Military Intelligence Liaison Officer, 15 March 1944.
42. SADDA, AG(POW) Box 1, file 1B, folio 1493, questions in House of Assembly, 18 Feb. 1944; SANA, SAP 101, SAP 1/75/43, vol. 2, Boffa case file, Mar.–Apr. 1944.
43. SADDA, CGS(War) Box 185/40/3, vol. 4, Ross to Forsyth, 12 and 18 Nov. 1943; *Natal Daily News*, 1 Nov. 1943; written testimony of events by Detective Head Constable Kuun, 27 Oct. 1943 and Major E. J. Burgess, Technical Service Corps, UDF, Kings Park, 26 Oct. 1943.
44. SADDA, SAP 101, SAP 1/75/43/1, Deputy Commissioner, SAP, Transvaal Division, to Baston, 15 Jan. 1944.
45. SADDA, Box 3077, DC 1472/29, Veronique Wilson to Blaine, 22 Mar. 1945.
46. Ibid, Supervisor, Government Baths, Warmbaths, to Blaine, 22 Feb. 1945; *Rand Daily Mail*, 'Italian POWs in Front Seats at Camp Show; UDF Men Walk Out', 26 Oct. 1945.
47. SANA, SAP 101, SAP 1/75/43/1, vol. 2, Deputy Commissioner, SAP, Kimberley Division, to Baston, 4 Aug. 1944.
48. Ibid, Prinsloo to Baston, 20 Jan. 1944; statement by D'Arcy-Searle, 26 Aug. 1943.
49. WO 222/1362, 'Annual Report of the Assistant Director of Medical Services (POW), 1/9/44–31/8/45', by Lieutenant-Colonel L. Blumberg. Also see his article, 'Italian POW in South Africa (Medical Services)', *Military History Journal*, 1, 4 (1969), 15–18.

50. WO 32/9905, POW censorship summary by Wilson, 15 Mar. 1944, p. 6; SADDA, Box 3077, DC 1472/29, Secretary for Interior to Blaine, 4 June 1943; AG(POW), Box 1, file 1B, folio 2590, questions in House of Assembly, 7 Mar. 1944; Box 3077, DC 1472/29, Wilson to Blaine, 3 Apr. 1942. In Feb. 1944 Smuts was asked in Parliament how many Italian POWs had married South African girls. The reply was two. See AG(POW), Box 1, file 1B, folio 2151, questions in House of Assembly, 29 Feb. 1944.

51. SADDA, Box 3066, DC 1472/1, chap. 5, questions in House of Assembly, 9 Mar. 1945.

52. WO 32/9905, R. R. Sedgwick, Office of UK High Commission, Pretoria, to A. W. Snelling, DO, 2 Sept. 1946; SADDA, Box 1075, DC 1472/26, chap. 2, POW capitation rates, Sept. 1946. In Dec. 1941 the rate had been set at 1s 6d, but by Oct. 1946 it had risen to 2s 2d. Blaine to Controller and Auditor General, 13 May 1947.

53. S.J. Butlin and C.B. Schedvin, *War Economy 1942–1945* (Canberra: Australian War Memorial, 1977), p. 379.

54. AA (Melbourne), MP 729/6, item 63/401/666, report of inter-departmental conference chaired by McCahon, 12 Feb. 1943 which was fed into War Cabinet Agendum no. 118/1943, 14 Mar. 1943. See AA, CRS A1308/1, item 712/1/11.

55. AA, CRS 1308/1, item 712/1/11, appendix B, Cumpston to F. R. Sinclair, Secretary, Department of the Army, 25 Jan. 1943; appendix C, Director-General of Medical Services to Adjutant-General, 17 Dec. 1942.

56. AA, CRS A989/1, item 44/925/1/52, Department of External Affairs (hereafter DEA) to Bruce, 20 May 1943; CRS A816/1, item 54/301/253, War Cabinet minute 2941, 14 May 1943.

57. Ibid, Bruce to DEA, 5 Aug. 1943.

58. National Archives of New Zealand, Wellington, EA 1, item 89/4/18, Foss Shanahan, Assistant Secretary to New Zealand War Cabinet, to NZ Minister of Supply, 28 Oct. 1943; Peter Fraser, NZ Minister of External Affairs, to Cranborne, 29 Feb. 1944; Walter Nash, NZ High Commissioner in London, to Fraser, 5 Apr. 1944; note tabled to NZ War Cabinet, 6 Apr. 1944; AA, CRS A373, item 6221, War Cabinet Agendum no. 170/1943, supplement no. 4, submitted by Forde, 1 Sept. 1944.

59. AA, CRS A816/1, item 54/301/253, War Cabinet Agendum no. 170/1943, submitted by Forde, 8 Apr. 1943; AA (Melbourne), MP 729/6, item 63/401/666, minutes by Sinclair and Harding, Apr. 1943.

60. AA, CRS A816/1, item 54/301/253, War Cabinet Agendum no. 170/1943, supplement no. 1, appendix A, proceedings of an inter-departmental conference held in Melbourne, 21 Apr. 1943.

61. Ibid, Sinclair to F. G. Shedden, Secretary, Department of Defence, 3 Sept. 1943 and Shedden's reply, 29 Sept. 1943; Cranborne to Curtin, 11 Oct. and 4 Nov. 1943; A816/1, item 54/301/253, War Cabinet Agendum no. 170/1943, supplement no. 2, 5 Nov. 1943; and attachment to notes on this Agendum, 8 Nov. 1943.

62. Ibid, War Cabinet minutes 3142, 3153 and 3283, 4 and 10 Nov. 1943 and 21 Jan. 1944; AA, CRS A373, item 6221, War Cabinet Agendum no. 170/1943, supplement no. 4, submitted by Forde, 1 Sept. 1944; AA, CRS 816/1, item 54/301/253, War Cabinet Agendum no. 170/1943, supplement no. 3, 5 Jan. 1944. Also see Barbara Winter, *Stalag Australia. German Prisoners of War in Australia* (Sydney: Angus & Robertson, 1986).

63. AA (Melbourne), MP 70/1, item 14/101/41, notes of conference on employment of Italian POWs without guards on work outside camps, 4 June 1943; Ibid, item 2/101/70, notes on conferences held at Hamilton and Colac, 30 and 31 May 1943; AWM 61, S56/2/575, secret memo by Adjutant-General's department on employment without guards by private employers, 2 June 1943; also attached is the Department of the Army's, 'Procedure for Employment of P. W. without Guards'; Ibid, S56/2/995, revised guidelines, 27 May 1944.

64. AA (Melbourne), B551/0, item 43/79/6382, *Hamilton Spectator*, 22 June 1943; O'Connor to Cameron, 24 June 1943; circular no. 361 from Cameron to all NSOs, land inspectors and War Agricultural Committees, 29 June 1943; Findlay to Cameron, 1 July 1943.

65. Ibid, I. A. Dorrington, NSO in Colac, to Cameron, 2 July 1943; Cameron to W. C. Wurth, Director-General of Manpower, 19 July 1943.

66. Butlin and Schedvin, *War Economy*, p. 379.

67. AA, CRS A373, item 6221, War Cabinet Agendum no. 170/1943, supplement no. 4, appendix A, June 1944; AA (Melbourne), MP 742/1, item 255/19/310, minute paper, Department of the Army, 21 Nov. 1944. There is some discrepancy in the figures. Fitzgerald has listed 96 POW Control Centres and 33 POW hostels established between 1943 and 1945; while in CRS A373, item 6221, a total of 144 POW Control Centres and hostels are listed together.

68. AA (Melbourne), MP 729/6, item 63/401/666, McCahon to Cumpston, 7 Oct. 1943; AA, CRS A816/1, item 54/301/253, War Cabinet minute 3548, 11 May 1944.

69. Ibid.; memo by E. J. Holloway, Minster for Labour and National Service, Aug. 1944; AA (Melbourne), B551/0, item 43/79/6382, Cameron to Wurth, 29 May 1944; Cumpston to Wurth, 6 Sept. 1944.

70. Ibid, War Cabinet Agendum no. 170/1943, supplement no. 2, 5 Nov. 1943.

71. AA, CRS A7711/1, item 1, 'History of the Directorate', p. 104.

72. Ibid.

73. AA, CRS A373, item 6221, War Cabinet Agendum no. 170/1943, supplement no. 4, appendix B, 1 Sept. 1944, copy of Bruce to DEA, 2 June 1944.

74. G. Cresciani, 'Captivity in Australia', *Studi Emigrazione*, no. 26 (1989), 203–4; AA, CRS A373, item 6221, War Cabinet Agendum no. 170/1943, supplement no. 4, 1 Sept. 1944, and appendix A, n.d.; W. B. Simpson, Director-General of Security, to Shedden, 3 July 1944.

75. AA, CRS A816/1, item 54/301/253, undated memo by Holloway; War Cabinet minute 3733, 23 Aug. 1944; War Cabinet Agendum no. 416/1944 and attached notes, 21 Aug. 1944; War Cabinet minute 3761, 6 Sept. 1944; F. Strahan, Secretary to the Cabinet, to Shedden, 2 Mar. 1945; AA, CRS A373, item 6221, War Cabinet Agendum no. 170/1943, supplement no. 4, appendix A, n.d.; Cresciani, 'Captivity in Australia', 204.

76. AA, CRS A989/1, item 43/44/925/1/111, DEA to Cranborne, 23 Oct. 1943.

77. AA, CRS A373, item 6221, statistics for the months ending 30 Apr. 1944 and 1945. The number of rejected applications was extremely low: 15 as of Apr. 1944 which had increased to only 29 one year later. Other regional breakdowns can be found in ibid, item 11638, part 2 (1943–49).

78. Kay Saunders, 'Down on the Farm', *Journal of Australian Studies*, no. 46 (1995), 24; AA, CRS A649/4, item 82/600/417, Sinclair to Watt, 9 Apr. 1944.

79. AA, CRS A649/4, item 82/600/417, financial statement and adjustments as of 30 Sept. 1945 made by Paymaster-in-Chief; H. C. Norman, Treasury, to Australian High Commission, London, 15 Mar. 1946.
80. AWM 54, item 780/3/2, notes from camp intelligence report no. 6, Murchison (21 May 1943), 15 June 1943.
81. Ibid, notes from camp intelligence report no. 7, Murchison (18 June 1943), 12 July 1943.
82. Ibid; notes from camp intelligence report no. 8, Hay (18 July 1943), 7 Aug. 1943.
83. Ibid, notes from camp intelligence report no. 9, Hay (19 Aug. 1943), 6 Sept. 1943.
84. Ibid, Cowra (15 Aug. 1943), 6 Sept. 1943.
85. Ibid, Hay (15 Aug. 1943) and Murchison (14 Aug. 1943), 6 Sept. 1943. For additional examples of the reaction to Mussolini's overthrow amongst POWs, enemy aliens and Australian nationals, see AA, CRS A373/1, item 681.
86. AWM 54, item 780/3/2, notes from camp intelligence report no. 10, Myrtleford (17 Sept. 1943), Murchison (10 Sept. 1943) and Hay (19 Sept. 1943), 6 Oct. 1943.
87. Ibid, notes from camp intelligence report no. 12, Yanco (28 Nov. 1943), 17 Dec. 1943.
88. Ibid, notes from camp intelligence report no. 16, Marrinup (27 May 1944), 6 July 1944.
89. Ibid, notes from camp intelligence report no. 19, Marrinup (31 Oct. 1944), 17 Nov. 1944.
90. Ibid, notes from camp intelligence reports nos. 9, 11 and 12, Myrtleford (19 Aug., 29 Oct. and 26 Nov. 1943), 6 Sept. , 17 Nov. and 17 Dec. 1943; Ibid, no. 16, Cowra (21 May 1944), 6 July 1944; Ibid, no. 21, Cowra (18 Feb. 1945), 6 Mar. 1945; AA, CRS A373/1, item 11181, notes from camp intelligence report no. 22, Myrtleford and Gaythorne (7 Apr. 1945), 25 Apr. 1945; AA (Sydney), SP 1714/1, item N45633, parts 5, 8 and 9, extracts from Cowra intelligence reports, Oct.–Nov. 1943 and 1944–5. For an excellent insight into how the Australians screened, processed and punished the ardent Fascists who arrived in Australia from India during 1945, see the numerous reports from the Gaythorne Camp in Queensland in AWM 54, item 780/3/2.
91. AWM 54, item 780/3/2, notes from camp intelligence report no. 11, 17 Nov. 1943, containing extract from South African intelligence summary. Also see AA (Melbourne), MP 70/1, item 37/101/185, Myrtleford part 1, South African intelligence summary no. 37, dealing with outside employment measures, 17 Apr. 1943.
92. AWM 54, item 780/3/2, notes from camp intelligence report no. 9, Myrtleford (19 Aug. 1943), 6 Sept. 1943.
93. AA (Sydney), SP 1714/1, item N45633, part 7, intelligence extract no. 107, Cowra (15–22 Oct. 1944), recording an act of indecent exposure on a nine-year-old girl; AA, CRS A472/1, item W25964, correspondence between the Premier's Department, Western Australia, and the Crown Solicitor's Office, Canberra (1944–45).
94. AA (Sydney), SP 1714/1, item N45633, part 6, intelligence extract no. 80, Cowra (2–9 Apr. 1944); part 8, intelligence extract no. 124 (18–25 Feb. 1945).

95. Ibid, SP 1714/1, item N45633, part 7, intelligence extract no. 107, Cowra (15–22 Oct. 1944).
96. Ibid, part 9, intelligence extract no. 114, Cowra (10–12 Dec. 1944).
97. Ibid, part 7, intelligence extract no. 106, Cowra (8–15 Oct. 1944); part 6, intelligence extract no. 74 (20–27 Feb. 1944). Also see Alan Fitzgerald, *The Italian Farming Soldiers*, (Melbourne: Melbourne University Press, 1981), pp. 129–34.
98. AA (Sydney), SP 1714/1, ibid, part 1, intelligence extract no. 8, Cowra (15 Nov. 1942) and no. 15, Cowra (27 Dec. 1942–3 Jan. 1943).
99. Cresciani, 'Captivity in Australia', 208–16.

9   The Long Road Home

1. Sir Harold Satow and M. J. Sée, *The Work of the Prisoners of War Department during the Second World War*, (London: Foreign Office, 1950), pp. 47–8.
2. The large number of Italian 'protected personnel' reflected the complete collapse of the Italian military forces in East Africa and capture of all the non-combatant elements as well as fighting men. Satow and Sée, *Prisoners of War Department*, pp. 50–1.
3. Satow and Sée, *Prisoners of War Department*, p. 57.
4. Ibid, pp. 57–8; WO 163/591, DPW paper no. 1 for Repatriation Committee, 'Repatriation Operation with Italy', 16 Mar. 1943. There was some considerable anger in government circles that the Italians had failed to repatriate all those eligible and had been in breach of a number of Geneva Convention Articles. Ibid, DPW, 'Notes on Recent Repatriation Operation with the Italian Government', n.d. Also see WO 201/2415 on exchange of POWs from Italy and repatriation details for Oct. 1942 to Mar. 1944.
5. Satow and Sée, *Prisoners of War Department*, pp. 58–9.
6. Ibid, p. 59.
7. WO 32/9890, IPOWC, minutes, Jan. 1945.
8. WO 32/10755, W. W. James, DPW, to A. R. Swinnerton, Principal, India Office, 1 May 1945.
9. FO 371/49859/ZM 1003 and ZM 1084, Sir Noel Charles, British Ambassador to Rome, to FO, 5 and 8 Feb. 1945.
10. The Office of the Italian Representative in London had officially taken over the protection of Italian rights in Britain on 1 Feb. 1945.
11. FO 916/1279, Ross, FO, to Lieutenant-Colonel R. Elwes, DPW, 24 Feb. 1945.
12. FO 371/49860/ZM 2241, memo from F. R. Hoyer Millar, Counsellor, FO, 30 Apr. 1945.
13. FO 916/1279, James to Ross, 13 Feb. 1945.
14. Ibid, Phillimore to Ross, 10 Mar. 1945.
15. FO 371/49860/ZM 2241, memo by Patrick Dean, Legal Adviser, FO, 20 Apr. 1945.
16. CAB 65/50, WM62(45)3, 18 May 1945.
17. WO 32/10755, Field Marshal Alexander, AFHQ, to WO, 28 May 1945; draft paper for War Cabinet, 'Repatriation of Italian Prisoners of War' by Phillimore, 1 June 1945.
18. CAB 66/67, CP(45)20, memo by R. A. Butler, Minister of Education, 'Italian Prisoners of War', 7 June 1945.

19. WO 32/10755, memo by Brigadier V. Blomfield, DPW, 9 June 1945; CAB 66/67, CP(45)20, memo by Butler, 7 June 1945.
20. WO 32/10755, ACS/B/1498, Army Council Secretariat, brief for Secretary of State, 13 June 1945.
21. CAB 65/53, CM9(45)2, 15 June 1945.
22. WO 32/10755, IPOWC, sub-committee A, 39th mtg, 13 Sept. 1944 cited in memo entitled, 'Repatriation of Italian Prisoners of War', Paper PWCA/P(45)28, 23 June 1945. This had included 40 men over sixty and 2,500 over fifty who had been interned for more than two years. AFHQ to WO, 7 and 26 Sept. 1944, Paper PWCA/P(44)33, 15 Aug. 1944.
23. FO 371/49861/ZM 3179, minute by Oliver Harvey, Assistant Under-Secretary of State, FO, 3 June 1945.
24. Ibid, ZM 3526, minutes of DPW mtg, 22 June 1945.
25. WO 32/10755, DPW mtg, on repatriation of POWs, 22 June 1945.
26. FO 371/49861/ZM 3523, Churchill to Cadogan, personal minute M654/5, 23 June 1945.
27. Ibid, minute by Hoyer Millar, 27 June 1945.
28. WO 32/10755, DPW mtg, 22 June 1945.
29. CAB 65/53, CM13(45)3, 10 July 1945; FO 898/14, confidential memo by PID, Italian Region, 30 Nov. 1945 quoting translation of *La Donna Qualunque*, 10 Nov. 1945.
30. Ibid, CM14(45)3, 12 July 1945; WO 203/3756, Labour Division records, South East Asian Command HQ, employment of Italian POW officers (Dec. 1944–May 1945); SANA, BLO PS 26/17/10, India Office to C. H. Taljaard, South African High Commission, London, 11 July 1945.
31. FO 371/49862/ZM 4394, draft memo by H. F. Rossetti, Assistant Secretary, Ministry of Labour, Aug. 1945, suggested that employers could pay the civilian rate for the work and that the prisoners then receive an agreed sum with the rest going to the exchequer. This safeguarded civil wage-rates and afforded some level of incentive for prisoners. Between Jan. and Mar. 1945 there was talk of recruiting 15,000 Italian civilians for Admiralty projects in the Far East, including 3,000 for ship repair work in India. With the contemplated repatriation (for political reasons) of the Italian POWs from India the labour shortage in Indian dockyards would be exacerbated. Oliver Harvey thought this 'almost unbelievable that 500 skilled workers cannot be found among India's teeming millions – not exactly a tribute to our rule!' In the end, the Indian authorities were allowed to recruit for 500 skilled workers in Italian shipyards with the resulting loss of capacity in Italy. FO 371/49875/ZM 1121, minute by Ross, 12 Feb. 1945; ZM 1489, A. A. F. Rumbold, Admiralty, to D. F. Howard, Counsellor, Southern Department, FO, 7 Mar. 1945, and minute by Harvey, 11 Mar. 1945; ZM 2002, CSA(45)55(O), 'Employment of Italian POWs on Ship Repairs in India', report to COS, 29 Mar. 1945.
32. WO 32/10755, interdepartmental meeting, 'Repatriation of Italian Prisoners of War now Employed on Agricultural Work', 19 July 1945.
33. FO 371/49862/ZM 4034, minute by Ross, 26 July 1945; ZM 4132, minutes by Harvey, 23 and 27 July 1945.
34. WO 32/9890, IPOWC, minutes, monthly meeting no. 48, May 1945.
35. Ibid, IPOWC reports, Jan.–Dec. 1945.

36. FO 371/49861/ZM 3730/G, Blomfield to Harvey, 3 July 1945.
37. Ibid
38. FO 371/49862/ZM 3907, report by Dr Raymond Klibansky, Head of Italian Intelligence Section, Political Intelligence Department, 9 Aug. 1945.
39. WO 32/10755, Blomfield to Major-General, the Viscount Bridgman, Deputy Adjutant-General, 4 Sept. 1945.
40. Ibid, Isaacs to Bevin, 30 Aug. 1945; note of conversation between Issacs and Baron Malfatti, Labour Attaché, Italian Embassy in London, 23 Aug. 1945.
41. FO 371/49863/ZM 4696, memo by Cadogan, 6 Sept. 1945.
42. CAB 129/2, CP(45)163, submitted to Cabinet by Bevin, 10 Sept. 1945.
43. CAB 128/1, CM33(45)2, 18 Sept. 1945.
44. WO 32/10755, conversation between Isaacs and Baron Malfatti, 23 Aug. 1945.
45. CAB 129/2, CP(45)163, submitted to Cabinet by Bevin, 10 Sept. 1945. See also FO 916/1288, PWD to British Embassy in Teheran, 3 Jan. 1945, and AFHQ to AGWAR for CCS, 3 Mar. 1945.
46. FO 371/49864/ZM 5180/G, note by Ross, 6 Oct. 1945; FO 371/49865/ZM 5531/G, memo by the Secretary of State for War to Defence Committee, DO(45)27, 31 Oct. 1945. This seems at odds with a letter sent by the PWD to the British Embassy in Teheran, 3 Jan. 1945, which claimed that 'some officers and men have been sent back for incorporation into the reconstituted Italian Armed Forces on account of their special qualification'. These repatriates may well have included captured *Carabinieri*. See FO 916/1288.
47. FO 371/49864/ZM 5180/G, note by Ross, 6 Oct. 1945.
48. WO 32/10755, IPOWC, sub-committee A, Paper PWCA/P(45)37, 'Repatriation of Italian Prisoners of War', 15 Oct. 1945. In addition, officers who were willing to co-operate but had remained non-co-operators due to lack of suitable work in India and the Middle East were also to be sent home in the early drafts. Sick prisoners and protected personnel were also to be given priority, the latter only insofar as they were not required for further administrative responsibilities.
49. FO 916/1279, A. J. Gardner, FO, to James, DPW, 15 Mar. 1945.
50. WO 32/10755, minutes of interdepartmental meeting on repatriation of POWs, 26 Oct. 1945.
51. FO 371/49865/ZM 5675, memo entitled, 'Repatriation of Italian Prisoners-of-War', 19 Oct. 1945, attached to urgent memo by DPW, 17 Nov. 1945.
52. FO 371/49864/ZM 5174, note by Hoyer Millar, 15 Oct. 1945. See also FO 371/60567/ZM 772, notes on the Foreign Labour Committee and minute by Ross, 6 Mar. 1946.
53. WO 32/10755, Isaacs to Bevin, 30 Aug. 1945.
54. CAB 129/4, CP(45)265, Bevin to Cabinet, 2 Nov. 1945; CAB 128/2, CM49(45)2, 6 Nov. 1945.
55. FO 371/49866/ZM 5998, J. N. Henderson to A. C. W. Drew, Private Secretary to Bevin, 15 Dec. 1945.
56. FO 371/49865/ZM 5619, progress report no. 9 on work among Italian POWs, 1–31 Oct. 1945.
57. FO 371/49865/ZM 5482, Carandini to Ross, 31 Oct. 1945.
58. FO 371/49863/ZM 4613, minute by Ross, 27 Aug. 1945.

59. The first two shipments were the SS *Malaya* which left for Italy on 17 Dec. with 16 officers and 2,658 men and the SS *Chittral* which left three days later with 1,050 officers and 762 men. FO 371/49866/ZM 6069, FO to Rome, 29 Dec. 1945.

60. WO 32/9890, IPOWC, minutes, July 1946.

61. LAB 8/91, memo by Miss M. F. Yates, Temporary Principal, Ministry of Labour, 16 Apr. 1946.

62. FO 371/49861/ZM 3620, Ross, FO, to J. M. Ross, Assistant Secretary, HO, 4 July 1945.

63. LAB 8/91, note by M. A. Bevan, Assistant Secretary, Industrial Relations and Trade Boards Department, Ministry of Labour, 10 Oct. 1946; memo by Yates, 21 Apr. 1947; minutes of a meeting at the Aliens Department, 28 Apr. 1947.

64. Ibid, undated report by Ministry of Labour, section 14.

65. FO 371/49866/ZM 6069, Charles to Bevin, 28 Nov. 1945. Also see WO 106/4083 on Italian impatience over repatriation issue July–Nov. 1945.

66. FO 371/60567/ZM 1016, Charles to Bevin, 15 Mar. 1946. When the *Italia Redenta* was repatriated in June 1946 it was noted by one intelligence officer at GHQ India that these men had done 'excellent' work for the British in India. IOL, L/WS/1/1616, GHQ(I), POW monthly intelligence summary, no. 56 (June 1946).

67. FO 371/49866/ZM 6192, Major-General Sir K. W. D. Strong, Director-General of PID, to Hoyer Millar, 12 Dec. 1945. This had been a fear since the early months of 1945 when the first prisoners were returned to southern Italy from North Africa. These men reportedly hated the western powers and still thought of the Germans as their brave allies. They despised Badoglio and the Italian civilians who supported the Anglo-American occupation. FO 371/49860/ZM 2939, PID report, 'Prisoners of War Returned by the Allies to Italy. A Social Problem', 22 May 1945.

68. AA, CRS CP 80/1/1, item S830/27, summary of repatriation proposal by Holloway, 29 Sept. 1945, and War Cabinet Agendum no. 472/45, 25 Oct. 1945; AA (Sydney), SP 1714/1, item N38486, morale assessment in Cowra POW Group, intelligence report no. 180, 27 Mar. 1946; FO 371/60569/ZM 3386, Norman R. Mighell, Australian High Commission, London, to Sir Eric Machtig, Permanent Under-Secretary of State, DO, 17 Sept. 1946.

69. FO 371/60569/ZM 3386, Mighell to Machtig, 17 Sept. 1946; ZM 3386, minute by John Wilson, 2 Oct. 1946.

70. FO 371/60569/ZM 2970, Alfred Barnes, Ministry of Transport, to Philip J. Noel-Baker, Minister of State, FO, 22 Aug. 1946.

71. WO 32/9890, IPOWC, monthly reports, Aug. 1946–Feb. 1947.

72. WO 32/11693, Colonel G. Tucker, HQ East Africa Command, to Sir Eric Speed, Permanent Under-Secretary of State for War, 30 May 1945.

73. FO 371/60575/ZM 2961, memo by Wilson, 23 Aug. 1946; WO 32/11693, Tucker to Speed, 30 May 1945.

74. FO 371/60575/ZM 3408, memo by Wilson, 9 Oct. 1946.

75. WO 32/9890, IPOWC, monthly reports, Dec. 1946 and Feb. 1947. The returns for the last three months of 1946 indicate that 876 officers and 8,784 other ranks were removed from the territory, but this was far short of the +20,000 reputed still to be there in October.

76. WO 32/10755, D. B. Sole, South African High Commission, London, to G. E. Boyd Shannon, DO, 3 Sept. 1945.
77. Ibid.
78. FO 371/60577/ZM 4047, P. W. H. Chapman, Staff Officer, South Eastern Region, Ministry of Home Security, HO, to Wilson, 29 Nov. 1946.
79. WO 32/9890, IPOWC, monthly report, Feb. 1947. The Australian authorities pursued with tremendous vigour their German and Italian escapees. On three ocassions the Chifley government (1945–9) had invited these men to give themselves up by the end of November 1947. Most of the 109 Italians still free in January 1947 had escaped after the war had finished. By Aug. 1948, 45 Italians were still at large despite the fact that for several years their photographs had been posted in public places throughout Australia. In Sept. 1948, 500 security officers under the supervision of the Department of Immigration launched one of the largest manhunts to date in Australian history. By June 1949, 17 Italian POWs continued to evade the authorities. The Minister for the Army in the Menzies government, Josiah Francis, was unwavering in his recommendations to cabinet that all POWs should be repatriated upon their apprehension. Harold Holt, Minister for Immigration and a future prime minister, requested leniency. The Australian cabinet decided in Holt's favour, probably because the numbers did not warrant such a rigid interpretation of the 1929 Geneva Convention. By Mar. 1953 three Italian POWs were still at large in the Commonwealth. AA (Melbourne), MP 742/1, item 255/18/730, draft Cabinet agendum by Francis, May 1950; Holt to Francis, 5 Apr. and 6 June 1950; *Sydney Sunday Telegraph*, 29 Aug. 1948; AA (Sydney), SP 1714/1, item N38319, part 8, memo by T. H. E. Heyes, 10 Mar. 1953.
80. FO 371/49862/ZM 4453, Carandini to Blomfield, 22 Aug. 1945.
81. FO 371/60568/ZM 2478, Ross to Western Department, FO, 8 July 1946. Raised as early as 15 Nov. 1945 in a letter from M. Follick MP (Loughborough) to Bevin, on girls who have had children by Italian POWs. Some would clearly marry the girls. FO advised that they were legally unable to marry. Also notes that British women who had married Italian ex-prisoners 'are having a difficult time in Italy'. FO 371/49865/ZM 5806, marginal note by unknown official, 30 Nov. 1945.
82. FO 371/49864/ZM 5304, memo by Blomfield to Hoyer Millar for Carandini, 19 Oct. 1945. Indeed, news of such liaisons reached Churchill himself when one distraught constituent wrote to him explaining that her daughter was expecting a baby, the father being an Italian POW. Churchill College Archive Centre, Chartwell Trust Papers, CHAR 7/87/A/79, fols. 30–6, Mrs A. E. Page to Churchill, 5 Oct. 1944; Mrs R. E. K. Hill, Churchill's personal private secretary, to Mrs H. M. de Groot, WO, 10 Oct. 1944 and de Groot's reply 25 Oct. 1944; Hill to Page, 26 Oct. 1944. There is a number of letters in this file dealing with Italian POWs wanting to marry English girls (1944–45). For a story about a proposal of marriage from an Italian POW, see IWM, 88/50/1, Mrs I. M. Corry mss.
83. FO 371/60570/Z 4065, British Consulate-General, Milan, to FO, 20 Nov. 1946.
84. FO 371/67784/Z 8218, Lieutenant-Colonel E. Collins, WO, to Captain F. D. W. Brown, Second Secretary, FO, 12 Sept. 1947.

85. Ibid, Z 9416, marginal note, illegible signature, 22 Oct. 1947.
86. FO 371/60569/ZM 2585, minutes by Miss E. Iredell, FO, 26 July 1946, and W. E. Beckett, Legal Adviser, 27 July 1946.
87. FO 371/60568/ZM 2478, Ross to Western Department, 8 July 1946.
88. FO 371/60567/ZM 637, Secretary, Kent County Military Welfare Organisation, to Command Welfare Officer, Eastern Command Headquarters, 12 Feb. 1946.
89. FO 371/60568/ZM 2478, Ross to Western Department, 8 July 1946.
90. Gabriele Sani, *History of the Italians in South Africa 1489–1989* (Zonderwater: Zonderwater Block South Africa, 1992), pp. 308–9; Mario Gazzini, *Zonderwater: I prigionieri in Sudafrica (1941–1947)* (Roma: Bonacci Editore, 1987), p. 332. Contained in Rhodes House Library is a proposal for a three-part documentary on 'Zonderwater: City of Prisoners' researched and directed by S. J. Moni. Nothing seems to have come of the idea.

Bibliography

Primary sources

Australian Archives (AA)
Canberra
CRS A373   Australian Security Intelligence Service, Correspondence files, single number series, 1941–49
CRS A367   Investigation Branch, Central Office, Correspondence files, 1916–1953
CRS A433   Department of the Interior, Correspondence files
CRS A472   Attorney-General's Department, Central Office, Correspondence files, War Series, 1939–1949
CRS A649   Correspondence files of the Treasury Department, Defence Division, 1941–62
CRS A816   Correspondence files of the Department of Defence 1935–39, Department of Defence Co-ordination 1939–42 and Department of Defence 1942–57, multiple number series (Class 301)
CRS A981   Correspondence files of the Department of External Affairs, series range 1925–42
CRS A989   Correspondence files of the Department of External Affairs, 1943–44
CRS A1066   Correspondence files of the Prime Minister's Department, secret and confidential war series, 1945
CRS A1067   Correspondence files of the Prime Minister's Department, secret and confidential war series, 1946
CRS A1308   Defence Division, Department of Treasury, Classified Correspondence files, multiple number series, 1941–1963
CRS A2684   Advisory War Council Minutes files
CRS A3269   Collection of Special Operations Australia, incorporating records of Far Eastern Liaison Office
CRS A5954   Records collected by Sir Frederick Shedden, Secretary, Department of Defence, 1937–71
CRS A7711   Report on the Directorate of Prisoners of War and Internees
CP 80   Records of the Department of War: Organisation of Industry. Register and Index to all 'S' Series Records

Melbourne
B 551   Department of Labour and National Service: Manpower Directorate. General Correspondence, 1942–49
MP 70   Southern Command – Victorian Lines of Communication. Security Classified Correspondence files, multiple number series, 1940–1945

MP 508	Department of the Army, AHQ: Central Registry, General Correspondence, 1939–42 System
MP 729	Army Registry: Secret Section 1937–45 (Class 401)
MP 742	Army AHQ, Secretariat Branch: Central Registry, General Correspondence, multiple number series, 1943–1951

Sydney
SP 1008/1	Army, HQ Eastern Command: Central Registry, General Correspondence, 1871–1965
SP 1714/1	Commonwealth Investigation Branch, NSW: Criminal Investigation files, 1914–1962

Australian War Memorial, Canberra
AWM 54	Written Records: War 1939–1945
AWM 61	Eastern Command Secret and other Security classified records
AWM 67	Official History, 1939–45 War: Records of Gavin Long
AWM 68	Official History, 1939–45 War: Records of Paul Hasluck
PR 84/370	Lieutenant-General Sir F. H. Berryman Papers
PR 88/178	Captain J. L. Hehir Papers
3 DRL 2529	Lieutenant-General Sir S. G. Savige Papers

Canada
National Archives of Canada, Ottawa
RG 24	Department of National Defence Records
RG 25	Department of External Affairs Records
RG 76	Department of Immigration Records

New Zealand
National Archives of New Zealand, Wellington
AD 1	Army Department, Series 1
AIR 120	Air Department, Series 120
EA 1	Department of External Affairs, Series 1
N 1	Navy Department, Series 1

South Africa
South African National Archives, Cape Town (KAB)

Magistrates Records

South African National Archives, Pretoria (CAD)
ARB	Ministry of Labour
BAO	Native Administration and Development
BLO	Ambassador, London
BNS	Ministry of the Interior
DGD	Director-General of Demobilisation
DGS	Director-General of Supplies
FIN	Ministry of Finance
FOR	Director of Forestry
LDB	Secretary of Agriculture
LDE	Ministry of Agriculture
SAP	South African Police (Commissioner)
A1	Prime Minister J. C. Smuts Papers

South African Department of Defence Archives, Pretoria
AG(POW)   Adjutant-General (Prisoners of War)
CGS(War)   Chief of the General Staff
DC   Secretary for Defence
UWH   Union War Histories

University of Natal, Killie Campbell Africana Library (Durban)
Dr E. G. Malherbe Papers

United Kingdom
British Library, India Office Library and Records, London
L/WS/1   War Staff Series Files 1921–50
L/MIL/5   Military Department Papers. Compilations and Miscellaneous
MSS Eur. F125 Lord Linlithgow Papers

National Archives of Scotland, Edinburgh
AP 54   Department of Agriculture and Fisheries for Scotland
HH 55   Police War Duties. Intelligence and Special Branch Reports

Public Record Office, Kew

Admiralty
ADM 1   Admiralty and Secretariat Papers
ADM 116   Admiralty and Secretariat Cases
ADM 199   War History Cases and Papers
ADM 223   Naval Intelligence Papers

Air Ministry
AIR 2   Air Ministry: Registered Files
AIR 8   Chief of the Air Staff
AIR 20   Unregistered Papers
AIR 22   Periodical Returns, Summaries and Bulletins
AIR 40   Directorate of Intelligence and other Intelligence Papers

Board of Trade
BT 168   Ministry of Production: Regional Boards for Industry

Cabinet Office
CAB 2   Committee of Imperial Defence: Minutes of Meetings
CAB 4   Committee of Imperial Defence: B Papers/Miscellaneous
             Memoranda
CAB 37   Cabinet Office: Photographic copies of Cabinet Papers 1880–1916
CAB 65   War Cabinet Minutes
CAB 66   War Cabinet Memoranda WP and CP Series
CAB 67   War Cabinet Memoranda WP(G) Series
CAB 78   War Cabinet Committees, Miscellaneous and General Series
CAB 79   War Cabinet, Chiefs of Staff Committee, Minutes of Meetings
CAB 81   War Cabinet, Chiefs of Staff Committees and Sub-Committees
             (Joint Intelligence Committee)
CAB 93   War Cabinet Home Defence Committee
CAB 95   War Cabinet Committees on Middle East and Africa
CAB 101   Cabinet Office: Historical Section: Official War Histories
             (Second World War), Military

CAB 102	Cabinet Office: Historical Section: Official War Histories (Second World War), Civil
CAB 103	Historical Section: Registered Files
CAB 105	War Cabinet Telegrams
CAB 106	Cabinet Office: Historical Section: Archivist and Librarian Files
CAB 114	Home Defence (Security) Executive: Secretary's Files
CAB 118	Various Ministers: Files
CAB 119	Joint Planning Staff: Files
CAB 120	Minister of Defence: Secretariat Files
CAB 122	British Joint Staff Mission: Washington Office Files
CAB 123	Lord President of the Council: Secretariat Files
CAB 127	Private Collections: Ministers and Officials
CAB 128	Cabinet: Minutes (CM and CC Series)
CAB 129	Cabinet: Memoranda (CP and S Series)
CAB 176	Joint Intelligence Committee: Secretariat Files, 1942–7

Colonial Office

CO 323	Colonies, General: Original Correspondence
CO 533	Kenya Original Correspondence
CO 537	Colonies, General: Supplementary Original Correspondence
CO 822	East Africa Original Correspondence
CO 967	Private Office Papers
CO 968	Defence: Original Correspondence
CO 980	Prisoners of War and Civilian Internees Department

Ministry of Defence

DEFE 1	Postal and Telegraph Censorship Department
DEFE 2	Combined Operations Headquarters Records

Dominions Office

DO 35	Dominions Office and Commonwealth Relations Office: Original Correspondence
DO 119	Governor of Cape Colony and High Commissioner for South Africa and Territories Archives: Correspondence
DO 121	Private Office Papers

Foreign Office

FO 371	Foreign Office: General Correspondence: Political
FO 898	Political Warfare Executive
FO 916	War of 1939 to 1945: Consular (War) Department: Prisoners of War and Internees
FO 939	Control Office: Prisoners of War
FO 954	Lord Avon Papers
FO 1011	Sir Percy Loraine Papers

Home Office

HO 45	Home Office Registered Papers
HO 213	Home Office: Aliens Department: General (GEN) files and Aliens' Naturalization and Nationality (ALN and NTY Symbol Series) files
HO 215	Internment: General files

Special Operations Executive
HS 3   SOE: Middle East and Africa files
HS 6   SOE: Western Europe files
HS 7   SOE: War Diaries and Headquarters files

Government Code and Cypher School
HW 14   Directorate Policy Papers

Ministry of Information
INF 1   Ministry of Information: Files of Correspondence

Ministry of Labour
LAB 8   Employment
LAB 76   Official Histories: Correspondence and Papers

Ministry of Agriculture and Fisheries
MAF 47   Labour and Wages: Correspondence and Papers
MAF 186   Registered Files: Manpower (MPB Series)

Metropolitan Police
MEPO 2   Metropolitan Police: Office of the Commissioner:
              Correspondence and Papers

Ministry of War Transport
MT 9   Marine: Correspondence and Papers

Prime Minster's Office
PREM 3   Operations Papers
PREM 4   Confidential Papers

War Office
WO 32   Registered Files: General Series
WO 106   Directorate of Military Operations and Intelligence
WO 141   Registered Papers: Special Series
WO 163   War Office Council and Army Council Records
WO 165   War of 1939 to 1945, War Diaries, War Office Directories
WO 169   War of 1939 to 1945, War Diaries, Middle East Forces
WO 177   War of 1939 to 1945, War Diaries, Medical Services
WO 193   Directorate of Military Operations: Collation Files
WO 199   War of 1939 to 1945, Military Headquarters Papers: Home
              Forces
WO 201   War of 1939 to 1945, Military Headquarters Papers: Middle East
              Forces
WO 203   War of 1939 to 1945, Military Headquarters Papers: Far East Forces
WO 208   Directorate of Military Intelligence
WO 214   Field Marshal Alexander Papers
WO 216   Chief of the (Imperial) General Staff Papers
WO 222   War of 1939 to 1945: Medical Historian Papers
WO 224   War of 1939 to 1945: Enemy Prisoners of War Camps: Reports of
              International Red Cross and Protecting Powers
WO 307   War of 1939 to 1945: Prisoners of War Information Bureau
WO 366   War Office: Department of the Permanent Under-Secretary of
              State: C3 Branch: Branch Memoranda on Historical Monographs

Public Record Office of Northern Ireland, Belfast
CAB 4   Cabinet conclusions

Churchill College Archives, Cambridge
DUFC   Duff Cooper Papers (1st Lord Norwich)
CHAR   Chartwell Trust Papers (W. S. Churchill)

Imperial War Museum, London
IWM 69/58A   General Sir William Platt Papers
IWM 78/38/1   Gunner F. C. Hawkridge, Royal Artillery
IWM 83/21/1   Major-General T. H. Birkbeck, 26th East African Brigade
IWM 84/36/1   Colonel J. H. S. Martin Papers
IWM 86/11/1   MSS by Lieutenant-Commander J. B. Lamb: 'Sidi Barrani to
              Derna, by Courtesy of Mussolini'
IWM 87/21/1   MSS by Mrs E. G. Yerbury
IWM 87/31/1   Diary of Lieutenant-Colonel K. Shirley-Smith, RAMC
IWM 88/1/1   MSS by Mrs E. H. Hughes; Mrs E. R. Hazell
IWM 88/43/1   MSS by Mrs M Waterhouse
IWM 88/50/1   MSS by Mrs I. M. Corry
IWM 88/59/1   Colonel H. S. Sell Papers
IWM 91/31/1   A. H. Hollick Papers
IWM 12861/2   Edie Ford (Sound Archive)
IWM Misc 952 MSS by Major-General James G. Elliott: 'An Account of the
              Battle of Keren, Eritrea, in March 1941'
IWM P469   Diary of Gunner J. W. Kelly, 51st Heavy Anti-Aircraft regiment

Liddell Hart Centre for Military Archives, King's College, London

Lieutenant-General Sir Ronald F. Adam Papers
Major-General F. H. N. Davidson Papers
Lieutenant-General Sir Richard O'Connor Papers
Air Chief Marshal Sir Robert Brooke-Popham Papers

Tom Harrisson, Mass Observation Archive, University of Sussex, Brighton

Rhodes House Library, Oxford

Air Chief Marshal Sir Robert Brooke-Popham Papers, MSS Afr. s 1120
Zonderwater: City of Prisoners. Proposal for a three-part documentary film series
researched and directed by S. J. Moni

John Rylands University Library of Manchester

General Sir Claude J. E. Auchinleck Papers

Diaries, memoirs and contemporary sources

Amery, L. S. *My Political Life*, vol. 2 (London: Hutchinson, 1953).
Badoglio, Pietro. *Italy in the Second World War. Memories and Documents* (Westport,
    CT: Greenwood Press, 1976 reprint) translated by Muriel Currey.
Barnes, John and David Nicholson (eds). *The Leo Amery Diaries*, 2 vols (London:
    Hutchinson, 1980 and 1988).
Bruce Lockhart, R. H. *Comes the Reckoning* (London: Putnam, 1947).

Butcher, Harry C. *Three Years with Eisenhower: The Personal Diary of Captain Harry C. Butcher* (London: W. Heinemann, 1946).

Churchill, Winston. *The Second World War*, vol. 2, *Their Finest Hour* (London: Cassell, 1971).

Dalton, Hugh. *The Fateful Years* (London: Muller, 1957).

Dulani, Mario. *The City Without Women*. Trans by Antonio Mazza (Oakville ON: Mosaic Books, 1994).

Gibson, Hugh (ed.). *The Ciano Diaries 1939–1943* (New York: Howard Fertig, 1973).

Hahn, Major J. E. *The Intelligence Service within the Canadian Corps 1914–1918* (Toronto: Macmillan Company of Canada, 1930).

International Committee of the Red Cross. *Report of the International Committee of the Red Cross on its activities during the Second World War (September 1, 1939– June 30, 1947)*, vol. 1, *General Activities* (Geneva, 1948).

Liddell Hart, B. H. (ed.). *The Rommel Papers* (London: Collins, 1953).

Mackenzie, W. J. M. *The Secret History of the SOE: The Special Operations Executive 1940–1945* (London: St Ermin's Press, 2000).

Ministero della Cultura Popolare. *Gli Italiani nei Campi di Concentrato in Francia: Documenti e Testimonianze A cura del Ministero della Cultura Popolare* (Roma: Società Editrice del Libero Italiano, 1940).

Ministry of Information. *Destruction of an Army: The First Campaign in Libya: September 1940–February 1941* (London: Ministry of Information, 1941).

Official History of New Zealand in the Second World War 1939–45: Documents, vols 1–2 (Wellington: War History Branch, Department of Internal Affairs, 1949–51).

Pimlott, Ben (ed.). *The Second World War Diary of Hugh Dalton 1940–45* (London: Jonathan Cape, 1986).

Satow, Sir Harold and M. J. Sée. *The Work of the Prisoners of War Department during the Second World War* (London: Foreign Office, 1950).

Scotland, A. P. *The London Cage* (London: Evans, 1957).

Swinton, Viscount. *I Remember* (London: Hutchinson, 1948).

Secondary sources

Books

Absalom, Roger. *A Strange Alliance. Aspects of Escape and Survival in Italy 1943–45* (Firenze: Leo S. Olschki Editoire, 1991).

Agarossi, Elena. *A Nation Collapses. The Italian Surrender of September 1943* (Cambridge: Cambridge University Press, 2000), translated by Harvey Fergusson II.

Andrew, Christopher. *Her Majesty's Secret Service* (New York: Viking, 1986).

Balfour, Michael. *Propaganda in War 1939–1945: Organisation, Policies and Publics in Britain and Germany* (London: Routledge & Kegan Paul, 1979).

Ball, Desmond and David Horner. *Breaking the Codes. Australia's KGB network, 1944–1950* (Sydney: Allen & Unwin, 1998).

Barker, A. J. *Eritrea 1941* (London: Faber & Faber, 1966).

——. *Behind Barbed Wire* (London: Purnell, 1974).

Barnett, Corelli. *The Desert Generals* (London: William Kimber, 1960).

Bassler, Gerhard P. *Sanctuary Denied. Refugees from the Third Reich and Newfoundland Immigration Policy* (St. John's, NFLD: Memorial University, 1992).

Benuzzi, Felice. *Fuga sul Kenia* (Milano: L'Eroica, 1947).

——. *No Picnic on Mount Kenya*, 3rd edn (Wellingborough, Northants: Patrick Stephens, 1989).

Berretta, Alfio. *Prigionieri di Churchill* (Milano: Edizioni Europee, 1951).

Bevege, Margaret. *Behind Barbed Wire. Internment in Australia during World War II* (St. Lucia, QLD: University of Queensland Press, 1993).

Biason, Renzo, Mario Tobino and Mario Rigoni Stern. *The Lost Legions* (London: MacGibbon & Kee, 1967).

Boog, Horst (ed.). *The Conduct of the Air War in the Second World War* (Oxford: Berg, 1992).

Bosworth, Richard and Romano Ugolini (eds). *War, Internment and Mass Migration: The Italo-Australian Experience 1940–1990* (Roma: Gruppo Editoriale Internazionale, 1992).

Brelsford, W. V. (ed.). *The Story of the Northern Rhodesia Regiment* (Lusaka: Government Printer, 1954).

Brode, Patrick. *Casual Slaughters and Accidental Judgements. Canadian War Crimes Prosecutions, 1944–1948* (Toronto: University of Toronto Press, 1997).

Brown, Donald. *Somerset v Hitler. Secret Operations in the Mendips 1939–1945* (Newbury, Berks: Countryside Books, 1999).

Bunbury, Bill. *Rabbits and Spaghetti. Captives and Comrades: Australians, Italians and the War* (Freemantle, WA: Freemantle Arts Centre Press, 1995).

Butler, J. R. M. *Grand Strategy*, vol. 2 (London: HMSO, 1957).

Butlin, S. J. and C. B. Schedvin, *War Economy 1942–1945* (Canberra: Australian War Memorial, 1977).

Casey, William. *The Secret War Against Hitler* (London: Simon & Schuster, 1989).

Cesarani, David and Tony Kushner (eds). *The Internment of Aliens in Twentieth Century Britain* (London: Frank Cass, 1993).

Clayton, Anthony. *Forearmed. A History of the Intelligence Corps* (London: Brassey's, 1993).

Connell, John. *Auchinleck. A Critical Biography* (London: Cassell, 1959).

Conti, Flavio Giovanni. *I prigionieri di guerra italiani 1940–1945* (Bologna: Il Mulino, 1986).

Cresciani, Gianfranco. *Fascism, Anti-Fascism and Italians in Australia 1922–1945* (Canberra, ANU Press, 1980).

Cruickshank, Charles. *The Fourth Arm: Psychological Warfare 1938–45* (London: Davis-Poynter, 1977).

——. *The German Occupation of the Channel Islands: The Official History of the Occupation Years*, 7th edn (Channel Islands: Oxford University Press, 1988).

Curry, John. *The Security Service 1908–1945. The Official History* (London: HMSO, 1999).

Dear, Ian. *Escape and Evasion. Prisoner of War Breakouts and the Routes to Safety in World War II* (London: Cassell, 1997).

De Guigand, Major General Sir Francis. *Operation Victory* (London: Hodder & Stoughton, 1947).

De Jong, Louis. *Het Koninkrijk der Nederlanden in de tweede Wereldoorlog*, vol. 3 (The Hague: Staatsuitgeverij, 1970).

Del Guercio, Alfonso. *Campo 25* (Roma: L'Arnia, 1951).

Della Santa, Nicola (ed.). *I militari italiani internati dai tedeschi dopo 1'8 settembre 1943* (Firenze: Giunti, 1986).

Dennis, Peter, Jeffrey Grey, Ewan Morris and Robin Prior (eds). *The Oxford Companion to Australian Military History* (Melbourne: Oxford University Press, 1995).

De Norman, Roderic. *For Führer and Fatherland: SS Murder and Mayhem in Wartime Britain* (Stroud: Sutton, 1996).

Durand, André. *From Sarajevo to Hiroshima: History of the International Committee of the Red Cross* (Geneva: Henri Dunant Institute, 1984).

Ellwood, David W. *Italy 1943–1945* (Leicester: Leicester University Press, 1985).

Faulk, Henry. *Group Captives. The Re-education of German Prisoners of War* (London: Chatto & Windus, 1977).

Ferretti, Camillo Milesi. *Ventimila rupi di taglia* (Roma: Danesi, 1948).

Finney, Patrick (ed.). *The Origins of the Second World War* (London: Arnold, 1997).

Fitzgerald, Alan. *The Italian Farming Soldiers. Prisoners of War in Australia 1941–47* (Melbourne: Melbourne University Press, 1981).

Fitzgibbon, C. *Denazification* (London: Michael Joseph, 1969).

Foot, M. R. D. and J. M. Langley. *MI9. Escape and Evasion 1939–1945* (London: Bodley Head, 1979).

Furlong, Patrick J. *Between Crown and Swastika. The Impact of the Radical Right on the Afrikaner Nationalist Movement in the Fascist Era* (Hanover, NH: Wesleyan University Press, 1991).

Gabrielli, Donatello. *I prigionieri di Saida* (Pisa: Industrie Grafische V. Lischi, 1947).

Gallo, P. Enrico. *Ricordi di Guerra e Prigionia* (Marino di Napoli: Società dei Missionari D'Africa, 1955).

Garrett, Richard. *P.O.W.* (Newton Abbot: David & Charles, 1981).

Gazzini, Mario. *Zonderwater: I prigionieri in Sudafrica (1941–1947)* (Roma: Bonacci Editore, 1987).

Gillman, Peter and Leni Gillman. *Collar the Lot! How Britain Interned and Expelled its Wartime Refugees* (London: Quartet Books, 1980).

Gilmore, Allison B. *You Can't Fight Tanks with Bayonets. Psychological Warfare against the Japanese Army in the Southwest Pacific* (Lincoln, NE: University of Nebraska Press, 1998).

Girvin, Brian and Geoffrey Roberts (eds). *Ireland and the Second World War. Politics, Society and Remembrance* (Dublin: Four Courts Press, 2000).

Glover, Michael. *An Improvised War: The Ethiopian Campaign 1940–1941* (London: Leo Cooper, 1987).

Gooch, John (ed.). *Decisive Campaigns of the Second World War* (London: Frank Cass, 1990).

Graham, Malcolm. *Oxfordshire at War* (London: Hutchinson, 1948).

Harper, Glyn. *Kippenberger. An Inspired New Zealand Commander* (Auckland: Harper Collins, 1997).

Harris, C. R. S. *Allied Military Administration of Italy, 1943–1945* (London: HMSO, 1957).

Harrison, Mark (ed.). *The Economics of World War II* (Cambridge: Cambridge University Press, 1998).

Hartley, Jenny (ed.). *Hearts Undefeated. Women's Writing of the Second World War* (London: Virago, 1996).

Hearnden, A. *The British in Germany: Educational Reconstruction after 1945* (London: Hamish Hamilton, 1984).

Herman, Michael. *Intelligence Power in Peace and War* (Cambridge: Cambridge University Press, 1996).

Hewison, W. S. *This Great Harbour – Scapa Flow* (Kirkwall: The Orkney Press, 1990).

Hinsley, F. H. *British Intelligence in the Second World War*, vols 1–2 (London: HMSO, 1979–81).

Hinsley, F. H. and C. A. G. Simkins, *British Intelligence in the Second World War*, vol. 4 (London: HMSO, 1990).

Hoare, Oliver (ed.). *Camp 020: MI5 and the Nazi Spies. The Official History of MI5's Wartime Interrogation Centre* (London: PRO, 2000).

Iacovetta, Franca, Roberto Perin and Angelo Principe (eds). *Enemies Within: Italian and Other Internees in Canada and Abroad* (Toronto: University of Toronto Press, 2000).

Jackson, Robert. *A Taste of Freedom* (London: Arthur Barker, 1964).

Johnston, Mark. *Fighting the Enemy. Australian Soldiers and their Adversaries in World War II* (Cambridge: Cambridge University Press, 2000).

Jones, R. V. *Most Secret War* (London: Hamish Hamilton, 1978).

Keefer, Louis E. *Italian Prisoners of War in America 1942–1946: Captives or Allies?* (New York: Praeger, 1992).

Kelley, Ninette and Michael Trebilcock. *The Making of the Mosaic. A History of Canadian Immigration Policy* (Toronto: University of Toronto Press, 1998).

Kemp, Paul. *U-Boats Destroyed. German Submarine Losses in the World Wars* (London: Arms and Armour, 1997).

Killingray, David and Richard Rathbone (eds). *Africa and the Second World War* (London: Macmillan, 1986).

Knox, MacGregor. *Mussolini Unleashed 1939–1941* (Cambridge: Cambridge University Press, 1986).

———. *Hitler's Italian Allies. Royal Armed Forces, Fascist Regime, and the War of 1940–1943* (Cambridge: Cambridge University Press, 2000).

Kogan, Norman. *Italy and the Allies* (Cambridge, MA: Harvard University Press, 1956).

Krammer, Arnold. *Nazi Prisoners of War in America* (New York: Stein & Day, 1979).

Larebo, Haile M. *The Building of an Empire. Italian Land Policy and Practice in Ethiopia 1935–1941* (Oxford: Clarendon Press, 1994).

Laurie, Clayton D. *The Propaganda Warriors: America's Crusade Against Nazi Germany* (Lawrence, KS: University of Kansas Press, 1996).

Lewis, George C. and John Mewha. *History of Prisoner of War Utilization by the United States Army 1776–1945* (Washington: Government Printer, 1955).

Long, Gavin. *To Benghazi* (Canberra: Australian War Memorial, 1952).

MacDonald, J. *Churchill's Prisoners. The Italians in Orkney 1942–1944* (Kirkwall: The Orkney Press, 1987).

MacDougall, Ian. *Voices from War* (Edinburgh: Mercat Press, 1995).

Maier, Klaus A., Horst Rohde, Bernd Stegemann and Hans Umbreit (eds). *Germany and the Second World War*, vol. 2 (Oxford: Clarendon Press, 1991).

Mallett, Robert. *The Italian Navy and Fascist Expansionism 1935–1940* (London: Frank Cass, 1998).

Margolian, Howard. *Conduct Unbecoming. The Story of the Murder of Canadian Prisoners of War in Normandy* (Toronto: University of Toronto Press, 1998).

Mars, Alistair. *British Submarines at War 1939–1945* (London: William Kimber, 1971).

Martin, H. J. and Neil Orpen. *South African Forces. World War II*, vol. 7, *South Africa at War* (Cape Town: Purnell, 1979).

Maughan, Barton. *Australia in the War of 1939–1945*, series 1, *Army*, vol. 3, *Tobruk and El Alamein*, 2nd edn (Canberra: Australian War Memorial, 1987).

Middlebrook, Martin. *Convoy* (New York: Quill/William Morrow, 1976).

Mieville, Roberto. *Fascists' Criminal Camp* (Roma: Edizioni Corso, 1947).

Miller, J. E. *The United States and Italy 1940–1950* (Chapel Hill, NC: Duke University Press, 1986).

Millett, Alan R. and Williamson Murray (eds). *Military Effectiveness*, vol. 3, *The Second World War* (Boston: Allen & Unwin, 1988)

Moore, Bob and Kent Fedorowich (eds). *Prisoners of War and their Captors during World War II* (Oxford: Berg, 1996).

Orpen, Neil. *South African Forces. World War II*, vol. 1, *East African and Abyssinian Campaigns* (Cape Town: Purnell, 1969).

——. *South African Forces. World War II*, vol. 3, *War in the Desert* (Cape Town: Purnell, 1972).

Parker, H. M. D. *Manpower: A Study of War-time Policy and Administration* (London: HMSO, 1957).

Pignatelli, Luigi. *Il Secondo Regno: I prigionieri italiani nell'ultimo conflitto* (Milano: Longanesi, 1969).

Pio, Cappuccino. *Convento e galera* (Siena: La Poligrafia, 1949).

Playfair, Major-General I. S. O. *History of the Second World War. The Mediterranean and Middle East*, vol. 1, *The Early Successes against Italy*; vol. 2, 'The Germans Come to the Help of their Ally (1941)' (London: HMSO, 1954–56).

Prasad, B. (ed.). *Official History of the Indian Armed Forces in the Second World War 1939–45. East African Campaign 1940–41* (Agra: Orient Longmans, 1963).

Rainero, Romain H. (ed.). *I prigionieri militari italiani durante la seconda guerra mondiale: aspetti e problemi storici* (Milano: Marzorati editore, 1984).

Rainero, Romain H. and Renato Sicurezza (eds). *L'italia nella 2ᵃ guerra mondiale: aspetti e problemi (1944–1994)* (Milano: Marzorati editore, 1996).

Reid, Pat and Maurice Michael. *Prisoner of War: The Inside Story of the POW from the Ancient World to Colditz and After* (London: Hamlyn, 1984).

Rennell, Lord. *British Military Administration of Occupied Territories in Africa, 1941–1947* (London: HMSO, 1948).

Robertson, K. G. *War, Resistance and Intelligence. Essays in Honour of M. R. D. Foot* (Barnsley: Leo Cooper, 1999).

Robertson, Seona and Les Wilson. *Scotland's War* (Edinburgh: Mainstream Publishing, 1995).

Robin, Ron. *The Barbed-Wire College: Reeducating German POWs in the United States during World War II* (Princeton: Princeton University Press, 1995).

Roskill, Stephen. *Churchill and the Admirals* (London: Collins, 1977).

Sadkovich, James J. *The Italian Navy in World War II* (Westport, CT: Greenwood Press, 1994).

Sani, Gabriele. *History of the Italians in South Africa 1489–1989* (Zonderwater: Zonderwater Block South Africa, 1992).

Saunders, Kay. *War on the Homefront. State Intervention in Queensland 1938–1948* (St. Lucia, Queensland: University of Queensland Press, 1993).

Shephard, Ben. *A War of Nerves. Soldiers and Psychiatrists 1914–1994* (London: Jonathan Cape, 2000).

Sherriff, David. *Bare Feet and Bandoliers* (London: The Radcliffe Press, 1995).

Smith, Jr, Arthur L. *The War for the German Mind: Re-educating Hitler's Soldiers* (Oxford: Berg, 1996).

Sullivan, M. B. *Thresholds of Peace: Four Hundred Thousand German Prisoners and the People of Britain 1944–48* (London: Hamish Hamilton, 1979).

Toscano, Mario. *Designs in Diplomacy. Pages from European Diplomatic History in the Twentieth Century* (Baltimore, MD: The John Hopkins Press, 1970).

Toschi, Elios. *In fuga oltre l'Himalaja* (Milano: Edizioni Europee, 1954).

Towle, Philip, Margaret Kosuge and Yoichi Kibata (eds). *Japanese Prisoners of War* (London: Hambledon, 2000).

Tyrer, Nicola. *They Fought in the Fields: The Women's Land Army. The Story of the Forgotten Victory* (London: Mandarin, 1996).

Visser, George Cloete. *OB. Traitors or Patriots?* (Johannesburg: Macmillan, 1976).

Waddington, Professor C. H. *O.R. in World War II. Operational Research against the U-Boat* (London: Paul Elek, 1973).

White, Louise. *The Comforts of Home. Prostitution in Colonial Nairobi* (Chicago: University of Chicago Press, 1990).

Whiting, Charles. *The March on London* (London: Leo Cooper, 1992).

Wilkinson, Peter and Joan Bright Astley. *Gubbins and SOE*, reprint (London: Leo Cooper, 1997).

Williams, Donald Mace. *Interlude in Umbarger: Italian POWs and a Texas Church* (Lubbock: Texas Tech University Press, 1992).

Williamson, Jr, Samuel R. and Peter Pastor (eds). *Essays on World War I: Origins and Prisoners of War* (New York: Columbia University Press, 1983).

Winter, Barbara. *Stalag Australia. German Prisoners of War in Australia* (Sydney: Angus & Robertson, 1986).

Wolff, H. *Die deutschen Kriegsgefangenen in Britischer Hand: Ein Überblick* (Munich: Gieseking Verlag, 1974).

Wynne, Mason W. *Prisoners-of-War. Official History of New Zealand in the Second World War 1939–45* (Wellington: War History Branch, Department of Internal Affairs, 1954).

Articles

Absalom, Roger. 'Hiding History: The Allies, the Resistance and the Others in Occupied Italy 1943–1945', *Historical Journal*, 38, 1 (1995), 111–31.

Anonymous author. 'I prigioneri Italiani nel mondo', *Revista Militare* (1987), 114–23.

Armstrong, Richard N. 'Hunting Tongues', *Journal of Soviet Military Studies*, 2, 4 (1989), 579–95.

Ball, J. A. 'Italian Prisoners of War in South Africa 1941–1947', *Military History Journal*, 1, 1 (1967), 21–3.

Blumberg, Lt. Col. L. 'Italian P.O.W. in South Africa (Medical Services)', *Military History Journal*, 1, 4 (1969), 15–18.

Boswell, Laird. 'Franco-Alsatian Conflict and the Crisis of National Sentiment during the Phoney War', *Journal of Modern History*, 71, 3 (1999), 552–84.

Brongers, E. H. 'De Meidagen van 1940: De afvoer van Duitse krijgsgevangenen naar Engeland', *Terugblik '40–'45*, 36, 12 (1998), 342–8.

Campbell, John P. 'Facing the German Airborne Threat to the United Kingdom, 1939–42', *War in History*, 4, 4 (1997), 411–33.

Cresciani, Gianfranco. 'Captivity in Australia: The Case of the Italian Prisoners of War, 1940–47', *Studi Emigrazione*, 26 (1989), 195–220.

Davis, Gerald H. 'Prisoners of War in Twentieth Century Economies', *Journal of Contemporary History*, 12, 4 (1977), 623–34.

Dubois, Colette. 'Internés et prisonniers de guerre Italiens dans les camps de l'empire français de 1940 à 1945', *Guerres mondiales et conflits contemporains*, 39 (1989), 56–65.

Fedorowich, Kent. 'Axis Prisoners of War as Sources for British Military Intelligence, 1939–42', *Intelligence and National Security*, 14, 2 (1999), 156–78.

Fedorowich, Kent and Bob Moore. 'Co-Belligerency and Prisoners of War: Britain and Italy, 1943–45', *International History Review*, 18, 1 (1996), 28–47.

Felici, Carlo. 'I prigionieri nella seconda guerra mondiale', *Revista Militare*, 1 (1988), 132–8.

Fickle, James E. and Donald W. Ellis. 'POWs in the Piney Woods: German Prisoners of War in the Southern Lumber Industry, 1943–45', *Journal of Southern History*, 66, 4 (1990), 695–725.

Furlong, Patrick J. 'Fascism, the Third Reich and Afrikaner Nationalism: An Assessment of the Historiography', *South African Historical Journal*, 27 (1992), 113–26.

Gat, Moshe. 'The Soviet Factor in British Policy Towards Italy, 1943–45', *The Historian*, 50, 4 (1988), 535–57.

Gladman, Brad W. 'Air Power and Intelligence in the Western Desert Campaign, 1940–43', *Intelligence and National Security*, 13, 4 (1998), 144–62.

Grundlingh, Albert. 'The King's Afrikaners? Enlistment and Ethnic Identity in the Union of South Africa's Defence Force During the Second World War, 1939–45', *Journal of African History*, 40, 3 (1999), 351–65.

Grundlingh, Louis. 'Prejudices, Promises and Poverty: The Experiences of Discharged and Demobilised Black South African Soldiers after the Second World War', *South African Historical Journal*, 26 (1992), 116–35.

Hagemann, Albrecht. 'Very Special Relations: The "Third Reich" and the Union of South Africa, 1933–39', *South African Historical Journal*, 27 (1992), 127–47.

Hellen, J. Anthony. 'Temporary Settlements and Transient Populations. The Legacy of Britain's Prisoner of War Camps: 1940–1948', *Erdkunde*, Band 53 (1999), 191–219.

Jones, Kevin. 'From the Horse's Mouth: Luftwaffe POWs as Sources for Air Ministry Intelligence During the Battle of Britain', *Intelligence and National Security*, 15, 4 (2000), 60–80.

Jürgensen, Kurt. 'British Occupation Policy after 1945 and the Problem of "Re-educating Germany"', *History*, 68 (1983), 225–44.

Keefer, Louis E. 'From Captive to Ally: Italian Prisoners of War in Virginia, 1943–1945', *Virginia Cavalcade* (Spring 1990).

Kelly, J. J. 'Intelligence and Counter-Intelligence in German Prisoner of War Camps in Canada During World War II', *Dalhousie Review*, 58, 2 (1978), 285–94.

Krammer, Arnold. 'American Treatment of German Generals During World War II', *Journal of Military History*, 54, 1 (1990), 27–46.

Laurie, Clayton D. 'The "Sauerkrauts": German Prisoners of War as OSS Agents, 1944–45', *Prologue*, 26 (1994), 49–60.

Linsenmeyer, William S. 'Italian Peace Feelers before the Fall of Mussolini', *Journal of Contemporary History*, 16, 4 (1981), 649–62.

Lloyd, Lorna. '"A Family Quarrel". The Development of the Dispute over Indians in South Africa', *Historical Journal*, 34, 3 (1991), 703–25.

MacKenzie, S. P. 'Essay and Reflection: On the *Other Losses* Debate', *International History Review*, 14, 4 (1992), 717–31.

——. 'The Treatment of Prisoners of War in World War II', *Journal of Modern History*, 66, 3 (1994), 487–520.

——. 'The Shackling Crisis: A Case Study in the Dynamics of Prisoner-of-War Diplomacy in the Second World War', *International History Review*, 17, 1 (1995), 78–98.

Marx, Christoph. '"Dear Listeners in South Africa": German Propaganda Broadcasts to South Africa, 1940–1941', *South African Historical Journal*, no. 27 (1992), 148–72.

——. 'The Ossewabrandwag as a Mass Movement, 1939–41', *Journal of Southern African Studies*, 20, 2 (1994), 195–219.

Miller, Dawn M. '"Raising the Tribes": British Policy in Italian East Africa, 1938–41', *Journal of Strategic Studies*, 22, 1 (1999), 96–123.

Moore, Bob. 'Turning Liabilities into Assets: British Government Policy towards German and Italian Prisoners of War during the Second World War', *Journal of Contemporary History*, 32, 1 (1997), 117–36.

——. 'The Last Phase of the Gentleman's War: British Handling of German Prisoners of War on Board HMT Pasteur, March 1942', *War and Society*, 17, 1 (1999), 41–55.

——. 'Unruly Allies: British Problems with the French Treatment of Axis Prisoners of War, 1943–1945', *War in History*, 7, 2 (2000), 180–98.

Petracarro, Domenico. 'The Italian Army in Africa 1940–43: An Attempt at Historical Perspective', *War and Society*, 9, 2 (1991), 103–27.

Rochat, Giorgio. 'I prigioneri di guerra, un problema rimosso', *Italia Contemporanea*, 171 (1988), 7–14.

Sadkovich, James J. 'Understanding Defeat: Reappraising Italy's Role in World War II', *Journal of Contemporary History*, 24, 1 (1989), 27–61.

——. 'Of Myths and Men: Rommel and the Italians in North Africa, 1940–1942', *International History Review*, 13, 2 (1991), 284–313.

Saunders, Kay. 'Down on the Farm: Italian POWs in Australia 1941–47', *Journal of Australian Studies*, no. 46 (1995), 20–33.

Schellack, Werner. 'The Afrikaners' Nazi Links Revisited', *South African Historical Journal*, no. 27 (1992), 173–85.

Stafford, David. 'The Detonator Concept: British Strategy, SOE and European Resistance after the Fall of France', *Journal of Contemporary History*, 10, 2 (1975), 185–218.

Weingartner, James J. 'Massacre at Biscari: Patton and an American War Crime', *The Historian*, 52, 1 (1989), 24–39.

White, Louise. 'Prostitution, Identity, and Class Consciousness in Nairobi during World War II', *Signs*, 11 (1986), 255–73.

Book chapters

Barton, Brian. 'Northern Ireland: The Impact of War, 1939–45', in Brian Girvin and Geoffrey Roberts (eds), *Ireland and the Second World War. Politics, Society and Remembrance* (Dublin: Four Courts Press, 2000), 47–75.

Bosworth, Michal. 'Fremantle interned: the Italian experience', in Richard Bosworth and Romano Ugolini (eds), *War, Internment and Mass Migration: The Italo-Australian Experience 1940–1990* (Roma: Gruppo Editoriale Internazionale, 1992), 75–88.

Ceva, Lucio. 'The North African Campaign 1940–43: A Reconsideration', in John Gooch (ed.), *Decisive Campaigns of the Second World War* (London: Frank Cass, 1990), 84–104.

Colpi, Terri. 'The Impact of the Second World War on the British Italian Community', in David Cesarani and Tony Kushner (eds), *The Internment of Aliens in Twentieth Century Britain* (London: Frank Cass, 1993), 167–87.

Connolly, Tracey. 'Irish Workers in Britain during World War II', in Brian Girvin and Geoffrey Roberts (eds), *Ireland and the Second World War. Politics, Society and Remembrance* (Dublin: Four Courts Press, 2000), 121–32.

Cox, Sebastian. 'The Sources and Organisation of RAF Intelligence and Its Influence on Operations', in Horst Boog (ed.), *The Conduct of the Air War in the Second World War* (Oxford: Berg, 1992), 553–79.

Cresciani, Gianfranco. 'The Bogey of the Italian Fifth Column: Internment and the Making of Italo-Australia', in Richard Bosworth and Romano Ugolini (eds), *War, Internment and Mass Migration: The Italo-Australian Experience 1940–1990* (Roma: Gruppo Editoriale Internazionale, 1992), 11–32.

Davis, Gerald H. 'The Life of Prisoners of War in Russia, 1914–1921', in Samuel R. Williamson, Jr and Peter Pastor (eds), *Essays on World War I: Origins and Prisoners of War* (New York: Columbia University Press, 1983), 163–98.

Dignan, Donald. 'The Internment of Italians in Queensland', in Richard Bosworth and Romano Ugolini (eds), *War, Internment and Mass Migration: The Italo-Australian Experience 1940–1990* (Roma: Gruppo Editoriale Internazionale, 1992), 61–74.

Fedorowich, Kent. 'Propaganda and Political Warfare: The Foreign Office, Italian POWs and the Free Italy Movement, 1940–3', in Bob Moore and Kent Fedorowich (eds), *Prisoners of War and their Captors during World War II* (Oxford: Berg, 1996), 119–48.

——. 'Understanding the Enemy: Military Intelligence, Political Warfare and Japanese Prisoners of War in Australia, 1942–45', in Philip Towle, Margaret Kosuge and Yoichi Kibata (eds), *Japanese Prisoners of War* (London: Hambledon, 2000), 59–86.

Foot, M. R. D. 'Prisoners-of-War' in I. C. B. Dear (ed.), *The Oxford Companion to the Second World War* (Oxford: Oxford University Press, 1995), 913–15.

Grundlingh, Louis. 'The Recruitment of South African Blacks for Participation in the Second World War', in David Killingray and Richard Rathbone (eds), *Africa and the Second World War* (London: Macmillan, 1986), 181–203.

Killingray, David. 'Africans and African Americans in Enemy Hands', in Bob Moore and Kent Fedorowich (eds), *Prisoners of War and their Captors during World War II* (Oxford: Berg, 1996), 181–204.

Klinkhammer, Lutz. 'Leben im Lager. Die italienischen Kriegsgefangenen und Deportierten im zweiten Weltkrieg. Ein Literaturbericht', *Quellen und Forschungen aus italienischen Archiven und Bibliotheken* (Tübingen: Max Niemeyer Verlag, 1987), 489–520.

Knox, MacGregor. 'The Italian Armed Forces, 1940–43', in Alan R. Millett and Williamson Murray (eds), *Military Effectiveness*, vol. 3, *The Second World War* (Boston: Allen & Unwin, 1988), 136–79.

——. 'The Fascist Regime, its Foreign Policy and its Wars: An "Anti-Anti-Fascist" Orthodoxy?', in Patrick Finney (ed.), *The Origins of the Second World War* (London: Arnold, 1997), 148–68.

Krammer, Arnold. 'Soviet Propaganda Among German and Austro-Hungarian Prisoners of War in Russia, 1917–1921', in Samuel R. Williamson, Jr and Peter Pastor (eds), *Essays on World War I: Origins and Prisoners of War* (New York: Columbia University Press, 1983), 249–64.

Lonsdale, John. 'The Depression and the Second World War in the Transformation of Kenya', in David Killingray and Richard Rathbone (eds), *Africa and the Second World War* (London: Macmillan, 1986), 97–142.

MacKenzie, S. P. 'Prisoners of War and Civilian Internees: The European and Mediterranean Theatres', in Loyd E. Lee (ed.), *World War II in Europe, Africa and the Americas, with General Sources* (Westport, CT: Greenwood, 1997), 302–12.

Maier, Klaus A. 'The Battle of Britain', in Klaus A. Maier, Horst Rohde, Bernd Stegemann and Hans Umbreit (eds), *Germany and the Second World War*, vol. 2 (Oxford: Clarendon Press, 1991), 374–407.

Miège, Jean Louis. 'I prigionieri di guerra italiani in Africa del Nord', in Romain H. Rainero (ed.), *I prigionieri militari italiani durante la seconda guerra mondiale: aspetti e problemi storici* (Milano: Marzorati editore, 1984), 171–82.

Moore, Bob. 'Axis Prisoners in Britain during the Second World War: A Comparative Survey', in Bob Moore and Kent Fedorowich (eds), *Prisoners of War and their Captors during World War II* (Oxford: Berg, 1996), 19–46.

O'Brien, Ilma Martinuzzi. 'The Internment of Australian Born and Naturalized British Subjects of Italian Origin', in Richard Bosworth and Romano Ugolini (eds), *War, Internment and Mass Migration: The Italo-Australian Experience 1940–1990* (Roma: Gruppo Editoriale Internazionale, 1992), 89–104.

Rainero, Romain H. 'I prigionieri italiani in Africa', in Romain H. Rainero (ed.), *I prigionieri militari italiani durante la seconda guerra mondiale: aspetti e problemi storici* (Milano: Marzorati editore, 1984), 149–70.

——. 'I prigionieri italiani in mani alleate', in Romain H. Rainero and Renato Sicurezza (eds), *L'italia nella 2ª guerra mondiale: aspetti e problemi (1944–1994)* (Milan: Marzorati editore, 1995), 383–401.

Rochat, Giorgio. 'Die italienischen Militärinternierten im zweiten Weltkrieg', in *Quellen und Forschungen aus italienischen Archiven und Bibliotheken* (Tübingen: Max Niemeyer Verlag, 1987), 336–420.

——. 'Bibliografia sull'internamento die militari italiani in Germania (1943–1945)', in Nicola Della Santa (ed.), *I militari italiani internati dai tedeschi dopo l'8 settembre 1943* (Firenze: Giunti, 1986), 197–210.

Rovighi, Alberto. 'Obiettivi, metodi e resultati dell'azione politica condotta dalla Gran Bretagna nei reguardi die prigionieri di guerra italiani', in Romain H. Rainero (ed.), *I prigionieri militari italiani durante la seconda guerra mondiale: aspetti e problemi storici* (Milano: Marzorati editore, 1984), 249–54.

Sadkovich, James J. 'North Africa and the Mediterranean Theater, 1939–1945', in Loyd E. Lee (ed.), *World War II in Europe, Africa and the Americas, with General Sources* (Westport, CT: Greenwood, 1997), 139–56.

Schreiber, Gerhard. 'Die italienischen Militärinternierten – Politische, humane und rassenideologische Geschichtspunkte einer besonderen Kriegsgefangenschaft', in Günther Bischof and Rüdiger Overmans, *Kriegsgefangenschaft in Zweiten Weltkrieg: Eine vergleichende Perspektive* (Ternitz: Höller, 1999), 393–406.

Sponza, Lucio. 'The British Government and the Internment of Italians', in David Cesarani and Tony Kushner (eds), *The Internment of Aliens in Twentieth Century Britain* (London: Frank Cass, 1993), 125–46.

Sponza, Lucio. 'Italian Prisoners of War in Great Britain, 1943–6', in Bob Moore and Kent Fedorowich (eds), *Prisoners of War and their Captors during World War II* (Oxford: Berg, 1996), 205–26.

Sullivan, Brian R. 'The Italian Soldier in Combat, June 1940 – September 1943: Myths, Realities and Explanations', in Paul Addison and Angus Calder (eds), *Time to Kill: The Soldier's Experience of War 1939–1945* (London: Pimlico, 1997), 177–205.

Ugolini, Romano. 'From POW to Emigrant: The Post-war Migrant Experience', in Richard Bosworth and Romano Ugolini (eds), *War, Internment and Mass Migration: The Italo-Australian Experience 1940–1990* (Roma: Gruppo Editoriale Internazionale, 1992), 125–37.

Zamagni, Vera. 'Italy: How to Lose the War and Win the Peace', in Mark Harrison (ed.), *The Economics of World War II* (Cambridge: Cambridge University Press, 1998), 177–223.

Newspapers

Bury Times	*Hamilton Spectator*
Cape Argus	*Melbourne Argus*
Cape Times	*Natal Daily News*
Daily Express	*News Chronicle*
Daily Herald	*Rand Daily Mail*
Daily Mail	*Sunday Pictorial*
Daily Sketch	*Sydney Morning Herald*
Daily Telegraph	*The Times*

Theses

Parkin, H. 'British Policy towards Italian Prisoners-of-War in Great Britain', BA (Hons) Humanities dissertation, Bristol Polytechnic, 1989.

Index